new
babycare

new
babycare

DR.miriam
stoppard
MD FRCP

DK

LONDON, NEW YORK, MELBOURNE, MUNICH, and DELHI

For Hazel, Oona, Tiberio, and Elias

Produced for Dorling Kindersley by **Cooling Brown**
Design **Arthur Brown, Peter Cooling, Tish Jones**
Editorial **Jemima Dunne**

Dorling Kindersley
Consultant Editor **Jinny Johnson**
Managing Editors **Penny Warren, Esther Ripley**
Managing Art Editor **Marianne Markham**
Editor **Emma Maule**
Senior Designers **Nicola Rodway, Anne Fisher**
Senior Production Editor **Jenny Woodcock**
Production Controller **Alice Holloway**
Creative Technical Support **Sonia Charbonnier**
Jacket Designer **Charlotte Seymour**
US Medical Consultant **Aviva Schein, MD**
US Editors **Shannon Beatty, Beth Hester**

First published in the United States in 2007 by DK Publishing

This revised edition published in 2009 by
DK Publishing, 375 Hudson Street, New York, New York 10014

Copyright © 1983, 1990, 2007, 2009 Dorling Kindersley Limited, London
Text copyright © 1983, 1990, 2007, 2009 Miriam Stoppard

09 10 11 12 13 10 9 8 7 6 5 4 3 2 1

ND148—1/2009

Published in Great Britain by Dorling Kindersley Limited

A catalog record for this book is available from the Library of Congress.
ISBN: 978-0-7566-4420-8

DK books are available at special discounts when purchased in bulk for sales promotions, premiums,
fund-raising, or educational use. For details, contact: DK Publishing Special Markets, 375 Hudson Street,
... 4 or SpecialSales@dk.com.

... apore by Colourscan;
... ed in London by Altaimage
... ina by L-Rex

... more at
... lk.com

Preface

I've learned a lot about babycare in the last five years or so. The lessons have come from my children (four sons), my stepchildren (two daughters), my daughters-in-law, and my 11 grandchildren.

The basics of child development and the principles of baby and child nurturing change little, but there's room for progress and improvement in all sorts of subtle ways. Some of these just nudge us in a different direction while others seem so fundamental we ask ourselves what took so long.

I'm grateful to all the new members of my extended family for all of them have taught me something useful—even the youngest, Maggie and Evie, my identical twin granddaughters.

It's been thrilling to listen to, observe, note, learn, and inwardly digest the hundreds of small things that have refined my thinking about baby and childcare. They're all reflected in this new edition of one of my favorite books.

Contents

	Introduction	8
1	The newborn	20
2	Equipment	32
3	Clothing	40
4	Holding and handling	50
5	All about diapers	58
6	Bathing and hygiene	70
7	Feeding	86
8	Bowel and bladder function	132
9	Sleeping	142
10	Crying	158
11	Physical development	178
12	Intellectual development	206
13	Social behavior	236
14	Playing	264
15	Outings and travel	282
16	Home safety	292
17	Home medicine	308

	Index	344
	Acknowledgments	352

Introduction

There must be parents who feel nothing but joy at the news that they are expecting a baby, but they are few and far between. Once the initial excitement is over, most parents would confess to having mixed feelings about the prospect of having a baby.

Your fears are natural

Probably the most common anxiety is simply fear of parenthood. This can be fear of whether you will be a good parent or of whether you can cope with bringing up a child, or both. On top of this will be the concern about your child's happiness if you don't do a good job of it.

There will be economic anxieties. Even if both parents are working, the money that was once enough for two now has to cover the needs of three, so it will be spread a little more thinly, and luxuries and comforts, expensive vacations, a new car, or redecorating the house may have to go by the board for a while.

Another cause for anxiety will be the undoubted loss of freedom. No longer will you both be able to jump into the car and whiz off anywhere you like, go to a party on the spur of the moment. You can still enjoy life, but you'll have to factor in the baby's needs too.

All of these fears and anxieties are natural. There's nothing abnormal about worrying that you won't make the grade as a parent. Your feelings may be easier to cope with if you understand that both you and your child will be constantly changing. Your family unit, the way it develops and the feelings it engenders, is dynamic. There is a natural rhythm to human relationships, especially relationships in the home. They are never at a standstill. Sometimes you may worry that your home seems less than harmonious, but this is normal family life. And as well as the lows, parenthood will give you some of the most exciting highs you've ever felt.

Mixed emotions

All the feelings of love that you have for your child will be mixed at one time or another with resentment, bitterness, anger, hostility, and frustration. This is inevitable, in the same way that it's inevitable in any human relationship. The difference is that you will gain rewards from your child that no other person can give you. One of the rules that I have learned about parenting is that whatever you put in you will get back five hundred times over. So not only will your freedom increase as your child gets older, but so will the pleasures that she gives you. The sacrifices you make when your baby is young will be replaced by more and more pleasures. One of the greatest will be to see your baby turn

Your new arrival
Many of your fears will be dispelled at the first sight of your newborn baby.

from a dependent, demanding creature into a charming, thoughtful companion, an entertaining friend, and a pal.

How a family evolves

The basic family unit as we know it today has been found in every race or tribe since people first inhabited the Earth. The family unit is, and always has been, the cornerstone of our society and its main function is to create a secure environment in which children can be raised.

There is no one to whom the family is more important than a baby; it forms her entire universe. Within the family your child learns all the basic aspects of human

relationships. And within its security, your child learns about the good things in life, the happiness, the love, and the laughter, as well as the bad things, the problems, the tensions, and the anxieties. As your child grows, the family will provide the steadying, optimistic, strengthening influence that will help her cope with new and possibly difficult situations. It should always be the sanctuary to which your child can return when any conflicts seem difficult to handle on her own.

The way the family is constructed and the roles played by the members of it vary from culture to culture and family to family. In modern Western society the man has traditionally taken the role of breadwinner, provider, and worker, while the woman has been the housekeeper and childrearer and was mainly confined to the home. While until not long ago society accepted this as the norm, it is in fact a very recent development in the evolution of the family.

The family unit

Prior to the Industrial Revolution in the nineteenth century, the family was a working unit with mother and father and children all working toward the common good. Because of this, many aspects of family life were shared experiences; no distinction was made between worker and nurturer of children as we do it today. Women and children were very often out in the fields along with the men, and there was never a sense that a woman's duty

Face to face
You're face to face with each other at last. Nothing bonds you more closely to your newborn baby—and him to you—than close eye contact.

was to rear children and do the household chores. It was a much more egalitarian arrangement in those days.

The Industrial Revolution tore apart this happy working family unit. Instead of being together, the family was split up. The wage earner, of whichever sex but usually the man, had to go to the factory in order to do his work instead of being close to his family. At about the same time, parents abdicated their role as educators of children to schools, so the family lost much of its educational function. The mother was often left at home with the children and—because the wage earner had to work long hours—she had to shoulder most of the responsibility for childrearing, everyday care, and discipline. Continuing industrialization and urbanization, and the increased scope for travel, resulted in families becoming geographically separate. Consequently mothers could no longer rely on their mothers, sisters, and grandmothers for help, as they had done in the past. They were left alone. The family unit became small, isolated, and unsupported; for the mother, it became boring, repetitive, tedious, and frustrating. She had no time to herself, suffered from a loss of identity, and had no other outlet for her skills and capabilities. Recently, and largely because of the feminist movement, there has been a move back to the kind of egalitarian marriage that existed before.

The modern mother

Twenty-first century mothers can be divided into two main categories. The first consists of those who feel that while their children are very young they want to look after them themselves and that this activity is the most worthwhile job they can do. However, even a mother who loves her child dearly will admit that looking after young children isn't easy. A woman who finds herself a mother shortly after leaving her job is unlikely to be very well prepared for the demands, not to mention the isolation, that can go with being a mother.

Motherhood has its pleasures and fulfillment but it is very tough. It's 24 hours a day, seven days a week. It's repetitious and tedious and extremely demanding and wearing. No mother undervalues what she is doing, but society does. Consequently, when a young mother, particularly one who has been well trained to do a job outside the home, is asked what she is doing and all she can say is that she's a mother, she feels that the admission classifies her as inferior to women who are holding down a job. It is up to society to have a more realistic view of motherhood than the present somewhat idealized one.

The working mother

The other category consists of working mother. For some reason the term "working mother" is still pejorative in our society. The general view seems to be that if women aren't prepared to devote themselves entirely to the upbringing of their children then they aren't maternal, or worse, they're selfish and heartless.

If we go back to the pre-Industrial Revolution family we find that mothers were always working mothers. They did the same amount of work as the father and they shared the work of the family with him. It is a natural instinct for a mother to want to go on working even though she has had children. Also, many women today work because they have to—either because they have no partner or because the family needs the income. Women have always made a vital contribution to the support of their families, whether by growing food, spinning wool, making pots, weaving cotton, grinding flour, curing bacon, or tanning leather. Over the centuries the economic importance of women has been equal to their domestic importance. It's only now that our priorities have become rather muddled.

Women who work nearly always have a strong drive to be independent outside the home. They want to have their own lives, their own interests, and their own source of income. They cherish their own area of activity, where they are respected and their efforts are prized and where they are needed for their skills and expertise. These are perfectly valid and reasonable motives for wanting to work after a child is born. However, the woman who opts to do this is putting herself into the category of people who work hardest and are the most stressed. In Western society today, the hardest-working person is the working mother. She has two full-time jobs; that of a mother and that of a wage-earner.

The modern father

This is a father who takes responsibility for the general care of his child. Fewer fathers today are prepared to be strangers to their children, missing out on all the good times in the family and, most important, missing out on their children growing up. The modern father is active rather than passive. He will arrange his day to come home early from work to see his children or work part-time so he can share the childcare with his partner. He'll spend as much time as he can playing with his children, showing them new things, helping them with their hobbies, taking them with him when he enjoys his own. He will participate from day one with the care of the baby, with changing diapers, with getting up in the middle of the night to do the 2 a.m. feeding, helping at bathtimes, reading stories, playing games, and singing songs before bedtime. The modern father is a full-time parent, not a part-time stranger, and everyone in the family benefits from this.

A father who is very interested in the pregnancy generally stays interested after the birth. Interest is positively related to how much he holds the baby in the first six weeks and whether he goes to the baby when she cries. Not unexpectedly, his attitude affects his partner's enjoyment of pregnancy and motherhood. The happier the father is about it and the more he looks forward to fatherhood, the more she enjoys the first weeks of her baby's life too and inevitably, the better the start for the baby. The better the father is at playing his role, the more important he becomes.

A new lifestyle

As a new parent you'll notice quite a few changes in the way you live. A life of free and easy egocentricity will now be regulated by your new baby's inner alarm clock, by the necessity to feed, to change diapers, and to tend your baby at any time of the day or night. It will be almost a complete reversal of lifestyle, which at first may not be easy to accept. Some parents don't accept it and never let the baby dominate their lives. They try to carry on

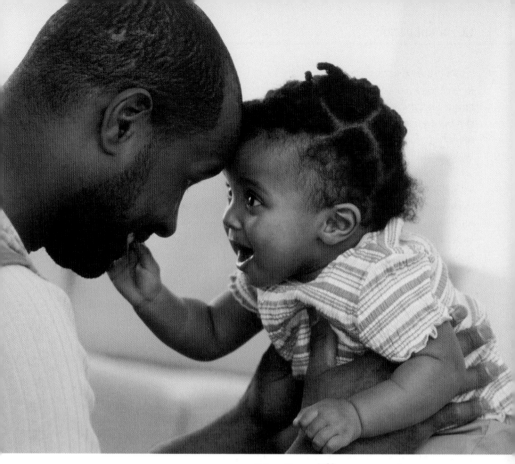

Your favorite playmate
You will be your child's favorite toy and playmate during her formative early years. Make the most of this privileged relationship whenever you can.

with their free and easy way of life with a baby carriage tagging along.

Other parents will do exactly the opposite and give up everything to look after their baby. The baby becomes the center of their lives and they devote all their energy toward his or her care.

Neither of these extremes of parenting is a good idea; far and away the best is a happy medium in which the needs and emotions of the baby and parents more or less dovetail together.

Meeting different needs

Children need certain things from their parents. They need security and love, they need to be introduced to new experiences, and they need to be recognized and loved as individuals. If a parent fulfills these needs, particularly for love and affection, which are the most important things that you can give a child, then that child will develop normally and establish a pattern for forming all future relationships.

After love, the next most important thing that you can give your child is stimulation. A young child is like a sponge soaking up practically every new idea and experience she comes in contact with. Your new baby has a great potential to develop and learn and is eager to be given the opportunity. So, to be good parents, it's important to start introducing your child to the outside world with all its wonders and excitements, first through yourselves and the immediate family, and then through your extended family.

Children also need to know that the adults they love most, their parents, approve of them. The way you should show this approval is by praise. It has often been noted that children respond much better to praise than to blame, and a positive attitude of teaching and education is far more effective than a negative one. A child who is loved has self-respect; a child who is unloved has none. She responds to this situation by being difficult to manage, and generally antisocial.

Although children have needs, parents have needs, too. Your needs don't disappear just because you've become a parent. The elation of having a baby will be quickly dispelled if you feel that your needs go completely unheeded. All parents make sacrifices, but there is no need for you to be a martyr. If your needs and those of your child are not well balanced, then resentment will build up and the chances of creating a happy, loving, domestic atmosphere will be small.

Parents' needs

The needs of both parents must be taken into consideration. In this day and age parents can be nothing but equal, and parenting and childrearing must be shared equally. It should really be viewed as a contract: you're equally responsible for your child's conception so you should take equal responsibility for rearing your child.

The least that must happen is that you and your partner are in agreement with each other about the roles that you have to play in parenting your child. It's just not good enough for a woman to be expected to take on all the childcare without any support, while the father leaves early in the morning and doesn't return home until after the baby is asleep. In this situation everyone is missing out.

In an ideal world, the needs of parents and children would complement each other. In other words, the need of the parents to love and nurture a small baby would be matched by the infant's dependency and need for care. One of the things that triggers conflict in a family is when the two sets of needs do not match—especially if the parents aren't mature enough to meet the demands of a young child.

Your role is important

As a parent you will be called upon to play many roles for your child. You will be your child's first friend and probably her best friend for life. At one time we thought a child was not alert to the world around it until it reacted overtly to what was going on. Indeed, Saint Thomas Aquinas took a broader view. He said, "Give me a boy until he's seven and then take him," the idea being that a person could be formed during the first seven years.

We now know that this formative time is much briefer than that. A child starts to absorb information about its environment from the moment it is born. The fact that it can't focus its eyes on a distant object until the age of about six weeks does not mean it cannot see. It can. A newborn baby can focus perfectly well at a distance of 8–10 inches (20–25 centimeters) and that's where your face and your hands should be if you want your baby to recognize you and watch you. Babies respond to sights, sounds, smells, touches, conversations, and ambiences as soon as they enter the world. If parents realize this and take this fact seriously it puts them in a highly responsible position. It means that they, and not teachers, are responsible for a child's first learning.

You will not only be teacher but playmate, counselor, educator, and disciplinarian. Your influence will be pivotal. A child learns from its parents' friendship and hostility, happiness and sadness, content and discontent—the blueprint for a loving relationship and the architecture of a conversation. (Indeed a baby is conversing in as short a time as two weeks so you need to know how to recognize primitive baby conversation.) All the early skills—walking, talking, socializing, and intellectual development—are absolutely in the parents' hands and no one else is culpable if things go wrong. This means that modern parents have to be active, interested parents who take their roles as teachers seriously and with dedication, from the moment the baby is born.

Children need consistency

All children require one strong, constant, emotional bond early in their lives. If this is missing because the parents are inconsistent in giving their child love, sympathy, and reassurance, or because the mother is replaced by several inadequate mother substitutes, their baby's early need for a secure relationship may be thwarted.

Part of your role will be to teach your child to respect other people's rights and property, and this will be enforced through discipline. For discipline to be effective it should be firm and consistent, but it should also always be sympathetic, understanding, and considerate.

Very often a child's delinquent act is directed at a neglectful parent with whom she cannot communicate. Parents who don't talk to their child have very little chance of influencing her, but parents who have observed and respected each step in a child's development and accepted her idiosyncrasies and failures will nearly always be in a position to talk over problems with that child.

Setting limits for children

Research has shown that children actually do not like a lack of boundaries nor do children thrive when they are undisciplined. In fact, children do best when the limits of behavior are clearly defined and constant; this makes them feel safe and secure. It is your role as parents to set standards for behavior and conduct appropriate to the age of your child, and to create a framework in which your child can live her life free of unnecessary control. Research has shown that both over-restrictiveness and inconsistency have adverse effects on children. Ideal parents are warm, affectionate, accepting, understanding, and always encouraging of independence in their children.

One of the most important aspects of parenting is being a model for your developing child. A boy observes his father and quickly realizes what is going to be expected of him as he grows up.

He models himself on his father, he copies what his father does, and he picks up habits from his father.

In the same way, a daughter learns from her mother what is expected of her and what it will be like to be a woman. It's the atmosphere and behavior in the home from which the children first learn social behavior and social roles. As they grow older they will determine their own moral values and their standards by those that are displayed by their parents. Children can still thrive with only one parent to learn from, but they are obviously better off with two models to check against rather than one.

It's my belief that children need the interest, the help, the support, the teaching, the counseling, and the love of fathers. Certainly in matters of discipline both parents are needed, because families should make important decisions as a unit, and children should see both their parents taking an interest in and making decisions about the important times in their lives.

The importance of touch

"Spare the rod and spoil the child" was something that my mother and many women of her generation quoted to her children, and most people of my age were disciplined not only with words, actions, rewards, and punishments, but with some kind of physical punishment.

To my mind the word "spoil" is a very dangerous one, because most people confuse spoiling with loving, and no baby or child can have too much loving. The first introduction to loving that a newborn baby experiences is the touch of her mother's arms. The second is the sound of her voice. I do believe that babies "bond" to these two things. In other words, they recognize the mother's touch, her smell, and the sound of her voice as belonging to the person who feeds and takes an interest in them, soothes away discomfort, and generally makes life happier and more pleasant. One of the most important aspects of this loving relationship is touch, and the first touches a baby experiences should be soft, gentle, welcoming, and cushioning.

We are not the only animal to whom touch is important; it is important throughout the whole animal kingdom, as some controversial and rather moving animal experiments show. Some of the first of these were done with baby Rhesus Monkeys. They were divided into two groups, having been taken away from their mothers at a young age, but old enough to survive on their own. The groups were given two substitute "mothers." One was a "wire mother," which was simply the shape and body of a mother monkey made out of wire. The other was a "soft mother": the wire body was covered in material such as lamb's wool. For the first group, the wire mother provided food via a nipple attachment; for the second group, the soft mother did. The experimenters thought that the monkeys would prefer the mother which had the food. However, it was found that the young monkeys clung to the soft mother whether it provided them with food or not, and only

Your baby's first conversations
At this magic distance—10 inches (25 centimeters)— between you, your baby can see you clearly and "speaks" to you with mouth and tongue movements.

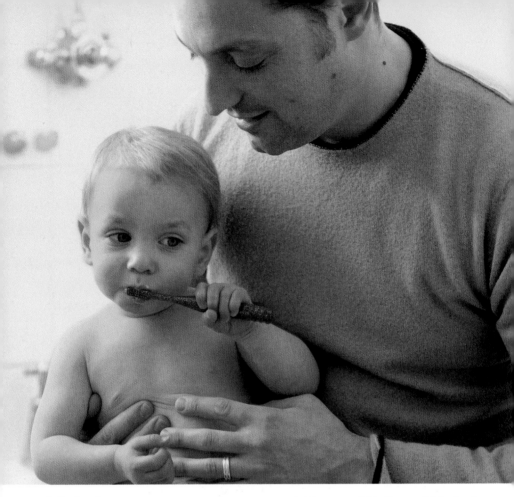

Father's role

There are so many things you can share with your child. For example, it's never too early to start showing him how to brush his teeth.

went to the wire surrogate occasionally to eat. Sometimes they were prepared to go without food in order to snuggle up to the soft mother, so great was their need for softness, comfort, and touching. In some intensive care units where premature babies are nurtured, the babies are put on soft fleecy sheets because this makes them feel like they are being touched. The astonishing fact is these babies thrive better and put on

weight more quickly than a child who lies on a linen or cotton sheet.

The upshot of all this is very important for a parent. If you want your baby to be happy, to thrive and to put on weight, one of the most important things you can do for her is to cuddle, and cuddle, and give more cuddles. Take every opportunity to stroke, pat, touch, and love your child through gestures. If you can accompany these touching movements with a soft, loving voice, a big smile, and keep your face 8–10 inches (20–25 cm) away from your newborn baby, you will be giving her a flying start in life.

Love is not exclusive

Until quite recently, the commonly held view of the mother–child bond was that it was exclusive. It was thought that a strong, healthy bond between mother and child was essential for a child's mental health, but more importantly that a child's care should be monopolized by one mother figure. It was also felt that a child was unable to form attachments to more than one person, that person being the mother. This placed a huge psychological burden on the mother and made her the subject of great pressure by everyone who cared to exert it, either partner or family.

Research has shown that this is almost certainly not the case. Babies are not confined to a single bond. Once your baby has reached the stage of forming an attachment to anyone, then she is probably capable of maintaining a number of attachments at the same time. As they grow up, most babies form specific attachments simultaneously—as many as five or more. By the time children are 18 months old almost a third have formed attachments with neighbors and grandparents, but, above all, with their fathers. Another aspect of the research has shown that being attached to several people at the same time does not mean that the baby has a shallower feeling toward each one. An infant's capacity for attachment is not like a cake that has to be cut. Love in babies has no limits.

Given a baby's ability to form attachments with several people, there is no reason why "mothering" can't be shared by several people. Furthermore, the mother need not be the biological mother. There is no evidence at all to suggest that firm attachments won't grow between children and unrelated adults who take on the parenting role by fostering or adoption, for instance. The belief that the mother, simply by virtue of being the biological mother, is uniquely capable of caring for her child is without foundation. There are no medical, physiological, or biological reasons for confining childcare to women. In fact, the argument in favor of equal sharing of parenting between both parents is irresistible.

Consistency of care

An infant can form multiple attachments and research has shown that such attachments depend more on the quality of the interaction than on its duration. Controversy about whether the mother has to be the infant's constant companion throughout each day is over. A minimum period of togetherness is desirable, but there is nothing definite that can be said about how much. It is the personal qualities that the adult brings to the interaction that are important. Provided that these can be fully expressed, there is no reason why mother and baby should not spend a portion of the day apart (while the mother at work, for instance, and the child is in a day-care arrangement that the family is comfortable with).

There is, however, one important proviso: the stability and quality of substitute care. If the people responsible for the child's care are constantly changing, the child could well become disturbed. A child may not need uniformity of care, but she does need consistency of care. It's your job to make sure this is given if neither you or your partner is going to stay at home.

1 The newborn

Soon after delivery, your baby will be examined and his weight, head circumference, and length will be measured in order to form a baseline against which his future development will be assessed. Don't try to compare your baby with others; doctors and midwives don't. The only comparisons that should be made are with himself at different stages. The average birth weight is 5 pounds 8 ounces–9 pounds 12 ounces (2.5–4.5 kilograms), but if your baby is smaller, don't worry. The normal range varies according to genetics, race, and nutrition. The average length of a new baby is 19–20 inches (48–51 centimeters), but again big variations are common.

Physical impressions

The head
Size The average newborn baby's head circumference is about 14 inches (35 centimeters). The head may seem large in comparison with the rest of his body since it comprises about a quarter of his length compared to an eighth in an adult.

Shape Your baby's head is unlikely to be perfectly rounded after birth, but no matter how bumpy or swollen it looks, the brain will not have been damaged. This is because the bones in the head are specially designed to move over each other during birth so that the head, the largest part of the baby's body, can pass down the birth canal easily. The head will soon regain its rounded shape.

Sometimes a baby has a large, firm swelling on one or both sides of the head that doesn't go down immediately. Called a cephalhematoma, it is caused by the natural pressure exerted by the uterine muscle during labor. It's really a large bruise of the scalp and it's outside the skull. The swelling puts no pressure on the baby's brain and subsides, without treatment, within a few weeks.

Bruising is quite common after a forceps delivery, as are shallow indentations on either side of the head. They are both rectified naturally within a couple of days.

The fontanelle The fontanelle is the soft spot in the top of your baby's head. It is the space where the skull bones have not yet joined; they don't fuse until your baby

Holding your newborn
Next to your skin, breathing in all those lovely reassuring body smells, will be your newborn baby's favorite position.

Your baby's body
A newborn baby's abdomen may seem very rounded and his limbs small and thin, but these proportions are normal and will soon change.

is about two years old. The baby's scalp covers this space and is very tough, but make sure that the fontanelle is never pressed very hard. The purpose of the fontanelle is to allow the soft skull bones to "mold" (this means to ride over one another) without damage to the baby's brain as the baby's head passes through the birth canal. No special care of the skin and hair that cover the fontanelle is needed. However, if you notice the skin over the area is taut, if there's a bulge, or if it looks abnormally shrunken, contact your doctor immediately.

The eyes

Condition Most babies are born with puffy eyes as a result of the natural pressure during birth. The swelling usually goes down within a couple of days.

Never consider a discharge from your baby's eyes normal. In all probability it's a common, mild infection called conjunctivitis, but it should always be treated by a doctor, not by you. Never use over-the-counter drops or ointments.
Color All babies are born with blue eyes.

This is because melanin, the body's natural pigment, is not present in the skin or eyes at birth. If a baby is going to have brown eyes or a dark brown skin, the color will gradually develop over a period of weeks or months. The eyes and skin may not reach their permanent color until the baby is six months old.

Eye function You may find it difficult to get your baby to open his eyes at first, but never try to force them open. One of the easiest ways I have found to get a baby to open his eyes is to hold him above my head. The tendency then is to open them.

You might notice when your baby does open his eyes he appears to squint. Don't worry about this. Your baby hasn't yet learned to use his eyes synchronously, as a pair, to focus on things. The squinting will gradually disappear as he learns to focus when he's one or two months old. Check with your doctor if your baby is still not focussing after three months.

Tears Tiny babies don't shed tears, as you'll find when your baby cries. It usually takes about four or five months for a baby to produce "real" tears when he cries.

The mouth

Lip blisters Such blisters, usually in the center of the mouth, are caused by the baby's sucking. They cause no harm and will go away on their own.

Tongue-tie Your baby's tongue may appear to be almost fully attached to the bottom of his mouth. This should not be a cause of worry. The baby's tongue grows mainly from the tip throughout the first year.

The skin

The vernix The skin of your newborn will probably be covered with a white, greasy substance. Some babies have vernix all over their face and body, while others have it only on isolated parts, like their face and hands. Hospital practices in the treatment of vernix vary. Whereas it used to be meticulously cleaned off after birth, today it is left on because it provides a natural barrier against minor skin infections. It is generally considered unnecessary to clean it off, not only because of the vernix's protective qualities, but also because it is naturally absorbed into the skin within two or three days. However, if there are large accumulations of vernix in skin folds it can be wiped away to avoid causing irritation.

Texture Your baby may be born with dry peeling skin (most noticeable on the palms of the hands and soles of the feet). This is not eczema nor does it mean that your baby will be permanently dry-skinned. In most cases the dryness soon disappears.

Color The top half of your baby's body may be pale while the lower half is red. This is because of the baby's immature circulation, which causes the blood to pool in the lower limbs. It is rectified by moving your baby.

You may notice that your baby's hands or feet have turned blue, especially if he's been lying down. Once again, this is because of your baby's relatively inefficient circulation. The color will change if you pick up or move him. Try to keep your baby's room at a consistent temperature, around 65–68°F (16–20°C). Blue marks (also called Mongolian spots), which look like bruises, often occur on the lower backs of babies with dark skin tones (nearly all African, Hispanic/Latino, and Asian babies have them). They are completely harmless and fade away naturally.

Jaundice Many healthy newborn infants develop slight jaundice—a yellowish discoloration of the skin and the whites of the eyes—on about the third day of life. This is known as physiological jaundice, because it is not a disease. It results from the baby's blood having a high content of primitive red cells, which are broken down after birth. When red cells are broken down, one of their constituent parts, the yellow pigment called bilirubin, increases in the blood and causes the skin and eyes to color. Physiological jaundice should clear by the end of the first week, as long as the baby is feeding well.

The umbilicus

Immediately after birth the umbilical cord is cut about 3–4 inches (8–10 centimeters) from the baby's abdomen. Pressure is exerted on it by a clamp and the stump shrivels and drops off within 10 days or so. Some babies develop umbilical hernias (small swellings near the navel), but these nearly always clear up within a year. If your baby has one and it enlarges or persists, check with your pediatrician.

The breasts

Both male and female babies can have swollen breasts at birth; they may even have a slight discharge of milk. This is caused by the presence of maternal hormones in the baby's body and it resolves naturally. Never try to squeeze any of the milk out. The swelling will subside within a couple of days.

The genitals

The genitals of both boys and girls are naturally larger at birth than the rest of their bodies. The scrotum or vulva may even look red and inflamed. This is a natural occurrence and is caused by the mother's hormones crossing the placenta into the baby's bloodstream. These hormones may also cause a clear or white discharge in female babies, and even a small amount of vaginal bleeding. Once again, this is perfectly normal and will clear up naturally after a couple of days. However, if you're at all worried by this, contact your doctor.

Stools

A baby's first stools are usually dark green and sticky and have very little smell. This is because they are mainly meconium, which is digested mucus from the mucus glands in the bowel. It is the only kind of motion your baby will pass for the first two or three days. Gradually over the next three or four days you will notice that the stools change color. The appearance and consistency of the stools will then depend on whether your baby is having breast-milk or formula (*see p.134*).

COMMON BLEMISHES

Birthmarks

Quite commonly there are small red marks on a baby's skin, particularly on the eyelids, on the forehead, and if you lift up the hair, at the back of the neck just under the hairline. They result from the enlargement of tiny blood vessels near the surface of the skin and are traditionally called stork bites. Both of my sons had them and they disappeared, as they do in most children, by the time they were six months old. In some babies, however, these marks may not disappear until they are about 18 months.

Another common birthmark is the so-called strawberry mark. This appears after a couple of days but fades before the child is three years old. If you're at all worried by your baby's birthmark, ask your pediatrician for advice and reassurance.

Pimples

It is not unusual for a baby to have small white pimples over the bridge of the nose, called milia. These pimples are not abnormal so never, ever squeeze them. They are caused by a temporary blockage of the sweat glands and sebaceous glands that secrete sebum to lubricate the skin. They nearly always disappear after a few days.

Rashes

Many babies develop a skin condition called *erythema toxicum*. The baby's skin becomes red and blotchy, with small white bumps that appear and disappear quite rapidly. The whole rash only lasts for a couple of days and will disappear without treatment. If you're in any doubt, you should talk to your pediatrician.

Body hair

Babies are born with varying amounts of hair, called lanugo, on their bodies. Some babies have only a soft down on their heads, others are covered in very coarse hair over their shoulders and down their spines. Both are quite normal, and the hair usually rubs off soon after birth.

Newborn behavior

If you concentrate on your baby and observe him carefully over the first two or three days of life, you will become familiar with normal infant behavior and will get accustomed to your baby's idiosyncrasies. It is essential that you learn to understand his signals; stay with him as much as possible, to watch him, nurse him, and play with him.

If you observe him closely you may notice that he does several unexpected things: he may shiver quite suddenly for no reason; he may make so many snuffling noises that you wonder if his nose and air passages are blocked; he may even stop breathing altogether for several seconds. None of these behaviors is abnormal. In the first weeks of life your baby will be given a hearing screening test by the hospital.

Sounds

Breathing A newborn baby's lungs are small and breathing will seem shallow when compared to ours. When you first go to your baby you may be unable to detect that he is breathing. Don't be frightened by this because the breathing will get stronger each day.

All newborn babies make strange sounds when they breathe. Sometimes the breathing is fast and noisy and at other times it may be irregular. Your baby may snuffle with each breath in and out and you may think he has got a cold. This is not necessarily so. In most babies it is because the bridge of the nose is low, and the snuffling noise is caused by the air trying to get through the very small nasal passages. As your baby grows older, the bridge of the nose will get higher and the snuffling sound will gradually stop.

On the other hand, if it interferes with your baby's freedom to suck then you should talk to your pediatrician or nurse-practitioner, because he may need treatment with nose drops before feeding. Nose drops should only be used under medical supervision.

You should, however, be concerned about your baby's breathing if it ever becomes labored, especially if you notice that the chest is being sharply drawn in with each breath and the breathing rate has risen to 60 or more breaths per minute. Any of these signs warrants immediate medical attention (*see p.310*).

Sneezing Babies are very sensitive to bright lights and sometimes sneeze whenever they open their eyes for the first few days. This is because the light stimulates the nerves to the nose as well as to the eyes. (You can try this out for yourself the next time you feel a sneeze coming on: if you look into a bright light you will find that you are able to precipitate the sneeze.) Even if your baby is sneezing a lot it doesn't necessarily mean that he has a cold. The lining of a baby's nose is very sensitive, and sneezing is essential as it clears out the nasal passages and prevents dust from getting down into the lungs.

Hiccups Newborn babies hiccup quite a lot. This is normal, too, and it shouldn't bother you. Hiccups are caused by sudden, irregular contractions of the diaphragm and are a sign that the muscles involved in respiration—those between the ribs, the diaphragm, and the abdomen—are getting stronger and trying to work in harmony.

Reflexes and movements

All newborn babies have reflexes, which are instinctive movements designed to protect them. These reflexes last until voluntary movements on your baby's part take their place, generally around three months old. Two of the most easy reflexes to elicit are those that protect the eyes and those that maintain breathing: your baby will close his eyes if you touch his eyelids and will make struggling movements with his hands if you gently hold his nose between your thumb and forefinger.

The rooting reflex If you gently stroke your baby's cheek you will find that he turns his head in the direction of your finger and opens his mouth. He makes this rooting movement when he is searching for your breast to start feeding (*see p.91*).

The sucking reflex Every baby is born with the reflex to suck and yours will begin to do so if something is put in his mouth or if you press on the upper palate just behind the gums. Sucking movements are extremely strong and they last for quite a long time after the stimulation to suck, such as a finger or a nipple, has been removed. If you want to breastfeed it is important that you put the baby to the breast as soon after delivery as possible. Your baby has to get used to the actual technique of breast-feeding, just as you do, so it helps if he has the powerful desire to suck as a stimulus.

The swallowing reflex All babies can swallow when they are born, so they can swallow colostrum or milk immediately.

The "walking" reflex A newborn baby will move his legs in a walking action if you hold him upright underneath the arms and let his feet touch a firm surface. This is not

NEWBORN REFLEXES

Crawling reflex
Your baby will take up a crawling position when he's placed on his stomach.

Rooting/sucking reflex
Your baby will instinctively turn his head in the direction of your finger when you gently stroke his cheek.

Walking/stepping reflex
When you hold your baby under the shoulders in an upright position with his feet touching a firm surface, he'll move his legs in a walking action.

the reflex that encourages a baby to stand upright and walk (*see p.188*). If you hold your baby upright and let the front of his legs gently touch the edge of a solid object, he'll automatically bring his foot up in a kind of stepping movement.

The "crawling" reflex When placed on his stomach your newborn baby will assume what appears to be a crawling position. This is because his legs are still curled up toward his body as they were in your womb. When your baby kicks his legs he may even be able to shuffle in a crawling manner and may actually move up slightly in his crib. This reflex will disappear as soon as his legs uncurl and he is able to lie flat.

The startle or Moro reflex If your baby hears a loud noise close to him, or if he's been roughly handled, he will throw out his arms and legs, with fingers outstretched, in an attempt to catch on to something. He'll let his limbs fall back slowly toward his body and will then bend his knees and clench his fists. This is a large or "gross" response to a stimulus and many newborn responses are like this. For instance, when your young baby sees you, he uses the whole of his body to greet you. It's only when he gets to about eight or nine months old that he simply smiles and reaches out his arms to you in a more mature greeting.

The grasp reflex A newborn baby will automatically tighten his fingers around anything that is pressed into the palm of his hand. He can grasp very tightly, and immediately after birth this reflex is so strong that his whole weight can be supported if he grasps your fingers. This reflex is lost by the time he is about three months old. If you touch the soles of your baby's feet, you will notice that his toes curl downward as if to grip something.

Moro reflex
Should your baby's head drop back, he will throw his limbs up with fingers outstretched, then let them fall back slowly towards his body.

Grasp reflex
If you put something, for example a finger, in the palm of your baby's hand, he will clench it surprisingly tightly.

Bonding

A newborn baby sleeps for most of his first days, so you should spend all of his waking time with him. Research has shown that physical contact with you, the sound of your voice, and the smell of your body, are very important during the first few days of life. During this time your baby forms a bond with you which, if encouraged, is unique and unbreakable.

This bonding process is nature's way of ensuring that children are nurtured and that the human race as a whole survives. However, in the normal course of events, whether you are breast-feeding or bottle-feeding your baby, he will automatically get the close contact he needs while you are feeding, changing, and holding him. He will get to know you, your smell, and the sound of your voice.

If, for any reason, your baby is taken to the nursery for observation, or to the neonatal (special care) unit, make every effort to visit him as often as possible. Even if he has to be cared for in an incubator, you can touch and caress him through the portholes, talk to him, and possibly feed him. It is important to take all the steps you can to reduce the time you are separated from your baby.

Eye contact is essential

All research points to the fact that physical contact between mother and baby should start as soon after birth as possible. Furthermore, eye contact should follow immediately after birth wherever possible. Most child development experts used to say that babies could not see properly until their eyes could focus, but babies can interpret shapes and outlines. The shape and outline of your face will be recognized by your baby within 36 hours. Research has shown that it is your eyes your baby searches for and concentrates on once he has found them. Furthermore, babies can do this within a few hours of birth. Certainly when my second son was born and I lifted him onto my stomach and called his name he opened his eyes instantly when he heard my voice and flicked them around the room until they came to rest on my face.

It has been shown that mothers who make early eye contact with their babies and continue to do so, particularly during feeding times when they face their babies and look deeply into their eyes, are much more likely to be mothers who are sympathetic and understanding. These mothers tend to solve problems calmly and by logical discussion. They rarely resort to physical punishment of their children.

Early physical contact

After the first few days, you should try to keep your baby in contact with you as much as possible. By contact I mean on your body, for instance, in a sling. It has been known for decades that children who are carried on their mother's backs, such as those in Indian, Inuit, and some African tribes, rarely cry. The newborn infant finds the close physical presence of the mother very reassuring. She is soft and warm, her smell is familiar. When the baby lays his head against the mother's body he hears the familiar heartbeat that he has heard for nine months in the womb. The baby feels secure and at home in his surroundings. It is more natural for your baby to be jogged about on his mother's body especially as it could bring back memories of his cushioned ride in the womb, than to lie completely still on a mattress in a crib.

The importance of smell

We know that your smell is one of the first associations your baby makes with you. You give off a smell to which your baby is very sensitive and to which he responds biologically. Whenever you go into your sleeping baby's room he wakes up. When other people, even your partner, go in to the room he will stay asleep. This is because your baby's very sensitive sense of smell picks up your chemicals, called pheromones, and he wakes because he recognizes you as his main source of comfort, pleasure, and food.

First impressions
Your newborn baby will be still covered in cheesy vernix. It's no longer washed off after birth—it's the best moisturizer known.

Sounds and their effects

Newborns do not like loud noises. While your baby is becoming used to your voice, speak or sing in a gentle, soothing, cooing voice. Research at Oxford University has shown that babies respond better to the high-pitched female voice than to the lower-pitched male voice. To a baby, the mother's voice is almost like therapy. You should chat, sing, or croon to your baby whenever you are with him. Even young babies enjoy nursery rhymes and simple songs, particularly if they have a pronounced rhythm and rhyming sound. Research suggests that children who were sung to early in their lives rapidly develop a feeling for and a facility with words and tend to speak and read slightly earlier.

Mother love

Most mothers are exhilarated, though exhausted, after the delivery of a baby and feel great love for the child. Some mothers, however, find they feel nothing at first.

We now know that mother love, put very simply, is a response to hormones. There are certain hormones produced in the brain almost immediately after delivery, namely oxytocin or prolactin, which trigger lactation and are also responsible for maternal feelings. Different women have different emotional responses to these hormones and some may find that their love for their babies takes longer to develop.

A mother's feelings for her baby can also be affected by other factors, including the delivery and her own expectations of

the birth and the baby. It's not uncommon for the baby's arrival to be something of an anticlimax. Even if it is short and perfectly normal, labor is a very dramatic event and it is a hard act to follow.

Conversely, if the labor has been very hard and long, and if drugs have been used, the mother may be too exhausted and numbed to feel great love for her child. Also, she may have unrealistic expectations of her response to her newborn baby. She may, for instance, expect to recognize him instantly as her

Instant recognition
In some babies you can immediately recognize their inherited features; in others they are less obvious. Parents will always know their own baby.

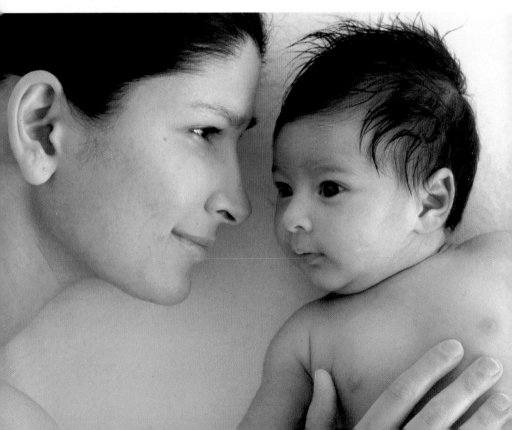

own flesh and blood, or for him to look physically similar to herself or his father. In fact, this is rarely the case, so it's important to be aware of it.

Most women, however, find that their love grows gradually over the 48 or 72 hours after their babies' births, until on the third day they feel a palpable love for their new babies. But don't be surprised if it takes two weeks or more.

Spend time with your baby

A mother's response to her baby can be affected by the amount of time she spends with him during the first few days of life. In one study, a group of mothers in a hospital ward were permitted only routine contact with their babies. Another group of mothers in the same ward were allowed to have contact with their babies for an extra 15 hours during their three days in the hospital. The two groups were interviewed one month after delivery and a year later. They revealed a number of very surprising differences. The mothers who had been given extended contact were found to be more reluctant to leave their babies, to be more responsive to their crying, to engage in more eye-to-eye contact during feeding, and to be generally more attentive. The remarkable thing is that these differences are accounted for by just 15 hours of additional contact during the first three days of life.

While it's undoubtedly true that early physical contact helps bonding, it's not the only factor involved in the development of maternal or paternal feelings. In a study of premature babies, who experience the most extreme form of early separation because they have to stay in an incubator

for an extended period, mothers were separated into two groups. In the first, the standard hospital procedure was used and each mother was only permitted to look at her baby during the several weeks he stayed in the incubator. In the second group, the mothers were permitted to handle their babies in the incubator from the second day onward.

Both groups of mothers were questioned after one week, after one month, and then after discharge from the hospital. It was impossible to find any consistent differences between the two groups. This important piece of research suggests that a mother's attachment to her baby may not be seriously affected by a temporary separation immediately after her baby's birth. That's just as well, otherwise there would be little hope for adoptive parents and their children.

Mothering instincts

Mothering is much more complex than a simple dependency on the hormonal changes that occur at childbirth. The most likely explanation for the way a woman develops mothering instincts is that they stem from the mother's own childhood. Love develops early on in life on a reciprocal basis. It stems from the experience of being loved by parents who give a child the capacity for loving others. It enables the child to return love when it is given and to transfer it to others later on in life. In other words, when a child is loved it makes him fit for love; if a child is deprived of this experience, the ability to love is stunted. This is why it's so important for your child to have your loving attention, care, and concern.

2 Equipment

Go shopping for equipment in the last couple of months before your baby is due, while you can still shop on your own and you feel reasonably energetic. You'll be faced with a seemingly endless choice of "essential" items, but don't be swayed by clever advertising. Ask friends or relatives which items of equipment they found useful and, more important, which ones they bought but never used.

Choosing equipment

Shop around and find out what's available before you make your final choices, and always think of the equipment in relation to your lifestyle. For example, if you feel perfectly relaxed about bathing your baby in the sink, don't bother buying a baby bath just because most people do.

Similarly, if you really like the idea of a large baby carriage and you have a large enough hall, an easy route to stores and parks, and you can afford one, then go ahead and buy a one. Some people think it is unlucky to buy too many things before the birth. Check to see if you can choose what you need but not pick it up until you're ready.

Second hand can be fine

It isn't essential to buy everything new. Babies grow so quickly that some items that are essential for a brief time are useless within a couple of months. Many families are happy to lend or sell such items, so keep an eye open on bulletin boards, in local papers, and your pediatrician's office as well as at house and garage sales and on Internet sites. The only stipulation I'd make when buying second hand, aside from checking for general wear and tear, is to check that all surfaces are smooth and rust-free and that, where applicable, they comply with the latest safety regulations.

However, never buy a second-hand car seat. It may have been damaged in an accident, probably won't have the original instructions and will be difficult to install.

Don't buy too many baby clothes before the birth. You will need to have the basics (see pp.40–42) ready, but you'll find that relatives and friends love buying for a new baby and you'll probably end up with many duplicated items.

Buy a car seat
You can't bring your baby home from the hospital in a car without a car seat. Check that it is comfortable to carry; some snap into a special stroller frame. Ideally, a car seat will have a fastening across the baby's chest.

CHANGING AND BATHING EQUIPMENT

New baby

- Changing unit with storage drawers
- Padded changing mat
- Changing bag for going out, with a folding changing mat
- Baby bathtub
- Cotton balls
- Baby wipes
- Baby oil
- Barrier cream
- Large soft towels
- Washcloth or sponge
- Baby's hair brush
- Blunt-ended scissors
- 4 packs disposable diapers

  or

- 24 cloth diapers

  Diaper liners

  Diaper pins

  Plastic pants

  2 diaper buckets

Older baby

- Toothbrush
- Bath seat and/or nonslip mat for big bath
- Potty
- Steps for reaching the sink

Choice of potties
Get a potty toward the end of the first year, before your child needs one.

Changing and bathing

If you like the idea of having a special changing area, but don't want to build one or convert a piece of furniture like a chest of drawers, then a changing unit is probably right for you. Make sure that it's stable and has plenty of storage space. Alternately, many parents find a padded changing mat on a chest of drawers or on the floor is sufficient.

If you don't want to bath your baby in the sink or a household basin, you'll need a baby bathtub. Some are designed to use on the floor while others fit on a stand or across a bath. Choose one that won't be too heavy when full and is easy to empty.

Baby bath and changing mat
For a young baby you can use a baby bathtub with a stand or you can rest it on a flat surface. A changing mat is an essential item for most parents.

Feeding

If you're breast-feeding you'll need the minimum of equipment—feeding bras and breast pads for you, and a couple of bottles and a breast pump if you want to express some milk. Bottle-feeding mothers will have to buy a complete feeding kit (*see right*). There are many kinds of bottles and nipples. Some nipples are molded to the shape of the baby's mouth; others are designed to move in and out like a human nipple when sucked.

When your baby starts on solids you'll need equipment for mashing food into a smooth enough purée. You'll also need unbreakable dishes to serve it in. Special dishes that keep the food hot are available, although they're not essential. Bibs, however, are. Probably the most efficient style is the plastic bib with a pouch that catches drips and pieces of food and can be washed easily.

For an older baby you'll also need some form of highchair and there is a wide variety to choose from. Make sure the chair is stable, and has washable surfaces, a tray with a rim to catch spilled liquids, and a safety harness. Make sure you can release the harness quickly if your baby chokes on food. Some highchairs have adaptable footrests and seats and can be used at the table for an older child for many years.

FEEDING EQUIPMENT

New baby/breast-feeding
- Nursing bra
- Breast pads
- Breast pump if you need to express milk
- Bottles or breast milk storage containers for expressed milk

New baby/bottle-feeding
- Bottles
- Nipples
- Formula
- Large pot for boiling bottles and sterillizing the nipples
- Bottle brush

Older baby
- Plastic bowls
- Baby spoons and forks
- Trainer cups
- Blender or liquidizer
- Bibs
- Highchair and/or booster seat
- Safety harness

Double breast pump
Expressing milk with a double pump is excellent for stimulating milk production. Each breast produces more milk and it's richer, creamier, and more nutritious.

Sleeping

The best choice for a newborn is a carrier, which is easy to move from room to room. Then a crib when the baby outgrows it.

Choose a crib with two mattress heights, so you don't have to bend too far in the early days, and with sides that drop down—it's much easier to get to the baby. Make sure that the crib's side rails are close together, so your baby's head can't get stuck. The crib mattress should fit snugly, allowing no more than one finger to slide between the mattress and the crib side. Foam mattresses are best; some have airholes that allow your child to breathe if she turns onto her tummy while asleep. Folding, fabric-sided travel cribs are useful for vacations and going out with the baby in the evening. Baby sleeping bags are useful for older babies. All equipment must comply with local safety standards.

Avoid bumpers and fleeces as they increase the risk of the baby overheating— babies who get too hot are at a greater risk of crib death. Don't put bumpers in cribs, or use a loose blanket for babies

Bassinet and bouncing chair
A bassinet makes a simple, lightweight bed for a newborn. A bouncing chair is useful for babies before they can sit up. Always place it on the floor.

under one year. As soon as your baby shows signs of being able to climb out of her crib, you'll need to buy a bed—some cribs are designed to convert into beds.

Outings and travel

Slings are a popular way of transporting a newborn baby; they're light and comfortable, and allow you to carry your baby close while keeping both hands free. The sling should be used with a neck attachment until your baby can support her own head. Backpacks, which have supportive frames that make it easier to bear a larger baby's weight, are suitable once your baby can sit up by herself.

You'll also need some form of stroller. The one you choose will depend on both your budget and your lifestyle. A large carriage is impractical if you live in a small apartment, three flights up; a folding lightweight stroller or a carriage with a removable carrier is more suitable.

SLEEP EQUIPMENT AND ACCESSORIES

New baby
- Baby carrier
- Waterproof sheet to protect mattress (tie-on sheets are good)
- Cotton sheets
- Cotton cellular blankets
- Fleecy blanket
- Baby monitor

Older baby
- Full-size crib with foam mattress
- Crib comforter (for babies over 12 months)

However, a carriage or a carriage/stroller is much more comfortable for a young baby than a lightweight stroller, which does not usually offer enough support. For the first three months, your baby must be able to lie flat in whatever you choose.

Any kind of stroller or carriage needs to be easy to push, have good brakes, a harness, or rings for one, and a mechanism to prevent the frame from collapsing. You will also need a waterproof cover and a sunshade for it.

Car seats

Whenever you take your child in a car you must comply with safety regulations. A car seat is one item you cannot do without if you intend to take your baby in your own or anyone else's car. Never buy a second-hand seat unless you can be certain that it has not been damaged in an accident.

All babies under one year old and up to 20 pounds (9 kilograms) should travel in a rear-facing seat, which provides better protection for a young baby's head, neck, and spine. These seats are portable so they can be used for carrying your baby to and from the car, and most can attach onto a stroller, as well. Never put a rear-facing seat in the front of the car.

An older baby can have a forward-facing seat, which must be fixed in the back seat of the car. These are designed to be left in the car. Some need to be installed; others use existing seat belts. Children up to the age of 3 years and 40 pounds (18 kilograms) should sit in a forward-facing car seat. Children up to the age of 8 years and 80 pounds (36 kilograms) must use a booster seat. A child should not sit in the front seat until at least 12 years old.

Additional equipment

Even young babies like to see what's going on around them and a bouncing baby chair is useful for a baby before she can sit. Always place the chair on the floor and make sure she is safely strapped in.

Although many people find playpens reminiscent of a baby prison, some find them invaluable. If you decide to buy one your choice will be between a collapsible nylon-meshed pen and rail, or a square wooden pen; both have a padded base.

CARRYING EQUIPMENT

- Front-carrying fabric sling with neck support for newborns. Make sure it's washable.
- Backpack for an older baby.
- Carriage with solid body and collapsible fabric hood,
  or
- Carriage with removable carrier,
  or
- Folding stroller that reclines for a young baby (there are many types available, ask other people which they prefer),
  or
- Carriage/carrier combination—can be used as a carrier on wheels for young baby and converts into a stroller. There are combinations called travel systems that include a car seat,
  or
- All-terrain, three-wheeler stroller.
- Sunshade for summer.
- Waterproof cover for stroller.
- Rear-facing car seat for baby up to 20 pounds (9 kilograms).
- Front-facing car seat for older child—this is compulsory in many states, up to various ages and weights. Check your local regulations
- Changing bag to carry spare clothes/diapers.

Your baby's room

A baby's room doesn't have to be stylish or filled with expensive furnishings, but it does need to be warm, clean, safe, and attractive. Make sure that the furniture is easy to wipe clean and has smooth, rounded edges. Any paint used should be nontoxic and lead-free.

Always use flameproof fabric for bedding, upholstery, and curtains. Most important, your baby's room should be fun, with plenty of bright colors, pictures, and mobiles to stimulate her senses. The colors of nature—blue, yellow, and green—are said to be soothing for your baby. Paint the walls in cheerful colors, use splashes of primary colors for curtains and accessories and put things to look at on the walls.

BASIC FURNISHINGS

- Baby carrier and stand.
- Crib (you can put a baby carrier in the crib to begin with).
- Changing area with storage for diapers and other items.
- Storage for clothes and toys.
- Baby monitor so you can hear her if she wakes or cries.
- Low chair where you can sit when feeding.
- Thick curtains or good blinds to keep the room warm and dark.
- Dimmer switch to provide low levels of light for night changing or feedings.
- Shelves for books and toys.
- Mobiles hung over the crib and changing area.
- Pictures on the walls and on a bulletin board in her room. Change the pictures regularly to keep her interested.

What your baby will need

You'll need plenty of storage space, especially above or to the side of the changing area. If you plan to build your own changing area you'll need a wide, flat surface on which to place the changing mat. Wide-topped chests of drawers make ideal changing tables because they have a large surface area and plenty of storage space for diapers and clothes. It is a good idea to build shelves above wherever you place it. Make sure that the surface is smooth, then cover it with a washable covering and put a padded changing mat on top. The floor covering should be heavy duty and easy to keep clean; consider cork tiles or vinyl with a couple of nonslip rugs. Carpet is warm and absorbs noise but is harder to keep clean.

Room temperature

A baby's room doesn't need to be very warm, but should be kept at a constant temperature. Around 65°F (18°C) is suitable if your baby is covered with two blankets and a sheet. If the room is warmer, use fewer blankets. If you don't want to heat the entire house to this level, put a thermostatically controlled heater in her room.

Adapting the room for a toddler

Your baby's room is going to have to evolve to suit her needs as she gets older and more mobile. She'll need plenty of floor space for crawling and taking her first steps so keep furniture to a minimum. What there is should be steady and stable

Planning a baby's room
A new baby's room doesn't need a lot of special furniture. The essentials are a crib, a diaper-changing area, and a comfortable chair for you when feeding.

so that she can use it to pull herself up without accidents. Be extra aware of the safety risks for small, inquisitive toddlers and follow the recommendations on p.296.

At some stage, she will need to move from her crib to a bed, but don't rush her. Most parents make the switch between the ages of two and four. You must do it when a child becomes able to climb out of a crib. Once she has a bed, she can get out of it by herself and explore her room, so you need to be certain that everything is safe.

Storage space

Make sure there are plenty of places to keep toys so it is easy for your child to keep her things in order. It's much more fun to play with toys if your child can find them easily and don't have to search in several different places for all the pieces. This does not need to be shelves, drawers, or ready-made toy boxes; wicker baskets, plastic stacking boxes, or laundry baskets all provide good storage for children's things. Don't worry too much about tidiness though—it's having a good time that counts.

A blackboard or a special wall area that your toddler knows she's allowed to chalk on may also be welcome as soon as she's ready to do so.

ADAPTING A ROOM FOR A TODDLER

- Nonslip rugs to make wooden floors cosier to sit on.
- Bedside table for nightlight and drinks; make sure she can't pull on cords.
- Low table and chair where your toddler can sit and draw and play.
- Low hook where she can hang up her coat.
- Bulletin board for her special pictures.
- Toy boxes on wheels.

3 Clothing

All parents take great pride in their new baby's appearance and it's very tempting for you and your family and friends to rush out and buy lots of clothes for him. It's up to you what you choose, but there's absolutely no need to spend a lot of money. Remember that your child is going to grow rapidly during these first years, and he will grow out of clothes very quickly. As far as your baby is concerned, he doesn't mind what he wears as long as it is soft and comfortable and can be put on and taken off without too much trouble.

Choosing clothes birth to 1 year

Your newborn baby won't be very active, but that does not mean he's going to stay scrupulously clean. There will inevitably be accidents and leaks from diapers, and he's bound to spit up and dribble sometimes—all of which will mean fairly frequent changes of clothing. Before your baby is born, make sure that you have enough clothes to keep up with his needs. Make sure, too, that everything is machine washable and colorfast.

Initially, there is no need to make a distinction between daywear and nightwear, and by far the most suitable nightclothes are one-piece stretchies. As your baby gets older, sleep suits make a cosy alternative. If you buy T-shirts or Onesies, buy wide-necked ones that go on over his head easily—babies hate having their faces covered. Onesies are useful because they can be fastened under the baby's diaper. Buy brightly patterned Onesies that can be used as T-shirts too.

BASICS FOR A NEW BABY

- 6–8 T-shirts/undershirts or Onesies
- 6–8 one-piece stretchies/pajamas
- 2 cardigans/sweaters (4 for winter babies)
- 2–3 pair of socks and padders
- 2 pair of mittens
- 2 nightgowns (choose one with drawstring bottoms to keep feet warm)
- 1 blanket or shawl
- Protective clothing and sunhat for sun protection
- One-piece snowsuit for winter

One-piece stretchies
These are ideal for babies of any age. Stretchies are easy to put on, they keep your baby warm, and allow for freedom of movement.

BUYING CLOTHES FOR A NEWBORN

- Whatever sizing system the manufacturer uses, make sure you buy a size that will last until your baby's at least two months old. He won't be uncomfortable if his clothes are slightly too big. It's more practical than buying the newborn size, which he'll quickly grow out of.
- Buy only machine-washable, colorfast clothing for your baby.
- Make sure any clothing you buy allows easy access to the diaper, so there's the minimum of undressing involved. One-piece stretchies with snaps in the crotch or down the front and legs are the easiest to put on.
- In the early weeks, you may find it simplest to use nightdresses that can just be lifted up to get at the diaper.
- Clothes that open down the front or have wide necks are the best because babies hate having their faces covered.
- Clothes that fasten up the front also mean you don't have to turn your baby over when you're dressing him.
- Material should be soft and comfortable with no hard seams or rough stitching; check the neck and waistband before buying. Buy terry cloth, cotton, or pure wool clothes; if you buy clothes made of man-made fibers check that they feel soft and comfortable.
- Buy nonflammable clothing.
- Avoid lacy shawls or cardigans—your baby's tiny fingers can easily get caught in the holes.
- Avoid white—it gets dirty quickly and needs more care when washing. Babies look as nice in bright colors as in the pastels traditionally specified for them.
- If you buy a hat, either buy one with a chinstrap, or sew some ribbon on it. Many babies hate wearing hats and pull them off unless they're tied on under the chin.

Additional clothing for a baby

The kind of clothes you buy in addition to the basics will be determined by finances and personal taste. There is no essential piece of clothing, but there are some items that are more practical than others.

In summer, for example, cotton T-shirts and shorts or cotton dresses are the most suitable because they're cool and leave the baby's limbs free; in winter, mini-tracksuits and overalls are practical alternatives to one-piece stretchies. Once your baby is mobile he'll need clothing that gives adequate knee protection. Just like when your baby was very young, stick to clothes that give you easy access to his diaper, because by the time he's crawling, he's not going to want to stay still for very long. All clothes you buy should be machine washable and colorfast.

Check fit regularly

Keep an eye on how tight the legs, neck, and wrists are on all clothes and buy the next size up accordingly. Bear in mind that clothes with snaps at the neck often last longer. Babies often outgrow clothes because their heads can no longer go through the neck opening; with snaps you can just leave them undone so the garment still goes over your baby's head.

You'll probably learn how to gauge your baby's size quite accurately, but if you're worried, always go by the height and weight charts given in stores, not by age. Different countries and manufacturers use varying sizing systems, so if you're confused about sizes ask a salesperson's advice. If in doubt, buy the larger size: looser-fitting clothes are much more comfortable than tight-fitting clothes, and your baby will soon grow into them.

Dressing a baby birth to 1 year

Babies need changing frequently in the first months and, initially, you may not be fully confident about supporting your floppy baby and dealing with his clothes at the same time. Don't worry: it's perfectly normal to be a bit awkward at first, and any fears you have are easily overcome with practice and patience on your part.

With a new baby, always dress and undress him on a flat surface: a changing mat, the bed, or the floor, is ideal because it allows you to have both hands free. Keep the amount of time he's undressed to a minimum and don't get flustered if your baby cries when you take off his clothes. Young babies hate being undressed; they're afraid of the air on their naked

bodies; the removal of the comforting fabric they were wearing makes them feel very insecure. When your baby feels like this he's going to cry, very loudly. It's not because of you, so don't think that you're a bad parent. Keep calm and continue the job, but always have something nearby to attract your baby's attention, like a mobile above the changing area.

Using your lap

When your baby has more muscle control and you feel more confident, you can sit him on your lap to take off his clothes. If you sit with your legs crossed, your baby can sit neatly in the hollow of your legs. Your arm should cradle your baby. You can

PUTTING ON A UNDERSHIRT

1 Lay your baby on his back on a flat, firm surface. Stretch the neck opening of the undershirt or Onesie as wide open as you can with both hands.

2 Slide the undershirt over your baby's head, gently lifting his head up to bring the undershirt over to the back of his neck, then lower his head.

3 Widen each sleeve or armhole with your fingers and bring your baby's arms through, fist first, one at a time. Draw the undershirt down over his body.

PUTTING ON A STRETCH SUIT

1 Undo all the snaps of the stretchie and lay it on a flat surface. Then lay your baby on top of it so that his neck lines up with the neck of the stretchie.

2 Put your baby's legs into the legs of the stretchie, one at a time, feet first. Fasten the stretchie under the diaper area so he can't kick it off again.

3 To put his arms in, roll back one arm of the stretchie and guide your baby's arm in, fist first. Roll the sleeve up into place. Repeat with the other arm.

also combine sitting your baby on your lap and using a flat surface. For example, it may be easier to put on the top layer in your lap, but to deal with the bottom half on a flat surface. You'll probably need to distract your baby in some way, so have some toys for him to hold.

Dressing an older baby

Once your baby can crawl, he won't want to stay still for long and dressing may take place "on the move." However, toward the end of the first year this will be coupled with an ability to help you put on his clothes. For example, if you ask your 11-month-old baby to make a fist, or stretch out an arm, he'll probably do so willingly and you'll be able to slide the sweater or jacket on without having to draw his hand through yourself.

Name the clothes as you put them on or take them off, and make a game out of the whole process. For example, make it

into a kind of hide and seek, Peek-a-boo game: "Where is your arm?" "Oh, look, here it comes!"

If he will not stay still, try to undress your baby when he's occupied with something else. For example, if your baby has a favorite song that he likes to sing with you, always sing it while you are dressing or undressing him.

Washing your baby's clothes

Once your baby starts eating solids, he's bound to get messy, even when he's wearing a bib, and once he starts walking his clothing will get dirtier, too. Make sure everything can go in the washing machine. If possible, have enough changes of clothes so you don't have to do the laundry every day.

If you need to use an enzyme-containing washing powder to remove stubborn stains, wash the garment in your usual detergent afterward to remove any traces of potentially irritating enzymes.

UNDRESSING A NEWBORN

1 First, unfasten your baby's stretchie. If his diaper needs to be changed, gently pull both legs out of the suit, leaving his top half covered while you change him.

2 Hold each sleeve by the cuff and slide his hand out, holding his arm at the elbow. Roll his undershirt up and gently pull his arms from the sleeves.

3 Pull the neck wide open and lift the undershirt over your baby's head, keeping the fabric off his face. Support his head while you carefully remove his undershirt.

DEALING WITH STAINS

Vomit/feces	Use an enzyme-containing detergent after you've removed the vomit and rinsed the garment with cold water.
Milk	Remove milk stains by rinsing the clothing thoroughly in cold water and then using an enzyme-containing detergent.
Egg	If there is an egg stain on clothing, soak in cold water for an hour before laundering in the usual way.
Fruit and chocolate	Douse tough stains such as chocolate or grape juice with seltzer, rub until the discoloration has gone, then wash as usual.
Blood	Soak bloodstains in cold water for thirty minutes. If they don't come out use an enzyme-containing detergent. If this fails, try a few drops of ammonia on the stain.
Lipstick	Dab stain with a soft white cloth that's been dipped in rubbing alcohol; or use a pre-wash stain stick, then wash as normal.
Grass	Remove grass stains with alcohol if they are resistant to laundering.
Chewing gum	Soften the gum with paint thinner before gently pulling the gum away from the fabric, or freeze the garment and scrape it off.

Choosing clothes 1 to 3 years

As your baby grows, your main concern when buying clothes will be that they're comfortable and, when he's more active, that they allow easy movement. Your baby will no longer spend most of the time asleep, and as he starts to move around more, he's going to need more clothes. They'll have to be suitable for various weather conditions (rain, cold, sun), and they'll also have to be tough enough to

withstand the wear and tear your toddler will give them. Once he can crawl he'll need sturdy protection for his knees, and once he can walk, he'll need shoes.

As before, buy clothing in a material that moves with your child so that however active he is there's no risk of him being uncomfortable or of the material tearing. Terry cloth, cotton, and corduroy are ideal. When he's learning to use the potty, clothing must be able to be pulled down or up easily. When he's learning how to dress or undress, avoid buying clothes with zippers or difficult fastenings, and use elastic waists for as long as possible.

Dressing himself

It'll take a while for your child to develop the coordination needed to dress himself, but by the time he's 18 months he'll be trying, even if he's just pulling off his socks. Any attempts at dressing or undressing should be encouraged. They're a sign of growing independence and maturity, not to mention coordination.

Try laying out his clothes in a way that your child can go up to them and maneuver them on easily. Even if he seems to be fumbling, don't step in until it's really necessary. You will, however, have to deal with buttons and snaps until your child has the dexterity to cope with them.

Room for growth
Overalls with buckles are ideal as they can be adjusted to fit your child as she grows, which means they can be worn for longer. And she'll enjoy learning how to manage the buckles for herself.

Buying clothes

Keep your child's measurements written down and, since your child is growing very quickly, make sure that you take new measurements frequently.

- Buy unisex clothes when you can. There is no reason why a girl shouldn't wear boys' clothes, and they are usually sturdier anyway.
- Get outdoor clothes on the large side so that extra layers can be worn underneath. Since such clothes are often more expensive, the larger size will allow your child to grow into it. For items that are worn every day, buy the best quality you can afford. This way they will last longer and may even be passed on to siblings or friends.
- Brightly colored clothes are useful if your toddler wanders away—he'll be easier to spot in the playground, for example.
- T-shirts can double as pajama tops.
- Buy patterned undershirts so they can double up as T-shirts.
- Put extra buttons on overall straps so that they can be lengthened as your child gets taller.
- Young children find short zippers difficult to manipulate, so buy pants with elastic waists for as long as possible.
- Buy tube socks without shaped heels so they grow with the child. Buy all socks in the same brand and the same color so that you don't have trouble matching them.
- Buy clothes with elastic waistbands and pants or skirts with shoulder straps so they can be let down.
- Avoid "fitted" clothes—your toddler will grow out of them more quickly.

- Avoid man-made fabrics—they don't "breathe" like natural fibers and could make your child uncomfortably hot, especially in summer. Look for natural fibers such as pure cotton or a fabric with a high cotton content.
- A loose coat, like a ski jacket coat, will last your child for two winters: one as a coat with the sleeves turned back, and the second as a jacket with the sleeves at their usual length.
- Some foot pajamas have plastic soles on the feet. To prevent your child's feet from sweating, cut a small hole in the middle to let the air circulate.

Dressing toddlers

- Keep your toddler's overall straps from slipping down by crossing them at the back (and front if necessary).
- When you're teaching your child to use buttons, show him how to button from the bottom up.

MAKING CLOTHES LAST

- When foot pajamas get too short for comfort, cut off the feet for an extra month's wear.
- Reinforce the knees on the inside of new jeans with the extra fabric you trim from the bottom of the legs, or use iron-on patches.
- Make summer shorts from long winter pants that are too short or have gotten worn at the knees.
- When your child outgrows an expensive jacket, you can cut out the sleeves and let her wear it as a vest.
- Run a dark blue crayon, indelible pencil, or a fountain pen filled with blue/black ink over the white line when jeans have been let down.

Getting dressed
By about the age of two, your child will be trying to dress herself. Choose pants with elastic waists to make the task easier.

- Wherever possible use Velcro, but don't use this near the neck because it may rub and cause sore patches.
- Tiny hands find zippers difficult to manage, so put a key ring through the zipper fastener for easy handling.
- When your child is learning to use a zipper, teach him to pull the zipper away from his skin and clothes to prevent the zipper from catching on his skin.
- Put a patch or clear marking on the front of a garment so that your child can tell front from back.
- Mark the hole in a belt that your child should use with a stick-on gold star or a piece of tape.

- Until your child learns to hold a sweater when he is putting on a coat, sew elastic loops inside the cuffs so that the child can hold onto those and keep the sleeves from being dragged up as the coat is being put on.
- If the zipper is sticking, run a soft lead pencil or a bar of soap over its teeth to make it run smoothly.
- If your child is unwilling to make a fist when you're putting on a sweater, put a small treat, like a raisin, into his hand. He will grasp it and make a fist, allowing you to push the sleeve on.
- Attach gloves or mittens to a long piece of string that you can thread through the arms of the coat.
- Wet shoelaces before tying—the bows won't slip and they will stay tied.
- When you first put on your baby's new shoes cover the slippery soles with a piece of tape so that he won't slide on a slippery floor, or score the soles with scissors so that they grip.
- If the ends of your child's shoelaces become frayed, coat them with clear nail polish or wrap some tape around them until you can replace them.
- Always buy boots large enough to accommodate an extra pair of socks. Rain boots aren't very warm, so put a pair of thick socks over your child's usual socks to keep his feet warm.
- When your child first starts to use buttons, sew large buttons onto his clothes so that he can handle them more easily and, if you can, sew them on with elastic thread.
- Once practical concerns are taken care of, let your child have a say in what you buy and choose his favorite colors.

CHOOSING SHOES FOR TODDLERS

There's no need to put your baby into shoes until he's walking. The bones in your baby's feet are soft and pliable—so pliable that even the pressure of tightly fitting socks can misshape toes if your baby wears them regularly. When it's very cold, or when he starts to crawl, you can put on socks or booties, but make sure there's plenty of room for his feet to move around.

When buying shoes, go to a reputable shoe store and make sure the assistant has been trained to measure and fit children's shoes. She should always measure the foot for width and length before bringing any shoes for your child to try on. Once the shoes are on, she should press the joints of the foot to check that the foot is not restricted in any way and be sure that the buckle or laces hold it firmly in place and don't let it slip. Ask your child to walk around in the shoes to be sure the toe doesn't crease up and hurt when he's walking and to double-check there's no slipping.

The type of shoe you buy will be determined by when and where it is to be worn. Your child will need a sturdy, well made pair of leather shoes once he is running around and playing outdoors, and

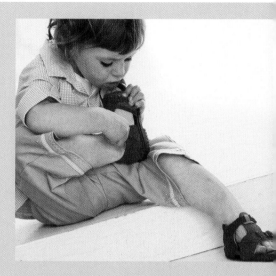

New independence
Children love having new shoes, and spend hours taking them on and off.

some rain boots for wet weather. In summer, leather sandals, canvas shoes, or sneakers are fine as long as they fit properly.

You should never buy second-hand shoes. Good shoes are an essential means of ensuring that your child has good feet in adult life.

Uppers should have no hard seams or stitching that might hurt the foot and cause chafing

Arch should be well formed to give support

Healthy feet
Good shoes are essential for the healthy development of your child's feet. At first, most young children find it easier to cope with buckles or Velcro than laces.

Toe should be wide enough for the child's toes to fan out without restriction. The box over the toe should be high enough that no pressure is exerted on the toenails

Sole should be light, flexible, and nonslip

Fastenings should be adjustable and hold the foot firmly in the shoe

The heel should grip snugly and shouldn't be higher than 1½ inches (14 centimeters)

4 Holding and handling

In the first few weeks of life your baby will seem very vulnerable, and many parents are afraid to pick up their newborns, fearful that they may somehow accidentally damage their child. It's important to get used to holding your baby properly, not just for her comfort but for your own sake. You'll never manage to feed or bath her successfully if you are unsure about holding her.

Handling your baby birth to 1 year

Most babies like to be handled in a firm way, especially in the early weeks when the sensation of being tightly enclosed (whether by your arms, by clothing, or by a receiving blanket), gives a great sense of security. When it comes to actually moving your baby, do it as slowly, as gently, and as quietly as you can.

It's an instinctive reaction to hold your baby close to you, and to talk soothingly and lovingly as you look into her face and eyes, and many experiments have shown that children do need and benefit from this physical contact. For example, premature babies gain more weight when they are laid on soft, downy sheets simply because the fluffy sheets give them the impression of being touched. Your newborn baby will be comforted by any kind of holding, cuddling, or caressing, and skin-to-skin contact, with both of you lying naked in bed, is probably the best of all. In this way she can smell your skin, feel its touch and warmth, and hear your heart beating.

Picking up your newborn baby

Don't worry about picking your baby up; she's much tougher than you think. The only thing that you really have to be careful of is her lolling head. Until she is about four weeks old she'll have little control over it, so whenever you pick her up do it in a way that supports the head.

Putting down your newborn baby

When you lay your baby down you must make sure her head is supported. Unless you do, it will flop back and may give her the sensation that she is going to fall; her body will jerk and she'll stretch out both arms and legs in the Moro or "startle" reflex (*see p.27*). Either put your baby down in the same way I suggested for picking her up, so that your whole arm supports her spine, neck, and head, or wrap your baby fairly tightly in a receiving blanket so her head is supported and her arms held close against her body. Once she is lying down in the crib, gently unwrap

Playing with an older baby
Your baby needs to be picked up and cuddled.
She'll enjoy conversations and contact with you.

HOW TO PICK UP A NEWBORN BABY

1 Slide one hand under your baby's neck to support her head. Slide the other under her back and bottom.

2 Pick her up gently and smoothly, so you don't startle her, making sure her whole body is well supported.

3 Gently swing her around so she is against your chest. Holding her close makes her feel safe, especially if she can see your face.

her. Swaddling her tightly makes her feel secure, so it's a useful way of comforting and calming a distressed baby.

Newborn and very young babies should be placed on their backs to sleep, with their feet against the foot of the crib. The latest medical opinion and research suggests this is the best and safest position in which to minimize the risk of crib death (Sudden Infant Death Syndrome), and it is no longer believed that, in this position, there is an increased risk of the baby spitting up and possibly choking. By four or five months, your baby will choose the position she finds most comfortable.

Carrying your young baby
When you are carrying your baby, gently support her head in the crook of your arm. Hold her so you can see her face and she can see yours.

Support your baby's head
Whenever you are putting your baby down to sleep, remember always to support her head and body to prevent her head from flopping back.

Carrying your newborn baby

In your arms There are two main positions in which to carry your baby in your arms. The first is with the baby's head in the crook of either arm, slightly higher than the rest of her body, which rests on the lower part of your arm encircled by your wrist and hand, which support her back and bottom. Your other arm provides additional support to the baby's bottom and legs. This position allows you to talk to and smile at your baby.

The second way is to hold your baby against the upper part of your chest, with your forearm across her back and her head resting on your shoulder, supported by your hand. This position leaves the other hand free, which is useful if you need to pick something up. Otherwise it can provide support to the baby's bottom.

In a sling There is no reason at all why your newborn shouldn't be carried in a sling, as long as it provides adequate support for the baby's neck and head and envelops the baby's body so she can't slip out of either side. The best kind of sling is the very soft, pouchlike one that allows the baby to rest in curled position. Most parents feel happiest wearing the sling on their chest where they can see and cuddle the baby easily and generally protect her more effectively.

Picking up your older baby

Once your baby has control of her head, there is no need to take the kind of care you did when she was a newborn. The head and body will now stay aligned when she's picked up. When she reaches this stage, the best way to pick her up is to put your hands under her armpits and lift her toward you. Once you've lifted her up, you can carry her in the crook of your arm or against your shoulder. As her back, neck, and head muscles become stronger, she can be carried on your hip with your arm across her back and holding her thigh.

Carrying your older baby

By the age of four or five months, most parents carry their baby on one of their hips; which one is determined by whether the parent is right- or left-handed. You'll inevitably develop your own methods of carrying your baby and these may well vary according to her mood. For longer journeys

HOW TO CARRY AN OLDER BABY

On one hip
Your baby is now able to support herself well enough to sit on your hip. This allows her to look all around while still feeling secure and close to you.

Facing forwards
Hold your baby securely around the waist, face outward, so that she can look around her. You can use your other hand to support her or keep it free.

Rocking
You can hold your baby under her tummy and make this a boisterous game by swinging her quite high, or just rock her gently from side to side to soothe her.

you can still carry her in a front sling (though she may be getting too heavy for that now) or in a backpack.

Putting down your older baby

You don't have to be as careful putting down an older baby as a newborn one. She is now stronger and can control her head so she can be put down in exactly the same way as she is picked up. Alternatively, you can support the upper part of your baby's body with one hand curved diagonally across her back and with the other hand supporting her bottom.

If you are lifting your child so you can put her into a highchair, support her under the armpits and let both legs dangle so she can place them easily between the tray and seat. Don't forget to strap her in every time you put her in the chair.

Handling your child 1 to 3 years

A toddler needs much less holding and carrying than a young baby but there will still be times when she'll signal that she wants to be carried, just like she used to be. If you ignore these signals she'll probably cry.

Cuddling and security

You may find she wants to be carried when she's tired, when you've been out for a long walk, when she's cutting a tooth, if she isn't feeling well, if she's fearful, or if you have been away. Don't hesitate to give this kind of physical support and affection. She will give you a very clear signal when she is feeling reassured, and will wriggle down and run off.

We never outgrow the need for physical affection. Always recognize this in your children. Never scoff at it and always give it. When my children were growing up, they liked to be cuddled every now and then, especially when they were tired or had had a difficult day at school, if they were fearful about my departure or absence, or if the world simply didn't feel right. Even when children are quite old they may still want to sit on your knee occasionally. In unfamiliar circumstances, they may even like to sit on your knee while eating, particularly if strangers are present and they feel they are under observation. Don't ridicule your·child for wanting this. If it is convenient, let her

Keep cuddling her
All babies love to be cuddled and as they grow up, they need the reassuring and loving embrace of caring parents more, not less.

AVOIDING BACK STRAIN

Babies and toddlers inevitably require lots of lifting and carrying, not to mention the carriages, strollers, and other equipment that go along with them. It is important for the protection of your back that you learn a lifting technique that avoids injury and strain. Don't lift with straight legs and curved back, because this puts strain on your back. Instead, keep your back straight, bend your knees, and lift, using your powerful thigh muscles to take the weight.

sit on your knee; there is absolutely nothing wrong with it, and a few moments of your touch will give your child the confidence to handle the situation in her own way. To my mind, a child should never have to go to bed without some hugging to provide a sense of security and the reassuring feeling that you really care.

Reassurance and sympathy

When your young child is hurt, worried, puzzled, or frightened, always be there with an encircling, comforting arm and a sympathetic word. But give these reassurances in the form that your child wants and don't overpower her with your physical affection when she makes obvious signs that she doesn't require it.

Of course there are some children who don't like to be handled or hugged very much. They usually show this from a very early age by stiffening their bodies and crying when you hold them. This can be quite difficult for a parent to cope with because it seems like rejection (*see p.239*). This kind of baby usually grows up to be a child who avoids physical contact and turns her head away if you lean to kiss her. They make no physical overtures themselves and can be quite difficult children to show affection to and to love in an overt way. They may never learn how to accept physical affection or to be comfortable with it. If your child is like this, the only way for you to treat her is to not make the discomfort worse by pushing physical affection on her. Respect your child's diffidence. Wait for her to come to you and only give her physical affection when she shows you by her actions that she wants it.

Holding and handling older children

As children get older they become more independent and we may think that they need less touching, stroking, holding, and cuddling. This is true, to a point, but don't make the mistake of thinking that they don't need physical affection at all—especially boys, who may feel that kissing and hugging are not masculine behavior.

I personally made it a rule to tell my children every day that I loved them, whenever the whim took me. I think that parents should make similar resolutions about holding and touching their children even if it's just letting them sit on your knee at the breakfast table, or putting an arm around your child when you read a book or look at the paper. Always give your children a hug as you talk over the day when you put them to bed.

Children need you

As your children get older, they often become somewhat shy about public demonstrations of affection, and even about the need for it. Always choose private moments to show your love and then your child won't feel self-conscious about luxuriating in your care, attention, and love.

If you have several young children it can be very difficult to spread yourself out between them evenly. I remember a friend of mine who had twins; out of necessity, she adopted a pragmatic approach to the problem. Instead of trying to ensure that each twin had an equal share of her time and attention every day, she concentrated instead on taking care of whichever twin needed her at any given moment, and assumed that over the months and years it would all even out.

This is the attitude I tried to pursue when my own children were growing up,

Kiss it better
When a young child is upset about something, nothing is as comforting as a hug from you and a kiss to make everything better again.

and it is an invaluable approach for a mother of twins. Of course, most of the time you will be giving your children equal attention, but if one demands more than the other, give it. She is asking for it because she needs it.

5 All about diapers

Until your child starts to use the potty, probably some time during the third year, he will have to wear diapers both day and night. During the first few months life may seem like an endless round of diaper changing. But don't despair. As your child grows and gains more control over bowel and bladder muscles, he will go for longer without excreting and urinating and the number of diapers you need to change will decrease. By about two and a half, he will probably become aware of wanting to go to the bathroom. It is at this point, and not before, that you should start toilet training.

Diapers and changing birth to 1 year

Your first choice in diapers will be between cloth and disposable types. Many parents prefer disposables, although an increasing debate on environmental issues has led other parents to consider cloth diapers.

Yet the issue is not clear cut: the detergents required to clean cloth diapers can be viewed as pollutants to the water supply, and the energy required to wash them might also be regarded as wasteful. While fabric diapers are cheaper than disposables in the long run, you need to consider the increased electricity bills for frequently running the washing machine, and the cost in your time.

What is clear is that, providing that the diaper is changed as often as necessary, and that the basic rules of hygiene are observed, your baby will be happy. The techniques for cleaning and caring for your baby's bottom will be the same.

When to change a diaper

Change your baby's diaper whenever you notice that it is soiled or wet. The number of times the diaper needs to be changed will vary from baby to baby and from day to day. However, you will probably always change the diaper when your baby wakes in the morning, when he's put to bed at night, and when he's been given a bath. In addition, you'll find that your baby will need changing after a feeding because of the gastrocolic reflex that stimulates the elimination of stools when food is taken in.

Always change your baby on a soft, warm, waterproof surface; padded changing mats are ideal for this. Usually

Diaper changing can be fun
Make diaper changing time a chance to chat with your baby and enjoy her company instead of a chore. She's less likely to get upset if you're talking and laughing.

made of a foam-filled, waterproof material, they have a slightly raised edge to prevent the baby from rolling off. They can be placed on whatever surface you prefer—floor, table, or bed. As your baby gets older and starts to wriggle when you change his diaper, you may find it safer and easier to change him on the floor or on a low bed, whether or not you use a mat. Never leave your baby alone on any surface that is above floor level.

Changing a diaper

This is always easier if you are prepared. Make sure everything you need is within easy reach. The last thing you want to discover halfway through changing your baby is that you've left the clean diapers downstairs and the cotton balls or baby wipes in the bathroom.

There is no need to wash your baby's bottom with soap at each change: just gently wipe off the feces with a corner of the diaper, then clean your baby's bottom with water or a baby wipe. If the diaper is only wet, use a water-soaked washcloth or cotton ball. When you change your baby, watch out for any redness and take the appropriate action (see p.68).

If your baby is very wriggly and restless when you change him, have a toy handy as a distraction. With an older baby, involve him in the process by letting him hold something, or give him a book to look at. Talk to your baby all the time—diaper changing is a great opportunity to interact with your baby.

Boys often urinate when their diaper is changed, so cover the penis with a clean diaper as you take the old one off.

CLEANING A GIRL

1 Lift your baby's legs by holding her feet or ankles. Use cotton balls dipped in warm water or baby wipes to clean the labia on the outside only.

2 Use a clean cotton ball or a baby wipe to clean the vulva, always wiping from front to back. Clean around the leg creases.

Disposable diapers birth to 1 year

This type of diaper makes diapering as simple as it can be. They are easy to put on—no folding, no pins, and no plastic pants—and can be discarded when they are wet or dirty. They are convenient when you're traveling because they are more absorbent, so you need fewer of them. You also need less space to change them in, and you don't have to carry wet, smelly diapers home with you to be washed. You will, however, need a constant supply so, to avoid carrying huge loads with your shopping, buy them in bulk and have them delivered to your home.

Even if you've chosen to use the fabric variety, it's always useful to keep a stock of disposables in the house. They're a good backup if you've run out of your usual diaper, or if your baby develops a rash because of your washing methods.

Disposable diapers are available in a variety of sizes, suitable for newborns to toddlers, and in a range of styles. They have elastic legs for added protection against leaks, a plastic outer covering, and an absorbent inner layer, sometimes topped with a one-way diaper liner. They are secured with adjustable adhesive tabs. There are special disposables for your baby to wear when swimming, and a pull-on type for toddlers, which can be pulled up and down like a pair of pants. Try different brands and styles until you find what's best for you and your baby.

CLEANING A BOY

1 Lift his legs by holding both ankles. Clean around the genital area. Use a new cotton ball each time you wipe.

2 Still holding your baby's legs, make sure all soiling is removed. Work from the baby's leg creases in toward the penis.

HOW TO PUT ON A DISPOSABLE DIAPER

1 *Open out the diaper, with the adhesive tabs at the top. Lift your baby's legs and slide the clean diaper under her, gently lifting her bottom into position.*

2 *Using both hands, bring the front of the diaper up between your baby's legs, as high as it will go. Tuck in the corners securely around her waist.*

3 *Holding the diaper firmly in place with one hand, fix the adhesive tabs to the front flap of the diaper. Make sure the diaper is not too tight.*

Disposing of a disposable

All disposable diapers are designed to be thrown away: the whole of an all-in-one diaper can be discarded, but not put down the toilet. You can throw used diapers straight into the garbage pail, or wrap them in old plastic bags if you prefer. You can also buy special closable, biodegradable diaper-disposal bags that reduce the smell—they are very useful when traveling or away from home.

Special diaper bins are now available. These are designed to wrap and seal individual soiled diapers in odor-proof plastic film, ready to put in the garbage.

CHOOSING DISPOSABLE DIAPERS

There are many different types of disposable diaper to choose from and they come in a variety of sizes to fit the age and weight of your baby. When trying them, consider the following:

- How absorbent is the diaper and does it keep your baby's bottom dry?
- Is it comfortable around the legs and does it fit around the body well? Check for any hard edges that might irritate your baby.
- You'll need to balance price against efficiency. Buying cheaper diapers might be a false economy if they are not as absorbent or effective as a more expensive brand.

Best for you both

Your baby will need to wear diapers for at least two years until he has full bowel and bladder control, so it's worth taking the time to find out what kind of diaper is best for you both.

Cloth diapers birth to 1 year

Although initially more expensive than disposables, cloth diapers can be cheaper over the years. Made of cotton or muslin, in a variety of styles, they have to be rinsed, sterilized, washed, and dried after use and therefore involve much more labor than disposables. Because they have to be washed regularly you will need a minimum of 24 diapers. Obviously, the more diapers you have the less often you'll have to do the wash (and the more economical your washes will be). Buy the best diapers you can afford. They will last longer and be more absorbent.

DIAPERS AND ACCESSORIES

Here is a selection of reusable diapers and equipment. Provided your baby is changed regularly he will be happy in any style.

PLASTIC COVER

FABRIC DIAPER WITH VELCRO FASTENER

FABRIC DIAPER LINER

LINERS AND SAFETY PINS

Cotton squares These traditional diapers are thick and absorbent and can be folded into a variety of shapes according to your baby's size and needs. They can be bulky on very small babies and newborns. Buy them ready-hemmed to avoid fraying when they are washed. Cotton squares are more absorbent than the majority of disposables and are therefore very useful at night. You can also use a disposable pad inside a cotton square for extra absorbency at night.

Muslin squares These are about the same size as cotton squares, but they are softer. They are ideal for newborn babies because they are soft and comfortable, but they are not very absorbent so need changing frequently.

Fitted cotton These T-shaped diapers are made of a softer, finer fabric than ordinary squares and have a triple-layered central panel for added absorbency. They are shaped to fit neatly around the baby's legs and are more straightforward to put on.

Plastic covers These covers, which come in several designs, are used over cloth diapers to prevent wet or dirty diapers from soiling clothes or bedding. Buy six initially. You'll need to replace them as they get old, torn, and unusable.

All-in-one reusables These offer all the features and convenience of a disposable diaper, but are produced using fewer chemicals, are made of cotton, and don't contain dyes, latex, or perfume. They're machine washable, can be brightly colored, and have Velcro closing tabs and elasticized legs. Made of several layers of absorbent fabric, they have a leak-proof outer layer, so you don't need to put plastic covers on top of them. Your baby's feces are collected in liners, and the used diapers can be stored in a diaper pail until you have enough to make up a load for your washing machine.

Diaper pins/diaper grippers Diaper pins are specially designed for use with fabric diapers and have locking heads. You'll need at least 12. Grippers are easier to use than pins, and safer too. These little plastic devices hook into the diaper and fasten it securely without the worry of pins.

Diaper liners These are placed inside the diaper and go next to the baby's skin. Choose the "one-way" variety, which is made of a special material that lets urine pass through but remains dry next to the baby's skin. This minimizes the risk of a sore bottom due to friction or moisture, so reduces diaper rash. They also catch most of the feces and prevent the diaper from getting badly soiled. Liners can be lifted out with any feces and flushed away if biodegradable, or if made of fabric, washed with the diapers.

HOW TO PUT ON AN ALL-IN-ONE CLOTH DIAPER

1 Cloth diapers are as easy to put on as disposables. Begin by sliding the clean diaper under your baby. Position it so your baby's waist aligns with the top edge of the diaper.

2 Bring the diaper up between his legs and hold it in place while you fold the sides into the center. Check that the diaper is fitting your baby snugly, then fasten with the Velcro tabs at the sides.

Baby on the move
Once your baby is crawling it's even more important that his diaper is comfortable and not too bulky so it doesn't restrict his movements.

then dried. Whenever you wash diapers use pure soap flakes or powder. Avoid strong detergents and biological powders, which irritate your baby's tender skin.

If you have to use a conditioner, because the fabric has become stiff, make sure you rinse it all out; despite manufacturers' claims to the contrary, it can cause irritation.

Unless the diapers are very stained, or have become rather gray, there is no need to boil them. Hot water is sufficient for both rinsing and washing after using sterilizing solution. Never add colored clothing to the sterilizing solution—the color will run. Even if the clothing has been soiled, just remove the worst of the mess, rinse the item and then wash as normal.

Diaper washing routine

To balance the chores of feeding, changing, and diaper washing try to develop a routine in which you wash the diapers in sufficiently large loads. The prerequisite of this routine is a large supply of diapers—I suggest no fewer than 24.

In order to sterilize the diapers you will need two plastic bins: one for soiled diapers, one for wet ones. They should be large enough to hold at least six diapers, plus solution, and they must have lids and strong, reliable handles. Don't, however, buy such a large bin that you can't carry it fully loaded to the washing machine or tub. Special diaper bins are sold, but any bin of a decent size with a lid is suitable.

Diaper washing and sterilization

Your baby's cloth diapers must be thoroughly washed to remove all traces of ammonia and fecal bacteria that would otherwise cause irritation and possible infection (*see p.68*). Special diaper sterilizers are now available that make this process much easier and less time-consuming. With this method, the diapers are soaked in a sterilizing solution for a specified length of time; then the soiled diapers are washed with soap; the wet diapers are simply rinsed out thoroughly,

Bins designed for beer-making are ideal and they are also reasonably priced.

Each morning, fill the bins with the required amounts of water and solution. Rinse a urine-soaked diaper in cold water, squeeze out the excess moisture and put it into the bin. Remove as much feces as possible in the toilet, then hold the soiled diaper under the water as you flush it to remove the excess. Wring out the diaper and submerge it in the solution. After the required time, wring out both sets of diapers. Rinse the urine-soaked ones thoroughly in hot water before drying them. Put the soiled ones through the hot cycle of the washing machine, then rinse and dry them.

To reduce the environmental impact of laundering reusable diapers, parents are advised to wash them in as large a load as possible at lower temperatures.

You might like to consider using a diaper-laundering service, available nationwide except in very isolated areas. You store dirty diapers in a deodorized bin that has a biodegradable liner. For a weekly fee, the diaper service takes away your dirty diapers and replaces them with fresh ones. You may need to have a bigger supply of diapers, though.

Washing plastic covers

If plastic covers become soiled or wet they should be washed in warm water with a little dishwashing soap. If the water is too hot or too cold, the plastic hardens and becomes unusable. Pat the pants dry after washing and let them air before using. One way of softening plastic pants is to warm them by puttting them in the drier to tumble with a load of towels.

TIPS FOR USING CLOTH DIAPERS

- Use a disposable inside a cloth diaper for extra absorbency at night. You can also use this method when you're traveling and want to avoid an awkward change.
- Use stretch fabric covers over plastic covers— they look neater than plastic covers on their own. Frilly and patterned plastic covers are also available if you want something prettier.
- Always keep your fingers between the diaper and the skin if fixing with a pin.
- When you've put on the diaper run your fingers around the legs to be sure it's not too tight.
- To save time, fold all the diapers ready for use and put the diaper liners in position.
- Make sure that the diaper fits snugly around your baby's body. It gradually gives, so if it's too loose it will slide down.

Tips for washing fabric diapers

- Keep plastic gloves near the sterilizing bucket for lifting diapers out; or use plastic tongs.
- If you use powder sterilizer, always put the water in before the powder. Otherwise the powder spreads through the air when you add the water and you may inhale it.
- Both drying in the open air and in a tumble drier keep the fabric softer. Drying on the radiator tends to harden the fabric. It's better to invest in a rack to place over the bath or use a pull-out clothesline if you can't dry outdoors or in a tumble drier.
- Keep any diapers changed at night in a separate bucket, or in a large plastic bag, and add them to the new day's solution the following morning.
- Some buckets have special holders for air fresheners. If yours doesn't, hook a piece of wire through a freshener and attach it above the waterline.

Diaper rash

If left for any length of time in a diaper or on the skin, urine is broken down to ammonia by bacteria from the baby's stools. Ammonia is an irritant; it burns the skin and results in diaper rash.

Diaper rash ranges from a mild redness, to inflamed broken skin and puss-filled pimples. The bacteria that produce diaper rash thrive in an alkaline medium. The stools of bottle-fed babies are alkaline, unlike those of breast-fed babies, which are acid. For this reason, bottle-fed babies are more prone to diaper rash.

To minimize the possibility of your baby suffering from diaper rash:

- Change your baby's diaper as often as necessary; never leave him in a wet diaper.
- Put a disposable diaper liner next to your baby's skin. This allows urine to pass through to the diaper below, and keeps the skin dry.
- Leave your baby's bottom open to the air whenever you can. Just slide a diaper under his bottom to catch any mess.
- Pay particular attention to washing fabric diapers. Make sure they are well rinsed to remove all the ammonia.
- At the first hint of diaper rash stop using plastic covers. These help keep the urine

DIAPER RASH CHART

Appearance	Cause	Treatment
Redness and broken skin in the leg folds.	Inadequate drying after bathing.	Meticulous and thorough drying. Do not use powder.
Rash that starts around the genitals rather than the anus. Strong smell of ammonia.	Ammonia dermatitis.	General diaper rash treatment, above. If this doesn't work, seek medical advice.
Spotty rash all over the genitals, bottom, groin, and thighs, which eventually leads to thick and wrinkled skin.	Extreme form of ammonia dermatitis.	Seek medical advice if rash persists after trying general treatment, above, first.
Rash that starts around the anus and moves onto the buttocks.	Thrush.	Get medical advice. You will probably be given nystatin cream and medicine.
Brownish-red scaly rash on the genitals and buttocks and anywhere the skin is greasy.	Seborrhoeic dermatitis.	Ointment for rash, prescribed by your doctor. You might also get a special lotion if the scalp is very scaly and sore.
Small blisters all over the diaper area.	Heat rash.	Don't use plastic covers, and leave off the diaper as much as possible.

close to the skin and promote the formation of ammonia.

- At the first sign of broken skin, start using a special cream for the prevention of diaper rash.
- Don't wash your baby's bottom with soap and water. This can dehydrate the skin and cause it to become cracked.
- Don't use talcum powder on a baby. Powder can become caked and irritating in the skin creases, which increases the risk of diaper rash.

Treating diaper rash

You may find, despite your precautions, that your baby develops a sore bottom. If you are satisfied that your baby doesn't require specific treatment (*see chart opposite*), then the most successful remedy will be a combination of the tips listed to the left, plus a few more:

- Change the diaper more frequently.
- At night, put a disposable pad inside a resusable diaper for extra absorbency. This is especially useful for older babies who are sleeping through the night and will therefore not be changed from evening until morning.
- Do not apply barrier cream when changing the diaper because they prevent air from getting to the skin. Though it also keeps the skin dry, it is more important that the skin be aired when your baby has diaper rash.

Using diapers 1 to 3 years

A one year old still urinates automatically, but because the bladder can hold an increasing amount of urine, he'll be dry for longer periods. You'll use fewer diapers—on average, 50 per week as opposed to the 80 used on a newborn. If you hesitated to use disposables before because of the price you may consider them now because they're neater and less bulky than fabric diapers. This is important because your increasingly mobile child will find it difficult to walk with a cumbersome wad of diaper between his legs. If you use cloth diapers, shaped all-in-one reusables may now be more suitable than folded muslin or cotton diapers.

When it comes to changing the diaper you'll find your toddler far less willing to lie still. Make sure that you've got some books or toys as distractions or you'll find that each change becomes a battleground. Clothes that give easy access to the diaper save time and energy.

Early bladder and bowel control

At some time during the third year your child will probably gain conscious control over his bowel and bladder muscles and your days of frequent diaper changes should be over. When your child stays dry during naps you can start skipping that diaper (*see p.138*). You may also want to use trainer pants that can be pulled down quickly when your child tells you that he wants to go to the bathroom. There are two types: plastic underpants lined with cotton, or special pull-up diapers. They're comfortable and provide some protection against the inevitable accidents.

6 Bathing and hygiene

Part of your daily routine is to keep your baby clean. This will be reasonably easy when she's very small, but as your baby becomes more active you'll find that you will not only have to clean her more often, but also that the daily bath will require more effort. By the time she's two she may want to try washing herself.

Washing your baby birth to 1 year

Most young babies don't need bathing very often because, except for their bottoms, faces, necks, and skin creases, they don't get very dirty. There is no reason why you shouldn't go for two or three days without bathing your baby as long as you clean her face, hands, and bottom every day. You can do this without even putting the baby in the baby bathtub by topping and tailing (see p.72). It's also advisable to wash her hair regularly to prevent cradle cap from forming (see p.75).

Some parents feel apprehensive the first few times they bath their baby. However, if you set aside half an hour, have everything you need around you, and try to relax, you will probably enjoy it. After the first two or three times it will become routine and you'll wonder what your first bathtime nervousness was all about.

Where to bath your baby

Until she's big enough to go into an adult tub you don't have to wash your baby in the bathroom. You can use your baby's room, the kitchen or any other room that is warm and has enough space to lay out everything you need to bath her in comfort. The baby's bathtub can be filled in the bathroom and then carried to the chosen room. (Make sure you don't fill it too full or the water will splash out as you walk from room to room.)

A small baby can be washed in a specially designed, sculpted plastic bathtub with a nonslip surface (see p.34). Because it is more comfortable for you if you don't have to bend too much, the bath should be placed on a table or worktop at a convenient height. You could place the baby's bathtub on an adjustable stand (although they tend to be rather flimsy) or on a rack that straddles the tub.

If, however, you don't have a baby bathtub, there are some inexpensive,

Keep her warm
After bathing your baby, wrap her in a towel immediately so she doesn't get cold. Pat her dry all over, being extra careful to reach folds and creases.

TOPPING AND TAILING A YOUNG BABY

This means cleaning your baby by washing her face, hands and diaper area, without undressing her completely. Remove her clothes, leaving her undershirt on. Place your baby on a changing mat or towel. Use cooled boiled water for her eyes and warm water for her face and body.

1 Using moistened cotton balls, gently wipe each eye from the inner corner outward. Use a new piece for each stroke and eye.

2 Wipe her face, ears and neck, then her hands and feet, using a clean cotton ball each time. Pat her dry thoroughly.

3 Clean her diaper area, then wipe with cotton balls moistened with warm water. Wipe from front to back, then pat dry.

practical alternatives you can use until your baby is old enough to go into the big tub. For example, a plastic household bowl functions in exactly the same way as a baby bathtub and is useful because, like a baby tub, it can be carried anywhere you choose. Kitchen or bathroom sinks are also practical because they are usually at a comfortable height, so you don't have to bend over too much, and they often have additional counter space on the side.

If you do use the kitchen sink, however, it's important to make sure that the faucets are well out of reach of your baby's kicking legs. If they aren't, wrap them with cloths or towels so they can cause no harm. If the "bath" surface is too slippery, either use a plastic suction mat or line the sink with a small towel or diaper to provide a nonslip surface for your baby's bottom.

Bathing a young baby

Get everything you need for washing, drying, and dressing ready before you start.

• Wear a waterproof apron, and lay a large, soft towel across your chest and onto your lap so that when you cuddle your baby after the bath she will feel warm and comfortable.

• Very young babies can't regulate their own temperatures very efficiently, so keep the time she's undressed to a minimum.

• Try using a towel with a hood: she'll feel even more secure and snuggly, especially if you put the towel over a radiator for a while first so that it's warm.

• Only fill the bathtub with a couple of inches of water until you are used to it.

• Never use baby powders. They are very drying to a baby's skin and may cake in the creases, causing irritation and rashes.

GIVING YOUR BABY A BATH

It is important that your baby doesn't get cold when being bathed, so make sure the room is warm and free of drafts, and that you have everything you need at hand: bath, two large towels, facecloth, cotton wool, diaper-changing equipment, clean diaper, and clean clothes.

1 *Fill the tub 2–3 inches (5–8 centimeters) deep, putting cold water in first. Test the temperature with your elbow or wrist; it should feel warm, not hot.*

2 *Undress your baby, clean her diaper area (see opposite) and wrap her in a towel. Clean her face and ears gently with moistened cotton balls.*

3 *Hold your baby under one arm like a football, lean over the bathtub and wash her head. Rinse well and pat dry. A gentle brushing is good for cradle cap.*

4 *Support your baby's shoulders with one hand, holding on to her upper arm, and support her legs or bottom with the other. Place her in the bathtub.*

5 *Keep one hand under your baby's shoulders so that her head and shoulders stay out of the water, and use your free hand to wash her. Talk to her soothingly.*

6 *When she is clean and rinsed, lift her gently onto a towel, supporting her as before, and dry her thoroughly. Don't use talcum powder, which can irritate her skin.*

GIVING YOUR BABY A SPONGE BATH

If you're nervous about giving your baby a bath, or if she really hates being undressed, give her a sponge bath. Get everything you need ready. Sit her on your lap and take off only the minimum amount of clothing at a time. You can also place your baby on a changing mat and use the same techniques.

1 *Have a bowl of warm water near you. Undress her top half and wash her front with a cloth or sponge. Dry her, then lean her forward and wash her back.*

2 *Put clean clothes on her top half and remove her lower clothing and her diaper. Clean her diaper area with a fresh cloth (see p.72) and dry thoroughly.*

3 *Using a sponge or cloth, wash your baby's legs and feet. Gently pat them dry, especially between her toes. Put on a clean diaper and dress her again.*

Using a bathtub

Between three and six months old your baby will outgrow most small tubs and you will have to start using an adult tub. If you think that your baby may be frightened by the size of the tub, you can continue to use the small one but place it inside the large, empty tub until she gets used to it.

It is much more awkward to wash a baby in a big tub. You must still hold onto your baby's arm until she can support herself. Don't bend over the bathtub or you'll strain your back. Instead, kneel by the tub and have everything you need on the floor next to you. Use a plastic suction mat on the bottom of the tub to prevent the baby from sliding around and keep the water shallow (no deeper than 4–5 inches/10–13 centimeters). It doesn't take much for a wriggly, kicking baby to slip under the water so you must be vigilant at all times. Never, ever, leave your baby alone in the tub, even for a moment; don't even turn away to do something else in the room. If the phone rings, either ignore it or take your wet baby with you. Leaving your baby, even for a second, is not worth the risk.

As your baby gets older she'll spend more and more time crawling around on the floor and, as a result, will need to be washed more often; baths will become a regular feature of the day. By this time she will no longer be afraid of being undressed and will feel very secure in the water. In fact, she will almost certainly have begun to enjoy bathtime. It's your job to make them fun and as trouble-free as possible.

As soon as your baby can sit up, always have a period at the end of the bath when she can enjoy splashing and playing with her bath toys. Have some boats, ducks, sponges, or plastic cups on hand so she can experiment with them and see what they do. If you have two children, occasionally try bathing them together so your older child can share games and teach your baby about the things that water does. It's exciting for your baby to see how containers can be filled and emptied or water poured from one to the other, and she'll love watching how some toys float and others sink slowly to the bottom.

Many household items can be adapted for bathtime. Babies love seeing water pour out of things and this makes plastic fruit containers with airholes ideal. Other good toys are: measuring spoons, small watering cans, ice-cube trays, and colanders.

Hair washing
Pick up your baby in a football hold by tucking her legs under your armpit and supporting her back along your arm. Cradle her head in your hand. Wash her hair using mild shampoo and rinse gently with warm water.

Care of the hair

To prevent cradle cap from forming you should wash your newborn's head every day with a soft bristle brush and a little baby shampoo. To prevent scales from forming, you should comb through the hair, even if she has very little. If cradle cap does appear, smear a little olive oil on her scalp and wash it off the following morning. This will dissolve the scales, making them soft, loose, and easy to wash away. Don't be tempted to pick them off.

After about 12–16 weeks, wash your baby's head with water every day and once or twice a week with baby shampoo. You can either use the football hold (if your baby is quite light) or you can sit on the edge of the tub with your baby across your legs, facing you. (This method is especially useful if she's afraid of the water.) Make sure that you use a nonsting variety of baby shampoo, but always take care to avoid getting it near her eyes. Don't worry about your newborn's fontanelles (soft spots). They are covered with a very sturdy membrane and you can do no harm if you are gentle. You do not need to scrub her hair. Modern shampoos remove dirt and oil within seconds, so you just have to bring

BATHTUB BATHING TIPS

- Always run cold water first. If you start with hot water, the bottom of the tub may be too hot and could burn the baby.
- Cover up hot faucets with a washcloth or towel so there's no risk of scalding.
- Don't pour more hot water into the tub while the baby is in it—she could be scalded.
- Make sure that you put your baby in the tub (and lift her out of the tub) with your back straight, taking the strain with your thighs.
- Don't let your baby stand up in the tub without your support—she could slip and fall.
- If your child starts to jump up and down in the tub—no doubt rejoicing in a newly found skill —be very firm about making her sit down again, or she could easily topple over.
- Don't be tempted to see if your baby can sit unsupported. She could easily tumble under the water and get a bad scare—bad enough to put her off baths for a while.
- Never, ever, leave your baby alone in the tub. Even if you turn around for a moment she could slip under the water and drown.
- Don't let the water out while the baby's in the tub. She may be frightened by the disappearing water and by the noise.
- Don't dust your baby with talcum powder after a bath—it's very drying to the skin and can cause irritation.
- If you're at work during the day, make the most of bathtime—it can be a great time to play and relax with your baby.
- Have some toys exclusively for use in the tub, to make bathtime a special treat.

the shampoo to a lather, count to 20, then rinse it off. One wash is enough, and your baby's hair will be absolutely clean at the end of the operation. Rinse your baby's hair simply by dipping the washcloth into the basin of warm water and wiping it over her head. Try to get as much lather off as possible, but if your child is complaining it really doesn't matter if you leave slight traces on the hair. Dry her head with the end of the towel, and be careful not to cover her face or she may become distressed and panicky.

Care of the skin

A newborn doesn't need soap. It is a de-fatting agent and your baby's skin is too delicate for it. She needs to preserve all her natural oils, so use only water until she's around six weeks. After that, any gentle soap can be used—you may want to try a special liquid soap that is simply added to the bath water and doesn't need to be rinsed off. Make sure that you wash any folds and creases well by running a soapy

Caring for the skin
Dry your baby's skin thoroughly after a sponge bath or bath. It is especially important to dry in any folds of skin, such as creases around her arms, legs, and neck.

finger along them, then rinsing well. Dry her skin thoroughly—moist creases will lead to irritations. Never use talcum powder as this also irritates the skin.

Care of the eyes

For a young baby, when you wash her eyes, squeeze a couple of cotton balls in cooled boiled water. Use a different cotton ball for each eye, starting from the inner part of the eye and working toward the outer part.

Care of the nose and ears

The nose and ears are self-cleaning organs, so you should never try to put anything up them or in them or interfere with them in any way. Pushing something the size of a Q-tip up a baby's nose or into a baby's ears, will only push whatever is there in further. It is much better to let whatever is in the nose come down naturally. Never put drops into the ears or nose unless your doctor advises it.

Never try to scrape wax out of a baby's ears even if you can see it. Wax is the natural secretion of the skin that lines the canal of the outer ear. It is antiseptic and it prevents dust and grit from getting into the ear drum. Some babies make more wax than others, but removing it will only result in the production of even more. Removing wax also irritates the skin, so leave it alone and check with your pediatrician if you are concerned. Wash your baby's ears and nose using moist cotton balls (*see p.73*).

Care of the nails

There is no need to cut a newborn baby's nails for about three or four weeks, unless she is scratching her skin. Nails are easiest

Trimming nails
If you're going to use scissors lay your baby on a flat surface, talk soothingly to her, and then gently cut the nails following the shape of the fingertips.

to cut when they are soft, so have a pair of small, blunt-ended scissors nearby when you take your baby out of the tub. If you do them right away you'll be able to cut the nails of her hands and toes in less than half a minute. But if you're worried about cutting your baby's nails try doing it when she is asleep.

Care of the navel

The umbilical cord was clamped and cut immediately after delivery, leaving a stump protruding 2–3 inches (5–8 centimeters) from your baby's abdomen. This may be clamped by a plastic clip. Over the next few days the cord dries and shrivels, and will then drop off. Let the area stay open to the air as much as possible to help speed up the shrinking and healing process. If you notice any redness, discharge, or other signs of infection, ask your pediatrician or nurse-practitioner for advice. You don't have to wait for the navel to heal before you give your baby a bath, as long as you dry it carefully and thoroughly afterward.

Some babies develop umbilical hernias (see p.23). They nearly always clear up within a year or two. If your baby has one and it enlarges or persists, seek medical advice.

Care of the genitals

You should never try to open the lips of your baby girl's vulva to clean inside; there is no need. Just wash the exterior diaper area (see p.60) and dry it well. However, you should take care to wipe from front to back—that is, toward the anus—whenever you are cleaning the diaper area. This minimizes the risk of bacteria spreading from the bowels to the bladder or vagina, causing infection.

An uncircumcised baby boy should not have his foreskin pulled back for cleaning.

It's very tight and could get stuck. Just wash the exterior of the diaper area as normal and dry carefully, particularly the skin creases; the foreskin will retract naturally at three or four years of age.

If your baby has been circumcised, it is important to watch carefully to make sure that his penis is not bleeding. A dressing may or may not be applied, but either way you will be given advice about bathing your baby taking special care of the penis. Following circumcision, the penis is nearly always swollen and slightly inflamed for a few days, and occasionally there may be a few drops of blood: this is normal and will gradually settle down. However, if bleeding persists or there is any sign of infection, get medical advice.

Possible bathtime problems birth to 1 year

Fear of undressing

Many young babies become extremely distressed when they are undressed. Babies hate the feeling of air on their bodies, preferring instead the security of being fully clothed or tightly wrapped. When your baby is very young, you can get around this by topping and tailing or giving a sponge bath (see pp.72–74).

Fear of bathing

If your baby is absolutely terrified of having a bath, skip it for a couple of days and then try again, very gently, using only a little water in the tub. Until your baby is ready to go back into the bathtub, give sponge baths or top and tail.

If, after some time, she still doesn't like being bathed and is still frightened of

water, try to overcome it by introducing bathtime in the context of play. In a warm room (but not the bathroom), lay out a towel with a large plastic bowl of water next to it. Put some floatable toys and plastic cups into the bowl, undress your baby, and encourage her to play with the toys. She'll gradually get used to the idea of being near the water.

When she seems happy and confident help your baby paddle in water: if your kitchen is warm put a towel on the counter, fill the sink with warm water and let your baby dangle her feet in it while she sits on the towel. Make sure you keep a firm grip on your baby with one hand while you play with toys and cups with the other, and that the faucets are bound up with cloths.

Bathtime games

The evening bath is a wonderful time for creative play. You'll find your baby is endlessly fascinated by filling things, pouring, and splashing water.

Do this a couple of times then swap the bowl or kitchen sink for a baby bath and let your baby play in the same way as before. You'll know she's overcome any fear when she struggles to get into the water with the toys. Let your baby do this a couple of times before you turn it into an occasion for washing as well.

Fear of the big bathtub

Once your baby is splashing around and making a mess in the small baby bathtub, she is ready to go into a big tub. However, if your child is afraid of getting into a big tub, you'll have to build up to it gradually. Place the baby bathtub inside the big tub and put a towel or a rubber mat next to it so that she can't slip. Sit her in the tub along with some toys and fill up the baby bathtub with warm water as usual. Then let her climb into the baby bathtub. Once she is happy doing this, you can introduce a few inches/centimeters of water into the big tub, with the towel or rubber mat in the bottom and all the toys, as before, and the baby bathtub full of warm water. She will probably climb in and out of the baby bathtub and quickly get used to sitting in the big tub in just a few inches/centimeters of water. You can then gradually increase the amount of water in the big tub, leaving the baby bathtub in the tub until she is no longer interested in it or needs it. This makes the transition to the bigger tub painless, and at the same time does a lot to increase your child's confidence.

Dislike of hair washing

A baby who thoroughly enjoys having a bath may hate hair washing, and she will probably develop this dislike at about eight or nine months old. Even though you may be gentle and take every precaution to make sure that your child isn't frightened or upset by hair washing, you may find that it remains a problem until she is of school age, so it is worth getting the technique right from the beginning.

Young children hate to get water in their eyes, let alone soap or shampoo. So you should do everything you can to keep your baby's face and eyes dry throughout the whole operation of hair washing.

Never pour water over your child's head just to prove that it won't hurt. Few children under the age of six can stand this, and if it is done suddenly they find it extremely unpleasant. Don't continue the hair washing if she screams or struggles, and never forcibly hold your child so you can get her hair washed. You may have an accident, like getting some soap into her eyes, which will make the whole incident much worse. It will also make all future attempts to wash your child's hair very difficult experiences for both of you.

Once your child strenuously objects to hair washing, give up and don't try again for a few weeks to give your child a chance to recover. Bathtimes are generally happy times for most children, so it is better to just exclude hair washing from bathtimes than risk your child developing a dislike for

Safety in the bathtub
When washing your baby in the bathtub, use a non-slip mat to prevent her from sliding around. Keep the water shallow—no more than 4–5 inches (10–13cm).

baths in general. Keep her hair reasonably clean by sponging it to remove any dirt or bits of food, or brushing it out with a soft, damp brush. It really doesn't matter if your child's hair is greasy for a week or two; it will come to no harm.

Another way of keeping water out of your baby's face is to use a specially designed shield. This fits like a halo around the hairline and allows you to rinse off shampoo without getting soapy water on your baby's face. You may find that your baby is less distressed if you wash her hair while she sits on your lap. Have a basin of warm water near you, and use a washcloth

Bathtime routine
Bathing is a perfect opportunity for hugging and playing that babies come to relish. Make it part of the bedtime routine, a signal to her it's time to wind down.

to wet her head before you apply a non-sting shampoo. So that no water gets on her face, wipe the shampoo off with a damp washcloth, not by pouring water over the head. She won't be disturbed by this because she won't feel any water trickling over her head or her body.

Washing your toddler 1 to 3 years

As your child gets older she will probably regard bathtime primarily as playtime. Most children love playing with water and the bathtub is one of the most convenient places for them to do it, so provide plastic cups, bowls, boats, and ducks, allow plenty of time, relax, and let bathtime be fun. Encourage your child to wash herself by having a special sponge that she can use. Until she's developed adequate coordination, she won't do a perfect job of it so be prepared to go over the same areas with another washcloth. Soap both of your child's hands by holding a bar of soap between them, and show her how to spread the soap over her body and arms.

Baths should be carefully supervised because children of this age are still at risk of slipping and falling under the water. Toddlers are generally eager to do things for themselves so there is the added risk that your child may turn on the hot water

ENCOURAGING DAILY HYGIENE

Face washing
If your child objects to washing her face, suggest that she use a sponge instead of a washcloth. This is more fun, and much softer on the skin.

Hand washing
Encourage your toddler from an early age to wash her hands. Give her a step so she can reach the sink and make sure she knows which is the hot faucet.

or grab the soap or shampoo and get some in her eyes. Covering the faucets with a towel is a good way to soften any falls or bangs.

Daily routine

Most children need to be washed in the morning, but it's probably best to wait until after breakfast. Children are often ravenously hungry when they wake up, and you'll only have time to change her diaper before food becomes imperative. After your child has eaten, she'll probably be more willing to stand still long enough to have her face and hands washed, teeth brushed (see p.203), and hair combed.

By the time she's about 18 months she'll be able to rinse both hands under water and, with improving coordination, will learn to soap them. Bear in mind, though, that she won't always remember the routine of hand washing: sleeves may not be rolled up, shirts may get wet, and soap may slip out of tiny fingers. So always be nearby to lend a hand if she needs it.

Hygiene

Start hygiene routines when your child is young and, when possible, teach by example. For instance, from the time your child starts to crawl and get her hands dirty, washing before eating should be automatic. If you start by washing your hands with your child (and I mean with), by getting your hands soapy together and washing each other's hands, it can be fun. While you're teaching your child how to wash, you can make a game of it by trying to blow bubbles in the soap film that forms between your forefinger and thumb when you make a circle. Dry your hands together

too. Afterward, let your child inspect your hands and then look at hers.

If you start like this, it makes it easier to apply hygiene rules at other times. For example, hand washing should always follow visits to the bathroom. But you should start at the potty stage and do it with your child every single time. You can help her become more independent by providing a stable, nonslip step stool in the bathroom so she can reach the sink and toilet easily and safely by herself.

Give your child a soft toothbrush to start with and encourage her to use it after meals, especially once her molars break through (see p.202).

Pets and hygiene

There are important advantages for your toddler in having a pet, but you may be concerned about the possible health risks. But, if you follow a few simple rules about handling pets, you should have no cause for concern. Encourage your child to wash her hands after playing with her pet—and especially before she touches or eats food. Also, it's important you stop your child from kissing her pet, especially near its nose and mouth.

The most common problems caused by pets are infestations of fleas and worms. Both of these are easily avoided by regular use of the appropriate preventive treatments. If infestations do occur, treat them promptly and keep your child from playing with the pet until the treatment has worked. Ringworm is a contagious skin condition that can be caught from pets and is commonly seen in children. If you suspect ringworm, ask your pharmacist or pediatrician for advice on treatment.

Possible problems 1 to 3 years

Fear of hair washing

If your child really hates having her hair washed, keep it very short so that it only needs sponging to keep it clean (*see p.80*). One of the major reasons why children hate having their hair washed is that they don't like water on their faces. To overcome this, you'll have to encourage your child to believe that hair washing won't hurt and that it won't feel bad when water is poured over her head. Use nonsting shampoo, and a hair-washing shield, even on an older child.

If your child has the kind of fine, curly hair that gets very tangled, this can make hair washing unpleasant. Combing through snarls after hair washing can be a nightmare. An option is to cut her hair short for a while. But if you don't want to, try using conditioner: after rinsing off the shampoo, work conditioner through her hair, gently comb it through with a wide-toothed comb, then rinse it off with a spray attachment. Then just pat her hair dry with a towel to absorb excess water. You can buy a detangling spray to put on dry hair before you brush it.

Family bathtime
Older children in the family will love helping to bath a baby and like to join in. Bathtime can become a riotous affair with lots of shouts and splashing!

You could make a game out of hair washing. It will become much more fun for your child if you get into the bathtub, too, and wash your own hair at the same time. Rinse it with a plastic container of water and show her that it's fun pouring water over your head.

If you have an older child, you can prove it doesn't hurt by letting the younger child help you wash her sibling's hair. Once you've lathered the shampoo, hold the frightened child and let her rub both of her hands through the bubbles. If possible, let her to help pour the rinse water, too. You can also wash a doll's hair in the tub with your toddler's assistance. Let your child help with the shampoo and rinse, then suggest that you do it to her hair. With any luck she'll take this as part of the game. You can encourage your child to wet her own hair with a washcloth, then put a tiny bit of shampoo into her hands so that she can put it on her hair.

An older child is also useful in proving that a wet face isn't unpleasant. For example, your older child may be proud of holding her breath under water. Once your toddler is about three, she might want to join in this game, even if it means only putting her nose and mouth under the surface while you count to five.

Fear of water

A few children hate water, and bathtime for these children and their parents will be very distressing. Probably the easiest way to overcome this fear is to make bathtime as happy and relaxing as possible, with plenty of playtime included. Try to discover what frightens your child: is it the size of the tub, or the amount of water in it? Is it because she has slipped and suddenly been ducked under the water?

If it is the size of the tub that causes her to worry, introduce alternatives, like the kitchen sink or a large basin. Your child will probably sit quite happily on a towel on the kitchen counter, playing and dipping her feet in the water. This should also help if she's afraid of the volume of water, and so will playing with a shower attachment or a garden hose (as long as the flow is gentle). Ironically, swimming can be used to overcome your child's fear of water, though you'll have to introduce the subject gently (*see below*).

GETTING HER USED TO WATER

Another way of getting your child used to water on her face is to take her swimming. Once she's got used to splashing and getting her hair wet, you'll be able to start hair washing. This is especially easy if you take a shower after swimming in the pool. You can then gently and deftly introduce the idea of having a shampoo in the shower, using a nonsting baby shampoo: a quick shampoo should only take a couple of minutes.

You can also use the shower attachment at home, encouraging your child to play with the spray, playing it up to her shoulders and eventually onto her hair and face. When she's used to wet hair, you can then quickly shampoo and rinse it.

If she likes swimming in a pool, take advantage of any swimming classes that you can attend with your child where you do most of the teaching (with help from an instructor if you need it). Being able to swim may save your child's life. If possible, it's a good idea to make sure that she has learned to swim before she starts school.

7 Feeding

The main aim of infant feeding is to provide adequate nutrition. It helps to bear in mind that while breast-feeding is undoubtedly best if, for any reason, you don't breast-feed your baby, he'll still thrive on bottle feeding. Don't feel guilty if you make this decision; concentrate on the needs of your baby. The love and affection that you give your baby while you're feeding is as important as any milk. And once he's on solids, the important rule to remember is to take your lead from your child; as long as you offer a wide variety of foods he doesn't have to have "essential" foods every day. Remember, above all, that food is a pleasure.

Nutritional needs birth to 1 year

A baby grows more quickly during the first six months than at any other time in his life. Most double their birth weight in about four months and triple it by the time they are about a year old. In order to grow, your baby needs protein, vitamins, minerals, and carbohydrates. Until he's at least six months old, your baby will receive these in the form of milk. When he's started on solids he will get all he needs from a well balanced diet. During the first six months a baby needs slightly more than 100 calories per 2 pounds (1 kilogram), and from six months to one year slightly less than 100 calories per 2 pounds (1 kilogram).

Protein

Most of the protein that a baby takes in is used for growth, and the protein requirements during the first year are correspondingly higher than at any other time of life; they are three times greater than those for adults. Milk, as long as it is given in adequate amounts, provides all the protein that a newborn infant needs.

Vitamins and minerals

Breast-milk contains everything except vitamin D. The main source of this is the sun, which stimulates the skin to manufacture it. In the US all exclusively breast-fed babies are given supplements containing vitamin D. If you bottle-feed your baby, all his vitamin needs will be satisfied by the formula.

The rapid growth of bone and muscle that takes place during the first year means that babies have a greater need for minerals like calcium, phosphorous, and magnesium than adults. All babies are born with a supply of iron that will last for up to four months. After this, iron has to be added to the baby's diet. The iron in breast-milk is very well absorbed and considered sufficient for a baby's needs. All routine formulas and baby cereals are fortified with iron.

Fats

The body needs minute traces of fatty acids for growth and repair. The fat content of both breast-milk and formula is about the same, but in human milk the droplets of fat are smaller and so more digestible.

Carbohydrates

These are the major energy providers. Both breast-milk and formula contain the same carbohydrates, although the level is slightly higher in breast-milk.

Feeding comfortably
Make sure you're comfortable when feeding. Sit with both feet firmly on the ground. Support your back and arms with pillows and place a pillow on your lap to raise and support your baby if necessary.

Trace elements

Your baby needs traces of certain minerals like zinc, copper, and fluoride. The first two are present in breast-milk and formula. Fluoride, however, is not, and infants need fluoride to protect them against dental decay. If it is added to the drinking water in your area a low-fluoride toothpaste will provide enough additional fluoride. If not, you may need to use a high-fluoride toothpaste for your child or even give supplements, but only with your dentist's guidance, as too much can cause damage to teeth. If in doubt, contact your dentist.

Breast-feeding birth to 1 year

Human breast-milk is tailor-made for a baby: it contains just the right amount of protein, carbohydrates, minerals, and vitamins to sustain your growing baby. Apart from its nutritional worth, breast-feeding makes sound sense for the following reasons:

- Breast-fed babies are less prone to illness than bottle-fed babies. There are fewer cases of gastroenteritis, chest infection, and measles and this is directly attributable to the antibodies that the baby receives. All babies receive some antibodies from their mother's placental blood, via the umbilical cord, but in the case of breast-fed babies these are supplemented by antibodies in both the colostrum (*see p.90*) and in the mother's milk. In your baby's first few days of life they exert a protective influence on the intestine (reducing the likelihood of intestinal disturbance), and because they are also absorbed into the bloodstream they form part of the body's protection against infections. Some antibodies, such as those against poliomyelitis, are in the breast-milk, so the mother can actively protect her newborn while he is breast-feeding. (The baby will still have to be immunized, however.)

- Breast-milk is more easily, and quickly, digested than formula. Breast-fed babies don't get constipated: they may pass stools infrequently but this is because the food is so efficiently and completely used up. The stools of breast-fed babies are soft and comparatively odorless, and they don't contain the bacteria that generally causes ammonia dermatitis, so these babies are less prone to diaper rash.

- Breast-fed babies rarely become overweight. Each baby has his own appetite and metabolic rate—it won't be the same as the baby next door, so don't worry if your baby is fatter or thinner than your neighbor's. He'll be the right weight for his own body.

- Breast-feeding is convenient. The milk is always at the right temperature, you don't have to waste your time sterilizing and making up bottles, and you save

Ensuring a good supply of breast-milk
When you are breast-feeding, make sure you are eating well and drinking lots of fluids, especially in hot weather when your baby will be more thirsty too.

money by not having to buy all the equipment. Breast-fed babies have less gas, sleep longer, spit up less, and the spit-up smells less unpleasant.

- Breast-feeding is good for your figure. Research has shown that most of the fat that is gained in pregnancy is shed if a woman breast-feeds. During breast-feeding a hormone called oxytocin is released and this encourages the uterus to return to its normal size, and stimulates the production of milk (*see p.90*). Your pelvis returns to normal more quickly and so does your waistline. Contrary to popular belief, breast-feeding does not affect the shape or size of your breasts. They may get bigger, smaller, or sag after pregnancy, but changes are not contingent upon breast-feeding; they are the result of being pregnant.
- Breast cancer is rarer in parts of the world where breast-feeding is traditional. Breast-feeding may provide some protection against the disease.

Breast-feeding and contraception

Because the hormone that activates milk production also suppresses ovulation, it is unlikely that you will conceive while breast-feeding. However, you should never rely on this as a means of contraception. See your doctor for advice.

Preparing to breast-feed

Ideally, try to decide whether or not you want to breast-feed your baby well before delivery so you can plan for it. If you are having your baby in the hospital, tell the nursing staff as soon as you are admitted that you intend to breast-feed. Be assertive about asking for help from them. Ask to

MILK SUPPLY AND DEMAND FEEDING

All mothers are anatomically equipped to feed their babies and there is no such thing as mother's milk that does not suit a baby: the milk the breasts produce is the baby's natural food.

- There is no such thing as a mother physically incapable of feeding her baby: the size of your breasts bears no relation to the amount of milk that you can produce, although breast enlargement or reduction surgery can affect your ability to breast-feed.
- Milk is produced in deeply buried glands, not the fatty tissue of the breasts, so don't worry if your breasts are small: they *are* adequate. The amount of milk that you produce is dependent on how much your baby takes, on the principle of supply and demand. For example, if your baby's appetite is not very great then your breasts will not produce very much milk because they're not being stimulated by your baby to do so. If your baby is an eager feeder, your breasts will respond and produce more milk. The amount of milk available for your baby will fluctuate throughout the whole time that you breast-feed, according to how much your baby takes.
- If your baby is hungry half an hour after being fed, don't worry. Your breasts will have produced some milk for your baby to feed on, and they'll soon build up a supply for his new needs. When the need for more food slows down, the breasts will produce less.
- A newborn needs 2–3½ fluid ounces (60–100 milliliters) of milk per 1 pound (500 grams) of body weight, so a 7 pound 11 ounce (3.5 kilogram) baby needs 14–24 fluid ounces (400–650 milliliters) daily. Each breast produces 1½–2 fluid ounces (40–60 milliliters) of milk in three hours so a daily output of 24–35 fluid ounces (700–1000 milliliters) is ample.

see a nurse or lactation consultant if necessary. Ask her to sit with you for an entire feeding, and to give clear instructions about what you should and shouldn't be doing. The best way to learn is to have someone who knows a lot about breast-feeding watch and encourage you right from the start.

Few women breast-feed without encountering any problems. So while you shouldn't necessarily expect to find it difficult, you shouldn't be surprised if you have a run of problems. The thing to bear in mind is that most breast-feeding difficulties can be corrected.

COLOSTRUM

During the 72 hours after delivery, the breasts don't produce milk. Instead, they manufacture a thin, yellow fluid called colostrum. This fluid is made up of water, protein and minerals and it takes care of all your baby's nutritional needs during the first days of his life before your breast milk comes in.

Benefits of colostrum

Colostrum contains invaluable antibodies that protect your baby against diseases like polio and influenza, as well as intestinal and respiratory infections. It has an additional laxative effect that stimulates the excretion of meconium (*see p.24*). It's important to give your baby the breast regularly in the first days, both to feed on the colostrum and to get used to latching on to the breast (*see opposite*).

Every time your baby cries in the early days you can give him your breast, but for only a couple of minutes each side at first so that the nipples don't get sore. Giving your baby the breast also helps the uterus to contract.

The first contact

It is good for both you and your baby to try nursing as soon as the baby is born. There are two important reasons for doing so: nursing naturally stimulates the production of oxytocin, a hormone that, among other things (*see p.89*), makes the uterus contract and expel the placenta soon after birth. Suckling also helps to form a very strong bond between mother and baby immediately after birth.

Incidentally, you shouldn't worry about your baby choking. The natural reflex to suck is very strong, and he is able to swallow at birth.

The let-down reflex

When your baby suckles at the breast the pituitary gland in the brain is stimulated to release two hormones: prolactin and oxytocin. Prolactin activates the manufacture of milk in the milk glands; oxytocin is responsible for the milk being passed from the milk glands to the milk reservoirs behind the areola. This process happens within seconds and is known as the let-down reflex. You may feel this reflex very powerfully: in fact, the very sight or sound of your baby may trigger it, and milk may actually leak out of your nipples in anticipation of feeding.

How to hold your baby

Support your baby along the length of his back and use your hand and fingers to support the back of his neck to bring him up to your breast. He should be able to reach your nipple without effort. Support your back and arms with pillows and place a pillow on your lap to raise and support your baby if necessary.

The rooting reflex

The first few times you give your baby the breast to feed he may need some encouragement and help to find the nipple. Cradle your baby in your arms and gently stroke the cheek nearest the breast. This will elicit the rooting reflex. Your baby will immediately turn toward your breast, mouth open and ready. If you put your nipple in his mouth he will happily clamp both lips around the areola and settle down to suckle. Many babies lick the nipple before they take it into their mouths and it sometimes helps to express some colostrum as an added incentive.

After a few days your baby will need no artificial stimulation and will happily turn and latch onto the breast as soon as he is picked up and held close to your body.

Never try to guide your baby's head to the nipple by holding both his cheeks between your fingers, or by squeezing the mouth

The sucking effect
The baby stimulates milk to flow by pressing the tip of his tongue against the areola. Then he presses the back of his tongue up towards his palate to squeeze milk from your nipple into his throat.

open. The baby will become very confused by the conflicting stimuli of both cheeks being touched and will turn from side-to-side in a desperate bid to find the nipple.

Giving your baby the breast

The key to happy, trouble-free breast-feeding is knowing how to get your baby's mouth correctly latched onto your breast. Try to get your nipple well inside your baby's mouth. This is important for two reasons. Firstly, unless he takes a good proportion of the areola into his mouth the milk will

GIVING A BREAST-FEED

1 Gently stroke the cheek nearest to you, so that your baby turns to your breast. He will turn to your touch, open-mouthed, searching for your nipple.

2 Cradle your baby's head in your hand and make sure he latches on correctly. The baby should take the nipple and a good proportion of the areola into his mouth.

3 To break the suction when he's finished or it's time to move to the other breast, slip your little finger into the corner of his mouth. Your breast will slip out easily.

not be successfully sucked from your breast. Your baby extracts milk from the breast in a kind of chomping, sucking motion: the baby's mouth forms a seal around the areola, and as he sucks, the tongue pushes the nipple up against the roof of the mouth. The milk is then drawn out in a rhythmic combination of sucking and squeezing. It can only be successful if the baby can exert pressure on the milk ducts behind the areola. Secondly, if you position the nipple well into the baby's mouth, you minimize the chances of developing sore or cracked nipples (see p.101). Your baby has a very strong sucking action and if only the nipple is in his mouth he will effectively shut off the openings of the milk ducts and little milk will get out. Your nipples will become extremely sore and your milk supply will eventually be reduced because the milk is not being depleted by the baby (see p.89). Your baby will quite naturally become frustrated and bad-tempered with hunger.

BREAST-FEEDING TIPS

- You may find that because your let-down reflex is too efficient, your milk pours out too quickly and chokes the baby as soon as he sucks. You can slow the flow down by expressing a little milk first (see p.96).
- If your nipple is soft and small and your baby has trouble finding it, put a cold, wet cloth on it for a moment—your nipple will firm up and protrude.
- Milk flows in both breasts at every nursing and it's best to use both breasts at each feeding. Start with the heavier breast.

Bonding
Once your baby is happily sucking at your breast, settle down and look at him. If your baby's eyes are open, make eye contact with him. Smile, talk, and chat softly to your baby while he is feeding so that he associates the pleasure of feeding with the sight of your face, the sound of your voice, and the smell of your skin.

How long on each breast
Your baby's sucking will be strongest in the first five minutes, when he will take 80 percent of his feeding. As a general rule, keep your baby on the breast for as long as he shows interest in sucking. If your baby continues to suck after your breasts have emptied, it may be that he is just enjoying the sensation; this is fine if it's not making your breasts sore. You'll find that your baby will show disinterest in his own individual way: he may start to play with your breast, slipping his mouth on and off the nipple; he may turn away; he may fall asleep. When he appears to have had enough of one breast gently take the baby off your nipple (see opposite) and put him at the other breast. If your baby falls asleep after feeding from both breasts he's probably had enough: you'll soon learn whether this is the case or whether he's going to wake, hungry again, after ten minutes or so. Similarly, if your baby appears to have taken all he wants from just one breast, don't worry. You can start the next feeding on the other breast.

Removing baby from breast
Never pull your baby off the breast—you'll only hurt your nipple. To get the baby off, slip your finger down between the areola

and your baby's cheek and put your little finger into the corner of the baby's mouth. This will make his mouth open, breaking the suction, and your breast will slip out of his mouth easily instead of being pulled out. This is particularly important in the first few days because your nipples are soft and they need a chance to become less sensitive.

What to wear to breast-feed

It is important that you wear a bra when you are breast-feeding. One that supports your breasts underneath, has front fastenings, and has wide straps to avoid hurting your shoulders is best. On top you should wear whatever you feel most comfortable in but, obviously, the top should allow easy access to your breasts. Large T-shirts are both comfortable and practical; front opening shirts are quick to open but some women feel more exposed in them when feeding.

Breast-feeding positions

You can feed your baby in whatever position you choose, as long as she can latch onto the nipple and you are comfortable and relaxed. Experiment and do whatever feels most natural. Try to change positions throughout the day— this will ensure your baby doesn't exert pressure only on one part of the areola, and minimizes the risk of a blocked milk duct. If you sit down to feed your baby, make sure you're comfortable, with your arms and back supported with cushions or pillows if necessary.

It's also nice to lie in bed to feed your baby, especially in the first few weeks and at night, and there's no reason why you shouldn't do this. Lie on your side, propped up with pillows if that's more comfortable, and gently cradle the baby's head and body alongside you. You may need to lay a small baby on a pillow so he's at the right height

BREAST-FEEDING POSITIONS

Sitting position
Make sure your arms and back are supported with cushions or pillows and you are relaxed. Use a pillow to raise your baby to a comfortable level.

Lying position
This is good when you're tired or to keep your baby off a Cesarean incision. Lie on your side and lay your baby alongside you so he can reach your lower breast.

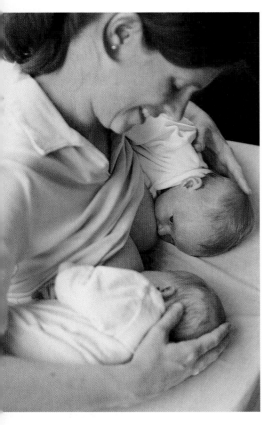

Feeding twins
While it can be easier to feed them singly in the early days, once breast-feeding is established you can try feeding your babies together.

for your nipple, but a larger baby should be able to lie on the bed next to you. Make sure the muscles under your arm aren't strained since this will slow down the flow of milk. Alternatively, lay your baby on a pillow under your arm, with his feet tucked behind you. Your hand can support your baby's head as he faces your breast. Always put your baby back in his own bed after feeding; don't fall asleep with him in your bed.

The position you choose initially may be affected by the delivery you've had. For example, if you've had an episiotomy you'll probably find sitting down extremely uncomfortable, so feeding on your side will be more suitable. Similarly, if you've had a Cesarean section, your stomach may be too tender for your baby to lie on, so try the football-hold position, with your baby's feet tucked under your arm. Alternatively, try feeding your baby while he's lying on the bed beside you.

Frequency of feeds
Babies need frequent feeding because of their body size. Breast-fed babies may need more feeds than bottle-fed babies because they digest their milk more quickly. Babies should be fed on demand (*see p.89*), and parents will quickly learn to recognize the cries that mean their baby is hungry (*see p.158*). Newborn babies may need to be fed every two hours, with as many as eight to ten feedings a day. By about one month, babies are usually taking food every three hours, and at two to three months approximately every four hours. However, every baby is different.

Most babies sleep through the night after their late evening feeding by the time they are three months old, but you shouldn't even consider trying to drop the night feeding unless your baby indicates his willingness by sleeping through the night.

Supplementary bottles
We have all heard tales about women not having enough milk to feed their babies, and even though the fear may be only subconscious, when problems arise during the early days of feedings a woman may

use this as an excuse to justify giving up on breast-feeding. Please don't succumb to this pressure; resist it even if your doctor mentions it to you, and certainly if friends and relatives do.

Every woman comes equipped with the means and capacity to feed her baby. Breasts respond to the demand for milk by producing it, so if your baby is not taking all your milk in the initial stages you should try to express the rest so the demand for milk from your breasts is kept up. Most breasts respond to this approach with a good flow of milk.

As your child gets older and perhaps has bouts of crying, someone will nudge you and say the baby is hungry. You may have just fed your baby, in which case he may simply be thirsty. This occurs, of course, as soon as you start mixed feeding because food needs liquid to dilute it and to be digested. So initially, try your baby with ½ fluid ounce (15 milliliters) of plain, cooled boiled water to quench his thirst.

Every new mother is worried about how well she can feed her baby and may feel a pressure to use supplementary bottles. The attraction of the bottle to an anxious mother is that she can see instantly how much milk the baby has taken—an assurance not available when breast-feeding. But try to be logical and rational about it, and above all have confidence in your ability to feed your baby. Remember that a baby takes 80 percent of the feeding in the first two to three minutes on each breast. So though the baby may become bored with being at your breast, if he has been sucking for at least five minutes, he has almost certainly had enough milk to satisfy his hunger.

ENSURING A GOOD MILK SUPPLY

- Rest as much as you can, particularly during the first weeks after the birth of your baby. This is a time when you should sit rather than stand, and lie rather than sit.
- Your milk flow will be affected if you are tense, so go through your prenatal relaxation routine and make sure that you have a period to yourself every day when you can lie down.
- Go to bed as early as you can. You will be very tired anyway since your sleep patterns will probably be broken by your baby.
- As far as the house is concerned, let the housework go. Don't do anything but the most urgent things.
- Make sure your diet is well balanced and protein-rich. Don't eat a lot of highly refined and processed carbohydrates (cakes, cookies, candy, or chocolates).
- You may need iron supplements and possibly some vitamin supplements; ask your doctor.
- Drink about 5 pints (3 liters) of fluid every day while you're breast-feeding; some women find they need a drink near them while feeding.
- Most of your milk is produced in the morning when you are rested, so if you constantly rush around or become tense during the day you'll find by evening that your supply is poor.
- If your baby doesn't take all the milk available in the early feedings of the day, express the remainder. This will ensure that the supply is restored up throughout the day.
- Get help and support from everyone around you who is positive and optimistic. Talk to your pediatrician, lactation consultant, or nurse practitioner; speak to friends who've had babies and get advice from them.
- If you are unable to give your baby a feeding because you're away or because you're ill, express the milk off to keep the supply going.

There may be times, such as when you have a blocked duct or a very sore nipple, when it is painful to breast-feed. Hard as it is, it's best to avoid giving your baby formula during these periods if you possibly can. There are too many benefits to your baby being exclusively breast-fed for the first six months if it's possible.

When feeding is painful, many mothers prefer to express milk from the affected breast and use it in a bottle. Giving supplementary formula feedings can undermine the production of breast-milk.

A baby who has become used to your nipple may dislike plastic nipples. Unfortunately, it can be difficult to tell whether your baby just dislikes the bottle, or is not hungry. If you persist, he'll eventually get used to the bottle, but you may then find that he doesn't want to go back to the breast. If your breasts are very sore, try giving your baby expressed milk from a sterilized spoon or cup.

Expressing milk

Bottles of your own expressed milk can be given to your baby when you are ill, extremely tired, or are leaving the baby with someone else. Expressed milk can be kept in sterile containers in the refrigerator for up to 48 hours, or frozen and kept in the freezer for up to six months. This will enable your partner or babysitter to feed your baby with your milk. Also, because breasts produce milk in response to demand, you may need to express milk in order to keep your supply going—if your baby is premature and can't yet breast-feed, for example.

Milk can be expressed by hand or with a breast pump. Electric pumps are more expensive but easier to use than the manual kind. They closely imitate a baby's natural sucking cycle and are best if you need to express often. Even if you use a pump, it is worth learning the technique of hand expressing in case you need to use it.

EXPRESSING BY HAND

1 Wash your hands. Massage your breasts with flat hands, beginning at your ribs and working toward your areola, gradually going over the whole breast.

2 Roll your fingers and thumb together below and above your areola so that you press on the wider milk ducts behind the nipple. Work gently and rhythmically.

3 If the milk doesn't begin to flow, keep on trying. Once it starts, continue for about five minutes, then move onto the second breast.

Before you start, get a bowl, a funnel and a container that can be sealed, and sterilize all of them, either in a sterilizing solution or with boiling water. Wash your hands.

Hand expressing is nearly always a little difficult in the first six weeks, since the breasts have not reached full production, but persevere. The best time to express milk is in the morning, when you'll have the most milk, although when your baby drops his night feeding you may find the evening the best time. You'll be able to express 1–2 fluid ounces (30–60 milliliters) without too much trouble.

The more relaxed you are, the easier it is to express milk. If the milk won't start to flow, place a warm washcloth over your breasts to open the ducts, or try expressing in the bathtub. If you have to lean over a low surface, expressing may give you a backache, so get comfortable and have the container at a convenient height.

EXPRESSING TIPS

- Expressing milk should never hurt. If it does, you're not doing it correctly. Stop immediately.
- Every piece of equipment and all containers should be sterile; your hands must be clean.
- If you're worried about your baby not going back to breast-feeding after a feeding from a bottle, try giving the expressed milk from a cup, with a spoon. They should both be sterilized.
- Milk must be stored correctly otherwise it will spoil and make your baby ill. As soon as you've expressed your milk, put it into the refrigerator until it is needed; it will keep for 48 hours. You can freeze the milk for up to six months; the expressed milk should be put into sterile plastic containers that can be sealed. Don't use glass; it might crack.

Using an electric pump
An electric pump is best if you need to express milk often. The operation varies from brand to brand so follow the manufacturer's instructions.

Using a manual pump
Start by fitting the funnel of the pump over your areola to form an airtight seal. You then operate the lever or plunger of the pump to express the milk.

Possible breast-feeding problems birth to 1 year

Some women find that breast-feeding goes without a hitch from the beginning, but be prepared to be clumsy the first few times, for your baby not to suck vigorously or for very long during the first 24 to 36 hours, and for your breasts to be a bit sore.

Refusing the breast

One of the most common reasons for a baby having problems taking the breast is that he has difficulty breathing. Your baby can't breathe through his nose and swallow at the same time, so always check to make sure that your breast is not covering his nostrils.

Your baby may be reluctant to take the breast if there has been a delay in starting to breast-feed after birth. For both you and your baby, the sooner you start the better. Babies learn to take the breast quickly in the first 48 hours but find it increasingly difficult the longer you wait. This does not mean, however, that your baby will never take to the breast. It just means that you will have to be patient and persevere. If, for example, your baby is premature, you can ask that he be given your expressed milk (so that your supply of milk continues), and when you get home you can introduce the breast.

Another reason for your baby refusing to take the breast may be that he's fretful. If he's wakes up hungry, only to find that he's either ignored, fussed over, or he's changed, you may well discover that he's too distressed to take your breast. If this happens you'll first have to hold your baby firmly and talk to him soothingly and not even try to feed him until he's calmed down.

"Sucky" babies

For many babies, sucking on their mother's breast is the most pleasant experience of the day. You'll soon learn to distinguish between sucking for food and sucking for comfort. During a feeding you may see and feel your baby making strong, rhythmic sucking movements, but if you look closely, you'll see that he isn't swallowing. There's no reason, however, why your baby shouldn't suck as long as he wants, as long as you are happy about it and your nipples aren't sore.

Sleeping through feedings

During the first few days your baby may not be all that interested in feeding. Don't be put off. Try suckling your baby for about five minutes on each breast at each feeding. If your baby goes to sleep at the breast don't worry; it is a very good sign that your baby is contented and doing well. (This is not the case with premature babies, who sleep a lot, and need to be awakened and fed frequently.)

Don't stick to a rigid routine. If your baby sleeps through a feeding, leave it for half an hour and then wake him up gently and try the breast. If he wants to go on sleeping, let him do so: just give the feeding when he wakes. If he is hungry he will perk up when food is offered.

Startled babies

Most babies are easily startled by sudden, loud noises or violent movements in their first few weeks. When you pick your baby up for a feeding, hold him firmly and talk to him soothingly. Lower your head toward your baby so your face and eyes are all he sees. Make sure the room is quiet and there are no disturbing noises around you and, if possible, pick your baby up before he starts to cry.

Biting

This is a natural impulse, and your baby may well bite you before his teeth have come in. When it happens, you will automatically jerk back and may even let out a cry. Your baby will be startled by this but if you say "NO", quite firmly but without shouting, he will quickly learn not to do it—even at a very early age.

Anxiousness on your part

If you meet a minor obstacle such as your baby refusing to have a feeding, try not to get worked up about it. Nervousness may lead to more difficulties, which will make you more discouraged and may even put you off breast-feeding permanently.

Nervousness may also affect your milk. As far as your baby's health is concerned, even a few days of colostrum and breast-milk give a good start to life and are better than none at all. You should never get worried about your baby going without food because you can always fall back on bottle-feeding. Don't let small problems lead you to hasty decisions. You may be tearful and easily upset during the first week or so after delivery anyway, and it would be a shame to give up breast-feeding when you are in this unsettled state. Try to persevere, and ask your doctor for advice.

If you are worried about breast-feeding, make it as easy on yourself as you can. If you are embarrassed about it, make sure you are not in a public place when feeding time comes around. Don't invite visitors to the house when you know you will be feeding, unless you are prepared to feed your baby in front of them if he wants food in a hurry.

Overfeeding/underfeeding

You cannot overfeed a breast-fed baby. He regulates how much he wants (*see p.89*), so unless you give him something other than breast-milk (like badly made-up supplementary bottles), he will take what he needs and his weight will be correct.

It is highly unlikely for a breast-fed baby to be underfed, but if you are worried that your baby isn't getting enough milk, talk to your pediatrician.

IF YOU'RE ILL

As long as you feel like breast-feeding, continue to do so—even if you have to go to the hospital. You may have to make special arrangements with the nursing staff, but if this is what you want, argue firmly for it, and don't be dissuaded.

- If you have to have an anesthetic you will not be able to breast-feed—not only will you be too groggy afterwards, but the drugs you have been given will have passed into your milk.
- If you have advance warning of an operation, try to express and freeze your milk. This way the baby will not miss your milk, even if he misses the pleasure of feeding from you.
- If you are confined to bed with a bad cold or flu, you can express your milk so your partner can feed the baby if you feel too weak.
- If you're too ill even to express milk your baby will have to be given formula milk by bottle or by spoon. He'll probably protest at first, but will acquiesce as he becomes hungrier.

Care of your breasts

Take good care of your breasts: they are going to be working quite hard for the next few months. The first step is to buy yourself a couple of the best maternity bras you can afford. Ask the assistant to measure you and make sure that the bra gives you good support both below your breasts and on your shoulders. The drop-front kind (see below) is very good because it makes feeding quick, convenient, and hygienic, and your breasts are never left to sag. Toward the end of the first week, when lactation becomes well established, your breasts may become full, sore, tender to the touch, and quite hard because there is so much milk. A good bra will minimize discomfort; so will expressing (*see p.96*).

Pay attention to the daily hygiene of your breasts and nipples. Wash them every day with water—don't use soap because it is drying to the skin and can aggravate a sore or cracked nipple. Always handle your breasts carefully: gently pat them dry after both feeding and washing. Leave your nipples open to the air whenever you can: still wear your bra for support, but leave the front flaps down.

Once the milk really starts to flow, it may leak out a lot during the day. Put breast pads or clean handkerchiefs inside your bra to soak up the leaking milk. Change the pad frequently for cleanliness.

While there are no muscles in the breasts themselves, exercise can help keep them in good shape. By shortening the connecting fibers that attach your breasts to your chest muscles, you draw them up and maintain their firmness. The following "top-lift" exercise is very beneficial after you've weaned your baby, but you can also use it once breast-feeding is well established. You can do the exercise either sitting or standing. Raise your arms to shoulder level; grasp the left forearm with your right hand and vice versa, and simultaneously, press and push with each hand towards the elbow with a jerky movement. Repeat for as long as feels comfortable. Do the exercise for a minimum of six weeks for the best results.

Nursing bras
A good supportive bra will minimize discomfort if your breasts become sore. Drop-front styles are convenient and easy to undo.

BREAST PROBLEMS

Problem	Prevention	Cure
Cracked nipples Shooting pain when the baby suckles.	Feed little and often in the first few days. Keep the nipples dry by using disposable breast pads or clean hankies.	Keep feeding if at all possible. If necessary, express the milk by hand (not by pump), and feed the baby by bottle or spoon.
Engorgement Extremely full and painful breasts with a swollen areola.	Feed your baby frequently and try to encourage him to empty your breasts regularly.	Have a hot bath and gently express some milk, or encourage it to flow by massaging toward the nipple.
Blocked duct A hard red patch on the outside of the breast where the duct lies. This can often occur as a result of engorgement or if your bra or clothes are too tight.	Same as for engorgement. Wear a properly fitting bra and keep feeding the baby in different positions throughout the day.	Frequent feeding, offering the breast with the blocked duct first so that it is properly emptied. Express the breast if necessary.
Mastitis Acute infection of the milk duct resulting in a pus-filled lump.	Same as for a blocked duct.	Antibiotics prescribed by your doctor. If this fails it will have to be drained surgically. You can, however, continue to feed, even if you need an operation.
Breast abcesses This infection, which results from an untreated blocked duct, can make you feel feverish; you may have a shiny red patch on your breast.	Same as for a blocked duct.	Same as for a blocked duct. You will probably be prescribed antibiotics by the doctor. Unless instructed otherwise, you can continue to feed your baby from the affected breast.

If you can, avoid all drugs when breast-feeding; many medications pass into the breast-milk and can affect your baby. If you are already taking medications, or if you see your doctor for any new problem, make sure he knows that you are breast-feeding.

Sore nipples

Painful nipples are the most common reason that women give up breast-feeding. However, there are ways to avoid this. Make sure your baby is correctly positioned and properly latched on, and never pull your baby off the nipple (see p.91). Ask your pediatrician or lactation consultant for advice if you have problems. Keep your nipples dry between feedings and make sure they are dry before replacing your bra. If they do become cracked, an ointment containing lanolin may be helpful. You can also try using a nipple shield, which is made of soft silicone and fits over your nipple. The baby sucks through a small teat on the nipple. Sterilize it before use.

Bottle-feeding birth to 1 year

Once you make the decision to bottle-feed, stick to it and don't feel guilty about it. Many babies are bottle-fed at some point, including those who started out on the breast. All of them thrive. Your baby will do well on infant formula. Just make sure he has the same attention and closeness at feeding times as he would have if you were breast-feeding.

Mother's milk is important to babies, but it is not as important as your love. Fill the hours you spend with your baby, particularly feeding times, with your love, affection, and care. These are just as important to your baby's physical and emotional well-being as your milk.

Most women feel pressure to breastfeed their babies, and worry quite a lot if they decide not to, but there are some good reasons for deciding that breast-feeding is not for you. Despite your best efforts you may simply not be successful at it. In that case, the best thing is to forget about it and concentrate on giving your baby a good bottle-fed diet.

He will do just as well. Some women find it emotionally or psychologically difficult, or feel too tied down by a breast-feeding routine that curtails many of their activities, including returning to work. Some couples are opposed to it because they feel it excludes the father.

One of the good things about bottle-feeding is that the new father can be just as involved as the new mother at feeding times. Make sure that your partner feeds the baby very soon after you get home from the hospital, so that he gets used to the technique and isn't afraid to handle the baby. The sooner he learns to do all the things that your baby needs the better. If possible, your partner should share the feeding equally. If not, he should give at least two out of the six feedings a day.

Choosing the bottles
Buy unbreakable bottles that have a wide neck so that they're easy to fill and to clean; the 10 fluid ounce (250 milliliter) size is the most suitable. The nipple should be shaped to fit the baby's mouth. Disposable bottles are useful for traveling, and when you run out of sterilized bottles.

Sterilizing the bottles
Buy your feeding equipment well in advance of having your baby so you can practice with it before your baby is born.

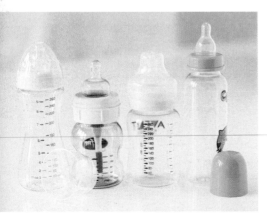

Bottles and nipples
There is a wide range of bottles and nipples now available. You may need to try a few to find out which kind is best for your baby.

Major department stores and drugstores sell bottle-feeding packs that contain all the essential equipment.

Although the water in many areas of the US is chlorinated and safe to drink, all feeding equipment should be sterilized to reduce the risk of your baby getting ill. There are a number of ways to sterilize bottles, including some countertop models that do not require any heat, but the easiest and most reliable sterilization method is to immerse all feeding equipment—not only all of the bottles but also any other equipment that you use to make up feedings—in boiling water for at least ten minutes (see below). Once your child is at least a year old, you can clean bottles in your dishwasher, but clean the nipples thoroughly before putting them in the dishwasher.

HYGIENE AND PREPARATION TIPS

- Always wash your hands before sterilizing, preparing, and feedings.
- Make sure that everything that comes into contact with your baby's food is thoroughly cleaned or sterilized before use and always clean the work surface before starting to prepare the formula.
- Sterilize every piece of equipment you use for making up your baby's bottles, as well as pacifiers and teething rings.
- Make up the bottles according to the instructions. Never add anything extra.
- Give the bottle to your baby as soon as it is ready. Do not make up bottles in advance.
- Never give your baby leftover milk. Throw away any milk that's left in the bottle.

CLEANING EQUIPMENT

Washing bottles and nipples
Wash all equipment in hot soapy water. Scrub the insides of bottles with a bottle brush and rub nipples thoroughly to remove milk. Rinse well in warm running water.

Boiling
To sterilize bottles by boiling, you should boil them for at least ten minutes. Then remove them from the water and allow them to cool down before using.

Cleaning in a dishwasher
Once your baby is more than 12 months old you can wash feeding equipment in a dishwasher. Clean nipples before they go in. Run the machine on the normal cycle.

The flow of milk

Milk simply runs out of the breast at the beginning of a feed so there is hardly any need for exertion when your baby is sucking. I feel that bottle-fed babies should find feeding just as easy. To make this possible for them, the hole in the nipple should be large enough to let drops fall in a steady stream when the bottle is inverted. If it takes a few seconds for a drop to form, then the hole is too small; if the stream is continuous, it is too big.

- You can buy nipples with different-sized holes; alternatively to make a hole bigger you need a fine, red-hot needle. Simply insert it gently through the hole in the nipple and the rubber, or plastic will melt. Have a few spare nipples as it is not as easy as it sounds, and you may end up with holes that are much too large. I did the first time I tried it.
- It is worth spending time getting the size of the hole just right, because if it is too large your baby will get too much too fast and will cough and splutter. If it is too small, your baby will get tired from sucking before he has taken a full meal, and he may swallow too much air.
- Buy sculpted nipples if possible. These are shaped to fit the baby's palate and allow the baby more control over the flow.

The first feeding

There is no artificial equivalent to colostrum. Even if you're not going to continue to breast-feed you will be giving

MAKING UP A POWDER FORMULA

Bottles must be mixed strictly in accordance with the powder-to-water proportions recommended by the manufacturer or by your doctor. Make bottles when you need them. Bacteria can multiply fast in bottles of warm formula, so don't make up bottles in advance and store them.

1 Fill the bottle to the correct level with fresh water that has been boiled and left to cool for half an hour. Fill the scoop with powder and level it off.

2 Add the powder to the water. Make sure you add exactly the right number of scoops of powder—no more and no less than the manufacturer recommends.

3 Put on the cap and nipple. Shake the bottle until you're sure there are no lumps or residue and the mixture is smooth.

your baby a great headstart if you breast-feed him for the first days (*see p.90*).

Don't worry if your baby doesn't gulp down everything in the bottle. It's perfectly normal for all babies, breast- or bottle-fed, not to take very much in their first 48 hours, and they take a while to get into the swing of feeding. Like a breast-fed baby, yours will let you know with a cry when he wants to be fed. Follow your baby's lead and develop the supply and demand system explained on p.107, just as for a breast-fed baby.

Formulas

A variety of formulas are available, all carefully formulated to make them as close as possible to breast-milk. In fact, formula milk has added vitamin D and iron, levels of which are low in breast-milk.

Most formulas are based on cow's milk. Some formulas are available both in powder and liquid forms. There are soy-based formulas available, but never give these to your baby without the advice of your baby's pediatrician. Pre-mixed milk comes in cartons or cans and is often ultra-heat treated (UHT), which means it is sterile and will keep in a cool place until the "expiration" date. Once formula has been opened, the milk will keep for 24 hours in a refrigerator. Liquid formula is more expensive than powdered formula, but it is very convenient when you are traveling.

Giving a bottle-feeding

Make sure that you have a quiet, comfortable place to sit and that your arms are well supported with cushions or pillows if necessary (*see p.93*). Lay your baby in your lap with his head in the crook of your

BOTTLE TEMPERATURE

Make sure that the milk is cooled to the right temperature before you feed your baby. Never keep warm milk in a thermos or leave a bottle standing overnight in a bottle warmer. Never warm a bottle in a microwave; microwaves cause "hot spots" that can scald your baby.

Testing temperature
Test the temperature of the milk on your wrist before feeding the baby: it should not be too hot nor cold to the touch.

Cooling a bottle
If the bottle is too hot, put it in a jug of cold water, or hold it under cold running water for a short time, then test again. Always leave the cap on the bottle covering the nipple.

elbow and his back supported by your forearm. Make sure your baby is not lying horizontally. He should be half-sitting, so breathing and swallowing are safe and easy and there's no risk of choking.

Just before you start feeding, test the heat of the milk by letting a couple of drops fall onto the inside of your wrist. The milk should not feel too hot or too cold. You should already have tested the flow of milk (see p.104). Loosen the cap of the bottle a little so that air can enter to take the place of the milk that your baby sucks out. If you don't do this, a lot of pressure can build up inside the bottle and will flatten the nipple and make sucking very hard work. Your baby will become bad-tempered and angry and refuse the rest of the bottle. If this happens, gently pull the bottle out of your baby's mouth so the air can get in and then continue feeding him as before.

To elicit the baby's sucking reflex so that he takes the bottle, gently stroke the cheek nearest to you. As your baby turns to your touch you can gently insert the nipple into his mouth. He should latch onto the nipple so that the tip is far back into his mouth, like a nipple would be. You should, however, be careful not to push it so far back that he gags on it.

Let your baby set the pace of feeding. He might want to pause a while to look around or play with the bottle and he

GIVING A BOTTLE-FEED

1 *Gently stroke your baby's nearest cheek to elicit his sucking reflex. Insert the nipple carefully into his mouth. If you push the nipple too far back he may gag.*

2 *Chat with your baby as you feed. Let him pause mid-feed if he likes. Change him onto the other arm at this stage to give him a new view, and your arm a rest.*

3 *If you want your baby to release the bottle from his mouth, gently slide your little finger into the corner of his mouth and lift it out.*

should be allowed this pleasure. From the very beginning, make feeding times as pleasant as possible. Face your baby and make eye contact. Don't sit in silence: talk, sing to him, make any kind of sound you like. Just make sure your voice sounds pleasant, happy, and responsive. This is the first conversation your baby will enjoy, and he will react to your movements, gestures, and smiles.

Halfway through the feed, change your baby onto the other arm. This will give your baby a new view to look at and your arm a rest. You may also want to burp your baby at this point (see p.108).

Bottle-feeding patterns

Bottle-fed babies tend to feed less frequently than breast-fed ones. This is because formula takes longer to digest. It also contains slightly more protein, which delays hunger for longer.

After the first two or three days bottle-fed babies usually settle on a four-hourly regime. They will have six feedings a day, probably one less than if they were being breast-fed. When your baby is first born he will probably not take more than 2 fluid ounces (60 milliliters) of milk at each feeding, but as he gets older, the feedings will get bigger and the number of feedings each day will be fewer.

Let your baby determine when he's ready to be fed. Never, ever, feed your baby according to the clock. Feed him when he tells you with his cries that he *is* hungry, not at a time when you *think* he should be hungry.

Don't feel that your baby has to finish every bottle. Like everybody else, your baby's appetite will vary, so if he seems satisfied, but there's a little left in the bottle, don't try to make him take it. He will only get too full and may spit it up (see p.109). What's more, he may become overfed and fat. On the other hand, if your baby always seems ravenous, give him some extra from another bottle. If your baby regularly wants more milk, then start to add the extra amount at every feed.

BOTTLE-FEEDING TIPS

- Don't feed your baby when he's lying flat; it is very difficult to swallow in this position and your baby may gag or even be sick.
- Never leave your baby with the bottle propped up on a pillow or cushion. Not only is it very dangerous because your baby could choke, but he could become very uncomfortable if he has to swallow a lot of air along with his formula because of the angle at which the bottle's been propped. Moreover, your baby misses out on the cuddling and affection that he should enjoy while he nurses.
- Don't try to force your baby to finish the bottle after he has stopped sucking: he knows when he's had enough.
- Even if you think the formula isn't right for your baby, don't change it without consulting your pediatrician or nurse practitioner. It is very rare for a brand of milk to be responsible for a baby not eating well. Sometimes a baby is allergic to cow's milk, and may have to have a hydrolized (broken down so it's more easily digested) formula. Always ask your doctor for advice. Never change to a substitute formula without checking with your pediatrician.

Possible bottle-feeding problems birth to 1 year

Overfeeding

Fat cells are produced by an infant in response to the amount of fat that is taken in with food. Once produced, these cells can't be removed, so if your baby develops an excessively large number, they will still be present when he's an adult and can lead to health problems.

If you overfeed your baby, he will become fat. Unfortunately, it is easier to overfeed a bottle-fed baby. There are two major reasons for this: firstly, it is tempting to put extra formula into the bottle. You should always follow the instructions to the letter (see p.104), otherwise you'll be giving the baby unseen (and unnecessary) calories. Secondly, because you can see the amount of formula he is taking it may be hard to resist encouraging him to finish the last drop. You should always let your baby decide whether he's had enough. Other causes of overfeeding include giving sweet, syrupy drinks and introducing solids to your baby too early.

Underfeeding

This is rare in bottle-fed babies, but it can happen. Your baby should be fed on demand and not according to the clock. Although most babies will be ready for a bottle every four hours by the time they are two to three months old, their individual appetites may vary from day to day. Say, for example, your baby's at the age when he can take five 6-fluid-ounce (180-milliliter) bottles a day, but at one feeding he only takes 4 fluid ounces (15 milliliters) out of the bottle. If you insist on feeding on a schedule, don't give any extra milk in the scheduled bottles, and don't offer any of the interim feedings that your baby will be crying for, he won't be able to catch up with the total volume of milk that he needs, and won't gain weight.

You should also be flexible about how much formula you make up. The figures on the package are given as a general estimate but, for example, if your child consistently drains each bottle you give and still seems fretful and upset, he may well be hungry. Make up an extra 2 fluid ounces (60 milliliters) of formula and see if he wants it. If he takes it then he needs it and won't put on extra weight.

If you find that your baby is demanding frequent feedings but doesn't drink much and remains fretful, check that the nipple hole isn't too small. It may well be that he's having a hard time actually sucking the milk out of the bottles and is not getting enough nourishment.

Burping

The point of burping is to bring up any air that has been swallowed during feeding or while crying before feeding. The reason for bringing up gas is to prevent it from causing your baby discomfort. Babies vary a great deal in their reaction to this, and in my experience the majority of them aren't noticeably happier or more contented for having been burped.

Babies also vary a great deal in the amount of air that they swallow during feeding. Some, including all breast-fed babies, swallow very little. Swallowing air is much more common in bottle-fed babies but even then it doesn't seem to be a problem.

Burping your baby
Hold your baby on your shoulder with a bib or a diaper beneath him to catch any dribble. Gently rub or pat the baby's back between the shoulder blades.

If very small quantities of air are swallowed during feeding they form small bubbles in the stomach that cannot be burped up until they have coalesced into a large bubble, and this can take a great deal of time. Small bubbles in the stomach are very unlikely to cause discomfort. The one point in favor of burping is that it makes you pause, relax, take things slowly, hold your baby gently, and stroke or pat him in a reassuring way. This is good for your baby and for you.

My attitude towards burping, therefore, is this: by all means do it, even if it is just for your peace of mind, but don't become fanatical about it. Don't pat or rub your baby too hard while you're burping, or you may jerk or jostle him and cause a spit up. A gentle upward stroking movement is usually preferable to firm pats.

Some experts advise that you stop the feeding halfway through to burp your baby. I don't think there is any need to do that. Wait until your baby pauses naturally during the feeding and take advantage of this little rest to try burping. As your baby gets older, you will probably find that he finishes his whole bottle quite comfortably without needing to burp.

Spitting up

Some babies never spit up at all. Others do so with surprising ease, and this can be a cause of concern to parents. My youngest son had a tendency to spit up, and I worried that he wasn't getting enough to eat. I simply followed my own instinct, which was to offer him more food. If he didn't take it, I assumed he had spit up the excess he didn't need. In very young babies, the commonest cause of spitting up is overfeeding. This is another reason why you should never insist your bottle-fed baby finishes his bottle.

If your bottle-fed baby shows a tendency to spit up, check the hole in the nipple. If it is too large, he may be taking too much, too quickly. If it is too small, he may be sucking in a lot of air because he has to suck very hard.

Forcible (projectile) vomiting, especially if it happens after consecutive feedings or goes on for more than a day, should be reported immediately to your doctor. Vomiting in a very small baby can quickly lead to dehydration, and you must get medical advice as soon as possible.

Night feedings birth to 1 year

Because you will be responding to all of your baby's demands for food, you may find that feeding him takes up quite a lot of your time—it can take at least 30 minutes per feeding. This will mean you are feeding for more than three hours out of every 24. With night feeding on top of all the other things that you have to do to take care of your baby, you may find yourself becoming extremely tired and tense. It won't be so much the number of hours sleep that you lose, but more the way in which your sleep patterns are broken up over long periods of time.

It is very important that you get adequate rest both day and night, so you need your partner to share the work with you. There should be equality of child-nurturing between you, and since you are doing most of the feeding it is only fair for him to take over some of the other jobs for the baby. In fact, even if you've decided to breast-feed, the night feeds shouldn't be solely your responsibility. If your baby sleeps in another room, ask your partner to bring him to you as soon as he cries, and get him to take the baby back and change his diaper after he's been fed. He can also take a turn by feeding with expressed milk.

TIPS FOR NIGHT FEEDS

- Feed your baby in bed so that you are warm and comfortable, but always put him back in his crib afterward.
- If you're very tired, and you are breast-feeding, express enough milk for the nightfeeding and put it into a sterile bottle, so your partner can give the baby the bottle.
- Keep some diaper-changing necessities in your bedroom so you can feed and change your baby with minimal disturbance.
- It's easy to get cold sitting up in bed so have a sweater or robe handy.
- Have a drink by your bedside in case you get thirsty while feeding.
- If your baby's in another room and you're concerned about not hearing his cries, invest in a baby monitor.

Reducing night feedings

Until your baby weighs about 11 pounds (5 kilograms), he won't be able to sleep for more than five hours at a time without waking up hungry. However, once this weight is reached, you can try stretching the time between feedings with the goal of giving yourself about six hours of undisturbed sleep, and getting your baby to drop the early morning feeding. Your baby will have his own routine, but as a general rule, it's sensible to try to juggle your baby's last feeding so it's given at around the time you go to bed.

But be flexible; it may be that your baby doesn't want to drop the early morning feeding, and no matter how much you try to alter the routine he will still wake up and want to nurse. If so, you'll just have to try to make the night feedings as straightforward as possible and look forward to when he drops them.

Introducing solids 6 months

At some stage during the first year, you will have to start to wean your baby off milk and on to solid food. Official advice is that breast milk or formula is sufficient for your baby for the first six months, but you may find that friends and relatives pressure you to start weaning your baby earlier.

You should, however, resist all such pressure for the following reasons: firstly, breast milk (or its formula equivalent) is the only food that your baby needs in the early months. Second, the introduction of solids to too young a baby can lessen the desire to suck. In the case of breast-fed babies, this decreases the amount taken from the breasts, which respond by producing less milk. Either way, your baby will end up having a diet that does not meet his needs. Third, until your baby is at least six months old, his digestive tract is incapable of digesting and absorbing complex foods. If you introduce solids before this, not only will they pass through largely undigested, but you will be putting an increased strain on his immature kidneys.

When to introduce solids

In the early months, milk provides all the calories required to make your baby grow. The more he grows, the more milk he'll need to drink. But your baby's stomach can only hold a certain amount of milk at each feeding, and he will eventually reach a point when he's drinking to full capacity at each feeding, but still won't have enough calories to keep going. This is the point at which you'll have to introduce solids. You'll recognize the sign when your baby starts to demand more milk and appears very unsatisfied after each feed. He may suddenly start demanding a sixth feed, having been quite content on five for the previous couple of months, or he may wake at night after previously sleeping through.

In many babies, this happens at around six months. It's also an ideal time to start solids because it generally coincides with the tapering off of your baby's intense desire to suck.

First tastes
Choose a time when he's not too hungry or tired, such as halfway through his midday feeding. Scoop some food onto a spoon and insert it gently between his lips.

What foods to give

Up until his sixth month your baby will have had a diet of milk. It is therefore only sensible to start with bland, semi-liquid, foods with a smooth, creamy consistency: unsweetened purées of fruit (bananas, dessert apples, ripe pears, and peaches) and vegetables (potatoes, carrots, and cauliflower), and gluten-free rice cereal are ideal. Although specially manufactured "first foods" are available, it's better to prepare your own. In addition to being cheaper, you'll know exactly what is in the food and that it has no additional sugar, salt, or preservatives.

Food safety

By the time your baby is ready for weaning you don't have to sterilize all cooking utensils meticulously—but you must follow the general principles of good hygiene. Wash your hands before preparing the baby's food and before feeding, and make sure all the utensils are clean and any made-up food is kept in the refrigerator. Purées of fruit and vegetables can be kept for two days in the refrigerator or frozen in individual portions in ice-cube trays.

Giving the first solids

Start off by giving your baby one or two teaspoons of food along with a normal milk feeding; the one around midday is ideal because your baby will be quite alert and not ravenously hungry. Though ready for the calories that solids provide, your baby will be hungry for what he knows is satisfying—milk—so feed from one breast first, or give half the usual bottle. As he gets more used to solids, he may want to be given them before he takes the milk.

Having decided which feeding to start the solids on, prepare the small amount that you'll need and then settle in your normal position to feed the baby. When you've given him half of the milk, put your baby on your lap, then, using a small spoon, scoop up some food and place it gently between his lips so that he can suck the food off. Be very careful not to push the spoon in too far or he may gag on the unexpected food on the back of his tongue. He's bound to be messy at first, maybe pushing more food out than he manages to take in. If so, gently scrape the excess off the baby's face and place the spoon onto his lips as before. Your baby will signal that he's had enough by turning away from the spoon with his lips shut, and may even cry. Never force your baby to take any more food than he wants. When he's taken the solid food, you can give him the rest of the milk.

TIPS FOR FEEDING

- Give your baby only one new food at a time and then wait for several days to see if there's an adverse reaction.
- Use dry infant cereals that you have to make up rather than ready-mixed cereals; they contain more iron and are more nutritious.
- Only give cereal once a day.
- If your baby doesn't like taking food from a spoon, dip a clean fingertip into the food and let him suck it off.
- If you find it difficult to feed your baby on your lap, put him in a baby seat on the floor.
- Keep plenty of paper towels nearby to mop up any mess.
- Even early solids, especially banana, can stain clothes, so put a small cloth bib on your baby.

Establishing solids 6 months to 1 year

Once your baby happily accepts one or two different solids, it's important to introduce a variety of textures and tastes. As the year goes on he'll be able to manage foods that have only been mashed or chopped and will learn to enjoy chewing and sucking on chunks of food. He'll soon move from the stage of milk feedings with "tastes" of solids to three solid meals a day with accompanying drinks of water, diluted fruit juice, or milk.

The amount of food you give your baby can be gradually increased over several weeks until he takes most of the calories that he requires for growth from solid food and not from milk. As the number of solid meals he takes increases, the amount of milk he needs correspondingly decreases. When your baby is thirsty, give him plain water or diluted fruit juice to drink, rather than milk. It is best to avoid encouraging a taste for sweet drinks, so never give your baby a commercial drink containing sugar and colorings. It's difficult to specify the amount a baby should be eating because every baby has different requirements and appetites. You'll be the best judge of how much your baby wants. If you are not sure, make slightly more of each food than you think he needs and feed your baby as much of each individual portion as he wants. Freeze the leftovers.

Finger foods
It won't be long before your baby starts wanting to feed herself. Start with easily held pieces of fruit or vegetables and be prepared for a mess. Never leave her alone while she is eating.

What foods to give

When your baby has got used to taking cereal and fruit or vegetable purées, you can start to introduce other foods—including meat, fish, and dairy products—into his diet, until he is eating virtually all the foods that you normally eat. As these gradually replace milk as the main source of his nutritional requirements, you will have to ensure that he has a balanced diet that includes foods from all the main food groups (*see p.122*).

When first starting on solids, your baby will cope best with foods of a smooth, creamy consistency. After cooking, mash, sieve or purée the food, then thin it with milk, stock, or the water you used to cook the vegetables.

By about nine months of age, your baby can gradually be introduced to food with a more lumpy texture. This can be mashed with a fork or finely chopped with a sharp knife. You don't have to wait for your baby's teeth to appear before introducing lumpy food, because he can chew with his gums.

Food safety

In the first few months of your baby's life, it is essential that all feeding equipment is sterilized by one of the various methods available (*see p.103*). By the time he starts eating solids, however, it is no longer necessary to sterilize everything used at feedtimes—but bottles and nipples used for milk should still be sterilized as before. For cups, bowls and cutlery, thorough washing in hot, soapy water followed by rinsing with hot water is adequate. However, as your baby is weaned onto solids and his diet expands to include a wider range of foods, more general questions of food safety become important, especially in the light of much publicized outbreaks of salmonella and listeria poisoning, as well as other concerns about food safety. Since babies— and the elderly, pregnant women, and people suffering from illness—are among those most vulnerable to the harmful effects of bacteria in food, it is vital to have clear guidelines about the safe preparation, storage and cooking of food for infants, but the advice is equally applicable to the whole family.

Kitchen hygiene

Wash your hands with soap and hot water before handling food. Ensure that you and your family wash your hands thoroughly (not at the kitchen sink) after using the toilet, after diaper changing, and after playing with pets.

Keep the kitchen scrupulously clean, especially the work surfaces, chopping boards, and utensils used in food preparation. Dry dishes with clean towels, or let them dry in a rack after rinsing with hot water. Wash your dishcloths regularly. Keep garbage pails clean and covered and empty them often.

Don't leave any food out without covering it first; also cover food before putting it in the fridge. If you are feeding your baby from jars of baby food, it's all

FOOD INTOLERANCE AND ALLERGY

Don't worry too much, but take sensible precautions with the foods you give your baby —especially if you or your relatives have allergies.

- Don't give your baby foods containing wheat flour or gluten before he is seven months old since he may find them difficult to digest.
- Avoid giving your baby soft-boiled eggs until he is about one year old.
- Don't give a baby under one years of age honey; it can cause infant botulism, a rare but serious disease.
- Don't give your baby very high-fiber breakfast cereals as they are too difficult to digest.
- Avoid unpasteurized cheese until your baby is at least two years old.
- If your baby has a relative who suffers from an allergic condition, avoid giving him peanuts, or foods containing peanuts, and shellfish until he is at least three years old.

right to give it to him straight from the jar if you know he is going to finish the contents at one meal. Otherwise, transfer some to a bowl and leave the remainder in the jar, replace the lid, and refrigerate until the next meal.

Buying food

The rule is to shop often, choosing fresh ingredients wherever possible and using them quickly. Avoid bruised or damaged fruit and vegetables, and wash fruit if it is not going to be peeled before eating. If you buy canned or bottled goods, check that there are no dents or signs of leakage on the cans, and that jar seals are unbroken. Check expiration dates, and avoid items that have reached them.

Storing food

Store food in clean, covered containers in the refrigerator, and use it as soon as possible. Don't store cooked and raw foods together, and put raw meat or fish on a plate at the bottom of the refrigerator so that juices cannot drip down onto foods below. Don't keep food in the freezer longer than the time recommended by the

TIPS FOR FOOD PREPARATION

- Before steaming and puréeing fruit, peel, remove the seeds and any parts that may choke the baby and cut up into small pieces. Do the same for the vegetables.
- Give your baby meat, cooked any way you like and then puréed. Don't forget fish, chicken, and chicken livers, which are cheap, quick, and easy to prepare. Thin down the puréed meat with vegetable water or soup.
- Always choose the freshest-looking vegetables (not wrinkled or dull-looking ones), and cook them as soon as possible.
- Handle fruit and vegetables gently. Don't cut them until you have to and don't crush and bruise them because this destroys the vitamin C in them.
- Cook vegetables and fruit in as little water as possible, with a tightly fitting lid on the pot, so they are steamed rather than boiled. This helps to retain the vitamins.
- Cook soft-skinned fruit and vegetables in their skins because this helps to retain the vitamins and will also give your child fiber. You may have to remove the skin if it's very tough and likely to choke your baby.

- Use cast-iron cooking pots. A little iron will be absorbed into the food and helps to boost your child's iron supply.
- Always make the food a suitable consistency for your baby's age. For example, a thick milk for your six-month-old baby; a thicker cream for your seven-month-old baby; and a slightly chunky mash for a nine month old.
- Don't use copper pans for green leafy vegetables as copper breaks down vitamin C.
- Don't cook canned foods for too long or you will destroy the vitamin content.
- Don't add salt or sugar to your child's food; the immature kidneys can't handle a heavy salt load and you will be doing your child a favor if you don't encourage a sweet tooth.
- Avoid using too many saturated fats in your cooking—use safflower or corn oil instead.
- Don't prepare vegetables or soak them in water a long time before you cook them or you will destroy the vitamin content.
- To discourage bacteria from growing, put your baby's food into the refrigerator as soon as it has cooled to room temperature.

manufacturer for your particular model. Foods that have been frozen must always be thoroughly defrosted before cooking, and never refreeze defrosted food.

Cooking and reheating food

The only safe rule as far as babies' food is concerned is always to cook thoroughly; this is especially true of meat, chicken and eggs. Never give raw eggs to babies. Try to avoid giving reheated leftovers to your baby, but if you do, make sure they are thoroughly heated through first. Chilled or frozen food should be heated up only once and any leftovers thrown away. If you're preparing food in advance, cool it as quickly as possible before storing it in the refrigerator or freezer. Putting hot food straight into the refrigerator may raise the temperature and warm other foods.

Ready-prepared foods

Whether you make up your baby's foods yourself or buy ready-made foods in jars is up to you. Bought foods are certainly convenient if you are traveling or you are in a hurry, but they are more expensive than home-made meals, and may not be nutritionally sound. However, there are now some excellent ranges of freshly prepared food. If you are going to use prepared foods on a regular basis, follow the guidelines listed below.

Preparing food for babies

You'll probably already have a liquidizer or food mill; if you don't, buy a cheap, easy-to-use, hand-operated blender. You'll only have to purée food for the first few months of your baby's new diet; after that it can be mashed or finely chopped. In the beginning, you may find it easier just to sieve the food, especially when you're not making up big batches. If you've frozen portions of food, a small pan is ideal for heating them up quickly.

For thinning down your home-prepared foods simply add water; the water in which you've steamed fruit or vegetables (with no additional salt or sugar) is ideal, but you can also add expressed milk, cow's milk, soup, or tomato, orange, or apple juice.

READY-PREPARED FOODS

- Check the list of ingredients on the can or jar. They are listed in order of concentration, so never buy anything in which water is listed first.
- Make sure that the jar is vacuum sealed when you open it, otherwise it may be contaminated.
- Don't buy "mixed dinners;" they usually contain a lot of thickener.
- If possible, buy meat and vegetable dishes separately and then combine them if you want a "mixed dinner."
- Don't keep opened jars in the refrigerator for longer than two days. Throw them away after that.

- Don't buy anything that has added salt, sugar, modified starch or monosodium glutamate (MSG).
- Never store food in opened cans; put it into a dish or bowl and keep it covered in the refrigerator.
- Don't heat the food up in the jar—it could crack.
- It is very unhygienic to feed the baby from the jar then keep the rest for a second meal, since it will have become contaminated with saliva. It's all right to feed your baby from a jar if he's going to eat it all or if, for example, you're on the move and you don't mind throwing away what's left when he's had enough.

For thickening, use ground, whole-grain cereals such as wheat germ or rice, cottage cheese, yogurt, or mashed potatoes. If you feel you need to sweeten foods, use naturally sweet fruit juice or dextrose. Never use refined sugar—brown or white. Our bodies don't need to have it, it's bad for our teeth, and it only encourages a sweet tooth.

Giving drinks

While you're introducing solids, milk will remain an important part of your baby's diet and will make up a large part of his daily caloric intake. By the time he's nine months old it will be safe for him to have cow's milk, either from a cup or in food. Although the milk doesn't have to be boiled, any containers that it is given in have to be thoroughly cleaned every time the baby's had a drink out of them.

As soon as your baby is having any quantity of solid food he will need water in addition to milk to drink. Start him off with ½ fluid ounce (15 milliliters) of water or natural, unsweetened, diluted fruit juice between and after meals (it is a good idea to try giving it from a cup, *see right*). After that, he can be given a drink whenever he's thirsty during the day. Keep this in mind, especially in the summer or in a warm environment. Avoid syrups and cola drinks and any drinks with added sugar or saccharin—these are very high in calories and also bad for your baby's teeth. Stick to water or natural, unsweetened, diluted fruit juice.

Where to feed your child

At first you will probably feed your baby on your lap or in an infant seat, but once your baby's back muscles are strong enough to

WEANING YOUR BABY ON TO A CUP

When he's six months old, introduce your baby to drinking from a cup as part of the process of weaning from breast or bottle. The best times to use a cup are at the lunchtime and late afternoon feeding when he'll probably be eager to eat solids. Give him solids first and then try the cup.

There are a variety of special cups available. Cups with spouts are best at the beginning because they let the liquid drip out and the baby has to half suck and half drink to get anything. Hold the cup yourself and offer only a few sips of milk at first, but release it as soon as he wants to take it from you. As he gets more dexterous, he can use a two-handled cup; the kind with slanted lips are ideal because they don't have to be tipped far before the liquid comes out. Some babies, however, prefer an open cup.

Your baby will gradually wean himself off the morning feeding. He'll still want a breast-feed or bottle before bedtime until he's at least a year old—more for comfort than for food.

Using a trainer cup
Give your child water or juice in a cup. You will need to hold it for him at first, but as he becomes more dexterous he will be able to hold it himself.

support him you'll probably want to get a highchair. Make sure the model you buy complies with safety standards. Chairs with a wide base are safest as they make it less likely that the chair could topple over if your child wriggles or jumps around. Check the chair regularly for any sharp edges or loose fittings. Always give the chair a good cleaning after meals so food doesn't gather in the nooks and crannies.

When your baby first starts using a highchair you may have to prop him up with cushions. Most highchairs have harnesses to keep the child from slipping or falling out. While these are important safety features and should be used, always make sure you know how to release them quickly in case your child should choke or gag while he's eating.

If he does gag on some food—and he's almost bound to at some stage—pat your child firmly on the back until whatever food is caught dislodges itself. When you give

your child a new texture, he may gag out of surprise. Talk soothingly and gently rub your child's back and he'll be able to swallow whatever was worrying him. It is essential that you know how to react quickly in any situation like this. A baby who is gagging should be left alone but if he is not making a sound, coughing, or breathing you must begin treatment, since he could become unconscious. For advice on first aid procedures, see p.299. Never, ever leave your child alone while he is eating.

Feeding your child

Your baby will soon look forward to solids—not only to eat, but to play with. Feeding times will become messier, so it's advisable to put newspaper or a plastic sheet beneath the highchair or table to catch the worst of the mess. Keep your baby away from expensively covered walls—remember, he can throw food now.

After about a month on solids, your baby will have grasped the technique of getting food off the spoon successfully, and by the time he's having two solid meals a day, he will be prepared to open his mouth to take the food.

Self-feeding

Your baby will leave you in no doubt when he wants to feed himself: he will simply take the spoon from you. Let your baby experiment and be prepared to put up with the mess. Encourage all attempts at self-feeding because it is such a huge step forward in your baby's development, both physically and intellectually, and also because it will give your baby a feeling of accomplishment and confidence. It will help him to become manually dexterous

SELF-FEEDING TIPS

- Tuck a few tissues under the neckline of your baby's bib to keep his neck from getting wet as he practices drinking.
- If a baby won't wear a bib, put a colored scarf round his neck to protect his clothes.
- If your baby is going to sneeze, get out of the way or you will get covered in food.
- Fit a kitchen towel holder on the back of the highchair or near it.
- Keep the highchair well away from your walls—your baby will be quite capable of throwing food by now.
- Get a nonslip bowl if you can since it will stay in place while your baby is trying to get food onto his spoon.

and to coordinate muscles and movements. There is nothing that will speed up his hand–eye coordination faster than getting a spoonful of food to his mouth.

Your baby will take several months to become proficient at self-feeding. Food will be a plaything and you may also worry because most of the food seems to be on the floor and not in your baby's stomach. Nature has taken care of this. At the time when a baby starts to self-feed, the initial growth spurt is beginning to slacken off and so he needs to eat less.

Until he can manage to get the food, into his mouth successfully, have a spoon, too. When he can't scoop the food up, swap your full spoon for the empty one.

Be flexible about feeding

Try not to get tense at mealtimes. This will be easier to do if you don't spend too much time preparing the food and then feel resentful if it isn't eaten, and if you

Preparing foods
Make sure cooked vegetables are easy to hold but soft enough to chew. Congratulate your baby when she manages to get the food into her mouth.

FINGER FOODS

If self-feeding with a spoon seems to frustrate your baby, but his appetite is good, try finger foods. Your baby will be able to handle them easily, and even if the food is hard he will suck it.

Fruit and vegetables
• Any fresh fruit that is easy to hold, cut into a slice, without the skin or seeds, e.g. bananas
• Any cooked vegetable that you can make into a stick or a shape that is easy to grasp, e.g., carrots
• Mashed potato

Grains and cereals
• Small pieces of sugarless dried cereal
• Little balls of cooked rice
• Whole-wheat bread (without the complete grains)
• Whole-wheat crackers (without complete grains)

Protein
• Cubes of low-fat cheese
• Macaroni and cheese
• Pieces of cheese on toast
• Hamburgers cut into small, easily held pieces
• Scrambled eggs
• Cottage cheese
• Any kind of meat, preferably white, in pieces that are easy to pick up
• Chunks of firm fish, taken off the bone
• Sliced hard-boiled eggs—only give him yolk until he's aged one year

take a few precautions so you don't have a lot of cleaning up to do. The most important rule of all is not to pit your will against your baby's. In the end, there is no way that you can force a baby to eat and you should never reach that point. Even if you are worried that your baby isn't getting enough food—he is. If he doesn't want to eat, his needs have temporarily shrunk. A child will always eat if he is hungry, and will eat to satisfy his needs. A period of eating very little will probably be followed by a period of eating a lot.

Balanced nutritional intake

Don't think of your baby's nutritional intake as what he has eaten that day, but look at what he has eaten that week, and try to balance it out in this time scale. You may find that for a couple of days your baby will refuse everything but cereal and then on the third day he'll go on a fruit-eating binge, or want only cheese. A baby, like most animals, is self-regulating. He knows what he wants and when he wants it.

As with many aspects of childrearing, take your cue from your baby on feeding. As a note of reassurance, a baby's chosen diet will be a balanced one, if he has the correct foods to choose from.

Daily eating patterns

Regardless of the guidelines already given, or what some baby books say about nutrition, your baby doesn't have to have every kind of food at each meal. He can take a whole day's supply of protein at one meal, and his day's carbohydrates at the next. Try to let go of the urge to control your baby's diet, and try not to think that being a good parent means that he has to eat "good" food at every meal. Think of a balanced diet as what he eats over the whole week rather than worrying about every meal he eats.

Your baby won't need more than one or two big meals a day. In between, he'll only need a snack. Don't confine eating to mealtimes; with a stubborn baby they can become pitched battlegrounds. Of course, encourage your baby to have regular feeding times, but if he is going through a difficult phase, bend a little and supplement a small meal with a snack later.

If he stands up or tries to get out of the highchair, take your baby out and forget about the feeding. He will come back to the food or ask for it when he is hungry. If you argue you will get upset, your baby will get upset, and mealtimes will become unpleasant. Your baby will come to associate mealtimes with unhappiness and this will lead to feeding problems.

Food and eating 1 to 2 years

For your toddler to be strong and healthy he must have a diet with sufficient amounts of protein, carbohydrate, fats, vitamins and minerals. He will get this if you provide a wide variety of foods from which to choose (*see p. 122*). The amount your child eats will largely be determined by how active he is and whether his body is going through a growth spurt. For example, the body slows down around the first birthday, but development speeds up again when the child learns to walk. By the time he's 18 months old, your baby will need about three times the number of calories per day for his body weight that an adult does, because of the speed of growth. To provide enough energy growth, your child should have roughly 45 calories for 1 pound (500 grams) of weight. He'll also need 1 ounce (25 grams) of protein a day. Although it's less than for infants, it is still twice that of adults.

New tastes
Now that your child is eating family meals, encourage him to try different tastes, and feed himself. Eating is still likely to be a very messy process.

What foods to give

By the second year your child will be able to eat more or less the same diet you eat. There is no one essential food that your child has to eat in order to be healthy—he just has to have plenty of sensibly cooked, fresh foods from which to build up a balanced diet. Milk will remain an important part of his diet as it is a useful source of protein, but drinks of water should also be given when he's thirsty.

Give your child at least one nutritious protein dish at each meal, and at least five servings of fruit and vegetables a day. He'll be able to eat an increasingly large amount

DON'T GIVE YOUR CHILD:

- Popcorn
- Whole nuts or very rough whole-wheat bread, with pieces of whole grain
- Small pieces of raw fruit or vegetable
- Fruits with stones or pits, such as plums
- Unpeeled fruit with thick skins
- Highly spiced dishes, unless he enjoys them and specifically requests them
- Salty foods
- Sugary drinks

FOOD GROUPS

Food group	Food	Content
High protein	Chicken, fish, lamb, beef, pork, offal, eggs, cheese, legumes	Protein, fat, iron, vitamins A, D, B
Milk and dairy products	Milk, cream, yogurt, ice cream, cheese	Protein, fat, calcium, vitamins A, D, B2
Green and yellow vegetables	Cabbage, sprouts, spinach, kale, green beans, squash, lettuce, celery, zucchini	Minerals, including calcium, chlorine, chromium, cobalt, copper, manganese, potassium, and sodium
Citrus fruit	Oranges, grapefruit, lemons	Vitamin C
Other vegetables and fruit	Potatoes, beets, corn, carrots, cauliflower, pineapples, apricots	Carbohydrates, vitamins A, B, C
Breads and cereals	Whole-wheat bread, noodles, rice	Protein, carbohydrates, vitamin B, iron, and calcium
Fats	Butter, margarine, vegetable oils	Vitamins A, D

of food at each meal; exactly how much will depend on his appetite, but he'll probably be able to take a third to a half of an adult portion each time.

Help your child to develop good eating habits by not sugaring or salting his food and by not giving "empty" calories in the form of cake, cookies, and candy. Don't give your child sweet desserts—fruit, yogurt, or fruit purée are much better.

Eating patterns
By the time your child is toddling he will eat three smallish meals a day with snacks in the morning and the afternoon. Be prepared for your child's appetite to be erratic this year: he may be starving one day and eat everything that you serve, and the next day eat hardly anything. Don't worry if your child goes on food binges,

eating only one food and refusing all others; it is perfectly normal at this age (see p.125). Similarly, don't be alarmed if he goes through periods of low appetite —your child knows exactly what he needs and will eat to keep pace with himself.

Giving candy
I believe that it is wrong to deprive children of candy. Deprivation very often leads to furtiveness and dishonesty. I believe, however, in treat rationing, but I am not beyond giving candies as a reward, since this kind of reward is immediately understood by your child. I rationed my own children to one treat after lunch and dinner. This worked with all four of them and encouraged self-control and good eating habits. Children should always brush their teeth after eating candy though.

SAMPLE DIET FOR A 14-MONTH-OLD CHILD

Day 1	Day 2	Day 3
Breakfast 1 egg, scrambled, ½ slice buttered whole-wheat toast	**Breakfast** 1 cup diluted orange juice, 5 ounces (25 grams) yogurt, 2 tablespoons baby muesli, with wheat germ, 1½ fluid ounces (50 milliliters) milk, ½ banana	**Breakfast** 2 ounces (50 grams) cereal plus milk, 1 cup diluted fresh orange juice, ½ banana
Mid-morning 1 cup diluted orange juice, 1 apple	**Mid-morning** 1 cup diluted fruit juice, 1 cookie	**Mid-morning** 1 cup water, 1 apple
Lunch 2 ounces (50 grams) white fish, ½ whole-wheat bread roll, 1 tablespoon green beans, 1 cup diluted fruit juice	**Lunch** 1 cup milk, 1 cup water, 2 fish fingers, 1 tablespoon peas	**Lunch** Egg florentine, (2 tablespoons spinach, 1 egg, 1–2 ounces/25–50 grams cheese), 1 pear, 1 yogurt (sugar-free), 1 cup milk
Mid-afternoon 1 cup water	**Mid-afternoon** 1 cup water	**Mid-afternoon** 2 cups diluted apple juice, 1 oatmeal cookie
Dinner 6 ounces (150 grams) beans, 2–3 ounces (50–75 grams) potatoes, 2 ounces (50 grams) cheese, ½ banana, 1 cup milk	**Dinner** 1 egg omelette with 1 ounce (25 grams) cheese, tablespoon fresh green beans, 1 cup milk, ¼ slice whole-wheat bread	**Dinner** Ham sandwich with whole-wheat bread, cubes of cheese, raw carrot, cubes of melon

Eating at the table

Introduce your toddler to family mealtimes by pulling the highchair up to the table when you eat. He'll be able to see everything that is going on and will gradually become more accustomed to family meals and to mealtime behavior and good manners. To make sure that he feels included, give your toddler the same food you are eating, but prepare it in a way he can manage to spoon or pick up without your help. This process will be much easier if your child is neat and able to eat without much mess. However, if your child is very messy you may find it better to feed him before the rest of the family and then to bring the child to the table with a few favorite finger foods to keep him happy when you are eating.

Don't expect your child to automatically adopt adult behavior, especially at the beginning. Around the age of 12 months he'll be used to crawling and "cruising" and will probably not be far from walking, so don't be surprised if he is unwilling to sit still for long. If he insists on getting down, let him do so; he'll probably come back for more food in a few minutes and will soon learn that food means sitting still and eating. If, however, he shows no signs of wanting to come back, don't insist that all his food is eaten. If he is hungry he'll make up for it at the next meal.

Messy eaters

Some children take so much pleasure in eating that they find it hard to concentrate on getting food from the plate to the mouth. Try to be philosophical about the mess your toddler makes at mealtimes. It is a transient phase during which he will be learning how to coordinate. You may think he's learning this at your expense, but try to stay cool and calm. Remember, being tidy is nowhere near as important as your child being happy and eating the way he wants to. Make your mealtimes pleasant and minimize cleaning up by following these tips.

- Stand the highchair on a plastic tablecloth so that you can wipe up spills easily; otherwise just surround the

Eating as a family
Even if your child has finished her own food, she will enjoy sitting at the table with you while you eat. Take the opportunity to let her try new tastes.

highchair with newspaper that can be thrown away after each meal.
- Draw a circle on the highchair tray to show your baby where he should put his cup down. Make the positioning of the cup into a game.
- Most toddlers don't like having their faces wiped with a cloth. Use your own hand dipped in water; for some reason, this is much more acceptable and will do the job just as well.
- If your child is very messy, take him to the sink to be washed. Make a game out of washing hands; let your child play some water games while you're there.
- Let your child dip both his hands into a bowl of water while he's still sitting in the highchair and then just dry them for him with a towel.

Possible feeding problems 1 to 2 years

Food fads

Between the age of one and two your child will begin to show pronounced preferences for certain foods. It is common for children to experience these fads, eating one food and refusing everything else. He may, for example, not want to eat meat and want only yogurt. A week of this may be followed by a dislike of yogurt and desire to eat cheese and fruit.

Being a good parent means not making a fuss about this. There is nothing magical about any one food and there is always a nutritious alternative to the one that your child rejects. Don't spend time cooking food that you know your toddler will refuse and then feel resentful when he does. Take the easy way out and cook what you know he really wants, even if it's something you disapprove of.

Research has shown that as long as you offer your child a wide variety of foods, the diet that he chooses will be balanced. There is, after all, no reason on earth why your toddler should eat the food you choose. His tastes are not necessarily yours and, if it is your child's happiness and well-being you are concerned about, you will soon realize it is better he eats something that he likes, than that he doesn't eat at all. So be flexible about what you give your toddler to eat.

Disliked foods

I really don't believe in camouflaging a disliked food, mixing it with a food that is well-liked, or bribing a child to have a spoonful of a disliked food with a spoonful of one he likes.

If your child dislikes something, give him an alternative food that provides the same nutrients and that you know he likes. If your baby shows a profound dislike for one food, trying to trick or bribe him into eating it may result in the child refusing other foods as well. When you introduce a new food, do it when you know your baby is hungry and he's more likely to take it.

The only thing that you should be on your guard against is your child excluding all of one food group. If this happens, then his diet will become unbalanced. Other than that, there is absolutely nothing wrong with fads. Don't forget, the more worked up you get about them, the more your toddler will display them because he very quickly learns that it is an effective way of manipulating you. Play them down.

Weight problems

If a baby is offered the right kind of food he cannot be underweight or overweight. Your baby will regulate his food and will take in enough to supply his needs at any particular time. An underweight or overweight baby is, therefore, the fault of the parent who offers the wrong kind of food to the baby.

Overweight Excess weight in a baby is nearly always a result of too much fatty meat, too many sweetened drinks, and refined carbohydrates (cakes, cookies, jams, and sweet foods) in the diet. It may also be because you curb your toddler's activity by keeping him in a carriage or playpen and not allowing him to use up energy by crawling and walking. Always encourage your child to be active by playing games with him yourself—the livelier the better.

Underweight Unless purposely deprived of food, very few toddlers are actually underweight, even if they weigh less than another baby of the same age and sex. Many parents worry unnecessarily about having a small, thin toddler. However, some children, like some adults, are just naturally (and healthily) small and thin.

If you are giving your baby a balanced diet and he is happy, contented, and developing normally (*see p.189*), then you probably have nothing to worry about. However, if you are concerned, check with your pediatrician.

Food and eating 2 to 3 years

Your child's daily caloric requirements will continue to increase as he grows, and during the third year he'll need roughly 50 calories a day for every 500g (1lb) that he weighs. His nutritional requirements will remain the same and he'll need a variety of well prepared foods with sufficient vitamins and minerals. Because he is growing, he still needs more protein and calories for his body weight than an adult.

TIPS FOR FEEDING TWO-YEAR-OLDS

* Always make sure that a meal contains at least one food you know your child likes.
* Always serve small amounts and allow second helpings. A full plate is intimidating to a child.
* Keep foods simple. Children like to see what they are eating: they don't like messy foods.
* Always offer a variety of foods to guarantee a balanced diet.
* Liven up your toddler's meal by using colorful food.
* Until your child is going to school, include a finger food in a meal when possible.
* Include foods that are fun to eat, like jelly, oven-baked potato chips, or an ice cream cone.

What foods to give

Between the ages of two and three, children tend to like dairy products like milk, yogurt, ice cream, and cottage cheese, as well as breads and cereals. They dislike, and may even reject, meat, fruit and vegetables. Don't get worked up about this; try, instead, to find a couple of meats and some fruit and vegetables that he does like and stick to them until your child seems to want a change.

Give your child two or three servings of protein, and five or more servings of fruit and vegetables a day. Provide four or more servings of whole-wheat bread and cereal—a serving of bread is half a slice, and one to two tablespoons of cereal. Avoid high-calorie, starchy foods.

Eating patterns

Your child may continue to have food fads (*see p.125*) throughout this year, and may also demand rituals at mealtimes. A ritual is something that your child has to have repeated. For instance, it may become a ritual to have a sandwich cut on the diagonal: your child will refuse a sandwich that is cut in any other way. Some children

Decorative food
One way to encourage your child to try different foods is to decorate it or make interesting shapes. Then ask your child to taste the whiskers, or eat the ears and nose.

want their plate placed in a certain way and will throw a tantrum if it is not. The best way to approach both of these rituals is with patience. After all, adults have food rituals, too: we sit in certain positions at the table, and may prefer our tables set in a certain way. As long as it is reasonable, you should indulge your child's ritual. On the other hand, if a ritual seriously interferes with the intake of food or disrupts the family, try to reason with your child and explain that such behavior is not fair to others. Be firm, but be prepared for it to take several attempts to break an undesirable ritual.

Organizing mealtimes

Your child should be getting very familiar with the social aspects of eating, but don't expect too much from him. It is very difficult for a child to concentrate on

eating with a spoon, not spilling his drink, not making a mess, and being quiet while eating at the table. He is trying to listen to what you are all saying, participate in the conversation, and concentrate on the food. He is also trying to learn a great many new skills at once. Viewed this way, it is not surprising he can get a bit excitable, just to break the tension, and there are bound to be accidents. Again, be understanding and flexible with him.

MAKING MEALTIMES FUN

As with all feeding, the key word is flexibility. You and your child should enjoy yourselves, so give a little thought to making mealtimes entertaining for all of you.

- Ice cream cones don't have to be used just for ice cream. Fill one with cheese and tomato chopped together or tuna fish salad. This allows you to give your three-year-old a snack on the move.
- Encourage your child to "build" his meal from sandwiches, cubes of cheese, vegetables, and dried fruit. He can build a house, a car, or a boat, and when it is finished, eat it.

- If he wants to use a knife, give your child a plastic or blunt-ended one.
- Let your child use a straw for drinking sometimes. So he won't tip the drink over, cut the straw off so there is no more than 2 inches (5 centimeters) above the cup, or use a flexible straw.
- Be open to innovation and occasionally serve your child's meal on a doll's plate or on a flat toy.
- Fill a cake pan with lots of different finger foods, like cubes of cheese, pieces of cold meat, raw vegetables, fruit, and tiny sandwiches, and let your child pick what he wants.

Possible feeding problems 2 to 3 years

The overweight toddler

Obesity in a young child is almost always caused by lack of exercise combined with a poor diet that is high in "empty" calories—for example, highly refined starches and carbohydrates, such as those found in cakes, cookies, candy, chocolate, ice cream, and sweet drinks. If your toddler is overweight, consider doing some of the following things:

- Look at the amount of sugar your child is consuming (especially "hidden" sugars added to foods). There is absolutely no need for your child to take in any sugar.
- If you have been adding sugar to food, stop now so your child gets used to the natural sweetness of food such as fruit.
- Look at the amount of food your child is eating as snacks. Try cutting down on them and changing to low-calorie, healthy snacks (see p.130).
- Reduce the amount of fat you use in food preparation. Don't use butter or margarine. Your child will probably not even notice. Don't fry in fat, broil instead; buy the leanest meat you can and trim off any fat; cut down on cheese; give him reduced-fat milk once he's over two.
- Make sure your child is getting every opportunity to be active and to play. Encourage active sports. Invite friends to the house for a game of football or go outside with your child and play an active game with him.
- Look at the amount of milk your child is consuming. If he is taking a lot of protein, and a lot of milk, he is probably getting too much. Cut down.

- Try giving your child more homemade and uncooked food. Prepackaged foods, especially salty, fatty snacks, are often high in calories.

Refusing to eat

This is one of the first signs that your child is not feeling well, so observe him carefully. Is he clumsier than normal, or pale and cranky? If so, check his temperature and get see the doctor if you're worried. At other times, your child simply may not be hungry. He may have had a lot of snacks before a meal—for example, if he's had a snack or a drink of milk in the hour before the meal, it's not fair to expect your child to eat with his normal enthusiasm.

Sometimes your child may refuse food for no apparent reason. What you must never do in this situation is try to force your child to eat, so don't be taken in by your child's capricious behavior. Try to be casual about it and pay attention to something else. If you insist, mealtimes can quickly become battlegrounds, and in the end you'll always lose. If you ignore your child, he'll eat when he's hungry; if he doesn't, don't worry. He'll make up for it at the next meal.

Food allergy

This should not be confused with food intolerance. Food intolerance simply means that some food doesn't sit with you as well as others. Food allergy, however, is quite specific and quite rare. Most cases of suspected food allergy turn out to be simple intolerance, or the combination of a fussy child and a fussy parent.

Picky eaters
Make a game out of eating. Give her little containers of different foods and some chopped vegetables so she can "make" her own meal.

Allergy is the body's reaction to a foreign protein or chemical. It is a protective mechanism and produces symptoms ranging from a headache, a slight rash and a feeling of indigestion, to profuse vomiting, swelling of the mouth, tongue, face, and eyes, widespread red blotches on the skin, diarrhea, and an extremely ill child. When first exposed to the allergen, the reaction may be very slight, but, if exposure is repeated, the allergic response may get worse and worse.

One of the reasons why food allergies have attracted so much attention is that they have been blamed for behavioral disturbances in children, but the number of cases where this can be proven is infinitesimal. The only proof of a true allergy as the cause of behavioral problems is when the food is withdrawn and the child's behavior changes markedly, then when the offending substance is reintroduced the child reverts to the previous bad behavior. Nothing else counts as proof. Improvement on its own is not proof; there has to be confirmation by the reappearance of the child's symptoms after the reintroduction of the substance.

In a very small number of cases there is proof, though even then it is very difficult to decide whether the child is responding to the removal of the food or to the added attention he has received from parents, doctors, nurses, and relatives. It may be, and in many cases it undoubtedly is true, that bad behavior is a cry for attention, love, and affection. If this is given, the behavior improves anyway. Parents should not sidestep this issue, and should try changing their ways before any food is withdrawn from a child's diet.

Talk to your pediatrician
The reason I am so concerned about allergy and intolerance is that many a child has needlessly had his diet seriously curtailed and robbed of nutritious foodstuffs in the name of an unproven association. Parents should never attempt to isolate a food allergy on their own or change the child's diet without a doctor's advice: a clear diagnosis from a pediatric allergist should always be the first step.

Snacks 1 to 3 years

Studies performed on the eating habits of children show that under the age of four or five children prefer to eat—in fact, their bodies require them to eat—frequently throughout the day. This is because their tiny stomachs can't cope with three adult-sized meals a day, and we shouldn't try to impose an adult eating pattern on them. The range of how often a child eats is quite wide—from three to 14 times a day,

with the average at around five to seven times. The size of the meal he'll want will vary throughout the day, but as a general rule the more often a child eats, the smaller the meals will be. On average, children take in the same amount of nutrients, regardless of the number of times they eat in a day. What is important is not the number of times your child eats, but what he eats.

Sensible snacks are those that provide adequate calories in a healthy and nutritious form but contribute little to tooth decay. They include fresh fruit and vegetables, cubes of cheese, cheese sandwiches with wholegrain bread, and fresh fruit juice.

Most commercial snack foods, especially those bought from vending machines and fast-food stores, are highly refined and processed, and contain a lot of calories and very few nutrients. Avoid foods like cookies, candy, cakes, ice cream, and raisins, and other dried foods.

Planning snacks

Snack food should contribute to the whole day's nutrition, so don't leave them to chance; plan them carefully. It is important to introduce variety, since snacks can become boring to children just like meals can. Some of the ways in which you can do this are as follows:

Fruit smoothies
Purée some soft fruit and add milk and/or yogurt to make your child a drink packed with vitamins and minerals. He might like to help you make it, too.

- Try to coordinate meals and snacks so you serve different foods in the snacks and the meals.
- Try to make snacks amusing. Put a tomato on top of an open wholegrain bread sandwich so it looks like a smiling face, for example, or cut up pieces of fruit in unusual shapes.
- Try to involve your child in planning and, more important, helping prepare part of the snack.
- Take advantage of the activity to make the snack exciting and even educational. For example, have your child help you shell peas or make bread and then use whatever you've prepared together as part of the snack.
- You can serve an ordinary food in a different form: yogurt, which your child might not like straight out of the container, becomes more like ice cream if you freeze it.
- Drinks are one of the best kinds of snacks, particularly if they are milk-based—though you should use reduced-fat milk once a child is over two. Milk-based snacks are nutritious because they contain protein, calcium, iron, and many of the B vitamins.

Snacks and tooth decay

Food encourages the development of tooth decay. Every time we eat, small amounts of food are left on and between the teeth, and these particles, particularly if they are starches, are broken down into acid by bacteria in the mouth. These acids dissolve the outer enamel layer of the tooth and cause tooth decay.

Carbohydrates and starches form the major food source of bacteria in the mouth. Refined sugar (sucrose) found in sweetened drinks, cake, and candy is more easily converted to acid by bacteria than any other form of food. It has been shown that the higher the sugar content of the food, the more acid can be made by the bacteria, and the greater the likelihood of tooth decay. Fruit juices can also be acidic and should be given with food or confined to mealtimes.

Not surprisingly, sticky foods such as raisins stay on the teeth for longer, so the bacteria are given more time to convert the starches into acid. Sticky foods, therefore, cause more tooth decay than sweet foods that don't remain in the mouth for long, by getting trapped between or coating the teeth. A sticky caramel, for example, will lead to tooth decay more easily than the same amount of sugar taken in a drink, because it stays on the teeth. The same applies to other chewy foods.

In considering the snacks that you give your child, you must consider the effect they will have on tooth decay. You can start early in your baby's life by never adding sugar to his food. Nobody needs to eat refined sugar; the body can manage perfectly well without it. Do your children a favor and don't encourage them to have a sweet tooth.

Another precaution you can take is to encourage your child to brush his teeth after their main meals. Ask your dentist for advice about which toothpaste you should use. In addition, you can avoid ending a meal with a sweet dessert. It is much better to finish off with fruit or, better still, a piece of cheese. Cheese is alkaline and neutralizes the acid in the mouth, helping prevent tooth decay in the long run.

8 Bowel and bladder function

The most important event that will occur in the process of bowel and bladder control will be when your child manages to stay dry and clean both day and night. However, this won't happen until she's physiologically and mentally mature enough to cooperate. You can't speed up this process—you can only help your child as she gradually gains control over her own body.

Passing urine birth to 1 year

In young babies, the bladder empties itself automatically, and a baby will pass urine frequently during the day and night. This is because the bladder is unable to hold urine for any length of time and as soon as it contains a little the bladder wall is stretched and stimulates emptying. This is perfectly normal, and you cannot expect your baby to behave any differently until the bladder has developed enough to hold urine. This rarely happens before the age of 15 months.

Bowel movements birth to 1 year

For the 24 hours after delivery your baby will excrete a sticky green-black substance called meconium. This filled the intestines when your baby was in the womb and has to be eliminated before normal digestion can take place.

Your baby will soon settle into a regular routine, and the stools will become firmer. As long as your baby is healthy, happy, and gaining weight, you should pay very little attention to her bowel movements. Don't become obsessive about them and don't worry about them.

Though babies vary a great deal in the number of stools they pass, there is a tendency for them to be fewer as the baby grows older. At the beginning, your baby may pass three or four a day, but at the end of a couple of weeks, she may only have a bowel movement every other day.

This is perfectly normal. In fact, all the following are normal: loose, unformed stools; a totally green stool; a bowel movement after every meal; or up to six stools in the first few days.

Using the potty
A baby who isn't ready can't be potty trained. A baby who is doesn't need any training. Don't try to force your child. Take your lead from him.

Stools of the breast-fed baby

During the first day or so, your baby's stools will be greenish black, smooth, sticky meconium; afterward, the light-yellow stools typical of the breast-fed baby will appear. The number of stools per day is quite unimportant. Some babies have several, some only have a few, and some may have a bowel movement every time they feed. The stools may be pasty or they may be no thicker than cream soup but they are rarely hard or smelly. Breast-fed babies hardly ever suffer from constipation. This is because they absorb practically all of the breast-milk they get so there is very little waste. It is logical therefore that they might not move their bowels more than once every third day.

Stools of the bottle-fed baby

Once the digestion has settled down, a baby fed on formula tends to have more frequent stools and the stools tend to be firmer, browner, and smellier than those of a breast-fed baby.

You may find that your baby's stools are soft, like scrambled eggs, but it's more common for the stools to be hard. The easiest way to fix this is to give your baby cooled, boiled water to drink in between feeding, tipping it gently into the mouth with a spoon. Once your baby is several months old, you can soften the stools by adding a little prune juice to her drink, or by giving her a few teaspoonfuls of sieved fruit thinned with water.

Never add sugar to your baby's bottles, but if the formula has a high sugar content, the stools may be loose, green, and curdy. If this happens, ask your pediatrician for advice.

Changes in bowel movements

As long as your baby is doing well, it really doesn't matter if the stools change in appearance from one day to the next. A slightly lighter or a slightly darker color doesn't mean anything serious. A slightly less well formed or a harder stool doesn't mean that there is anything wrong. If you are ever worried, however, consult your pediatrician, who will be glad to give you advice. Looseness of the stools per se doesn't indicate an abnormality or an infection. On the other hand, watery stools that are accompanied by a sudden change in color, or a sudden change in the frequency of passing stools, and a change in the smell of the stools, should be mentioned to your pediatrician, especially if you feel that your baby is listless or not quite right. As a general rule, changes in the number and color of the movements are much less important than changes in the smell of and the amount of water in the stools.

As your baby gets older, be prepared for the stools to change whenever you add a new food, particularly fruit and vegetables. If the stools become very loose after introducing a new food, don't give it again for several days and then try it again in a very small quantity. Don't forget that beets can turn the stools red and that it is quite normal for a stool to turn brown or green if it's exposed to the air.

Streaks of blood in the stools are never normal. Even if the cause is quite minor, like a tiny crack in the skin around the anus, you should consult your pediatrician. Large amounts of blood, pus, or mucus may herald an intestinal infection, so contact the doctor immediately.

Possible bowel problems birth to 1 year

Constipation

Bowel movements that occur less often than every three or four days, and stool hard enough to cause discomfort or pain may mean that your baby is constipated. Constipation itself cannot make a child ill, and old theories that constipation poisoned the system were discarded long ago.

Without any other signs of illness this is nothing to worry about. However, if your baby is straining to pass a hard stool, you should consult the pediatrician to see if it is necessary to get any medicine to soften the stool. Doctors are loathe to use laxatives or purgatives for a young child, and it is hardly ever necessary to resort to such treatments. In a very small baby, constipation is rare and it is nearly always a result of not giving the baby enough water. It can nearly always be corrected by giving your baby more to drink or by adding a little extra water to each bottle. Don't try the old-fashioned remedy of adding a little sugar to your baby's bottle—it won't work, your baby doesn't need sugar, and it will only encourage a sweet tooth.

By far the best way to soften stools is to alter the diet and to add a little more fiber and roughage. A couple of teaspoons of prune juice added to your baby's water will help, and when she's on solids, two teaspoons of sieved stewed prunes with the evening meal should bring results.

Once your child is on a varied diet, he should never be constipated unless his meals don't include enough fresh fruit, vegetables, whole-wheat breads and whole grains. It is very easy to prevent him becoming constipated once he is eating solids: simply add more of these foods to his diet. In a young child, the bowel always responds to the addition of complex carbohydrates (contained in root and green vegetables), because the cellulose in them holds water in the stools and makes them bulkier and softer.

There are only two reasons why a child could become chronically constipated. The first is an over-fussy parent who has become obsessive about the regularity of the child's bowel movements. The second is if a child has previously felt discomfort or pain when trying to pass a stool, and retains the stools to prevent recurrence.

It is fairly common for a child to have a few days of constipation after an illness and a high temperature. This is partly because she has eaten very little food, so there are no waste products to pass, and partly because of the loss of water from sweating out the fever. The body conserves all the moisture it can by absorbing it from the stools and this makes the movements hard. This kind of constipation needs no treatment at all and will correct itself when your child goes back onto a proper diet. Don't use over-the-counter medicines, laxatives, suppositories, or enemas without seeking medical advice.

Diarrhea

True diarrhea—very loose, frequent, watery stools—is a sign that the intestines are irritated and that the food is "hurrying" along. Once your child is on solids, a change of diet, including the introduction of a new fruit or vegetable, may be enough to cause it.

Diarrhea in young babies is always serious because the intestines are not given sufficient time to absorb the water essential for life, and severe dehydration can develop quite rapidly. There is no need to be concerned about the odd loose stool if your baby is acting well, eating normally and is happy. However, if your baby has very green, smelly, and watery stools, refuses food, has a fever of 100°F (38°C) or more, has blood or pus in the stools, and is listless and has dark rings under her eyes, contact the pediatrician immediately.

If your baby is very young (under four months), go to the pediatrician or hospital emergency room as soon as possible. With an older baby, the AAP recommends a regular diet, allowing your baby or child to eat whatever appeals. If she has is vomiting as well, an electrolyte solution such as Pedialyte is suggested. If your baby has had diarrhea for quite a few days, avoiding milk or milk products may be recommended (such as switching to a soy formula). Juice should also be avoided since it can make diarrhea worse. If your baby has mild diarrhea and no other symptoms, you can start treatment yourself. If you are breast-feeding your baby continue to nurse. Diarrhea usually clears up well on breast-milk. If your baby can't tolerate normal formula, a soy-based one may be recommended. Let your baby take as much of this mixture as she likes, as often as she likes. She may not want food, or takes small amounts, and will become hungry more quickly. If mild diarrhea doesn't improve within two days, call the doctor.

Once diarrhea has cleared up you can re-introduce normal food. The best foods to start off with are mild, milky ones. Start off with a third to a half of the usual serving and on the second day a half to two thirds of the usual amount. On the third day, if there is no recurrence, you can go back to regular servings.

Gaining control 1 to 2 years

I believe that there's only one way to approach the whole subject of bowel and bladder control, and that is to take signals from your child and to help—not train—your child. Control over the bowel or bladder is rare before the age of 15 or 18 months; sometimes it occurs much later.

Gaining bowel control

It is not uncommon for babies to empty their bowels during a meal or very soon after as early as three months. Some parents take this to be an early sign of readiness for toilet training. It is not. It is simply the working of the gastro-colic reflex that stimulates the passage of food down the intestines to the bowels when food is eaten.

Your child will be ready for your help when she can make the connection between inner sensations and the physical reality of urinating and passing feces. You'll notice this awareness when, for example, she suddenly stops what she's doing and points to her diaper, or attracts your attention with a cry or a shout then dirties her diaper. Your child's awareness of having a full rectum and a full bladder will probably occur at about the same time, but her ability to deal with the two sensations will be different.

Introducing a potty

It's much easier to "hold on" to a full rectum than it is to a full bladder, and your child will probably achieve bowel control first. Because of this, it's wise to help your child use the potty for bowel movements first. It's also sensible from your point of view, because bowel movements are more predictable, and you can prepare for them on your child's behalf. When your child makes her special movements or sounds, suggest that she use the potty. Make things easier by deliberately leaving off

clothes or diapers so that nothing hinders her getting onto the potty in time.

After she's been on the potty, wipe her bottom (front-to-back in girls) with toilet paper and put the paper in the potty. Flush the contents of the potty down the toilet. Remove any trace of feces and rinse it out, then wash it with disinfectant.

Never force your child to sit on the potty—it will have the opposite effect you seek, and when you next suggest that she use it you might be faced with a point-blank refusal or even a tantrum. Instead, just forget about the potty for a few days and then reintroduce it in a casual way.

Using a potty
Keeping a potty for your child's favorite doll or teddy bear can encourage her to sit on the potty, too.

Gaining bladder control

This process will have to be gradual and for it to be successful your child's bladder will have to be capable of holding more than a little urine without spontaneously emptying. One of the first signs of this maturity is your child's diaper being dry after a reasonable length of time (for example, after an afternoon nap). Once your child stays dry regularly throughout this nap, you can start to leave off that diaper. Before you put your child down for her nap, encourage her to empty her bladder. If she does, congratulate her; if she doesn't, don't make a fuss, just try it again another day.

When she can do this successfully and can indicate to you that she wants to go to the potty, you can start leaving off diapers completely during the day. Never start this until she can wait quite comfortably for a few minutes while you take down her clothes.

TIPS

- Let your child develop at her own pace. There is no way that you can speed up the process. You can only be there to help your child along.
- Let your child decide whether to sit on the potty. You can suggest that she does but you should never force the issue.
- Treat your child's feces in a sensible manner, and never show disgust or dislike for them. They're a natural part of your child and initially she'll be very proud of them.
- Do not delay once your child has signaled she wants the potty, since control is only possible for a short time.
- Always praise your child and treat her control as an accomplishment.

There will be accidents, so be prepared for them and always be sympathetic. Never scold your toddler if she has an accident: it's not her fault. Just clean up and change her clothing without a fuss.

Toilet "training"

I am wholeheartedly against toilet training. For me, there are no arguments in favor of it; there are only arguments against it. I believe that toilet training and the attitudes that advocate "training" a child's bowel movements and bladder function should be completely eradicated from child care and child development.

The reasons I feel this so strongly are simple. It is impossible to train a child to do anything unless her body has developed to a point where it is anatomically and physiologically able to perform the tasks that you demand of it.

When applied to bowel and bladder function, this means that it is impossible for your child to control either of these until the bowel and the bladder muscles are strong enough to hold urine and feces, and that, at a signal from the brain, the nerves to the bowel and bladder are mature enough to obey the order to evacuate. If this level of development has not been reached, there is nothing that your child can do to adhere to your "training" program.

You can see immediately what a dreadful position this puts your child in. She is aware of what you want, but her body is unable to do it. Your toddler's desire to please you overrides almost all of her other desires, and she will be frustrated and unhappy at not being able to. She may feel inadequate, ashamed, guilty, or resentful.

If you insist on toilet training when your child is not ready for it, the result can only be sadness. Your relationship with your child will deteriorate. You will become a source of unhappiness, and bowel movements and potty training will become a battleground of your baby's will against your nerves, and you will always be the loser. You cannot make your baby pass a stool or keep a diaper dry, and if you try, you'll simply make your child miserable every time the inevitable accident occurs.

Gaining control 2 to 3 years

While it is likely that your child has already shown signs of muscle control and has an awareness of urination and bowel movements, it is also possible that she hasn't. If this is the case, don't worry. The procedure for helping your child to understand her bodily requirements is the same, no matter what age she starts.

If, however, your child has gained some control, you'll find that she'll continue to improve during this year. It has been shown that by two-and-a-half years old approximately 90 percent of girls and 75 percent of boys have complete bowel control and even go to the bathroom alone. However, the same study also showed that more than half the children that age were still wet at night, although they could go without a diaper during the day.

Staying dry at night

Bladder control at night comes last of all. It is often not possible for a two-and-a-half-year-old child to hold urine for much longer than four to five hours, and it is often much less than that. The signal to start leaving off the night-time diaper is when she wakes up regularly with a dry diaper. When this happens, leave off the diaper, but take the child to the potty and encourage her to empty her bladder before she goes to sleep. Leave a potty beside the bed and suggest she use it if necessary during the night. Leave a nightlight on so that she can see what she's doing and be prepared to help her if necessary.

It's a big step for your child to stop relying on you and to take responsibility for using the potty herself. Encourage your child as soon as she shows any sign of taking this responsibility because it is important that you help and that she feels a sense of confidence.

Be prepared for accidents, but never get upset by them. You can minimize the amount of work by:
- protecting the mattress with a rubber sheet, with your usual sheet on top.
- putting a small rubber sheet on top of the child's ordinary sheet, with a half sheet over that. If there's an accident you can quickly remove the half sheet and spare the undersheet.
- making sure that nightwear is free of zippers so that your child can take down her clothes without any trouble.
- avoiding any confrontation by not forcing your child in any way. Gentleness and understanding invariably pay off.

Getting used to the toilet

Once your child is using the potty regularly, introduce her to the idea of using the toilet. To help your child feel safe and secure, get a special seat for her to sit on that fits in the rim of the toilet bowl. If she's worried, suggest that she hold onto the sides of the seat, and always stay close by. You'll probably need to put a small step or box in front of the toilet so that she can climb up easily. Show your little boy how to stand in front of the toilet and aim at the bowl. Put a piece of toilet paper in the bowl for him to aim at.

If your child wants to do everything alone, respect her wishes. However, do teach your child how to wipe her or himself after using the toilet, especially your little girl. It is very important that she learns to wipe from the front to the back to avoid spreading any bacteria from the rectum to the vagina.

Possible bowel and bladder problems 2 to 3 years

Late developers

Some children acquire bowel and bladder control much later than others, and this may present a problem to the parents. In nearly all cases it is wrong to blame the child. Often there is a family history of lateness in acquiring bladder control.

If your child is wet during the day and night, most pediatricians feel that there is no need to investigate this difficulty before your child is three years old. If she is only wet at night, your doctor may feel that these investigations may be put off until she is five years old. Whenever you go to the pediatrician about a urinary problem, take a specimen of urine.

Bed-wetting

Many children, especially boys, will not be able to be dry at night until well past four years of age, and this is perfectly normal. If they are dry, then a change of routine or surroundings—such as the arrival of another baby, an illness, a spell of unhappiness, or starting school—may cause them to start wetting the bed again. If your child has a bed-wetting problem, lightly suggest that she think about going the whole night staying dry—positive

Encourage good hygiene
Girls are generally more receptive to being taught good hygiene than boys. Let her flush the toilet if she wants to, but remind her to wash her hands afterward.

TIPS

- Whenever you travel, make sure that you have a potty with you so that your child can go under any circumstances without having to wait. Put the potty on the floor in the back of your car so that you can stop anywhere along the road instead of having to worry about finding a public restroom in a hurry.
- If she sits down and can't do anything, turn on the faucets; this works for babies as well.
- If you keep star charts for different accomplishments, keep one for each success.
- If you have a potty in the bathroom, you and your child can go to the toilet at the same time.

- Let your child accompany you to the bathroom at an early age so that she can learn from watching you. This works particularly well with boys.
- Tell your child quite firmly and sympathetically that accidents will always be ignored and forgiven, and that she should not worry about them.
- Get a potty well before you think your child will need it. You can explain why it is there and that when she is old enough she'll be able to use it. This may give your child an incentive to try.
- Be wary of flushing the toilet when your child's with you—many are frightened by the noise, and by the fact that "part of them" is being taken away.

thinking may help. Don't make a big thing of it—she'll worry and you'll have defeated your purpose. No matter how long it goes on, assure your child that it will eventually stop, because it does. She will just outgrow it, so be calm and sympathetic at all times.

Regression

If your child suddenly seems to lose bladder and bowel control and regresses to an earlier stage, the cause could well be a physical illness or an emotional disturbance. Sometimes the cause is obvious—a new baby, for example, may make your child feel dethroned and rejected. It would be normal for her to try attention-seeking behavior to detract from the new baby, which may include wetting and soiling her clothes. Starting nursery school, moving to a new house, or your absence could all stimulate the same pattern of behavior. If none of these have occurred, consult a doctor. She may have developed an infection or may

have a minor anatomical abnormality in her urinary tract.

Toddler diarrhea

Some toddlers, who are healthy and eat well, often have diarrhea that contains undigested food. The exact cause of this toddler diarrhea is not known, but may be linked to drinking too much fluid, particularly fruit juice, not eating enough fat, or in some cases, eating too quickly. If your child is otherwise well and there is no underlying illness, changes in her diet usually help.

- Give your child water or milk to drink instead of fruit juice. Clear apple juice seems to be a likely culprit.
- Slightly increase your child's fat intake. Give her whole milk, add butter to her meals, and don't give her low-fat foods.
- Encourage her to eat plenty of fruit and vegetables but don't give her excessive amounts of fiber.

9 Sleeping

A newborn baby spends most of the time asleep but as he gets older regular sleeping patterns will emerge. By the time he's three months old he'll have one main wakeful period a day, usually at the same time and often in the late afternoon or early evening. By the time your child is 12 months old, he'll probably be having two naps a day, one in the morning and one in the afternoon, and will be sleeping through the night. Although the sleeping patterns will gradually come to resemble those of an adult during the second and third year, your child will still need a brief nap during the day because of the energy he's using in growing and in play.

All about sleeping birth to 1 year

Unless your newborn baby is hungry, cold, or otherwise uncomfortable, he'll spend most of the time between feedings asleep. The amount of time he sleeps will depend on individual physiology, but the average is about 60 percent of the day. Don't, however, expect your baby to sleep all the time and don't get worried when he doesn't. Some babies are naturally more wakeful right from the start; others are more sleepy.

Even though your baby will follow his own sleep pattern, it is important that he learns to differentiate between day and night, and there are several ways of helping your baby to do this. For example, when you put your baby in his crib in the evening, make sure that the room is darkened and make an extra effort to see that he's comfortable and contented.

When he wakes to be fed during the night, feed him but don't play or otherwise distract him. As he gets older and more aware of what's going on, develop an evening routine so that he has the evening feeding, a bath, a story, games, and songs before going to bed happy.

Occasionally a baby is sociable rather than sleepy after a meal and this is something to enjoy, although it shouldn't stop you from trying to set up the routine of bed after the evening meal.

If your baby is habitually wakeful after this meal, don't cause unhappiness for all of you by insisting that he stays in his crib. He'll only get upset and you'll end up with a baby who is very hard to pacify and your nerves will be worn to shreds. If, like me, you are a working mother and spend a good deal of your time away from home, your child will naturally see the night-time as mothering time and will want to spend that time with you. The probability is that you will want to spend time with him, too, in which case there is nothing wrong with being flexible about what time he goes to bed. In our house, when we discovered that we had two sleepless young children, we had to abandon the idea of routine bedtimes and the household was happier for it. However, we didn't abandon bedtime routines.

Where your baby should sleep

As long as your baby is warm and comfortable he'll be able to sleep almost anywhere. Most parents start their baby off in a basket or carrier (see p.36), because that way the baby is portable, and they can therefore keep him close day and night. However, when your baby outgrows whichever of these you've used, he'll have to be put in a crib—preferably one with

Keep him close by
Your young baby will be happiest going to sleep hearing your voices in the background so keep his carrier or bassinet near you.

drop sides and an adjustable mattress height (see p.36), so he can be picked up and put down easily.

Whatever room you put your baby to sleep in, it must be warm. Your young baby doesn't have full control over his body temperature: he'll lose body heat easily but won't be able to generate it again by moving about or by shivering. For this reason you must keep the room at a constant temperature of about 60–68°F (16–20°C). If you don't want to keep your whole house that warm, you can buy a thermostatically controlled room heater (approved by a recognized safety board) that will keep the baby's room at a constant temperature.

Whenever you leave your baby sleeping outside, make sure that he's not in direct sunlight. Either put the carriage under a shady tree or use a sunshade. If there's a breeze, put the hood up and point the front of the carriage into the wind so that there's an effective windbreak. In addition make sure you always put a cat net over the front of the carriage, even if you don't have cats yourself.

What your baby should wear

Young babies don't like being changed, so in the early weeks, when he's going to need changing frequently, you'll want something that gives easy access to his diaper but causes the minimum of disturbance. Nightdresses are useful initially, but once your baby has settled down, probably within a month, one-piece "stretchies" are equally practical.

When your baby's about four months old, you may want to use a sleeping bag, especially in the winter (see p.36). Your

WHAT BEDDING TO USE

Temperature	What to use
57°F (14°C)	Sheet and four blankets or more
60°F (16°C)	Sheet and three blankets
65°F (18°C)	Sheet and two blankets
68°F (20°C)	Sheet and one blanket
75°F (24°C)	Sheet only

baby will stay snugly warm inside and there will be no risk of the blankets being kicked off on a cold night. Choose a lightweight bag and make sure it is the right size so your baby can't slide down into it. If the weather's very cold, put your baby in a stretchie first. Or just leave on his undershirt and diaper. In summer he may not need a cover, though you'll probably want to put him in a T-shirt or body suit.

Many parents worry about whether their baby's too hot or too cold once he's been put down. You can tell by touching the back of his neck, but make sure that your hand isn't too hot or too cold before you do this. If the back of his neck feels about the same temperature as your skin then he's at the right temperature; if it feels damp and sweaty he's probably too hot. If you've got blankets in his crib, take one off. If his neck feels cool, add an extra blanket (but check the room temperature—see chart above). Never judge your baby's temperature by feeling his hands. Babies' extremities are often cooler than the rest of their bodies, and are often bluish in color. This is nothing to worry about.

BED-MAKING TIPS

- Your baby will be most comfortable wrapped in sheets and blankets made of natural fibre—cotton is ideal.
- Do not use blankets with fringes—he may suck on them.
- Avoid lacy, openwork shawls because your baby's fingers might get stuck in the holes.
- You can use your own old sheets, cut to the correct size, in addition to new ones. The more you have, the less frequently you'll have to do the wash.
- Use a pillowcase as a sheet—just slide the mattress into it. When one side gets dirty just turn the mattress over.

Putting your baby down to sleep

The safest position in which to lay your baby down to sleep is on his back. He will not be more liable to choke in this position. Research has shown doctors that the risk of Sudden Infant Death Syndrome (crib death) is reduced when the baby lies on his back. When he is about four or five months old, he will be able to roll over to find the most comfortable position regardless of how you put him down. Put your baby down with his feet touching, or close to, the bottom of the basket or crib.

It's best not to use a bumper because it impedes air circulation and later on your baby may use it to try to climb out of the crib. Once your baby has fallen asleep, don't change his position or he's bound to wake up. Similarly, don't keep going into the room to check that he's all right. However, there's nothing wrong with carrying your baby in a sling while he's asleep; he'll enjoy being soothed by your constant closeness.

There's no need to keep the house quiet when you put your baby to bed. In fact, it's good to encourage him to get used to going to sleep while the household noises go on.

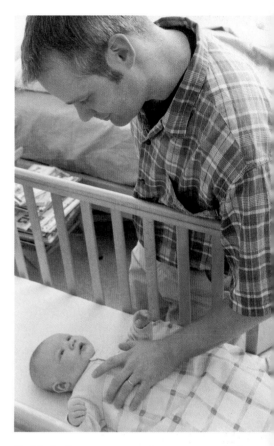

Feet to foot
Lay your baby on his back with his feet touching the foot of the crib, even if his head is halfway down the mattress. That way he can't wriggle under the covers.

Getting your young baby to sleep

Your newborn baby will undoubtedly fall asleep whenever he's tired, and in almost any situation, but there are a few precautions that you should take to guarantee this:

- Wrap your baby before he's put down, at least during the first month. He'll feel much more secure and contented with something firmly wrapped around him. Swaddle him in something that is not too heavy, however, and make sure his head is uncovered. Note that swaddling is used instead of, not in addition to, other bedding, and don't let him get too hot.
- Darken your baby's room at night.
- Make sure that the room is warm enough (*see p.143*).
- Place your hand on your baby's back or on one of his limbs to soothe him, or rock your baby gently.

- In the winter leave a hot-water bottle in the bed for half an hour before he's put down. Don't forget to remove it before putting your baby to bed.
- Use a musical mobile.

Getting your older baby to sleep

By the time your baby's about nine months old he'll be able to keep himself awake even when he's sleepy. As a result, he can become overtired and so tense that sleep is impossible. The main reason he does this is his attachment to you; you provide love, security, and excitement and he doesn't want to lose these, even for a moment.

Another reason, which is linked to the desire for security, is that he doesn't like routines being changed. For example, if you've been on vacation or if your baby has been moved to another room, he may become disturbed by the change. Whatever the cause, this period of insecurity will be brief, so treat it as calmly and sensibly as possible and remember that your child isn't the only child in the world who refuses to go to sleep at night.

Security objects

By about nine weeks your baby may be showing signs of becoming attached to a comfort object such as a blanket, a piece of cloth, a handkerchief, a doll, or his own thumb. There is nothing wrong with him using any of these.

There's no particular age at which "comforters" should or shouldn't be used and, like bed-wetting, children grow out of them. So if your baby takes up a security object, don't try to prevent it. If you really feel doubtful about letting him have one, look at it in this way: by using one, your child is showing self-reliance; he has found a way of coping without you. I think the time to question your baby's use of a security object is if he uses it all the time, even when you are there. If he clings to it occasionally when he's feeling sick, or when he's very tired, that's understandable. But if he persistently uses it there's a good chance you're not providing the kind of comfort and love he needs, so your baby's having to resort to an artificial source of comfort instead of you.

SLEEPING TIPS

- Keep pre-bedtime as happy and pleasant as possible.
- Try giving a comfort suck from the breast or the bottle just before he's put to bed.
- Develop a routine and stick to it. Don't put your baby straight to bed: work out a routine of play, then bath, bed, story, song, and then goodnight. But don't leave the room; quietly tidy up so that your baby learns that he can drift off to sleep without actually "losing" you.
- Let your baby develop comfort habits (see above).
- Rock your baby's crib if he finds that soothing.

- Play a musical mobile. Many babies are fascinated by the movements they make and are soothed by the sound.
- Don't take your older baby out with you in the evenings, even if you used to do this earlier with no problems. He'll be used to his own routine and his own room and will be frightened by being moved somewhere else.
- When he does cry, always go back but don't pick him up immediately. See what's wrong first—he may just need you to change his position or adjust the temperature in the room.

Naps

Once your baby sleeps through the night he'll need one or two naps during the day to revive his energy. What time he takes the naps depends on the individual baby— it may be after breakfast, it may be mid-morning, after lunch, or at four o'clock. At the beginning, the time may change from day to day and from week to week. By the end of the first year, a set pattern will probably emerge. Apart from special occasions (when, for example, you want your baby to be awake at a special time), the length of the nap should be left to your baby—some sleep only 20 minutes a day, others need four hours. However, if he wants to sleep through the afternoon but then stays up for most of the evening you may want to encourage him to wake up earlier so that he'll go to sleep at a more sociable time for you. This won't harm your baby and it will make life easier for the whole family if the routines of adult and child dovetail.

Going out at night

Until your baby is about six months old and really requires a regular routine at bedtime, you can take him with you whenever you go out at night. In fact, it's a very good thing for the parents, and the mother especially, to have some relaxation in the early period, and because your baby will sleep anywhere it's easy to do this.

However, once he starts sleeping through the night, it's advisable to try to stick to a regular bedtime routine. You can't expect your baby to be as adaptable as an adult, and if you want trouble-free bedtimes it's best to follow a routine.

Possible problems birth to 1 year

Early wakers

From the very beginning, try to encourage your baby to be happy alone in bed when he wakes. Put an interesting mobile just above the crib that will swing in the currents of the air and make moving patterns for your baby whenever he's awake. Put a round-edged mirror on one side of the crib so that he can look at his own reflection and not feel lonely. Once your baby can reach up, put a string of objects within arm's reach so that he can move and play with them. However, be sure that the string is not long enough to be caught aroiund the baby's neck. Be sure that any items on the string are not so small that your baby could choke on them.

These need not be expensive and can be household articles, such as a small wooden spoon or an empty spool of thread, strung onto a length of string. It will also help if you put a few favorite toys in the crib so there is always something interesting to play with. Make sure the room isn't too dark in the mornings so he can at least see what he's playing with. If the room is very dark, leave a nightlight near the crib or consider sheerer curtains.

You can help to train your baby to stay happily in bed by training yourself first. Don't lie there waiting for the first wakening murmur and then leap out of bed to see if he is all right. Leave your baby to snuffle and chatter to himself as long as

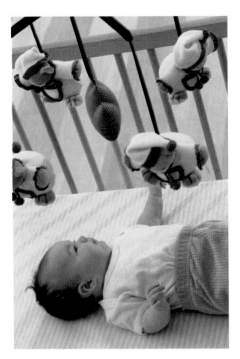

Keeping your baby amused
Unless your baby is hungry or uncomfortably wet he'll lie happily if he has something to hold his attention. A bright mobile above the crib stimulates young eyes.

end result will be a baby who's difficult to pacify and a fraught parent. Until your baby drops the night feeding and sleeps through the night, you're always going to have to get up at some stage during the night. To cope with this you should try doing the following:

- Work out a routine with your partner so you can go to bed early at least once or twice a week.
- If you are bottle-feeding, get your partner to give some night feedings.
- If you are breast-feeding, and your milk is well established, you could make the night feeding a bottle of expressed milk that your partner can give. There is absolutely no reason why you shouldn't do this, though your baby may not accept the rubber nipple (*see p.96*).
- If you breast-feed your baby, make sure your partner helps you by getting the baby if he's in another room, by changing the diaper after he nurses, and by putting the baby back to sleep.
- Many mothers find it difficult to get back to sleep if they have been woken up. Don't lie there fuming with resentment because you'd rather sleep: try some relaxation exercises, read a book, tackle some work, or get up and do some task you've been putting off.
- If you've lost sleep during the night, you must make it up the following day. Completely relax your routine and do as little as possible in the house so you can have a nap when the baby's sleeping.

you possibly can, and only get up if he appears to be getting restless and upset. Always wait to see if he quiets down; you will be teaching your baby self-reliance and independence if you do so, even at this early age. If, however, he becomes fretful, don't delay; go at once and give all the comfort and affection you can.

Night wakers

Young babies It is absolutely essential that you get enough rest. If you have a baby who wakes at night, you and your partner should bear the burden equally from the very beginning and take alternate nights on and off duty. Whatever the cause of the crying, you should always go to your baby immediately. If you don't, he'll become increasingly distressed and the

Older babies In the second half of the year your baby should sleep through the night. However, there may be occasions when, for whatever reason, he wakes up. Try the following:

• Check that your baby is not too hot; if he is, remove some clothing or blankets.

• Make sure that he's not too cold after kicking off his blanket. Either use a sleeping bag (see p.36) or more blankets, or leave a safety heater in the baby's room to provide a constant temperature.

• Check that he doesn't have diaper rash. If he does, the discomfort of it could wake him up. Treat the rash (see p.68).

• Don't go into the baby's room constantly to check that he's sleeping well—your anxiety will be more of a disturbance.

• If he's had a nightmare, provide comfort and stay until he's asleep again. If it happens on more than one night in succession look for some external reason—are you getting upset with him a lot? Is he being looked after by a new babysitter? Is he disturbed by your not being there during the day?

Wakeful babies

Some babies just don't need as much sleep as others and as a result are much more demanding of their parents' time and energy. Such babies should never be left lying alone in their cribs with no amusement. They should either have mobiles or activity centers in their crib, or should be carried by the parent if they're moving around a lot. For example, you could put your baby in a sling and still move quite easily around the house. Whatever you do, don't fret because your baby sleeps less than anticipated. When he's awake he's learning all the time, and you'll inevitably be rewarded with an eager, bright child.

All about sleeping 1 to 2 years

Most toddlers will sleep an average of 11 hours through the night, and will make up any extra sleep that they need in naps. If your baby needed a lot of sleep in the first year he'll probably continue to do so in the second; if he needed little sleep, then this trend will continue, too. Even though he sleeps through the night, he'll still need two naps a day. How long these naps last will depend, as before, on your baby. What may change this year will be the times at which he wants to nap. For example, you may find that the nap that he used to take at around 9 or 9:30 a.m. gets later and later. This means he'll want to sleep immediately after lunch, at around 1:30 or 2 p.m. On other days, however, he may take a nap late in the morning but then not want another one until the middle of the afternoon. As far as these changes are concerned, you have to take the lead from your child; there's no point in trying to make him sleep to order and you'll have to accept that the napping pattern varies from day to day. Fit into your baby's routine. If he establishes a pattern in which he gets sleepy around 11:30 a.m. and wants to have a nap around noon, you should start giving him lunch around 11:30. Then he'll be able to have a satisfying nap after lunch, and you'll have a much less grumpy baby. You could also wait until he wakes up before having lunch—it depends on your baby.

Around the age of 15 months your toddler will reach a period where two naps a day are too many and one nap a day is not quite enough. He'll happily play through the first nap, but because he can't last without sleep until the second one he has to have a later nap than usual. This inevitably means that he's alert enough to go through the usual afternoon one, but then because he's too tired to last out until bedtime he has to go to bed early. As with everything else in child care, you have to be flexible. The period in which he drops one nap won't last long and he'll soon acheive his own napping routine. By the end of the second year he'll probably only take a single nap at the end of the morning, or in the early afternoon.

Until he settles into a napping routine, make sure that he is having adequate rest during the day. Even if he doesn't seem to be all that tired and is rushing around, eager to learn new games or play with exciting toys, it's easy for him to become overtired. Keep an eye on your child and if he starts to become bad-tempered or fretful, or shows a sudden lack of coordination, then make sure he rests or plays a quiet game.

Whenever your toddler takes a nap, give him a chance to wake up gently. It may be a restorative sleep, but he's unlikely to wake up perfectly refreshed and active. He'll need a quarter of an hour or so of being cuddled and talked to gently and quietly before he's ready to be active again. If you have to go out immediately after your toddler's nap, make sure that you leave enough time for the recovery of his good humor.

HELPING YOUR TODDLER TO SLEEP

During the day

- Make up a nap time box for your child with favorite toys and books that he can look at as he gets sleepy before a nap. Don't include good or expensive books—they may get ripped up. Use board books or old books. A good alternative is to make up your own books by pasting interesting pictures from magazines onto cardboard and then covering them with clear plastic.
- Give your child a occasional treat by letting him take a nap in your bed, or somewhere near you.
- If your child won't take a nap, make sure that he has a rest time where he is calm and quiet.
- If your toddler won't go to sleep, put on a long-playing tape or CD. Teach your child that the rest time is not over until the music stops.

In the evening

- Don't put your child to bed immediately after an exciting game or rough-and-tumble—he will have great difficulty settling down, which will be frustrating for you. Give him 10–15 minutes to quiet down, sitting with you watching TV or looking at a book.
- Even a small child likes to look at a book in bed so, if your baby is quite happy, leave him with a favorite, nonscary book.
- Put a dab of your perfume or aftershave on your child's pillow and suggest that he breathe it in deeply. Deep breathing is relaxing and calming and will help your child get to sleep.
- Give your toddler a bath before bedtime and follow this with a warm drink and a story in bed.

Bedtime routines

Your baby's bedtime routine will change this year. He'll need more diverting games and more of your attention; give him both. The essential thing to remember is that bedtimes should be play times and happy times, and even though you're worn out, you should try to be calm and relaxed throughout. If you are not, your baby will pick up your anxiety and be fretful, and you may have to spend twice as long trying to put him to sleep than if he had had an extra five minutes of your undivided attention in a quiet way.

Where your toddler should sleep

At some time during this year your baby may try to get out of his crib to come to you. Obviously a fall from the top of a crib could be dangerous, so either lower the mattress to keep the top of the rails out of reach, or put your child into a single bed. If your toddler is young when he's first put into a "big" bed get a safety guard for the side of the bed, or put cushions or a mattress on the floor beside the bed.

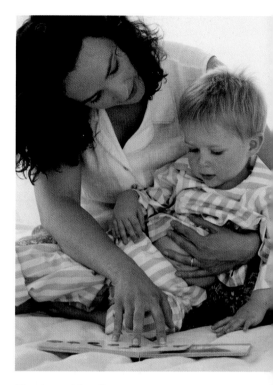

Time to read together
Children like routines, and bedtime is a great time to sit down quietly together and read a favorite book; he may even want the same book every day.

Possible problems 1 to 2 years

Waking in the night

It's been estimated that 15 percent of two-year-olds wake regularly in the night. This can be a source of great worry to parents who also need sleep. No matter how often this happens, or how irritating it may be, don't let your toddler cry; go to him immediately, provide comfort and try to find out what the problem is. It may be something easily remedied—he may be cold because the blanket or quilt has fallen off; he may be too hot; he may be thirsty; he may be teething.

On the other hand, it may be something less tangible: he may have woken up for none of these reasons and may just be afraid after a bad dream. The difficulty is that he can't explain what's upsetting him and you can't tell your toddler that he doesn't have to be afraid. What you should always do is provide love and affection, without fear of spoiling him.

Dealing with a sleepless child

I'm very sympathetic to parents with sleepless children having had two myself, one of whom spit up if he wasn't reached within a minute or so of starting to cry. I would like to give the parents of such children a hopeful message. Neither my husband nor I enjoyed an unbroken night's sleep for six years and on many days we were almost too tired to drag ourselves around; but we got through it and we've forgotten the dawn vigils. When I look at our two loving, outgoing, affectionate sons I sometimes think that I wouldn't have had it any other way. We gave them love in the night, and they gave us five hundred times as much back every day.

At the time, we were so desperate for sleep that it became our overriding priority. Once it did, our worries were half over. We decided to do anything to ensure a full night's sleep, at least now and then. I had never believed that taking the baby into our bed could do him or us any harm. I could not believe staying with my baby when he wanted me could do him any harm, so I followed my instincts and threw the so-called rules to the wind. If you feel it's necessary to try something like this I suggest that you try it sooner rather than later. I'm convinced you're not buying

Early risers
Leave some special toys or board books beside your child's bed to keep her occupied when she first wakes in the morning, or after her nap.

problems, you're only being a good parent to your child. Never take your baby into bed, however, if you have been drinking alcohol, taking drugs, or using medications that make you drowsy. Keep his head uncovered and use lightweight blankets.
- My husband and I alternated nights "on duty": one stayed with the child; the other remained sleeping unless there was a real emergency.

TIPS FOR EARLY WAKERS

- Put a pile of cloth or board books at the bottom of the crib or bed for early morning "reading." Make sure that there is enough light to see by; if there isn't, leave on a low-wattage nightlight when you put your toddler to bed.
- Put a soft box or plastic bucket at the side of the bed or crib with small toys, crayons, paper, bits of

cloth, or interesting household articles in it, so he can play with them.
- Leave a paper bag with some fresh fruit or bread at the bottom of the bed; never put the food in a plastic bag for safety reasons.
- Leave a drink of water in a plastic cup within reach of your child.

- We put up a cot next to the crib, and later the bed, so that we could put out a reassuring hand to pat him when he started to cry. This way neither of us really woke up at all.
- We gave the child 15 minutes to respond to our strategies, then if that failed we tried taking him in to our own bed— a sure-fire success.
- We only gave drinks of water at night, never milk, so he would not become accustomed to food, nor juice because it can cause cavities if the teeth are not brushed afterward.

Refusing to go to bed

Judging by the correspondence I get, there are more "difficult" babies around than most people realize, and they pose great problems for their parents. The baby who doesn't go to sleep at night is classically intelligent, physically very active, interested in everything that is going on around him, and openly affectionate. During the day these difficult children are delightful and very rewarding, but you pay the penalty at night.

Two of my four sons were sleepless, demanding babies, so I devised a few principles for coping. You have to get your priorities right: no one can function properly for long without adequate sleep and a parent is no exception. Sleep is too important to miss and you are justified in doing whatever is necessary to get it. Why not adopt a few pragmatic rules in place of the old-fashioned dogmatic ones?

- There is nothing magical about bedrooms. Let your child go to sleep where he is most comfortable: at your feet on the floor, on a couch, in your lap.
- Be flexible about bedtime. Left to themselves, most children go to sleep at around seven or eight o'clock in the evening, whether you put them to bed or not. Why should they be unhappy in a room on their own, instead of happy in your company?
- Give your child an early evening bath. This often relaxes children and makes them sleepy.
- If your child is proving difficult to get to go to bed, put on his pajamas before he's brought into the living room. If he falls asleep, you won't have to wake him up again. You can put him straight in bed.
- If problems persist, talk to your pediatrician, who is trained to support parents coping with common behavior problems and should be able to suggest helpful strategies and techniques.

Rapid-return technique

If, for some reason, your baby starts to get out of bed every night or calls for you constantly, cries when put down, and won't settle in his bed at night, try this technique. It can take a few nights, but it does work.

- Go in, remain silent, and put your baby down again.
- Repeat this immediate action of settling your baby back down in his crib as many times as it takes.
- Be patient and don't give in. You may have to repeat these actions up to 50 times on the first night.
- Follow through on the second night. You still may have to go to your baby as many as 20 times.
- The third night will be much better and your baby should be back to normal in about four nights.

All about sleeping 2 to 3 years

By the time your child is two years old, he usually needs 12 hours of sleep at night and about one or two hours of napping during the day; the actual amount will depend on the child. In general, the nap or rest time will shorten during the year, but bedtime will usually stay the same. The amount of time your child sleeps at night won't decrease until he's around six years old, when he'll reduce it half an hour at a time, per year.

Around the age of three, many children stop having naps, although the majority still need a rest period indoors after lunch until they are about five or six.

Sleep routine

Children about the age of two and three sometimes start delaying tactics at bedtime. He may ask to go to the bathroom or to have a drink and, of course, there's the possibility that he may just appear at your side with no excuse, wakeful and charming. In these circumstances, I think you have to decide how to act according to what your previous routine has been. If you have been pretty flexible about bedtime and never insisted that your child went to bed in his room, crib, or bed, then you can't suddenly change tactics when your child is two or three: he will not accept the inconsistency, and he will quite rightly balk at the new regime. In these circumstances, I think it is better to be practical and to let your child play in the room with you until he is tired, then let your child fall asleep on the chair beside you, and then carry him up to his bed.

On the other hand, if the bedtime routine has been carefully set and this new behavior is a departure, then I think your child will only benefit from your being firm about the reestablishment of routine.

TIPS FOR MAKING BEDTIMES EASY

- Mark bedtime with an alarm or a timer, so that you can give your children five minutes warning.
- For a young child, have a toy clock next to the real clock and set the hands of the toy clock to bedtime. When the hands of the real clock match up with the toy clock, it is time for bed.
- Keep a child's bedtime as near the same time as you can every night to help establish regular sleeping patterns.
- Children are often not sleepy at their bedtimes. They like the time to slow down just lying in bed looking at a new toy, reading a new book, or chatting to one another. It is a good idea to have children who are near each other's own age sharing a bedroom until they require privacy.
- Once your children get into a bed, lie down with them before you leave them to go to sleep. It is very nice for them; it warms up the bed, and their last memories are of your closeness. It is also very relaxing for you: I did it with my children and I nearly always found that I dropped off before they did. It was a tradition we started when they were young but continued after they went to school.

Night-time comfort

It is about this age that a child may like to take a particular doll or toy to bed with her. If this happens, keep an identical spare in case the first is lost.

No doubt you will get a few whimpers and a few sorrowful pleas, but you have already established with your child that you are loving and will come if he is in real need, so you can afford to be firm. You have a lot of credit to draw on and your child will learn this lesson quickly, and stop repeating the new behavior. However, if you give in to your child now, he will pick it up as a new habit and try it every evening.

The way you handle these situations depends quite a lot on how much energy you have left and how much you are prepared to have your evenings interrupted. If you have been with your children all day, you probably feel with justification that the night-time is your own. If you've brought your children up to recognize this, you can be quite firm in insisting on it.

Keeping bedtimes happy

It is important to keep bedtimes happy. Personally, I was prepared to make quite a lot of concessions to make sure that my children didn't go to sleep unhappy. I forgave certain misdemeanors that would normally have been punished earlier in the day, so that they didn't go to bed with the memory of my angry voice ringing in their ears. I tried to avoid letting them feel upset or crying with distress. It is worth making pre-bedtime activities especially joyful and friendly: as your child gets older spend the time between dinner and bed (about 30 minutes) in their company—even if you are only sitting in the same room reading a newspaper, or paying bills. Having your presence in the room is very comforting and consoling and this will calm your child so that he'll be in a happy mood when he makes the transition from the living room to the bedroom. If you can, watch a suitable television program or a DVD together, read a book, or play a quiet game before you take your child to his bedroom.

Bedroom rituals

Most children like a bedtime ritual. Mine always had half a dozen favorite songs they liked me to sing, and a storybook they liked their father to read. When we were home together we would share the bedtime routine: ten minutes with me singing and ten minutes with him reading a storybook. We would both stay in the bedroom and, since there were three children going to bed, bedtimes were communal, with the children sitting or lying on each other's beds. It was a family time. My husband would lie on the bed while I sang the songs. I stayed and laid on a bed while he read a story.

When the story and songs were over, it was lights out, except for a low nightlight, although we often stayed and talked over what had happened during the day. Sometimes we stayed under the blankets for a while to give our children the extra loving companionship.

In our household this sometimes rather protracted but worthwhile bedtime routine worked. The last thing we did was to switch on the hall light so that the children could see their way to the bathroom during the night or to our room if they needed us. A light with a dimmer switch gives a low enough light so no doors have to be shut.

Possible sleep problems 2 to 3 years

Delaying tactics

Your child may try to keep you from leaving by saying that he simply doesn't want you to go. You have a choice in this situation. You can stay with your child until his fears have gone and he is feeling calm enough to go to sleep, either with you or without you. Or you can call your child's bluff and leave. I think the latter action is dangerous, as it can cause your child to get so frightened that he becomes hysterical. This is bad both in the short term—he will have great difficulties going to sleep that night—and in the long term—you may make your child fearful of going to bed for several years to come. I would never advocate it.

Another possibility is to say "If you lie still for five minutes I will come back," and then come back in exactly five minutes. Make sure that he's comfortable and say that you will come back in another five minutes, and do so again. In your absence, leave music playing, let your child continue to read the book he has been reading, or to enjoy the game he has been playing, so that he is not left alone with fearful thoughts, waiting for you to return. On the third or fourth occasion, you'll probably find he's asleep.

As a last resort, take your child downstairs with you. Rest assured that there is absolutely no harm in it, although you will have to be prepared for this to become a long-term habit. It can make for some very rewarding family evenings, as long as you don't get too tired and you aren't too jealous of your privacy. Use the method most suitable for you all.

Fear of the dark

If your child delays going to bed because he is fearful of being left alone or of being in the dark, then you can allay both of these fears. If your child is afraid of being alone in the dark, sit and distract him by reading a story, playing a game, or singing nursery rhymes. Make sure he is calm and sleepy, and sit and pat his back until he has quietly dropped off. Fear of the dark is perfectly normal and reasonable in a small child, so don't insist on the bedroom being dark. Provide a him with a low-voltage nightlight, which will be a comfort to him and will also help you to see your way to your child's bedroom at night.

Bad dreams and sleepwalking

Your child probably won't have a nightmare before the age of three, although children sometimes wake up with a scream and a frightened look, suggesting that they have had a bad dream. Many children have an occasional nightmare and this is normal, although it can be quite frightening for the parent if the child doesn't become conscious right away. Nightmares are not abnormal unless they happen often or are accompanied by regular sleepwalking. This behavior suggests that the child is having to exercise a great deal of self-control to overcome anxieties when he's awake and only loses this control when he is asleep. The treatment is to find out the cause of the tension if you can, and to remove it. If the cause isn't obvious, like a new baby at home, or starting at school, talking things over with your pediatrician may help. If nightmares are a problem, your pediatrician may recommend a child psychologist.

A night terror is different. Your child's eyes may be open although he won't actually see you. He may shout abuse at you in a strange, garbled language and be rude and angry. Ignore all this; he is not in control of himself and, during the night terror he is very frightened.

Very often there is little you can do to relieve your child's fear, even though that is your greatest wish. There's no point in trying to speak to him rationally about what's going on. In many cases, he can't even understand the words you say. During the nightmare, don't ask your child to do anything. This puts further pressure on him and only increases his anxiety. The only way for you to behave, even though the nightmare may last as long as half an hour, is to remain by his side and be entirely sympathetic, calm, soft-spoken and caring. Never, ever, leave your child with a night terror. Stay until the nightmare is over. Your nearness and comfort are all that is required. Speak soothingly and quietly about anything you like; don't suggest that he try to calm down; never raise your voice and never scold your child, as this may make him hysterical.

Locked doors

Never lock your child's door to keep him separate from you. This is just admitting to a failure in your ability to handle your child and is cruel. Locked doors and gates shouldn't be used as childcare devices. They are no substitute for you teaching your child, even as early as two years old, about respecting other people's privacy, including your own. A three-year-old child is able to reason and you can explain to him that he cannot get out of bed whenever he pleases, and that you will put him back no matter how often he does it. If you are firm but reasonable, your child should respond.

If your child habitually gets out of bed, put a guard across his bedroom door at the top of the stairs, for his own safety.

10 Crying

Many newborn babies cry a lot, so be prepared for it. If you expect your baby to cry, and treat it as normal when she does, you'll find it easier to cope with. If your baby is one of the few who doesn't cry much, think of it as a bonus. In order to understand why your baby is crying, and how you can provide comfort, bear in mind that what upsets a baby, and what comforts her, changes as she develops. A new baby may cry when she's undressed for a bath; a one-year-old may cry when you leave the room. The new baby will be comforted by being snugly wrapped up in a towel; the one-year-old will be comforted by the sight of you returning.

All about crying birth to 1 year

Your newborn baby has a limited repertoire of communication, and crying is almost her only way of telling you that something is wrong. Remember that for several months she's been floating gently in the dark, in a constant temperature with a constant food supply. As a result, bright lights and hard surfaces are unexpected, so it's not surprising if she cries when she's cold and hungry. But crying doesn't necessarily mean that your baby is in danger.

Recognizing different cries
Cries can be identified accurately by mothers and fathers who become increasingly able to distinguish different kinds of cries from their baby during the weeks following birth. This is not a one-sided ability; a baby becomes increasingly able to anticipate her mother's responses

to her cries. Most new parents worry a lot about why their baby is crying, and the interpretations seem endless. Is it hunger, boredom, anger, loneliness, overtiredness, stomach pains, or colic? Does she want a hug or is she just plain miserable?

After the first four weeks, mothers start to pay much less attention to the type of cry, than to lots of other information, such as how long is it since the baby was fed? Did she eat well last time? Is she too cold or too hot?

Responding to crying
The way you respond to your baby's distress can affect how your baby behaves and how she grows up. Your response to her cries and the way you comfort her can influence the bond that grows between you over the years. This goes beyond the issue of

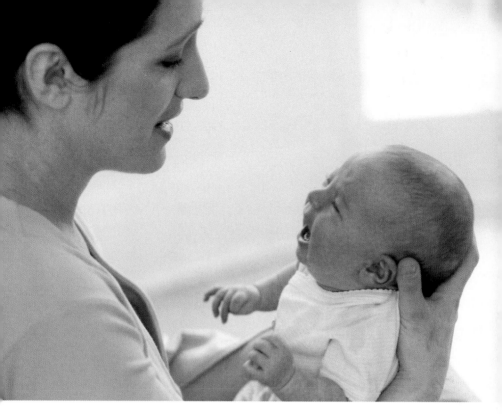

spoiling your baby to the central question of how your child's early experiences with you will affect her later development.

Some research with mothers and newborn babies has shown that over the first few days of life a slow response to crying may well lead to more, rather than less, crying. Another study found that babies whose crying was ignored early on tended to cry more frequently and more persistently later in the first year, and that after the first six months this persistent crying discouraged the mothers from responding. The same research showed that mothers who had responded quickly to their babies had children who were much more likely to be advanced in "communication skills," as measured by a comparison of the range of facial expressions of each baby.

The newborn baby
Crying is her only way of communicating with you in the early days. Always respond to her, and she will come to learn and recognize the sound of your voice.

Further studies paint a picture in which the sensitive and prompt response of a mother promoted a harmonious relationship with a child, who was content, obedient, secure, and competent as a result. This research supports the belief that mothers are programmed to respond immediately to their babies.

Some psychologists have attributed the difficulty mothers have with demanding children to the erosion of a natural mother and baby relationship, produced by anxiety about spoiling the child. They see mothers who do not respond promptly to their babies as "going against nature."

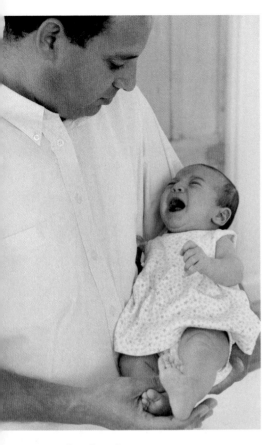

Comfort through movement
When your baby cries, rock her in your arms to comfort her. Most babies are soothed by gentle rocking movements; it is what they were used to in the womb.

Never leave your baby to cry

The factors that prevent a child from forming deep, loving relationships with parents are parental apathy and lack of response. They are more important inhibitors of a child's attachment ability than a parent causing distress, say by physical violence.

I have heard mothers say, "If she is clean and dry, burped and well-fed, let her cry," or "He needs to cry for an hour. It is the only exercise his lungs get, so leave him alone." I am very strongly against these attitudes. In my opinion, a baby should never be left to cry. In the first place, a crying baby can swallow air, which will cause discomfort and make feeding difficult. Prolonged crying may make your baby feel very tired, even exhausted, and she will become irritable and difficult to soothe. More important than either of these reasons is that she will quickly learn that pleas for attention go unheeded, and that there is no loving human response when she needs it.

All the research I have read supports not letting your baby cry. It also suggests that if you let her cry she'll very soon stop asking for attention, which may seriously damage her ability to form relationships with others while growing up. A baby's pattern of behavior, first with the mother, then with the father, and later on with family and friends, is worked out during the first year of life and probably starts as early as the first six weeks. If friendship is denied to a child in these early weeks, she may grow up introverted, withdrawn, shy of displays of affection, and repulsed by physical contact. Don't give your child such an unfair start in life.

Spoiling your baby?

In my opinion a baby cannot be loved too much. I don't share the belief that too much picking up or nursing will spoil a child. A child under one year cannot be "spoiled" enough, if picking up, nursing, loving, and cuddling mean spoiling. To me, none of this behavior constitutes spoiling. A child who is picked up and nursed is learning about loving human behavior. The model for this behavior, which she'll retain for life, is that important early relationship with her parents.

What we tend to call spoiling is both a natural response of a mother to a distressed child, and the natural need of the baby. A mother's behavior is "built in" just as much as the behavior of the baby. A mother is genetically programmed to respond to her baby's crying, although she may suppress her instinctive response with a learned response that interferes with her natural drives—which are to pick up, soothe, and nurse her crying baby. Society has suggested that she will spoil her baby if she does this, and so she is torn. She should not be; she should follow her natural instincts. The protective instinct in a mother (which is what she is displaying when she picks up and tries to soothe her crying child) is the basis of her maternal instinct, and essential to her biological function as a mother. Babies require this physical contact with a soft, warm, loving human being. The need for this is so strong that it almost overrides the need for food.

The mother's response

Crying, and your prompt response to it, undoubtedly play an important part in the way your baby becomes attached to you. Every child in a family will become attached to both parents, but the quality of the attachment depends on the sensitivity of the mother. It is the promptness and appropriateness of the mother's response to the child's distress—in other words how much she is attuned to her child, which is the most important part of this sensitivity. It is critical for the development of a stable

and happy relationship between baby and mother and then between baby and other people as she grows up.

So my unequivocal answer to the question, "Is it possible to spoil a baby?" is definitely "No."

Crying spells

Spells of crying are likely to go on for three, four, or even six weeks, while your baby becomes acclimated to the outside world. When she has developed a routine that takes account of her likes and dislikes, the frequency of crying usually decreases.

Everyone finds it harder to cope with crying during the night. When your sleep is interrupted, you will feel, like every other parent, a high degree of impatience. Your feelings aren't abnormal; everyone has them. Don't panic when your baby starts to cry. It is inevitable that she will, and your tenseness will only make matters worse.

If you feel that your baby seems to be crying a lot, you can take comfort in some research that has shown that babies may cry quite independently of any discomfort they may be feeling or of the effectiveness of the comfort you give. For instance, babies who were born after a long labor, or whose mothers were given drugs during labor, were more likely to cry frequently and sleep in short bouts.

Mothers who were highly anxious during pregnancy tend to have more irritable and difficult babies. It is also well known that male babies are more vulnerable to stress at the time of birth than female babies, and at least one American study has shown that boys are more irritable at the age of three weeks than girls.

Causes of crying birth to 6 months

Hunger

This is the most common cause of crying in young babies, and parents soon learn to recognize it. Studies have confirmed what parents know—babies cry more before feeding than after. Experiments have shown that it is the actual feeling of a full stomach that brings the most comfort, not being held, sucking, or swallowing.

GENERAL CRYING CURES

If your baby still seems fretful, try some, or all, of the following remedies as part of your crying cure. Most babies are soothed by movement and sound, and many parents find it relaxing, too.

Movement
- Rock your baby—rocking chairs and swings are ideal for this.
- Walk or dance with your baby.
- Bounce your baby gently in your arms or on a bed or in the crib.
- Put your baby in a bouncy seat, and rock it gently for her.
- Take your baby for a ride in the car, or a walk in her carriage, stroller, or sling, even at night.
- If you are on your own, put your baby in a sling and just let her cry. Keep doing whatever you want to do and try to ignore the crying.

Sound
- Talk, sing, or croon to your baby.
- Put on the radio or television.
- Put on the vacuum cleaner, or let a faucet run forcefully into the sink for a few minutes.
- Give your baby a noisy toy. Shake and rattle it.
- Play tapes or CDs of calm music.

- Feed on demand. Don't be inflexible about feeding times, and never feed by the clock. Remember, she's very young; she may want to eat every two or three hours and a feeding 15–30 minutes earlier than expected will do your baby no harm at all.
- If your baby seems only to want to suck, give her cooled boiled water between feedings (from a sterilized spoon).
- Give your baby a pacifier to suck; hold it in the baby's mouth if necessary. You can also use a clean finger.

Lack of contact

Some babies cry whenever you put them down in their cribs, but stop as soon as you pick them up again. This is perfectly natural, and means that your baby feels happiest when she is physically close to you. In many cultures, babies are swaddled or held in close contact with their mothers' bodies, and these babies rarely cry.
- Pick your baby up as soon as she cries.
- Carry your baby around with you in a sling or a shawl so that she can hear and feel your heart beating.
- Rock your baby until you get tired, then hand her over to your partner until the baby is calm again.
- Wrap your baby tightly. The texture of the cloth should be warm and fluffy—cool fabrics are far less effective.
- Lay your baby across your lap, tummy down, and massage her back and her arms and legs.
- Lay your baby across a warm hot-water bottle on your lap or on a bed.

Temperature

Heat and cold (and humidity) have important effects on the amount of time that a baby sleeps, cries, and is active. Young babies sleep more and cry less if they are in relatively warm environments (65–68°F/16–20°C), but they do not like to be too hot either.

Wet or dirty diapers don't in themselves cause a baby to cry, unless the wet diaper gets cold, too, in which case it is the drop in temperature that is a potent cause of distress in a baby.

- Make sure your baby's room is at the desired temperature.
- Feel the back of your baby's neck to test whether she's too hot or too cold (if it feels sweaty, for example, she's too hot). Either add another layer of clothing if she's too cold or take a layer off if she feels too hot.
- Check your baby's diaper to see if it's wet or dirty; change it if necessary.

Undressing

Most babies hate being undressed, even when the room is warm and they are awake and contented immediately before their clothes are removed. The effect of undressing is consistent and it gets worse over the second and third weeks: as soon as the baby senses that the clothes are being removed she tenses up and finally breaks down when the piece of clothing nearest to her skin comes off. The cause is not the cold, but the fact that her skin is no longer in contact with the familiar and reassuring texture of the clothing.

- Keep undressing to a minimum in the early weeks. Try topping and tailing your baby (see p.72), so that you only have to undress her a little at a time.
- Whenever you have to undress your baby fully, lay a towel across her body—the contact with the fabric will help her.
- Talk soothingly and reassuringly, and try to get the undressing over quickly.

IF CRYING IS DIFFICULT TO COPE WITH

One of the things you should be aware of is that every parent at some time or other contemplates doing something physically violent to her or his children. Most mothers with newborn babies who are exhausted and trying to pacify a screaming baby will confess that they have thought of doing anything to stop the baby crying. It is not abnormal to think such things. It's only abnormal to do them.

A crying baby can be particularly difficult to handle before your period. Mothers who are ideal parents—very loving and caring, sympathetic, and patient for the rest of the month—can find the few days prior to menstruation a challenging time.

Most mothers are aware when they begin to lose hold of themselves and are able to control violent behavior against their children. But if you feel yourself sliding down a slippery slope, you should seek help, first from your partner, or from a friend, but also from your doctor.

Get help if necessary

If you ever find yourself hitting or shaking your baby, don't feel that it is an admission of failure to seek help. You must do so immediately, both for your child's sake and your own. Don't stand by and let your partner injure your child either: try to make him or her see that what he or she is doing is wrong. If he or she is impervious to your pleas, seek help on behalf of both of you. Contact your doctor, or the police immediately.

COLIC

This term describes unexplained recurrent bouts of crying usually in the late afternoon or evening, though they can occur any time. The crying may be intense and brief or last for hours, and is not generally pacified by the usual remedies. The baby's face gets red and she draws her legs up.

Many causes have been suggested, such as overfeeding, underfeeding, gas, being picked up too much or too little, indigestion and tension. It has always seemed to me that tension is the most likely cause. You're busy in the evening and it's likely that your baby picks up on the tension and responds by crying.

Since your baby is likely to cry every night for 12 weeks, I'm against using medicine to prevent it. Of course, try to soothe your baby, but don't expect her to respond readily. Take comfort from the fact that these colicky spells come only at night and usually only last for three months. Colic generally stops without you doing anything and is rarely serious.

Colicky babies
It's not known why colic occurs, but it usually starts in the first three weeks of a baby's life. Try laying her across your lap, supporting her abdomen, and gently massaging her back.

Pain

This is a very definite cause of crying, but the actual cause of the pain may be hard to determine. It may be the discomfort of colic (*see left*), or it may be something quite obvious like a sore bottom or a very tightly fitting garment. If, for example, the pain is caused by an earache, you'll probably see your baby putting her fist against the affected ear.

- Go to your baby immediately. Hold your baby close to you, cuddle, and talk soothingly to her.
- Always remove the source of pain if it's easily discernible.
- Stay with your baby until she's completely calmed down.
- If no amount of comforting on your part works, and your baby seems ill, see your baby's pediatrician for advice.

Violent or sudden stimulation

Sudden changes in the level of stimulation—whether it is light, noise, jerking movements, being played with too roughly, or the sensation of falling—will cause your baby great distress. In the latter case your startled baby will throw out her arms and legs in the Moro reflex (*see p.27*), and will invariably begin to cry.

- Hold your baby close to you and use the general pacifying methods of contact, movement, and sound.
- Avoid moving your baby in such a sudden way next time.
- Avoid sudden stimulation with bright lights, loud noises, or jerky movements. A baby can tolerate very loud noises or bright lights over a long period of time, but a sudden change will cause her immediate distress.

Fatigue

Many babies cry when they are tired. It took me almost two weeks to understand my tired newborn son's message. "Clever baby," I thought, "dumb mother." Some babies (like adults) twitch or jerk as they are dropping off to sleep. This may cause a baby to wake up again and, if it continues, will result in a fretful sleep.

• Put your baby to sleep in a quiet, warm, dimly lit room.
• If she's particularly twitchy, wrap her up firmly before you put her down.

Misreading your baby's signals

Not reading your baby's signals to you, whether they mean "I'm hungry," "I'm tired," or "I want to be cuddled not played with," can all result in tears. For example, if your baby is ready for feeding, but you ignore this and give her a bath first, then she is bound to cry. If, while you're breast-feeding, you fail to notice that your baby can't suck on your nipple properly because she's being smothered by your breast and is finding it difficult to breathe, then she's bound to cry.

• Be alert. Look at your baby, listen to her gurgles and grumbles and try to interpret what she's saying to you. She is telling you something if you are attentive enough to understand.
• Resolve whatever is causing the alarm immediately to reduce her stress.
• Use the general crying cures (see p.162) to soothe your baby.

Causes of crying 6 months to 1 year

Your baby will still cry if she's hungry, if she's in pain and if she's too hot, or too cold and the cures for these are the same as for newborns (see pp.162–163). However, as she gets older she will be distressed by new things too.

Boredom

Your baby will spend longer periods awake during the latter half of this year and she may cry out of sheer boredom if she's just left alone with nothing to look at or play with. She'll be eager to stay with you and see what you're doing all the time, because at this time you're a constant source of amusement and affection. When you leave your baby, especially if she can hear you elsewhere, she's bound to cry.

• Hang a mobile or similar toy above your baby's crib so that she can swipe at it and watch how it moves. Leaves on trees, curtains blowing by an open window, lamp shades moving—they all provide amusement for your baby.
• You'll have a more contented baby if you keep her near you when she's awake; she will always sense your presence.

Anxiety

Your baby may well become increasingly wary and afraid, especially of strangers and of your going away. During the second half of this year your baby will be extremely clingy. At the same time as this increasing dependence on you emerges, she will form attachments to comforters like her own

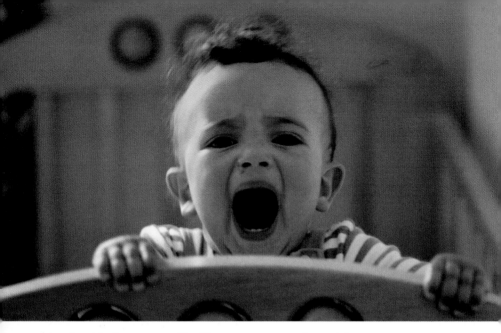

thumb, a blanket, or a pacifier. The source of comfort varies with individual children, but the need for it is common to all of them. The intensity and persistence of these attachments can last for two to three years. The objects are usually suckable or strokable, and children use them in moments of anxiety and tiredness to simulate the effects of continuous stroking and contact.

- Understand that this is a period in your child's development that she has to go through.
- Never force her to go to a stranger if she really doesn't want to.
- Let your baby have a comforter, even if it's a pacifier. She'll grow out of using it in time.
- Give your baby lots of affection and hugs.

Frustration

Your baby's increasing physical capabilities may well lead to tears of frustration. Once she's started crawling she'll be able to

Boredom and frustration

Your baby may cry because she wants to be with you all the time, but she may also cry because she is bored. Try leaving a few toys in her crib for when she wakes.

move away from you more quickly and will want to explore her surroundings. What this means is that she'll have to be checked frequently, and stopped from doing what she wants to do sometimes, for her own safety as well as to protect whatever it is she's trying to explore.

- Make your home as childproof as possible by removing breakable objects from low tables and shelves and by using the correct safety fittings throughout your home (see pp.292–298).
- Remove the baby from the source of frustration. If, for example, she keeps going up to a dog and pulling its tail, either remove the dog or the baby from the room. Your baby's memory is very short at this time, so she'll soon forget the object of her curiosity.
- Distract your baby with other games.

All about crying 1 to 2 years

In the one- to two-year-old, most crying is the result of emotional disturbance: fear, anxiety, separation, or deprivation of mother love.

Insecurity

Between the ages of one and three, children spend less and less of their time being physically close to, and touching, their mothers. But in contrast to this apparent independence, there will also be moments when your toddler becomes frightened and anxious.

There is usually a period around the age of one when this occurs. You may notice that she's quieter and less mischievous than usual; that she's become very shy of strangers and strange situations and clings desperately to your legs. She may even lose her appetite. These are all signs of anxiety, which you should respond to immediately.

- The best way of coping with these anxieties is to give your toddler extra affection and, while doing this, to encourage her to be curious and adventurous, and to have a growing sense of self-confidence. Praise and reward each feat and new achievement. Your toddler requires your approval and will do almost anything to get it, including showing off her new independence, so it really is very easy to encourage her.

- A child who is securely attached to at least one of her parents (mother or father) uses that parent as a base from which to explore, and will go on to explore confidently. Much research has demonstrated that the presence of the person with whom the child has a secure attachment enables her to cope with new, possibly fearful, experiences and with the accompanying anxiety.

Fear of separation

Because a toddler is so attached to the parent, separation becomes one of the greatest causes of distress, and fear of separation is one of the most potent causes of anxiety. When fear, insecurity, anxiety, or separation cause great distress, crying ensues. The degree of distress varies according to your child's age (you may find that it is much less by the time she is 15 months than when she was 10 months); the way you actually leave the toddler; and the familiarity of the situation. Of course, it also depends upon your toddler's previous experiences of being separated. If it was unpleasant the first time, your toddler is likely to find it more unpleasant when it happens a second time.

Children undoubtedly don't like being left. In a way, the better parent you are, the more your toddler is likely to cry when separated from you.

- Never be scornful of fears and always try to be sympathetic and supportive. Reassure your child, more by actions than by words, that you are to be trusted and relied upon. If you say you will come back in half an hour, do it. If you say you are going into the next room, don't go any further. If you say you'll pop back in five minutes to check on a game, come back. One of your baby's greatest sources of confidence is that she can trust you.

- In your attempts at sympathy and reliability, do your best not to be overprotective. This will only curb your child's adventurous spirit and stop her from building her self-confidence.

Frustration

Toward the end of the second year, your toddler's sense of adventure will almost certainly outstrip her coordination and degree of mobility. She will attempt tasks that are beyond her dexterity, sense of balance, and physical strength, and this will cause great frustration. It's also inevitable that you'll be the source of frustration because you stop her from doing certain things she wants to do, for her own safety.

- Try to be patient. The best form of support you can give is your help: help with the painting; help with building a tower of blocks; help with climbing; help making sand castles; help propping up toy soldiers or farmyard animals. If the frustration at her inability causes crying, you can easily distract your child into another favorite game.

- If she gets frustrated when she tries to copy older children's games, or if she tries something an older child can do easily, suggest that you play a game together that you know she can physically cope with. While it's important for your toddler to try new things, and to continue trying when she doesn't immediately succeed, too many defeats can have a retrogressive effect.

- Don't be drawn into battles with your toddler—whether they're over using the potty or eating a certain food. She'll want to assert her independence and, when possible, respect this and don't force the issue. Let her decide whether she wants to use the potty, and don't worry if she only wants to eat green beans and ice cream. A calm acceptance of facts is better than arguing.

Possible crying problems 1 to 2 years

Temper tantrums

A temper tantrum is an attention-seeking device. The tantrum will go on as long as you are giving your child your attention; it will be shortened abruptly if you withdraw it. The best thing to do is to leave the room; your child will come to no harm. Holding her breath is self-limiting. Your child will take a breath as soon as she becomes short of oxygen. If she is kicking and screaming, simply move articles out of reach that could hurt her and let her kick and scream. Don't be tempted to cajole your child, to lose your temper, to smack, or to threaten punishments. They will do nothing to bring the tantrum to an end, or to avert the next one—they can make the situation worse. The only course of action is to leave your child alone.

Nighttime crying

Many babies cry as they are going to bed at night. You can do a lot to avoid this if you establish a bedtime routine. This doesn't mean that you are inflexible, rather that you give the evening a rhythm that you and your baby get used to. Bedtime and bathtime should be happy. From the time your baby is six months old she should be enjoying her bath and if you treat it as playtime you are off to a good start. By the time bathing is over, your baby should be relaxed and getting a little sleepy. If dinner is also casual, informal, and happy, with a drink, a story, a game, or a song—whichever your child prefers— followed by bed and a firm but loving goodnight, then just leaving your baby should work. As children get older they tend to express preferences for particular songs that they even like sung in a certain sequence, or favorite stories that they will follow with you in their storybook. Some of them will drop off to sleep by listening to music or while you sit by them quietly reading or singing. Find the bedtime routine that suits your child best and follow it every night without fail (see p.151). Familiarity brings security and that brings a happy child at bedtime, who is more likely to go to sleep without fussing.

Prolonged separation

The effect of prolonged separation varies a great deal with age. Before the age of six or seven months, there are usually no signs of distress when, for example, babies are admitted to the hospital or are separated from their parents for extended periods. From the age of six months to four or five years, however, children are acutely distressed, and it is possible that boys are more disturbed by separation than girls. If young children have had an unhappy first experience of separation, they are more likely to be upset by a second. The longer the separation, the more disturbance the child shows, especially if it is separation from mother, father, and siblings.

The effects can be mitigated by mothering from another individual, say a foster parent or a loving nurse, especially if the following things are done:

- Care is given to follow your baby's known daily routine and the pattern of childrearing that she is used to.
- A brief period of familiarization is arranged so that the child can meet the person who is going to take care of her before the separation occurs.
- Memories of the past are kept fresh in the child's mind by the caregiver talking about them.

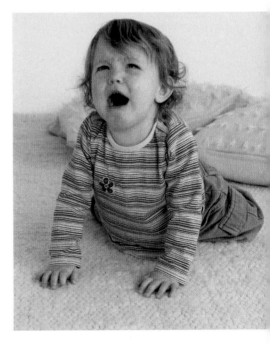

Comfort while you're away
Leaving one of your garments that smells of you, such as a scarf or a sweater, may go a long way toward easing the pangs of separation.

All about crying 2 to 3 years

As your baby gets older the reasons for crying become much more complicated. Her thinking becomes increasingly sophisticated, and she has a much wider appreciation of the world and what is going on in it; she has insight into your motivations and understands your more subtle expressions of approval and disapproval; she is becoming acutely aware of her own position in the family, among friends, and in the world in general; she has new insecurities and anxieties. Fears are no longer confined to simple ones like the fear of separation. There are all sorts of new and unusual things happening every day that may cause fear. Because your child's appreciation of the world is growing, there is increasing potential for her to become upset by things. While she is gaining in self-confidence, she is also becoming sensitive and more likely to feel shame, resentment, frustration, anger, jealousy, and dislike, all of which may upset her and make her cry. Because she knows more of the world, she is becoming aware of the threats that are around her and how they might affect her. She has to face many of them alone. This is not easy for anyone, let alone a young child, and it is not surprising that she often resorts to tears.

TIPS FOR MAKING SEPARATION EASIER

Separation anxieties

Children over the age of three still dislike being separated from their parents, even if they are only going to spend the evening out of the house. Up to the age of five or six it is quite normal for a child to shed a few tears until she is reassured about some of the details of the evening.

One of the most difficult separations for a child of this age is when her mother goes into hospital for the birth of a new baby. In addition to the jealousy that most children feel at this time (*see p.253*), there is the upheaval of being separated from the mother. Prepare your toddler well in advance of the birth by talking about the new baby, about your going into hospital, and about who will take care of her while you are away. Ideally it should be someone she knows well who understands her routine and can ensure that it continues while you are away. Try to let her visit you as often as possible while you are in hospital.

Making separation easier

- Always spend a few minutes with your child quietly doing something nice before you leave. Never rush off without a proper goodbye.
- If you make a promise that you will be back by a certain time, keep it and, when you go, remind your child that you will always come back. If you are delayed, call to explain why.
- Have a goodbye ritual—tell a story or play a game, give a hug, blow a kiss as you get into the car, wave to your child as she stands on the step.
- Think up a few games—kiss a child's palm and fold her fingers around it. Tell her if she needs a kiss from you while you're away there is one for her in her hand.
- Never keep the fact that you're going out a secret from your child. Talk about it ahead of time.
- If you are going to have a babysitter, ask her to come a half hour before you leave so she can start a game with your child before you go.

Fears real and imagined

Children suffer from classic fears between the ages of two and three. The fact that your child suffers from them is not a sign of abnormality. Two of the most common are described below.

Fear of the dark This is very common and not at all abnormal. Help your child by leaving a nightlight on in the bedroom. You don't have to go to any expense; just replace the standard bulb in her bedroom lamp with a low-wattage colored one. You can also help your child by showing that darkness is nothing to be afraid of. Go for a walk at night and point out all sorts of interesting things that you don't normally see during the day, like the stars, the moon, or nocturnal animals (the nocturnal house in a zoo, in which you often have to walk through in darkness, may also be a good idea). In the summer, take your child out in the backyard and lie on the grass, covered by a blanket.

Fear of thunder Most children are fearful of thunder and lightning. The best you can do is to distract your child while it's overhead. You can tell a favorite story,

Walk away
A child won't persist with a tantrum if there's no audience. Try to walk away slowly so your child can catch up with you for reconciliation and lots of hugs.

turn the television set up loud, play music, or get out that game you bought especially "for a rainy day."

Dealing with fears

Encourage your child to talk about fears as soon as she is able to. Listen intently and show your child that you are interested and sympathetic. Hear her out even if she finds it difficult to put her fears into words. Try to help by giving examples, and show that you identify with such fears.

Never tease or shame your child about what she is feeling—that will only encourage her to hide her fears, and could drive your child away from you. You should always be the sympathetic friend who will give help and comfort in a frightening situation. You are going to have to show your child how to face up to fears and there are several different ways that you can do it (*see overleaf*).

- One of the best ways of reassuring your child is to show her that you are exactly the same as she is. All children love hearing stories about when you were little, like them. Tell your child some of the fears that you had, and explain how you managed to overcome them with your parents' help.

- If your child develops fear of a piece of household equipment, for instance, the washing machine, help her overcome it by explaining what it's for and how it works. Tell your child that machinery is nothing to be afraid of and to prove it, hold her in your arms while you fill it, and give a running commentary of exactly what you are doing. Go through the routine of putting in the detergent and starting the machine. Put your hand on it to feel the vibration and then slowly and gently put your child's hand on it with yours on top so that she knows that you are not frightened, and that with your support she doesn't have to be frightened either.

- If your child is afraid of getting lost or of being in an accident, talk her through it. For instance, you can say things like, "If you got lost, what is the first thing you could do? Well, I think probably the best thing would be to go to the first store you come to, go to the counter, and say, 'I am Jane Brown. My address is... my telephone number is... Please will you call my mommy and daddy?'"

- Never ever brush off a fear as if it isn't serious. It is serious to your child and you should treat it as such. If your child is worried by the lamp in her bedroom, which casts an unpleasant shadow on the wall, try moving the light, or the bed, to a position where there are no shadows any more.

Dealing with irrational fears

One of the best ways to deal with irrational fears is to dispel them with some kind of physical activity. If your child is afraid of monsters or ghosts, say that you are a parent who can do magical things to them. Say that you are able to blow them away and give a big blow; promise that you will be able to get rid of them with the vacuum cleaner and turn it on; guarantee that you can flush them down the toilet and do it. There are some people who say indicating to your child that you believe in monsters and ghosts in this way encourages your child to believe in them too, and that a better alternative is to say

DEALING WITH INJURIES

You don't want your child to grow up being babyish about minor injuries, but you should never underestimate one, especially if you can see the damage. There is no point in saying that a small scratch doesn't hurt, because the sight of blood will scare your child and she will use pain as an excuse for your attention. Whenever your child comes to you with an injury give sympathy and support and use placebos whenever you can. The best possible placebo is a kiss and a cuddle and a gentle word. Next, try a favorite drink or snack, then suggest a small treat—perhaps your child's favorite food for the next meal, or having a tea party in the garden. Always keep your "magic" ointment handy. In our house it is a simple antiseptic that can be used for all cuts and abrasions. It is very soothing and if your child believes that an ointment will work and take away the pain, you are halfway there.

that there are no such things as ghosts. The one trouble with this ploy is that your child won't believe you. She can't. She can only believe you if her fears are rational, which they aren't.

Crying from overtiredness

This is one of the most common reasons for crying, especially in the evening. The child may have been allowed to stay up later than usual, perhaps because of a visit from friends or relatives, or on a special occasion such as Christmas, when children tend to be thrown out of their usual routines with more excitement than they can cope with. The result is an exhausted child whose overexcitement will spill over into tears at the slightest motivation. And the more you try to jolly her out of the crying (and this is especially true when visitors are involved), the more hysterical and inconsolable her crying will become. It is clearly better to prevent these situations from developing in the first place, by trying not to let your child become overexcited and by ensuring that she has a rest in the middle of the day if you expect to let her stay up later than usual in the evening.

If you haven't been able to avoid it, and your child does become overtired and tearful, try to deal with her as calmly as possible. Take her off quietly to her room and hold her until she has calmed down; if she has a favorite book or song, and she has quietened down enough to be receptive, read or sing to her. Or let her have a quiet, relaxing bath, get her ready for bed, and stay with her until you are sure that she has completely relaxed and is ready for sleep.

Pre-school nerves

There are very few children who skip off happily to playgroup or nursery school with a cheerful goodbye and hardly a backward look. Prepare your child in advance, no matter how self-confident she seems.

The first thing you must do is look at the various schools in your area. Visit each one, talk to the teachers at length, and sit in on at least a couple of classes. Get a good feel for the atmosphere and for how interested the teachers are in the children and how much individual attention they are prepared to give during different activities. One of the most important things you have to establish is that there is a rapport between you and the teachers. If there isn't, there is no point in sending your child there, no matter how good the school appears to be.

Take your child to the nursery

Most nursery schools suggest that you take your child for a brief visit several weeks ahead of starting school. Don't make a big thing of it. Fit it in between errands and don't stay for any longer than about 15 minutes. Don't push her into it. Make the point of your visit a talk with one of the teachers and just let your child look, listen, observe, and absorb. Let her wander around, touch, pick up, and play with things, but don't force your child to do so. Some nursery schools will let your child visit more than once.

On the first morning, be prepared for a shaky start, and for the necessity of staying with your child for the whole morning. Many nursery schools welcome this and they will suggest that you help your child by participating in the lessons and staying

near her. This may not be necessary. As soon as your child feels that you are not going to leave, she will be quite happy if you sit at the back of the room. Take some work or a book along with you so that it is not a complete waste of time as far as you are concerned. If your child seems happy, say that you are just going to run out to get something from the car and will be back in five minutes. Come back in exactly five minutes. If your child is distressed when you leave, don't go. If, on the other hand, she is quite happy, you might let another half hour pass and say that you are just going to do an errand and will be back in 20 minutes. Be sure you are there in time though.

Take the lead from your child

Over the next few days, using your child's reaction as a guide, see if you can leave her for longer. Some children adapt very quickly to nursery school and you won't need to stay after a few days. Others may still want you to stay for about half an hour

at the end of two weeks. Just fit in with them. The most important thing is that your child should feel that school is a happy place and that it is not associated with the unhappiness of being separated from you and feeling entirely alone. A good teacher, who feels confident about your child and confident about herself, will very firmly suggest that you leave when she thinks the time is right. Being overprotective about your child at nursery school only makes it harder rather than easier for your child, especially if she's capable of coping without you. If you have a good rapport with the teacher you should feel happy taking her advice about this.

All of my children liked a ritual when they first arrived at nursery school. No matter what it was, we always did something that took about five to seven minutes before I said goodbye, and then they always came to the window and waved. This seemed to keep a child of not yet three happy when I departed, and you may like to try something similar.

Possible crying problems 2 to 3 years

Temper tantrums

A good method of handling temper tantrums when you are on your own with your child, and in the privacy of your own home, is to ignore them completely (*see p.168*). You can also try to distract your child by saying something unusual,

Fear and anxiety
When a young child is upset about something, there's nothing like a cuddle from his mom or dad to make everything feel better.

amusing, or silly, or by switching the light on and off, or opening and closing the door several times.

However, as your child gets older, and there is a greater chance of her throwing a tantrum in a public place, there are a few different ways that you can handle them. The majority of temper tantrums are caused by anger and frustration—anger that she can't have her own way or that her body is not physically strong enough or well coordinated enough to do what she wants it to do. Every now and then your child, like everybody else, needs to give vent to this anger. You can help her by doing some of the following:

- If your child is having a temper tantrum in a public place, don't get flustered; just take her out of the room into another as calmly as you can. If you're in a store, take her out into the street, or even to your car. If you're in a restaurant, take her to the bathroom. It is easier to deal with the tantrum calmly when there are fewer people around.
- Don't ever forget to congratulate your child and praise her when the tantrum is over and she has got control again. After all, it's only a stage she's going through.
- A lot of anger and aggression can be got rid of by physically active games outdoors. That is why toys such as tricycles, scooters and footballs are so good, because strenuous physical activity redirects antisocial behavior.
- If your child is expressing anger by shouting, join in for a few sentences and then gradually lower your voice, encouraging her to do the same, until you are both whispering. Then laugh about it together later.

BREATH HOLDING

As your child gets older she may try holding her breath and her face might become quite blue during them. In this instance, try any of the following tips:

- Blow gently on your child's face.
- Sprinkle a few drops of cold water on your child's face or apply a cold cloth.
- Gently pinch your child's nostrils together for a second or two.

- Give your child some paper and crayons or finger paints and ask her to paint or draw exactly what she is feeling.
- Teach your child that she has a set of "angry" toys, like a drum to beat loudly, or a musical instrument like a xylophone, to play, or a marching song that can be shouted.
- It can help your child a lot to talk about anger and to let her know that you consider it to be a reasonable and valuable emotion to feel. It lets off steam but it also draws boundaries. Your anger will tell her when she has overstepped your boundaries. Her own anger can be just as useful.
- Try to discuss the causes of anger with your child. Try to get to the root of the problem. It is one of the ways you can teach your child about sharing, tolerance, love, kindness, and thoughtfulness for others. If you think that such anger is justified, say so, and tell her why you think it is reasonable to be angry about something that has happened and then discuss the different ways that she might have reacted that wouldn't have been so hurtful and destructive.
- Show your child that anger is expressed just as well in words as in physical violence or destructiveness and let her know that angry words are much more acceptable to you than hitting or breaking things.

Phobias

A phobia is different from an ordinary fear. If your child is afraid of snakes, she is only afraid when she meets one at fairly close quarters. The rest of the time she doesn't give snakes a second thought. However, if your child has a phobia about snakes, she will become hysterical when she actually sees one, when she sees a picture of one, when she thinks of one, or when something reminds her of one.

One of the things you have to understand is that, even as your child gets older, explaining away a phobia doesn't make any difference: she is not open to rational explanations. The only way you can help your child overcome a phobia is to convince her in some way that the object of her fear is harmless. There are a variety of ways in which you can help her understand this:

- You can help your child realize that such fears are unfounded by letting her know that you don't have the same fear, but don't do it in a way that makes your child feel inferior.
- Another way is to show her that her peers aren't afraid of the phobic objects. If, for example, your child is afraid of dogs, it is a good idea to ask one of your friends who has a dog to bring it to the nursery school when you pick your child up, so she can see that the other children are not afraid of it.
- Never, ever ridicule your child's fears. No matter how unrealistic they seem to you, they are very real to her. Give rational explanations whenever you can and always behave in a sympathetic, helpful, and rational way.
- If the phobia starts suddenly, look for something in your child's life that is causing stress. If the phobia is associated with things like a parent going away, the death of a pet, or your child starting nursery school, then there is a very good chance that it will be transient.
- Your child may be emotionally upset about something that is difficult to fathom. You can try to very gently introduce the object of her phobia while she is doing something very pleasant, for example, while she is eating one of her favorite foods, like ice cream.

FAMILY CONFLICT

Your children have to grow up knowing the facts of life, one of which is that adults disagree occasionally, get angry, and have quarrels, but for heaven's sake, don't let them be frequent.

Don't argue in front of the children

If your partnership is going through a difficult period, don't fight in front of the children. Children, of course, want their parents to inhabit an ideal world where there is no arguing, no anger, and no acrimony, and they get very insecure when the people they love most don't seem to love each other. The greatest deterrent to having a quarrel with my husband came when my second-youngest son, at four-and-a-half years old, snuggled up next to me right after we had had an argument, looking very doleful. When asked what was wrong he said, "I don't know, but the world doesn't feel right."

Most children have an instinct to be peace-makers; mine certainly did. As soon as they heard a raised voice or an opinion vehemently expressed, they'd start diversion tactics like, "Do you want a cup of coffee, mom," and then actually interject with, "Please don't get in a woos," their term for getting upset. It is very hard to lose your temper when a child is pleading with you to stay calm. Remembering the damaging effect that witnessing an argument can have on a child is a great deterrent.

11 Physical development

Watching your baby grow and develop is one of the most exciting aspects of being a parent, and during the first year you'll be astounded by how quickly your child changes. With each passing week, he'll gain control over the various muscles in his body so his coordination will improve, and with this improved coordination he'll be able to sit, crawl, stand, and, eventually, walk and run. His manipulation abilities will improve and gradually, over the months, he'll develop fine control over his movements.

General development birth to 1 year

Every child develops at his own rate, and the ages given for the achievement of various skills or aspects of coordination are only approximate. Never try to force your child to go more quickly than he wants to—it will serve no purpose. Let him learn new skills at his own pace, while at the same time providing all the encouragement and help that you can.

The main changes that occur in your baby's general appearance in this first year of life, besides those of size and weight, are his proportions, posture, and body control. Your baby's head gradually gets smaller in proportion to the rest of his body, and his limbs lengthen and strengthen, ready for walking. During the first year your baby gains general control of his body; it's becoming less floppy and able to move purposefully.

Your baby goes through the fastest growing phase of life in the womb. Growth and weight will continue to be rapid during the first six months, but the rate will slow down toward the end of the first year. In general, a baby of average weight will increase his length by a quarter during the first six months, and double his weight. His head will increase in circumference by about twice as much in the first 12 months as it will in the next 11 years.

Long-term changes
Most size/weight charts plot the baby's weight in pounds or kilograms against the baby's age in weeks and his length in inches or centimeters. Except for the first few weeks of life when weight gain is watched rather closely, it's best not to watch your baby's weight obsessively. If your baby looks and acts healthy, it's highly unlikely that there's anything wrong. Long-term trends in growth and weight gain are important than day-to-day changes.

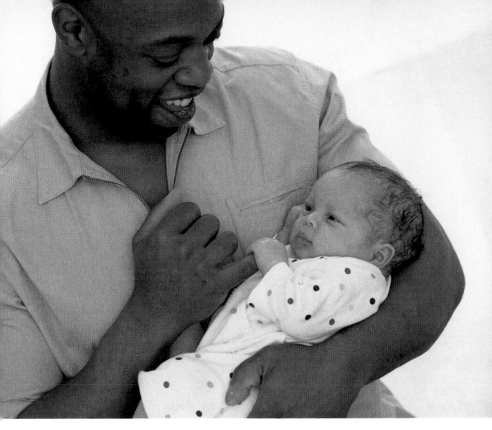

When you look at your baby's growth you should pay attention to the regularity of weight gain rather than the amount. As long as your baby's weight is increasing over the weeks, even if it is a bit erratic, and he shows signs of being happy and thriving, then you should not worry about weighing him too often. Furthermore, all size/weight charts are constructed for an "average" child. The average child is a theoretical statistic. Your baby is unique and his pattern of growth and weight gain will probably be very different from any other babies that you know. That doesn't mean he's abnormal.

Milestones

These are stages or "punctuations" in a baby's growth and development. They

Grasp reflex
Your baby is born with a "grasp reflex," which means that he will keep his fingers tightly closed over anything that is put into them. He loses this after a few weeks.

always follow the same order, as each one depends on the previous stage. They come along with such regularity that it is possible to forecast with some accuracy when they will occur for most babies.

This does not mean, however, that all babies will develop at the same speed. Just as there is a wide spread in the growth of size and weight, so there is for the development of physical capabilities. While no two babies develop at the same rate or in the same way, there are general principles that apply to physical development in all babies.

MILESTONES: BIRTH TO 6 MONTHS

Month	Milestone
Birth	• **Head control when on his back** If you grasp your baby around the upper chest and lift his body from the mattress, his head will be so heavy and floppy that it will just hang back. This is why it is so important to support his neck and head carefully. • **Sitting** Your baby won't be able to sit up at all without support. If you hold him in a sitting position his back will be round and his head will loll forward. He'll be very wobbly, and will collapse immediately unless supported. • **Crawling** Your baby will be born with a crawling reflex (*see p.26*), but will lose this as soon as his body uncurls from the fetal position.
1	• **Mobility** Your baby will have lost his newborn appearance, but his legs will still be bent. He may lift his head. • **Manipulation** Your baby's hand will be held in a tight fist; he'll reflexively grasp anything put in his palm. • **Head control when on his stomach** Your baby will lie with his head to one side, with his bottom pushed up in the air, and his knees slightly bent underneath his body. • **Sitting** Your baby's back will still be rounded and he'll only be a little steadier. However, he'll try and hold his head up for a second or two when held by you.
2	• **Mobility** Your baby continues to stretch himself. When lying on the floor, he can lift his head to a 45-degree angle and hold it for a few moments. • **Manipulation** He'll hold his hand open more often and his grasp will become voluntary. • **Head control when on his back** If you lift your baby from the mattress by holding on to his hands, he'll be able to hold his head in line with the rest of his body for a second or so. • **Head control when on his stomach** Your baby's body will be more fully stretched out and he'll be able to lift his head from the mattress for a moment or two.
3	• **Mobility** Your baby's body will be completely uncurled and his legs will be extended. He'll hold up his head. • **Manipulation** His hands will generally stay open although he may not be able to grasp anything for long. • **Head control when on his back** If you pull your baby up from a lying position by his hands, he will keep his head up in line with the rest of his body without additional help from you. • **Head control when on his stomach** He will now lie quite flat and be able to raise his head and hold it in this position for quite a long time. He'll begin to take the weight of his shoulders and head on slightly outstretched forearms. • **Standing** Once your baby can support his head, he'll enjoy being held facing you with his feet touching your knees. Lift him up and down so he feels his feet in contact with your legs and learns the sensation of taking his weight.

AT THREE MONTHS

Month	Milestone
4	• **Mobility** Your baby should be able to roll from side to side and on to his back. He'll support himself on his forearms. • **Manipulation** Your baby will have discovered his own hands, which he'll suck and play with. • **Head control when on his stomach** Your baby will be able to raise both legs off the mattress. He'll be able to support his chest and head by propping himself up on his forearms. This way he'll be able to see what's going on around him. • **Sitting** If you hold your baby in the sitting position, he will be able to sit with his head held up; the lower part of his back will still be rounded, but the upper part will be almost straight. • **Crawling** Your baby will probably raise chest and legs off the floor while making swimming movements with his arms.
5	• **Mobility** When placed on his stomach, your baby will push his head off the mattress. He'll roll from back to side. • **Manipulation** Your baby will be able to grasp objects between his hands and will love sucking his own feet this way.
6	• **Mobility** Your baby will be able to twist in all directions and may sit briefly unsupported. • **Manipulation** Your baby will be able to hold an object between finger and thumb and may be able to rotate his wrist. • **Head control when on his back** Your baby's head and neck will be so strong and well-controlled that he'll be able to raise his head from the mattress and look at his toes. • **Head control when on his stomach** Your baby will be able to take the weight of his head, shoulders, and torso on his outstretched hands, and roll from his back to his side. • **Sitting** Your baby will be able to sit up without support, but only for a few seconds. • **Crawling** Your baby will be able to support the top half of his body on outstretched arms, and you may see the first signs of crawling when he bends his knees up below his body. Although he's moving into the crawling position he probably won't yet have got the hang of it, the result of which will be his rocking back and forth. • **Standing** By now he'll probably make jumping movements by bending and straightening his knees and hips whenever he's held in a standing position.

AT FOUR MONTHS

AT SIX MONTHS

MILESTONES: 7 MONTHS TO 1 YEAR

Month	Milestone
7	• **Mobility** Your baby's ability to sit will improve, although he may have to bend forward to balance himself. • **Manipulation** The finger and thumb become completely opposable. Your baby will hold an object in each hand and can transfer small objects from one hand to the other. • **Sitting** He will be able to sit alone but will be very unsteady. His back will still be rounded and he will have to support himself with both arms, probably by placing them in front of his body as a kind of brace. However, in this position he won't be able to move his hands in any way because he'll be relying on them for balance. Any movement will result in his tumbling over. • **Crawling** Probably within a month of the previous stage your baby will have begun to take his body's weight on one outstretched arm when he wants to. • **Standing** He may start a sort of dancing movement instead of jumping and he'll also start to hop from one foot to another. Babies quite often place one foot on top of the other then pull out the underneath foot and repeat the whole movement over and over again.
8	• **Manipulation** Your baby's dexterity will improve and he'll use a pincer movement to grasp small objects. • **Sitting** Your baby will be able to sit up completely unsupported and will be able to turn around. He will still be a bit unsteady so always make sure that he is surrounded by soft cushions in case he topples over. • **Crawling** Your baby will have begun to pull himself forward on the floor with his head held erect, making kicking movements. • **Standing** If he hadn't started his dancing movement instead of jumping, this will begin about now and he'll start hopping from one foot to another. He may also start standing on one of his feet, pulling out the lower foot and repeat it endlessly.

AT SEVEN MONTHS   AT EIGHT MONTHS

Month	Milestone
9	• **Mobility** Your baby will make determined efforts to crawl and may be able to support himself on his hands and knees. • **Manipulation** Dexterity continues to improve. He begins to poke his index finger into holes in toys. • **Sitting** Your baby's balance will be so well-developed that he'll be able to swing his torso to look around and will be able to reach forward without losing his balance. • **Standing** He can take his full weight on his feet, but can't balance yet. If you support your baby firmly underneath the arms, he will be able to take his weight on his legs and will try to move one foot in front of the other. Supported on your lap, he will try to take a step or two forward. At this stage, you must support your baby very securely to take most of the weight, because his balance is still primitive.
10	• **Mobility** Your baby will be able to crawl with both his arms and legs straight. He'll pull himself to a standing position. • **Manipulation** Your baby will be able to hold two objects in one hand. He'll be a little clumsy in releasing them. • **Standing** The muscle control of his knees and feet will have improved and he will begin to pull himself up to a standing position on furniture, despite the fact that his balance is still far from good.
11–12	• **Mobility** Your baby will probably be able to toddle when supported but will "cruise" along furniture by himself (*see p.188*). • **Manipulation** Your baby will be able to hold crayons, feed himself, and give and take objects. Coordination will improve daily.

AT TEN MONTHS   AT ONE YEAR

Physical milestones

There are key developmental milestones that each child goes through.

- All milestones are reached in the same order and your baby will usually not go on to another milestone before the previous one has been mastered.
- The rate of development is rarely constant. It goes through periods where it is very fast (growth spurts), then may slow down considerably. While development is continuous, many children can take huge steps forward in a developmental spurt, and then slow down for a while.
- A primitive reflex or movement has to be lost before a baby can acquire a particular skill. For example, your baby has to lose the primitive grasp reflex (see p.27) before he can acquire the skill to grasp an object purposefully.
- Development always proceeds from head to toe. The first milestone to be reached is control of the head; control of the body then progresses downward to the arms, then to the trunk, and finally to the legs.
- When your baby is very young his movements are usually jerky. As he gets older the movements become smoother and more precise.
- A generalized activity very often makes way for a specific activity. Your baby at six months old may be making apparently purposeless leg movements that resemble walking, although they are different from the movements that your one-year-old child will make when he eventually does start to walk.
- Development is measured not only in terms of what is done but how it is done.

In other words, as your baby develops so do his skills.

- The brain and the nervous system control movement and coordination, so your baby can only reach the milestones when the brain is ready. For instance, your baby will only learn to pick up a small object between his fingers and thumb when the nerve connections to the finger and thumb are fully developed.
- When a new skill is being mastered, your baby may appear to lose a previously learned skill. This is simply because he is concentrating on the new one. As soon as it is mastered, the old ones will reappear later.
- Milestones can be affected by your child's personality. Independent, determined children nearly always try out then and practice new movements more than others so it's not surprising that they master them earlier. A friendly, outgoing child often has a very strong desire to communicate with others and may develop speech earlier than other children. You can encourage both of these characteristics in your child by the way you behave toward him (see p.225).

Sitting

Bear in mind that before your baby is able to sit up he has to develop sufficient strength in his neck, shoulders, and trunk to control his head and keep his torso upright steadily. He also has to learn how to balance himself so that he doesn't topple over every time he tries to pick something up, or twist around to see what's behind him. Most babies don't achieve this skill before the age of about eight or nine months.

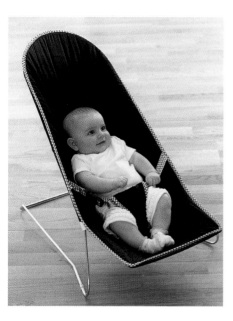

New view of the world
Propped up in a bouncing chair, your young baby will enjoy seeing what's going on around him and watching what you're doing.

- You can help your baby learn to sit up from the age of about two months by supporting his tummy and shoulders and by talking to him so that he momentarily tries to raise his head to look at you.
- By the time your baby is three months old he'll be able to control head, neck, and shoulders, but his back will need support because it's still rounded.
- At four months, he'll hold his head, neck, and most of his back straight, and all you have to do is hold on to his arms to keep his bottom steady and stop him from bending too much at the hips.

Helping your baby to sit up

Now that you know how a baby learns to control his head and to sit up, you can help your baby by playing similar sorts of physical games as those played in the first months of life. These games will introduce your baby to the use of the muscles he needs for grasping, pulling, and pushing.

Propping your baby up

From as early as six weeks your baby should be included in what's going on. Prop him up with cushions in his carriage or in a bouncing chair. With all of my children I found the bouncing chair the best way of propping them up. The chair

---

SAFETY TIPS WHEN PROPPING YOUR BABY UP

- At about five to six months old, most babies learn to roll over from their back to their sides and then from their front on to their back. Once your baby acquires this skill, he must never be left lying anywhere except on the floor, in a space that you've cleared of all hard or sharp objects. You should never leave your baby alone anywhere.
- When your baby is propped up, surround him with cushions. By the age of six months, when only his lower back needs support, he should still be padded around the bottom with cushions.

- Never leave him propped up on a chair or bed —he should always be on the floor.
- At about seven months old, when your baby will start to sit up, but topple over many times while attempting to do so. You must surround him with cushions or pillows so that he does not get hurt.
- Beware of leaving lightweight cribs, furniture (chairs, for example), or carriages within his reach. Your baby could easily pull them over by grabbing the side of something unstable and attempting to pull himself upright.

is soft and molds to the baby's rounded shape; it can be safely padded with soft pillows and cushions. But the baby must be safely strapped into it to prevent him from slipping, and his head must be supported with a cushion or pillow. Because the chair is so springy, it responds to your baby's jerky arm movements and kicking, so he is encouraged to try to make things happen for himself. Never put a bouncing chair on a table or other raised surface in case your baby's movements "bounce" it off.

SAFETY TIPS

- Never leave your baby alone.
- Remove furniture with sharp edges and corners.
- Remove anything breakable from a surface that is less than 3 feet (1 meter) from the floor.
- Don't leave wires trailing across the floor.
- Cover sockets with safety plugs.
- Make sure that there are no electric switches less than 3 feet (1 meter) from the floor.
- Put safety gates across doorways and at the bottom of the stairs.
- Try to keep the floor clear of small, sharp toys.
- Make sure all fireplaces are guarded.
- Don't leave any cloths hanging from tables, which a baby could reach up and pull.
- Make sure that all furniture is sturdy and fixtures are safely attached to the wall.
- Never leave anything hot on the table in the same room as your baby.
- Make sure that stair balusters are not wide enough apart for a child to squeeze through.
- Make sure that all cabinet doors are closed firmly and that the handles are out of a crawling baby's reach; if they aren't, lock them or seal them with masking tape.
- Make sure that all containers of poisonous substances are locked away or out of reach.

Crawling

Before your baby can crawl, he has to be able to get into the right position. He has to be able to straighten his body so that his legs are outstretched. He has to learn adequate control of his head and neck. He has to have the strength to push up on both of his arms so that his chest and head are clear of the floor.

It's difficult to specify at exactly what age a baby will start to crawl, so you should regard the times on pages 181–183 as stages more than ages. What's more, you shouldn't worry if your baby shows no interest in crawling. Some babies hate lying on their tummies and they are usually the ones who love seeing what's going on around them. They will probably leave crawling to a later stage; indeed, some babies never learn to crawl at all, but still walk perfectly.

Helping your baby crawl

While I am very much against teaching your baby to make orthodox crawling movements, you can encourage him to start moving forward from a lying or sitting position.

- The best possible way is for you to sit a few feet from your baby and to encourage him to come toward you, possibly using one of his favorite toys as an enticement.
- Help your baby whenever you think he needs it, particularly if he's getting tired and frustrated because his efforts are unsuccessful, and make sure that you always praise any efforts that he makes.
- As your baby becomes more adventurous, you can help him by placing a toy just out of reach so that he has to

use all his own resources, including his determination, to get it.

- Babies learn by mimicry from a very early age so once he starts trying to crawl it's not a bad idea for you to get down on the floor yourself and crawl with him.
- Slippery floors, although usually dangerous, can be encouraging for crawling babies because even the slightest movement is rewarded with forward motion.

Shuffling

To move forward your baby has to coordinate hand movements and knee movements. Initially he may find this difficult and may devise a unique shuffling movement to propel himself forward and backward. This can be anything from a sideways crab-like movement to a kind of shuffling on his bottom with one leg tucked underneath for leverage. It doesn't matter what style of movement your baby adopts—all are acceptable. The important thing is that he's mastered the art of moving; it's a great achievement, and he should receive a lot of praise for doing so. Don't discourage your baby from any odd movements he makes, but rather let him discover how to control and move his body in his own particular way.

The crawling baby

Once a baby has learned the knack of crawling (or shuffling), he can pick up speed very quickly, so he needs to be watched constantly. He'll also need a lot of room so that he can move around to the full extent of his capabilities. For this reason, and to encourage your child to be as curious and adventurous as possible,

try to give him plenty of clear floor space. Your crawling baby is getting stronger every day, so beware of anything that's rickety or fragile because he could break it very quickly.

Your baby will also get much dirtier now, and will put any object he finds on the floor straight into his mouth. Be sure that he doesn't go near pets' feeding bowls or litter pans. Your baby's knees will take quite a bashing, so put him into overalls or pants. Try to ensure that the floor is very smooth or covered with something soft to prevent abrasions. Your baby doesn't need shoes and should go shoeless until he's walking.

Standing

Because a baby's development progresses from head to toe, control over the muscles of the knees, lower legs, and feet is rarely achieved before ten or 11 months. It's only at this time that he's strong enough and has sufficient balance to take his whole weight on his feet and stand up.

Sitting down

Standing up is easy compared to sitting down, and it usually takes a baby three or four weeks to master getting back down to the floor again from a standing position. He usually does this by sitting down backward with a thump, or by carefully sliding his hands down the support until his bottom is on the floor.

Until he's mastered this, he'll probably just stand still and scream for your help. There may be a period of frustration for both of you before he learns to drop down into a sitting position. You can help your baby by lowering him down gently so that he gains confidence in the movement. You can also help by not getting angry when you have to do it over and over again.

"Cruising"

After your baby has gained sufficient confidence from pulling himself up into a standing position and getting back down on to the floor again it will probably be about four weeks before he starts "cruising." He does this by facing what he's holding onto and then gradually inching his hands along the support; he then brings the rest of his body into line with his hands by taking small sideways steps, one foot after the other. As he gets confident with this method, he'll hold on to the support at arm's length and will only use it for balance.

Once your baby has reached this stage, it's only a few weeks before he will let go of the support and move forward to the next piece of furniture. These first few steps are very unsteady. To increase the width of the base, he will keep his feet wide apart and balance by holding his

Cruising around the furniture
If you have low, sturdy furniture, your baby will be able to pull himself up against it and "walk" around it by supporting himself with his hands.

arms up and forward, slightly bent at the elbows. It is not until your baby has become proficient at walking that he will bring his feet closer together and let his hands drop to his sides.

HELPING YOUR BABY STAND

- Don't put socks or shoes on your baby's feet. He has much better grip and balance when his feet are bare. If your house is cold, put booties with suede soles on your baby's feet. Make sure that all your baby's clothing is loose so that movement isn't restricted.
- All the furniture in the room should be heavy, firm, and stable so that there's no risk of it toppling on the baby as he holds onto it.
- Resist the temptation to hurry your baby with standing or walking. He'll do it in his own good time and nothing you do can rush the process.

- Don't play tricks on your baby by suddenly removing your support. This will give your baby a bad fright and could damage his trust in you, because until that moment you were the one thing he could rely on.
- Don't start to use sleeping bags for the first time now—your baby will try to stand and will fall. If he's used to one it's all right to continue with it.
- Make sure that all wires and cords are tucked away or firmly tacked down. He may start by cruising around furniture, but a cord may seem an ideal "hold" once he's on the move.

General development 1 to 2 years

During the second year, your baby's body grows in length, loses its rather plump, pudgy appearance, becomes firmer, stronger, and more muscular, and starts to take on adult proportions. His balance and coordination will have improved and fine movements are mastered.

Size and weight vary very much from one child to another, just as they do from adult to adult. Your child's weight gain will be proportional to your child's size, so small children will gain less weight, and less quickly, than large children.

Physical milestones

At 13 to 15 months Your baby should be able to stand by himself and take one or two steps to reach a support. However, he won't be able to get up from the sitting to the standing position without support (from you or by holding onto furniture).

At 15 to 18 months Your baby will be able to raise himself to the standing position unaided. He will probably begin to walk without any support in the early position of feet wide apart and elbows high. Practice more leg movements with your baby, using a large soft ball that he can try to kick to you. This also helps his balance.

At 18 to 20 months Walking will become steadier and his arms will drop down to his side. Your toddler will almost certainly want to walk upstairs.

At 21 to 24 months Your toddler will be able to maintain his balance while he bends over to pick something up and will not fall over. Dance with him to help him practice a wide range of movements.

Manipulation milestones

At 12 months Your baby will have mastered the adult grip, which is a fine movement achieved by bringing the finger and thumb together. If you ask your baby for something, he will give it to you, and will be able to roll a ball across the floor.

At 13 to 15 months Your baby will be able to hold two small objects in one hand, he will be able to put one block on top of another, and may try to make marks with a pencil. When it is time to be undressed, he may start taking off his shoes.

At 18 months Your baby can build a tower of blocks, possibly three or four blocks high. He will be more skilled at manipulating food with a spoon. If you show him how, he'll pull down a zipper.

At 2 years Your baby will have learned turning and screwing movements with his hands so he'll be able to open a door with the doorknob and may be able to unscrew a loose lid. He'll enjoy washing his hands.

Turning pages
By the time he is about 18 months, your baby will be able to turn the pages of a book.

Walking 1 to 2 years

There is no right age for your baby to start to walk. Your baby's first unsupported steps will probably occur sometime between nine and 15 months, but there's a wide variation on either side of these figures. The reason for this is not known, although very often there's a family history of early or late walking. Despite the very wide variation in the age at which babies learn to walk, they all have to pass through the same well defined stages of development before they can walk with confidence and good balance.

Babies can stay for a variable length of time in each phase and you should never make the mistake of trying to push your baby too hard to move from one phase to the next. You will give the greatest help if you are there with encouraging words so that your baby doesn't lose heart. Learning to walk is one of the most difficult things he'll ever have to do, so make your baby proud of his achievements.

Stages of walking

1 Your baby may have started cruising around the furniture before he reached the age of one. He'll slide both hands along the support and bring his feet along to align with the rest of his body. Balance will be a problem.

2 He'll still cruise, but he'll stand further away from the furniture and take more of his weight on his feet. He'll start to move one hand over the other instead of sliding them together and, as he becomes more confident, will start to move his hands and feet together. He has the confidence and the balance to take all his weight briefly on one foot.

3 Your baby will enjoy the independence of moving around rooms using any support he can, and the next stage will be the negotiation of the space between two supports. He will only do this if he can hold on to both supports at once. At this stage he still has to feel securely

HELPING YOUR CHILD WALK

- Arrange the furniture around the room so that he can go down one side, across, and up the other.
- Initially, spaces between furniture should be no bigger than the width of your baby's arms so that he can hang on to something with one hand and stretch out the other to reach the next support easily. If the gaps are too big, your baby won't be able to reach the support that will enable him to cross the space.
- While your baby is learning to walk, make sure that the floors aren't slippery—one bad bang may keep him from walking for several weeks.

- Make sure the room is baby-proofed, with no cords or objects that can be pulled over.
- He doesn't need shoes or socks; bare feet are safer not only because there'll be no risk of malformed feet but also because he'll be able to grip well and get used to the sensation of weight.
- A useful aid to complement cruising and your baby's first steps is a pushing toy or cart. Make sure it has a stable wide base so it won't topple over. Don't use a baby walker.
- Always stay nearby when your baby is taking his first steps.

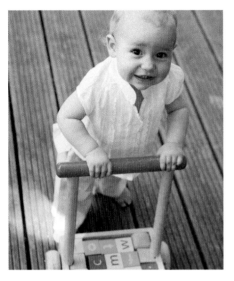

Walking toys
Your toddler's mobility and independence will be greatly enhanced by sturdy, wheeled, walking toys such as this one.

supported, and will only let go of one support when he's holding firmly on to the other.

4 Your baby will start to cross spaces that are wider than an arm's span. While still holding on to one support with one hand, he will move into the center of the gap and, having achieved balance, will release one support and take a step toward the next one, making a grab for it with both hands.

5 Your baby will begin to "toddle." He will manage to stagger a couple of paces to reach the second support.

6 Your baby will launch himself into an open space and take several unsupported steps with confidence. He may only take half a dozen steps before losing his balance and sitting down with a thud. However, he sets off to reach a goal and waddles bowleggedly to get to it.

SAFETY TIPS

- Remember that once your toddler can walk he'll also be able to climb, so install childproofing devices on all windows: either bars or special fasteners that allow the window to be opened only a few inches.
- Keep possible hiding places like cabinets or chests securely locked so that your baby can't disappear and get locked in.
- Door locks must be out of reach.
- Do not allow your unsupervised child into a backyard with access to the street. Teach the street-training drill as soon as possible.
- Teach your toddler how to negotiate stairs properly, by sitting on the top stair, putting his legs down to the one below, and then following with his hands.
- Keep all the handles of pans turned away from the front of the stove.
- Never leave anything hot lying where your toddler can reach it. Keep it out of his reach until it is absolutely cold.
- Glass doors should never be so clean that your toddler bumps into them. Put colored paper or stickers on the glass to make them visible.
- Keep all medicine in a medicine chest, high up and always locked. Never carry medicine around in your purse.
- Move cleaning products out of reach or store them in a locked cabinet.
- Don't put rugs on polished floors unless they are backed with double-sided tape or carpet grip to stop them from slipping.
- Don't let your child near anything that is small enough to be swallowed or pushed up his nose or into his ear.
- Keep all sharp instruments, including kitchen equipment, out of your child's reach.
- Never leave sewing materials or tools around.
- Never leave your child alone near water.

Your toddling child

When your baby first starts to toddle, he will have very little control over his movements. However, by about 19 months, he'll be able to walk backward as well as forward and may even have mastered running. Once he can run, he'll be able to jump.

By two years old, he'll be able to veer and swerve while he's running and will be able to glance over his shoulder without losing balance. He will be able to stop suddenly without toppling over and will have sufficient balance to be able to bend down to pick something up without having to sit down first. If you encourage him, he'll be able to kick a ball, although it will be a dragging kind of kick because he can't maintain his balance on one leg for very long.

Your toddler will want, very naturally, to race around as much as possible, but outdoors you'll have to be careful. He'll have no road sense yet so you'll either have to hold his hand or use a harness.

Starting to toddle
When your baby first starts to toddle she'll only be able to travel in one direction and will be incapable of swerving or stopping once she's gotten up speed.

I believe that a harness is the most satisfactory solution for both of you: it hurts neither your arm nor your toddler's arm (like a wrist strap might) and will give him far greater freedom than he would have holding your hand. Although your toddler's strength will increase during this year, don't expect him to walk much further than a couple of hundred yards at a time. If you're in a hurry, or can't bear the idea of constant stops and starts to look at things, take a stroller for him to sit in when he gets tired.

If your baby has a setback in the development of walking, don't worry. He's learning so much at the moment, it's understandable that he may slow down in one aspect of his development in order to concentrate on another. He may also suffer lapses after an illness. Just relax and let your baby develop at his own pace.

General development 2 to 3 years

By your child's third year, his rate of growth and development will have slowed down. He will have almost complete control over his body, and many movements will have become automatic—he'll no longer have to concentrate or make an effort to do things requiring fine coordination or physical maneuvering. He will have the coordination to build a tower of blocks, he will try to get dressed and undressed, and he may even manage to undo buttons.

Physical milestones

At two years Your child will be able to go up and down stairs alone, but he'll put two feet on each step before moving on to the next. He'll kick a ball successfully without falling over.

At two and a half years He'll be able to walk on tiptoe, and jump in the air, and on and off objects. However, he won't be able to stand on one foot yet.

At three years He'll walk upstairs with a foot on each step but will have to put both feet on the same stair coming down; he'll jump off the bottom step. He'll be able to stand for a few seconds on one foot but he won't be able to skip yet.

Manipulation milestones

At two years He'll put on his own gloves, socks, and shoes successfully. He'll manage to rotate his elbow accurately so that he can turn a door handle or unscrew a lid. He'll begin to draw pictures with pencils and crayons.

At two and a half years He'll be able to take off his pants and underpants by himself. He'll be able to thread big beads onto a string and will be able to fasten large, easily placed buttons.

At three years He'll be able to dress and undress himself completely as long as all the fastenings are within his reach; he'll handle a Velcro fastening on his shoes and possibly even the buckle on his shoes. He'll be able to hold a pencil well enough to draw and color quite accurately now, and he may also begin to master the difficult skill of using scissors.

Learning pencil control
He will be able to hold a pencil and will enjoy scribbling on paper. Give him washable felt pens since he won't necessarily confine his work to the paper.

Coordination birth to 1 year

During the first six weeks, your baby's hands will be held in fists, although they'll probably open and close when he cries. By about eight weeks, your baby's hands will be open more often, and the grasp reflex (*see p.27*) will be replaced by a voluntary movement on your baby's part. Some parents worry at this stage because their baby doesn't hold on to objects as tightly as before. Don't worry—your baby is simply learning a new skill that he will perfect within a couple of months.

Up to this age, he won't have tried to coordinate the movements of fingers and hands. Instead, he'll spend a great deal of time discovering how they look, feel, and move. He'll hold them open most of the time and will move his fingers and watch them closely. It's as though he's assessing his powers before starting to use them.

Playing with his feet
As your baby develops coordination, he will try to grab everything. He will play with his feet and toys put within his grasp, and everything goes into his mouth.

Developing control

Between four and five months old he'll have voluntary control over reaching—he'll probably move both arms toward an object and grasp it between his hands. At about six months old, your baby will try to hold an object, either between his hands or in one hand, by squeezing it between the palm and fingers. He has no fine control yet.

However, he'll be able to differentiate between large and small objects and will open his hand accordingly. He'll love the feel of things, so provide lots of different textures to clutch and handle, as well as different shapes. When he's lying down, he'll probably reach out, grab a foot, and put it in his mouth. He won't know exactly what to do with all objects, so if you offer a cube he may hold on to it, but if you offer a second one, he'll drop the first one without thinking. About this time, he'll start to explore how he can use his hands in feeding. Hand–eye coordination will be developed enough for your baby to pick up finger foods and start feeding himself, but it will not be accurate.

Learning how to let go

At about eight months old your baby will hold something out to you but will not yet have learned how to let it go and give it to you. He will not reach this milestone until he's about a year old, when dropping things deliberately from his highchair or stroller becomes a very entertaining game. From now on your baby's ability to grasp becomes more and more refined. By the

HAND–EYE COORDINATION

Month	Skill	How to help
Up to 2	Until he is about eight weeks old your baby will not have learned to use his hands. He'll be learning to focus; the maximum distance at which he'll be able to focus will be about 8–10 inches (20–25 centimeters).	Your baby will try to focus on anything that is moving, for instance a colorful mobile. However, your face will be the most interesting object in his life, so make sure he sees it often and close. Hang interesting objects in his line of sight, no further than 10 inches (25 centimeters) away.
2–2½	Your baby will have opened his hands and will watch them with fascination. Focusing distance is not much more than 12 inches (30 centimeters) so he'll bring hands and fingers up to his face so he can watch them moving.	As soon as your baby's hands are open, they are ready to have things put into them. The most interesting toys are the ones that make a noise, like a rattle. They are also useful because your baby starts to make a connection between what his hands are doing, what his eyes are seeing, and what he can hear.
2½–3	Your baby will watch his hands very carefully and with a lot of concentration. When he does this you'll know that he has made the connection between seeing and doing. At about this age your baby may make a clumsy movement with either hand to get near an object.	Your baby is learning to judge distances and to move his hands to where his eyes think something interesting is happening. Put a string above his crib or carriage with lots of interesting objects hanging from it. Let them swing freely so that your baby can reach up and touch them and see them move as a result of his action.
3–4	Your baby will touch everything in sight, and will be learning how to measure distances using his hands and eyes. He'll look at an object and then confirm the distance by trying to reach it. Instead of using an open hand, he will try to make a fist before he connects with it.	Your baby will now be too old for swinging things. If something goes out of reach it will only frustrate him because he wants to grasp it. Instead of having objects dangling from a string, secure them to the sides of the crib. You can hold out an object so that he can try to get hold of it. Always wait until he's touched it before handing it over.
4–6	Your baby's hand–eye coordination will be developing rapidly, so he judges distance well and his eyes will be mature enough to focus on objects at any distance. He will also be learning to grasp, so when he reaches out and touches an object he'll open his fingers and curl them around whatever he wants to hold.	Your baby really needs lots of practice at reaching out and grasping things; he'll also have a great deal of fun doing it. You can encourage him to do this by holding out the most interesting objects you can find, for example, anything that makes a noise or is an interesting shape. It could be a plastic bottle, a ball of wool, or car keys.

time he is nine months old, he will have stopped holding an object in the palm of his hand and will hold it instead between his thumb and the side of his index finger, and once he's one year old he'll be able to pick up a small object between the tips of his finger and thumb, and will usually point at it with his index finger before picking it up. He'll be able to pass an object from one hand to another, and hold two objects, one in each hand, at once.

Manipulation

Between eight and ten months, your baby really learns to manipulate. He squeezes things, slaps, slides, pokes, rubs, scrapes, and bangs them. He explores every new substance with his hands, including food, and will mix, smear, and splash anything liquid or runny. Most objects find their way to his mouth, whether they're feet, fingers, plastic lids, or toys.

As he gets more skilled at manipulation the fascination with putting things in his mouth begins to wane, and he begins to play games like pat-a-cake. He'll also have developed the social skill of being able to wave goodbye.

Right- and left-handedness

If both you and your partner are left-handed, there's a one in three chance that your children will be left-handed; the chances of this happening with two right-handed parents is one in ten. There is no natural law that states that one hand is

superior to the other, so it should never bother you if your child is left-handed.

Your child has no control over which of his hands is dominant; it is decided by the developing brain. Think of the brain as two linked halves, each of which controls different activities. One of these sides becomes dominant as your baby's brain develops. If the left side dominates, the baby is right-handed, and vice versa.

In the first months your baby may seem to have no preferences, but in fact most newborns turn their heads more to the right than to the left. As your baby's coordination improves, you may find that he starts to use one hand more than the other. Don't be worried if he doesn't do this; a baby will develop at his own speed.

Never, ever, try to dissuade your baby from being left-handed. You could risk causing psychological side effects like stuttering as well as reading and writing difficulties by altering what your baby's brain naturally wants to do.

Children love to copy
Sit and draw with your baby; he may not have enough coordination to draw for himself, but he'll quickly get the idea from watching you.

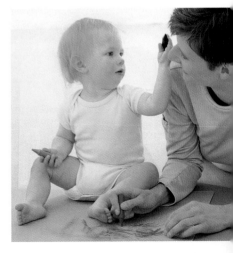

Coordination 1 to 3 years

By the time he's a year old, he'll be able to pick up something very small, like a button, between thumb and forefinger. If you take a pencil or crayon and make marks on a piece of paper, your child will take the pencil and try to imitate your marks.

By about 13 months your baby will have learned to hold more than one object in his hand. His coordination will also be improving so if you show him how to build a tower of blocks he'll follow your example, putting one block on top of another. He'll start to remove items of clothing (see p.46), and will love pulling a toy around on a string, hammering pegs through holes, and fitting different shapes into the appropriate openings. He'll be able to feed himself without any help and without making too much mess by the time he's 15 months old. He will attempt to brush his hair if shown how and will be eager to help you around the house.

New accomplishments

By the time he is about 18 months old, your baby will be able to build a tower of blocks, four or five high, and turn over the pages of a book, probably two or three pages at a time. By the time your child is two years old his hands will be very well coordinated and he'll manage the complex movement of twisting something around in his hands so he can open a door by turning the doorknob and unscrew a loose cap from a jar. Washing and drying the hands will be a favorite pastime. Two-year-olds usually start to make their first attempts to dress and undress themselves.

They can usually manage things like putting on their shoes but probably need help with their socks.

Always remember that your child will proceed at his own pace and that he cannot develop muscular coordination faster than his brain and nervous system are developing. No two children develop at the same rate. Don't make the mistake of expecting more from your child than he is capable of. He has a tremendous desire to please, and if you constantly set your goals higher than he's naturally capable of reaching he will feel demoralized because he has let you down. Worse still, he may become resentful and frustrated if he aspires to do things that are more complicated than his body allows. Your role is to help and encourage your child, not to set unachievable goals.

Skills to master

By the time your child is three years old, he'll probably be cabable of the following:

- Building a tower of blocks, up to eight or nine blocks high.
- He'll continue to dress and undress himself with increasing skill.
- He'll undo buttons in easy reach but may not be able to button them.
- He will help with any household task or chore that you suggest and will love playing games that imitate the kind of jobs that you do, whether it's fixing something or washing the dishes.
- He'll be capable of carrying plates and dishes to the table, and will be a much more cooperative member of the family.

How to improve coordination

Between the ages of two and three, your child is a great experimenter, so feed this curiosity by opening up his world and planning new discoveries. This is the age when children find out about (and understand) the force of gravity—something always falls down; anything that is round will roll but something that is square will not; liquids flow and have no shape but take up the shape of their container. Clay and dough can be squeezed and made into different shapes.

These discoveries can only be made if your child's coordination, not just of the hand and the eye, but also of the body and the limbs, develops and matures. Toys that demand good coordination will help your child develop it. You can help him improve balance simply by encouraging him to walk along narrow steps. Always stay nearby;

otherwise, your child could lose his confidence and fall. You can improve his ball sense by throwing and catching with him, initially using something large and soft like a beach ball.

Encouraging adventurousness

Once your child becomes mobile, it is better to encourage a spirit of adventure than to be over-protective. Of course your child will fall a few times—that is inevitable—but that's better than having a child who has no sense of physical freedom or confidence. If you don't you would be doing your child a disservice, because for the next seven or eight years most of his pleasures will be derived from physical activities. If he can't move with the same pace and accuracy as other children, he may be left out of many enjoyable activities by his friends.

An overprotective parent is one who insists on holding the child's hand if he wants to climb along the edge of a low wall. Conversely, a parent who encourages physical activity will be one who introduces a child to balancing on a fairly narrow surface, practicing at home on a plank supported by stacks of magazines.

One of the best ways of encouraging activity in your child is to join in and do it yourself. You are the best person to introduce your child to new physical activities. Just by imitating your physical movements, he will be learning new skills, without either of you knowing it.

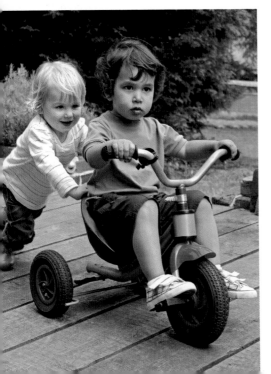

Adventurous spirit
Exercise is vital for your child so encourage him in active play whenever your can. He'll have lots of fun with a wheeled toy such as a tricycle.

Vision birth to 1 year

People used to think that newborn babies could not see. It was thought that since they could not focus very well, their visual world did not need to be stimulating and could even be neglected. We now know that this is far from the truth. A newborn baby can see. The only difference between a newborn baby and an older one with mature eyesight is that the newborn baby cannot see as much, as easily, or as well. In other words, your newborn baby sees in a limited way, and you have to fit the visual world into a range he can perceive.

Your baby's visual powers will not be fully developed until he's between three and six months old. He won't be able to focus on anything more than 10 inches (25 centimeters) from his face. As his eye muscles become stronger and he develops binocular vision, his acuity greatly improves.

Even though your newborn baby's eyesight is limited, his eyes are very sensitive to two things: the human face, and anything that moves. If you bring your face to within 8 inches (20 centimeters) of your baby's, you'll notice his eyes move and his expression change. Even a baby only a few hours old can bring both eyes together on an object (convergence) and follow it if it moves. As he gets older, his whole body may react with excited jerking movements when your face comes into focus.

Color vision

When your baby is born, the cells in the retina of the eye that see colors are not fully developed, so your newborn baby only sees the world in muted shades.

The first colors that your baby detects are red and blue, then green and yellow. For the first few months of life your baby can only see the brightest of colors, so make sure that you have brightly colored objects around him. Babies are also attracted to graphic black-and-white pictures or objects.

Three-dimensional vision

Because your baby can only focus on objects that are closer than 10 inches (25 centimeters) from his face, the world appears flat and many details are not seen. However, even at two weeks a baby will automatically raise a hand to protect himself from something moving toward him quickly. It is necessary for your baby to have three-dimensional vision before he becomes mobile. He probably won't crawl until he sees and understands the third dimension. A complete, three-dimensional picture of the world is not usually built up until your baby is about four months old, and may not be perfect until six months old.

Checking eyesight

During the first few months of your baby's life, you are the best person to check his sight, although you shouldn't become obsessive about it. By the age of four months even an inattentive or lazy baby should focus on a brightly colored object held 8–10 inches (20–25 centimeters) from his face, especially if it makes a noise, like a rattle, and especially if it is moved. One of the most joyful sights in your child's life is your face, and he should also react to

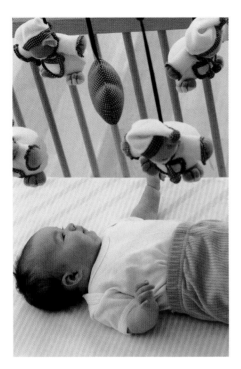

Something to watch
Your young baby is attracted to moving objects. String some brightly colored shapes or a special mobile over her crib and she will love to watch them.

your smile and the bobbing movement of your head as you talk by around four months or so. If he isn't, don't be too concerned but do mention it to your pediatrician at your next visit.

Stimulating your baby's eyesight

You can stimulate your baby's eyesight in many different ways.

- Put a large photograph of your face (or any face cut out of a magazine) at the side of your baby's crib so that he can practice focusing on one of his favorite objects—the human face. On the other side of the crib firmly attach a mirror so that he can look at his own face and see it moving when he wriggles near it.
- Put very simple brightly colored pictures around the rest of the crib within the baby's range of vision (but no more than 10 inches/25 centimeters away for the first month).
- Put a mobile over the crib. This doesn't have to be an expensive item. It can be a couple of soft toys or a few household objects hung on a coat hanger, or on a wooden pole attached to the crib.
- String some interesting objects on elastic across the hinges of the carriage hood so that your baby can watch them.
- If your baby's crib is near the wall, you can use toys with rubber suction pads to stick out from the wall between the bars of the crib for your child to watch and focus on.
- As your child gets older, it is important that toys move and make a noise, so dangle soft, light objects on strings so that they swing when your baby swipes at them. Anything that jingles, like a rattle or a toy with bells, is fun.
- In the car, stick toys onto the back of the seat. You can also hang them from the side windows or the roof, as long as they don't dangerously cut your visibility.
- Your baby's never too young to go to museums or art galleries with you. If he's in a backpack, he'll be able to look at exactly the same things as you.
- When you and your baby are outside in the yard, suspend some toys or mobiles from a tree branch or from a washing line. Even clothes drying on the line are fun to watch as they blow in the wind.

Vision 1 to 3 years

Around one year, your child begins to see and rapidly follow moving objects, and his vision now is about as good as it ever will be in adult life.

The main changes that occur during your child's formative years have to do with the ability to interpret what he sees so that he can use it to express ideas in words, pictures, and movements. In other words, it is the connections in the brain between the eyes, the tongue, the pen, the brush, the intellectual thought, the hand and the rest of the body that mature, not the ability to see per se. As with other aspects of your child's growth you should try to encourage the development in his eye/brain and eye/body connections so that he can reach his full potential. You can do this by providing stimulating ideas, plenty of books, interesting toys, and a varied range of activities.

Look out for changes

I don't think regular eye checkups are necessary in a child who is developing normally, but you should be on the lookout for any changes in the appearance of your child's eyes—that is, a lazy eye, a drooping eyelid, or a squint. Be responsive to signs that your child can't see clearly, for example, bumping into furniture or not being able to follow the trajectory of a ball that's thrown to him. Seek medical advice at once; don't wait to see if an abnormality clears up. Like a disused limb, a disused eye deteriorates rapidly.

Teeth birth to 1 year

There is no correct time for your baby to cut his first tooth. Some babies are born with a tooth (although this is rare), and yet it is still within the normal range to have none at 12 months old. It would therefore be misleading to give dates when you should expect your child to cut certain teeth, although it is possible to make a generalization about the order in which teeth erupt.

As a general rule, teething starts at about six months old, after which many teeth appear up to the end of your baby's first year. The order in which the teeth come very rarely differs between children (*see overleaf*).

Teething

If you are on the lookout, you will probably notice your baby's first tooth as it starts to push its way through the gum and form a small, pale bump. The only normal symptoms of teething are fretfulness and dribbling. You should never blame any other symptoms on cutting a tooth; it is a myth that teething can cause fever, diarrhea, vomiting, convulsions, rashes, or loss of appetite. Don't make the mistake of attributing any illness to teething; if you're at all worried get medical advice immediately. No parent likes to see their child in discomfort, so I would suggest doing the following to help relieve any pain or discomfort:

- Offer your baby something firm to chew on like a cooled teething ring. Your baby may find sucking painful, so give drinks from a cup instead.
- Try just gently rubbing your child's gums with your own little finger—this can help as much as anything. Certainly your attention and concern about his pain will bring him comfort.
- Avoid taking your child out in a cold wind, which always seems to make the pain of teething worse. When you go out in the winter, try to cover most of your child's face and head with a warm hat or a hood and put a scarf around his neck and chin.
- Don't put teething gels containing local anesthetics on his gums. They only have a transient effect, and local anesthetics can cause allergies.
- Don't use over-the-counter teething remedies. Your baby has many teeth to cut, and if you use anything regularly you will be exposing your baby to a large amount of medication, much of which may be unnecessary and all of which may be accompanied by side effects.
- Be careful if you use the water-filled teething rings that can be frozen if placed in the freezer. Careless use of these teething rings has been known to cause frostbite in babies. These rings can be used quite safely to cool down the mouth if they are kept in the refrigerator instead of the freezer.
- Avoid the frequent use of aceominophen. It is useful, but should not be given with any regularity except under doctor's orders. If you need it to soothe your fretful baby for more than two doses, then you should consult your pediatrician or nurse practitioner.

HOW THE TEETH COME IN

The first to erupt are usually the lower front incisors, then the two upper incisors. The two upper lateral incisors come next, followed by the lower ones. After this, the first upper molars erupt and then the first lower molars. The upper canines come in next, one on each side, followed by the lower ones. The second molars erupt first in the lower jaw, and then in the upper jaw.

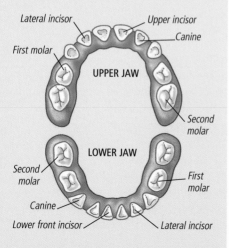

Lateral incisor
Upper incisor
Canine
First molar
UPPER JAW
Second molar
LOWER JAW
Second molar
First molar
Canine
Lower front incisor
Lateral incisor

Caring for teeth

When your baby has several teeth, you can start good habits early by encouraging him with a game of tooth brushing. First of all, let your child watch you so that he can see how brushing should be done. Then just offer a soft toothbrush as something to play with. He will almost certainly want to do what he has just seen you do and will try to make the same kind of movements by putting the brush into his mouth and moving it to and fro. Cleaning the teeth

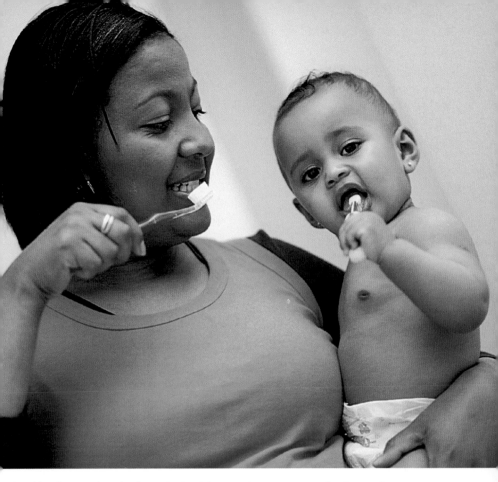

shouldn't be a serious business; it should be playful. You are teaching your child to like and want to look after his teeth, so you should avoid being censorious and make it a big laugh instead of a chore.

To actually get the teeth clean, take a piece of gauze with some nonfluoride toothpaste on it and gently rub it across the gums and any teeth that your baby has. It's important to clean the baby's gums even if there are no teeth because this keeps the mouth free of the bacteria that cause plaque. It also provides a good environment for milk teeth and, later, permanent teeth to grow into. The easiest position to clean his teeth and gums will

First attempts at cleaning teeth
Encourage your baby to want to brush his teeth from an early age. At first give him a toothbrush to play with whenever you are brushing your own teeth.

probably be with him on your lap, with his mouth tilted up toward you.

For infants and toddlers under the age of three, always use a special baby toothpaste that does not contain flouride. Your baby may want to eat the toothpaste, but you should try to dissuade him. Clean the teeth once if not twice a day and always after he's been given any medicine, which are often sweet and sticky to make them more palatable.

Fighting tooth decay

The three most important factors in the care of your baby's teeth are diet and the absence of sugar, good dental hygiene, and regular checkups.

One of the best ways to take care of your baby's teeth as soon as he has them is to see that his diet does not contain sugary foods such as candy, chocolates, cakes, cookies, and very sweet drinks. Sugar, whether its white or brown, is the arch-villain in tooth decay. No child needs sugar. It is not necessary for health and you will be doing your child a favor if you don't encourage a sweet tooth, not only for his teeth but also for his weight.

Never leave a bottle containing milk or a sweet drink lying around for your baby to suck on. His teeth will be constantly bathed in a sugary fluid, which will encourage decay. Give him a pacifier if he wants to suck something.

Make sure that your baby's diet contains plenty of calcium and vitamin D, which are essential for the healthy formation of the permanent teeth already growing in your baby's jawbones. Foods that are rich in both of these nutrients are dairy products and fish; oily fish such as salmon, herring and sardines are particularly good.

Many people think that dental hygiene isn't important until your child has his permanent teeth. This is not true, so follow a sensible cleaning program for your child's teeth from the beginning and, as soon as he's about two, start taking him for regular dental checkups.

Teeth 1 to 3 years

At one time it was thought that milk teeth were not very important, but we now know that it is important to look after them. First of all, they guide in the adult teeth so that they grow in the correct position, and second, if the primary teeth are lost through decay, the bone behind the teeth can be affected, eroding the support the adult teeth need. Your baby will be teething for most of the second year, so be prepared for the molars to be a bit upsetting. The first molars are usually cut between 12 and 15 months, when the upper molars appear, followed by the lower ones. The second molars appear between 20 and 24 months, in the lower jaw first and then in the upper jaw. In general, the later teeth are cut, the less trouble they cause.

Once your child has all his teeth, give him plenty of chewy foods, particularly fresh fruit and raw vegetables to encourage the development of strong jaw muscles. As it happens, this kind of food also has a cleansing effect, as the fibers within them are shredded by the teeth. Take your child for regular checkups.

Dental hygiene and care

The mineral fluoride has been proven to improve dental health and to reduce tooth decay. All water contains some fluoride but in most states fluoride is added to drinking water. Dentists also recommend using

Gaining independence
Get your child into a tooth-brushing routine, which should include always cleaning her teeth in the morning and before going to sleep at night.

fluoride toothpastes, but when water has added fluoride children under seven may be advised to use toothpaste containing lower levels of fluoride to avoid taking in too much (an excess could cause fluorosis, which damages the teeth). Check with your dentist. He or she may even recommend supplements, but these should only be given under dental supervision.

Help toddlers with tooth brushing

Until your child has reached the age of about six or seven he won't be capable of cleaning his own teeth thoroughly, so you'll need to help him. He may object to this at first, and clamp his jaws firmly shut. The best way around this is to make it into a game using a disclosing tablet. These expose plaque as a dense area of color, which can be brushed off.

Dentists generally agree that it doesn't matter how a toothbrush is used, as long as it removes plaque. At one time we were encouraged to brush the top teeth downward and the bottom ones upward so that the gum margins were protected. The best method, especially for children who don't have a great deal of coordination, is small circular movements

on all surfaces of the teeth. Make sure that the bristles have rounded tips and aren't too hard. Stifff bristles may cause the gums to bleed, then recede, and the teeth to eventually become loose.

Always encourage your child to have a regular tooth-brushing routine, morning and evening. Most children will put up a fight if they have to brush their teeth every time they have a sweet drink or a cookie, but you could help by giving them a piece of cheese at the end of every meal. This makes the saliva alkaline and counteracts the sugary acid that erodes the enamel of the teeth and causes cavities.

VISITING THE DENTIST

Take your child for his first dental check-up before his third birthday, and make sure that this visit is as relaxed and pleasant as possible. Take your child for this visit when his teeth are healthy rather than waiting for signs of problems.

Get your child used to the sight of the instruments and the smell of the surroundings by taking him with you when you go for your own checkup. If he can be trusted, and if your dentist has no objections, sit the child on your lap and let him watch while the dentist examines you. He'll no doubt be fascinated and will be delighted to copy your example. Just before your child's visit, play a game of going to the dentist and look into each other's mouths. Then, when you actually get to the office, prearrange for the dentist to look at your mouth before he looks at your child's.

12 Intellectual development

Your baby is the most responsive and rewarding pupil you will ever meet. She wants to do more things, explore more areas, and widen her horizons more than anyone else you know. She also wants to please you, and the combination of these qualities gives her an appetite for learning that should thrill you. One of the most important things to remember is that she is never too young to learn, though you'll have to tailor the way you introduce her to new experiences or the ways you try to teach her. Don't set her tasks that are beyond her capabilities, as this will only lead to frustration. Guide her in all things, but never try to force her.

Learning birth to 1 year

Whatever you do, don't waste the first crucial six weeks of your baby's life. Many people still think that because a baby isn't making sounds and moving very much, she can't respond to what is happening around her and she can't learn. We know this to be entirely incorrect. Your baby's emotional and intellectual development during the first weeks of life is moving at exactly the same rate as every other kind of her development, from her size and weight to her ability to coordinate.

I believe that, initially, the most important person in a baby's life is the one who most consistently looks after her. In the majority of cases this is the mother. You are her most important teacher. As adults, we learn the most important and the most memorable lessons of our lives from people we like and with whom we

have a good rapport. If there is a special feeling of closeness, common ground, empathy, and understanding with the teacher, then the lessons can be even more salutary and lasting. Exactly the same applies to your baby. All her learning will be made easier if she establishes strong bonds with you, her teacher, very early in life. A close runner-up to you is your partner. Your partner is your baby's next best friend; he should form a strong relationship with your baby as early as possible and be involved in as much of the "teaching" as you are.

The teaching you give your child is not teaching in a formal sense; there are no specific rules and no particular targets that your child has to reach. You should "teach" your baby by making the world interesting for her. Introduce her to new

The five senses
Your baby has five senses and she wants to learn through all of them. She is eager and keen to meet new sights, sounds, smells, tastes, and touches.

WHAT YOUR BABY UNDERSTANDS

Newborn baby Your baby will concentrate on your face if you bring it close to her, and she can distinguish your voice from other people's. When she hears your voice her eyes will move in the direction of your face and she will try to follow it if you move your face close to her. She can recognize your face if you place it about 8–10 inches (20–25 centimeters) away from the time she's 36 hours old.

Four weeks If your face is close enough for her to focus on, she'll watch you while you are talking and she'll mimic your talking by opening and closing her mouth. She may stop crying when you pick her up because she knows you are a source of comfort. She imitates the movements of your face: she can use the right muscles to smile and grimace.

Six weeks She will smile back at you and her eyes will follow a moving toy.

Eight weeks If you hold something brightly colored above her head, she will take a few seconds to focus on it and will then follow it as you move it from side to side.

Three months She will immediately see a toy held above her. She will smile when you speak and will squeal and gurgle with pleasure. There will be obvious signs of curiosity and interest in what is going on around her.

Four months At feeding times, she will show signs of excitement. She will laugh and chuckle when played with. She will love being propped up because she'll be able to see what is going on; she will turn her head in the direction of sounds.

Five months She'll be aware of strange situations and can express fear, disgust, and anger.

Six months Your baby will become very interested in mirrors and in seeing herself in one.

Eight months She will know her name and will understand the word "No." She will probably have developed little sound signals like a cough to attract your attention when she reaches out for something she wants. She'll probably want to feed herself at around this time.

Nine months She'll show a will of her own and may stop you when you try to wash her face. She will concentrate very hard on toys and games and will even turn a toy over in her hand so that she can examine it carefully. When an object is hidden under a cloth, she'll lift the cloth up to see the object.

Ten months She'll probably be able to clap her hands and wave bye-bye. She'll show that she understands a small number of words, and very short, simple statements.

Eleven months She'll know, and will enjoy, simple games like "Peek-a-boo." Her other favorite game will be dropping things and having you pick them up. She'll become very noisy and will want to shake and bang anything that makes a noise.

Twelve months She will do anything to make you laugh and will repeat it over and over again. She'll enjoy "reading" simple books with you and will help you undress her by lifting up her arms when you take off her clothes. She may know a few simple words like bottle, bath, ball, and drink.

Stimulating games
Hold a mirror up so your baby can see herself. Point at her reflection and say her name as you do so.

experiences, explain everything you see, and, above all, join in with every activity so that you and your baby learn together. You have to give encouragement at all times, give praise when even the smallest thing is achieved, and provide her with constant support, especially if your child fails to do something she really wants to do. Without your support, your child won't gain the confidence she needs.

Look at your baby

In the early days, it is a prerequisite to face your baby; facial contact is extremely important. One of the few things that a baby responds to visually in the first days of life is a human face (see p.28). Your newborn baby has to see that face as close as 8–10 inches (20–25 centimeters) from her own, so bring your face up close to your baby's and make it interesting. Move your head as you talk, raise your eyebrows and, most important of all, smile. Look deep into your baby's eyes all the time, and make constant eye contact. It has been shown that parents who face their children while they are feeding or playing with them and look into their eyes are much less likely to use corporal punishment to discipline their children as they grow up. It's hardly surprising that the children of such parents are much better able to form relationships with people as they get older.

Have conversations

Your baby holds her first conversation with smiles. The conversation goes something like this: you are chatting away to your baby about any subject you like with your face about 8–10 inches (20–25 centimeters) away. You are animated and

you smile a lot. Your baby sees this as a friendly approach. Every baby has the natural human desire to respond in a friendly way, so she smiles back. You are delighted with her recognition, her response, and her friendly smile. You smile some more, you may laugh, you may cuddle her, you may kiss her. She loves that, so she smiles more to please you. You do more things to please her, and so the conversation goes on.

What is interesting about this kind of interaction between parent and baby is that your baby has learned two very important lessons. A smile from her gets a smile back. It may even get more substantial reward like hugs and cuddles, as well as praise and approval. The second lesson is that she has found a way to please you and interact with you. She will learn that she can initiate this interaction and she'll go on to use this method with other people. It is well known that the amount of smiling a baby does is related to her intelligence, because it shows that she has learned that if she smiles the world will like her and life will be more pleasant. You have given her a very good start in coming to terms with and managing her world.

Read to your baby

Your child will love books and respond to them from a surprisingly early age if you look at them together and read to her from them. Reading books together will teach your child about colors, the alphabet, numbers, and the names of simple objects. Your baby's never too young to be read to—your voice will be soothing to her, and you'll soon find that books at bedtime are a useful and pacifying part of your evening

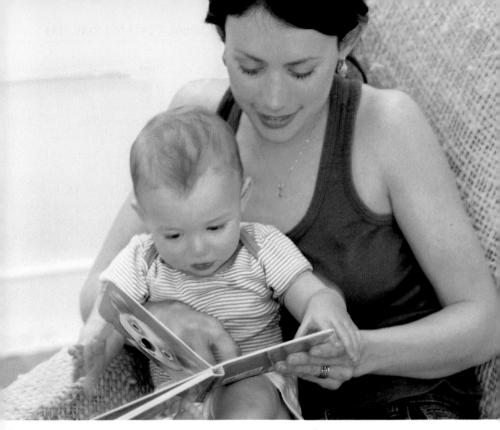

Reading together every day

Settle into a comfortable chair and read a story to your baby. She will enjoy turning the pages of the book and looking at the pictures with you.

routine. The bonus you may never have expected is that once you have introduced your child to books, she may want to read them by herself too. You'll have done her a great service because you'll not only have introduced her to the idea of entertaining herself, but also to a pleasure that will last her for the rest of her life—reading and learning from books.

I suggest you start off with board books because they are brightly colored and sturdy. For variety, buy some popup books, too, but resign yourself to your baby's rough treatment of them.

Learning spurts

Your baby doesn't grow, develop, and learn at a constant rate. Learning spurts are well known and every child has them. During a learning spurt, your baby will gobble up new ideas, acquire new skills, and put them into practice immediately. However, while she's going through these learning spurts, some activities, and possibly certain skills that she's already learned, may appear to slip. Don't worry. They have not gone for good. It is just that your baby is using all her concentration to learn something new, but once it is learned she'll regain all the other skills.

During a learning spurt, you should try to make your child's life as interesting as possible. Of course, if your child shows that certain things are enjoyable, then you should do them as often as you can, but don't hesitate to introduce your baby to new things, too; she is ready to learn and absorb information at a very fast rate. Don't be too discriminating about the kind of entertainment you give either. Babies simply focus on what they prefer and understand, and let the rest go by. In the first year learning is an entirely piecemeal process, so you'll help your baby most if you provide as wide and interesting a range of things as possible.

Learning spurts are invariably followed by periods when development appears to slow down. Treat them as recovery periods during which your baby consolidates newly learned skills and prepares herself for the next spurt. Don't get anxious about this— just let her practice the skills that she has already learned. You can help during these slower learning times by practicing with her, saying something like, "Let's sing that song again," or "Why don't we try to push the peg through that hole again?"

Let your child guide you

All the way through life, teachers who succeed do so by helping us develop and reach our full potential. They help us maximize our strengths and minimize our weaknesses. As your baby's teacher, it's important to try to make the best of her good points and play down her bad ones. You also have to give your child the kind of help she needs when she needs it. Giving help is worthless if the person who

is being helped doesn't really require it or like it, so while you have to be an active helper, don't be an interfering one. Your baby should not be learning what you want her to learn, she should be learning what she wants to learn. This should be your first priority.

You have to suppress any ideas about what you think a child of her age ought to be doing and respond to what she wants to do. This means that you have to be guided by your child. You have to respond to her needs. While it is your job as a good parent to introduce her to as wide a range of interesting things as possible, it is not your job to decide which of those things she should find interesting. In other words, having presented her with the menu, you must let her choose her own dishes.

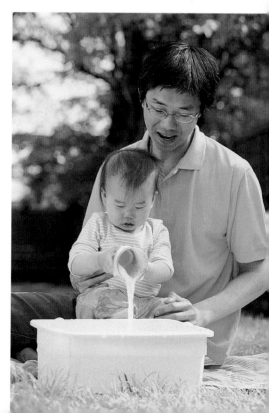

Water play
All babies enjoy playing with water. Fill a plastic bowl with water and give your baby lots of unbreakable containers to pour and fill.

Learning 1 to 2 years

During the first year of your baby's life the emphasis was on learning physical skills: she learned to crawl, to stand up, and possibly even to take a few steps. The ability to do these things brought with it a sense of physical achievement and a sense of independence. She was able to go and explore the world without having to wait for you to bring it to her.

During this second year, she'll not only consolidate all the physical skills she acquired in her first year, but she'll also master one of the most difficult intellectual ones—speech (see p.229). Your child will be struggling to express her thoughts and desires through speech, and with her increasingly able brain she'll now see herself as a separate entity from you—she'll be aware of "self." She'll probably be very frustrated this year, and you may notice that more tantrums occur during this period. She'll need a lot of affection, encouragement, and support.

Learning and speech

This is one of the most important intellectual lessons your child will ever master. Without it, many of the other learning skills are delayed and may even be prohibited. Learning to speak is almost an act of survival; a child quickly learns that she has to communicate to survive.

Early communication, as we have seen, is not with words; initially it's with cries. The first conversation is usually with smiles; later it may just be with a head movement.

INTELLECTUAL DEVELOPMENT

12 months Your baby likes looking at simple books with you and loves a joke—she will repeat anything that makes you laugh. She'll understand that she should hold up her arms when you dress her and she knows the meaning of simple, frequently used words like shoe, bottle, and bath. She may even say one or two intelligible words.

15 months She will show you that she wants to brush her own hair. She'll know what kissing means and will give you a kiss if asked. She'll be very thrilled by any new skill and will want to help you with household chores like dusting. Even though she doesn't understand individual words she can understand quite complex sentences.

18 months When you are reading together she will point to things, like a dog, ball, or cow. She will recognize a cow and say "Cow." She'll know the different parts of her body: if you ask her where her foot is she will point to it, and to her hand, her nose, her mouth, and her eyes. She'll know the difference between her nose and Mommy's nose. If you ask her to fetch something she will.

21 months She will come to you, attract your attention, and take you to things that she is interested in or has a problem with. She'll love scribbling with a pencil. She'll begin to understand and obey simple requests and questions.

2 years She likes her own company and will play happily on her own. Instead of just scribbling with a pencil, she will make up-and-down strokes in imitation of writing. She knows the names of many familiar objects and toys and will use the words with meaning. Once she learns the meaning of a word she may repeat it continuously.

You may notice that your child just bobs her head to say thank you, and then a little later she may stand close to something she wants and shout for your attention. Once she has got it, she will point to the object. These early lessons tell her that life will be a lot easier if she can communicate with the world around her in the language that is commonly used—that is, with words rather than gestures.

In learning to use words, a child learns about the world around her and how people behave in it. Very often she will try to guess at the meaning of a word from the general sense of what is being said and the tone of voice that is used to say it. In discovering language, your child makes connections between sounds and what she understands about the nature of things that surround her.

When she first uses words she'll use them generically, and they'll have a much wider meaning for her than they do for an adult. For example, "nana" (banana) may be her word for all fruit because that's the name she remembers first learning for a single fruit. However, with your help, your child will learn the difference between a car and a truck, even though they both move on four wheels, and between a cat and a dog, even though they are of similar size and shape and have tails.

Talk to your child

Your child is learning the art of communication. For this to happen, you must communicate with her. If she wants something, tell her that you understand what she wants and give it to her, naming the object as you do. Don't talk to her without looking at her. If she wants your attention, stop whatever you are doing, turn to face her, and listen. When your child first starts to learn language she learns it in broad strokes, so while she may not understand individual words, she very often gets the gist of the sentence. Give her lots of clues to help her with this. In the evening, when it's time for bed, start straightening up the playroom, ask her to help you put the toys away, stack everything neatly in its place, then go to the door and say, "It's time for bed now," and put your hand out for her. Although she may not yet understand the words, she'll have understood the sense of them.

During the early stages of learning to talk, you can give your child a great deal of help in learning to understand language.

Eye contact
Always give your child your full attention when you're talking together and make your meaning clear by your expressions and gestures.

Children love the sound of speech and they love your attention. You can combine the two by talking to your child as often as you can. Make sure that while you are talking you look directly at your child and make eye contact. Exaggerate your facial expressions and your gestures. Exaggerate the emphasis you put on words, your inflection, and your tone of voice. Try to match your words with actions. For instance, if you say "I think it is time for your bath,"—go into the bathroom and start running the water. When you say, "Let's comb your hair,"pick up the comb and start combing her hair.

Learning and playing

To a child, play is learning; it's also very hard work. While she is playing, she is learning and growing up. Play helps learning in many ways:

- It can improve manual dexterity. Building a tower of blocks or, when she is older, doing a simple jigsaw puzzle, teaches a child she can make her hands work for her as tools and prepares her for using her hands in delicate and refined ways.

- Playing with other children can help teach a child how important it is to get along with others. Having playmates come over teaches her to overcome shyness and introduces her to sharing. It presents her with problems to solve without help from adults, and teaches her to control outbursts of antisocial behavior. Through a special friend, your child may learn to love people and understand feelings that she can't easily put into words. At the same time, she'll be learning about the feelings of others.

- Through play, a child will learn to communicate. Playing with other children demands a more complicated use of language. Talking while playing may be one of the most complicated tests for your child, because the more imaginative the play, the more complex the ideas, and these have to be expressed in words that her friends can understand.

- Play undoubtedly helps a child's physical coordination. In fact, it helps both physical and intellectual development.

Play helps coordination
By playing with a shopping basket she's imitating you, communicating that she is interested in what you are doing, and improving her hand–eye coordination.

The freedom to swing, climb, skip, run, and jump helps perfect muscular coordination and physical skills. It also improves hearing and vision.

Provide the right games

Your child makes no distinction between learning and playing. You'll help learn a great deal simply by choosing material for her to play with, and by the kinds of toys you introduce her to.

From a very early age, all four of my children loved playing with water, whether it was outside in a small wading pool or just standing on a chair at the kitchen sink with a bowl of water and an assortment of plastic dishes, cups, jugs, containers, and funnels nearby.

Other games you can play

Water games were always good for an hour's concentration, and all the time my children were learning lessons: that water feels wet, that it will pour, that you can fill things with it, that you can empty them, that you can blow bubbles in it, that things will float on it, things will sink through it, and that vegetable dyes will make it turn color and that other liquids won't, that when the faucet drips it forms drops, and that cupped hands aren't watertight. This wasn't the only game:

- Materials like play dough or pastry dough was interesting, too, because it could be molded by their hands. They soon discovered that it would keep its shape if left to dry out, or they could roll it into a ball and start all over again.
- Sand, whether in the sandbox or at the beach, was also interesting because it was halfway between a liquid and a

solid. It felt like a solid but it poured like a liquid. If the sand was wet, it would keep the shape of the bucket, and the children could make sand castles; if it was dry, the castles crumbled.

Helping the learning process

One of the most important concepts that a child grasps during her second year is that of classification—of sameness and difference. Toys can help the formation of this idea. Farmyard toys, with a variety of horses, cows, and chickens, allow your child to sort the animals that look the same, especially if you assist by showing her the differences and naming the animals repeatedly as you both put them into little groups. The same procedure can be applied to many other objects—fruit, cars, shapes, or cans.

Children like being part of the domestic routine and learn a lot about what goes on in the house and what people have to do if they are allowed to participate. A young child can be given a little bowl with some flour to mix each time you bake, she can help carry things, and she can be given her own brush and dustpan to help clean.

For years, an essential part of our playroom was the dressing-up box, into which we put all sorts of old clothes, uniforms, hats, and shoes. Most children get enormous pleasure from imitating other people. This is a very important learning step for a child, because she is beginning to recognize that she has to share the world with other people and get along with them. Dressing up to look like them is one of her ways of coming to terms with this.

Children of both sexes like dolls. Boys should have dolls, too: they are their imaginary friends, their imaginary families, and they help create an imaginary world into which they can escape. While your child is playing with dolls, she is learning about, and possibly mimicking, human emotions. She will mother the doll, she'll feed it, talk to it very firmly, correct it, then put it to bed, and kiss it goodnight. Through this, your child is working out the things that happen to her, and is learning to understand them fully and relate them to other people.

Creative games

Long before she'll be able to write or draw, your child will love scribbling and using colors. A box of colored chalk, a blackboard, and an easel will be attractive because she'll be able to "draw" then erase the scribbles and start again. Attach a sheet of paper to the easel and give your child a set of finger paints and let her make her own design of splodges, hand prints, and smears on the paper.

Most children are musical and like to be sung to from the day they are born. Many children have mastered the tune of their favorite song or nursery rhyme long before they can talk. As soon as your child is old enough, buy her a simple musical instrument like a xylophone or a keyboard. Join in with marching and clapping and singing. She'll enjoy it even more if you have your own instrument, too.

Help if she is frustrated

The best way to help your child learning is to join in her learning activities, especially if you make suggestions about how to do

something new with a toy and then demonstrate how to do it. However, you must do it tactfully and without interfering, and allow her to decide whether she wants to follow your advice. Many of your child's games can't be played without a partner. You should offer to be "It" whenever you can, but only join in for as long as she wants you to; don't overdo it. Let her take the initiative; she may want you to fill the bucket of sand and ask for your help, but the last thing she'll want is for you to turn the bucket upside down for her to make the sand castle.

Your child's attention span is increasing, but she may still have problems concentrating on something difficult. You can help her concentrate by making a task easier or by giving her a helping hand. If you show her how a task can be completed, you'll give your child a goal to work toward. She needs your loving support and encouragement; if you give it readily, she will probably find the determination to go on longer than she would without you. Doing his will give your child a great sense of achievement.

Let your child play alone

Some parents make the mistake of thinking that their child's every waking hour has to be filled with interesting diversions and stimulating activities. This is wrong and can even be harmful. One of the most important lessons that your child has to learn, and will learn willingly if left to her own devices, is that she can be the source of her own entertainment. Very often a child wishes to be left to play by herself, and to make her own decisions about what to play with and for how long. Let your child follow through on little tasks that she has set herself, alone. If she can't do them, she will ask for your help; if she doesn't, don't interfere. Interfering, interrupting, or introducing a different activity will do the opposite of making her life more entertaining. It will make it boring, because she'll never have the opportunity to see an activity through to the end. She will miss out on the sense of achievement that every child needs.

Another common mistake is to believe that children need to play with toys. Many of the most popular play activities don't involve toys at all. They may involve physical activities like swimming, climbing or running, playing with a bat and ball, building a camp out of twigs and leaves, carrying water to the sandbox and filling the moat, or collecting pebbles or shells. Give your child the scope and the autonomy to do these things. If you don't encourage private activities, your child will have a very uncomfortable sense of withdrawal or even deprivation when she is forced to entertain herself if you are absent, and this may lead her into mischief, delinquent behavior or, even worse, danger. You should be pleased if your child shows signs of self-sufficiency, of being able to do without you and entertain herself while excluding you.

Coping with a mess

Leaving your child alone, however, will mean that you'll have to either ignore a mess or anticipate one. If she's playing water games, cover the kitchen floor with newspaper or old towels that will soak up the water. If she's painting, cover the

Costumes and dressing up
Children love dressing up, so keep a special box and fill it with old shoes, hats, and clothes that you and your partner don't wear any more.

carpet with a sheet of plastic. If she's playing with mud or clay, cover your child's clothes with an apron and ignore the mess on her face and on her hair; it can all be washed off when she's finished.

Learning 2 to 3 years

The way your child learns changes a lot in the third year, particularly in the second half. As a toddler, your child was learning about separate things, single events, one experience at a time. She may have satisfied her curiosity and explored that experience as far as she could, absorbing a great deal of new information in the process, but she rarely related it to anything else in her life.

Learning from experiences

In the third year, your child starts to think about her experiences and to learn from them. As your child develops the ability to think about new learning experiences, her mind starts to work for the first time like a mini-computer. Information is sorted and sifted, matched up to other experiences to see if they fit together or if they differ very much, then put into similar or different pigeonholes. Your child starts to think and plan ahead, and becomes much more creative and imaginative. Gradually, all the information she has absorbed over the past years becomes available to her to apply to a given situation. Your child suddenly has an orchestra of thoughts that she can command at will.

This new ability to think, imagine, and create changes your child's world considerably. Many familiar things in the house or backyard no longer contain the same interest or excitement for her. She now needs wider horizons; she needs to be able explore, to push the frontiers of her experience and knowledge further out.

Your child becomes very interested in how things work at this time, and her conversation will now be constantly punctuated with, "Why?" She is eager for information and constantly asks questions. It's as if her brain wants more and more information to put into the computer and

INTELLECTUAL DEVELOPMENT

2 years and 3 months She will try to build houses and castles with blocks and will repeat new words when you encourage her. She knows who she is and can say her name. She'll begin to pit her will against yours, and may become negative. She'll say the word "No" more often and won't always conform to your wishes.

2 years and 6 months She loves helping you and will help with chores, putting things away, and bringing things to the table. She'll know both her first name and last name. She can draw horizontal lines and vertical lines and can name several common objects. A boy will notice that his sex organs stick out from his body wheras those of his mother, and of his little girlfriends, do not.

2 years and 9 months She'll begin to ask questions. She'll know the difference between boys and girls. She'll learn nursery rhymes and will be able to repeat them. She'll begin to understand numbers. She'll try to draw a circle but won't be able to complete it successfully without help.

3 years She'll like to play with other children. She'll know more nursery rhymes and will almost be able to draw a circle. She'll know the difference between words such as on, under, and behind, and will be able to form complicated sentences.

start using immediately. One of the most important steps in your child's intellectual development is when she understands that time is not just the present, but that there was a past and there will be a future, when she understands yesterday and tomorrow. Planning for the future is one of the most critical aspects of our intellect, and makes us different from lower animals. Because of this development, it is during this third year that you will hear your child say for the first time, "I'll eat that later," or "We can go tomorrow."

Learning and speech

As your child grows older, speech plays a more and more important role in communication and becomes more and more important in helping your child to learn. By now your child has got the hang of the basic rules of conversation. She knows, for instance, that people usually take turns at speaking, they know when it is their turn, and they don't try to dominate a conversation. She also knows that instead of accompanying single words with gestures to explain what she means, she can vary the intonation of the words. She knows that an intonation that rises usually means a question, and that a falling pitch indicates a statement. When your child was younger, speech was part of a simple pattern of communication that told you what she wanted or didn't want—it was used as a greeting or as a label. As your child's world widens, she needs more sophisticated ways to express her thoughts.

One of the first expressions of this is her use of the possessive pronoun—"my doll, Mommy coat, Daddy nose." Another is the negative. Your younger child would

Learning colors
All children love to paint and draw and you can take the chance to name the colors of the paints and point out other things with the same colors.

just have said "No;" now she says, "Can't" or "Won't." A little later she will start to express actions—"Dolly fall," "Dog bark," "Car bump." Another characteristic she'll develop is the increasing use of questions combined with statements. "Daddy sleep, why Daddy sleep?" "Mommy go shop, why Mommy go shop?" "Daddy gone out, where Daddy gone?"

By the time your child is three, she will be asking quite complicated questions in parallel with the way her thinking is developing. The following sentences contain quite sophisticated ideas: "I go get pencil and draw." "What that on table?" "See, this one better. But this not better."

Don't "talk down"

The kind of language you use with your child is very important. It's well known that adults change the way they speak to children as they get older. Sentences become more complex, contain longer words, and describe abstract ideas. Don't fall into the trap of talking down to your child and don't use baby language when it is no longer needed. Throw an occasional word into your conversation that you know is unfamiliar to your child, but that she can guess at from the gist of the sentence. This way, she'll learn new words and will learn how to use them and how to express herself in an articulate way. Research has proven that the children of articulate parents who don't tailor their speech to their children, use words more easily and freely at an earlier age than the children of parents who persist in simplifying language.

Learning and playing

In keeping with your child's expanding way of thinking, she starts to get more out of playing. Playing still involves learning, but it's about learning different things.

- Play now starts to put the world around her into perspective. Before, a game like a farmyard with animals was simply a question of sorting the animals into different types and putting them in the right place. Now she sees it with different eyes. It introduces her to an aspect of life that she knows is different from the one she leads. After all, she is probably not surrounded by animals most of the time, so it helps to reduce the world to a scale she can handle.
- Play increasingly becomes an outlet for emotions. Even an action-man type of

doll can bring out feelings of protectiveness and gentleness. She can also use the same toy to get rid of aggressive instincts, which, if directed against other children, would be labeled naughty and antisocial.

- Play creates an interest in other people. If the dress-up box has a cowboy outfit or a nurse's uniform, your child can dress up and play a role. Even if she just puts a hat on at an angle and wears a pair of high-heeled shoes too big for her she can pretend to be her aunt. By acting out what she thinks her aunt does, she is getting insight into her life and into other people's lives.
- Play develops a sense of territory and ownership. Safeguarding a new and cherished toy or her own private place to play, like a den, tent, or a play house, teaches a child to respect the belongings and privacy of others. Play stimulates curiosity, independence, an adventurous spirit, and intellectual growth. Mechanical toys and puzzles stimulate analytical thought. Painting, drawing, making shapes with clay, and fitting together patterns encourage creativity. When your child gets older, toys like a microscope, telescope, chemistry set, or a magician's outfit allow experimentation. These kinds of toys teach her to meet challenges and master difficulties.
- As your child gets older, play helps teach her how to cope with events beyond her control. She may break a treasured toy, she may fail to make a mechanical toy work, or she may not have the competence to do what she wants to do. All these experiences help her to learn how to cope with problems that arise in

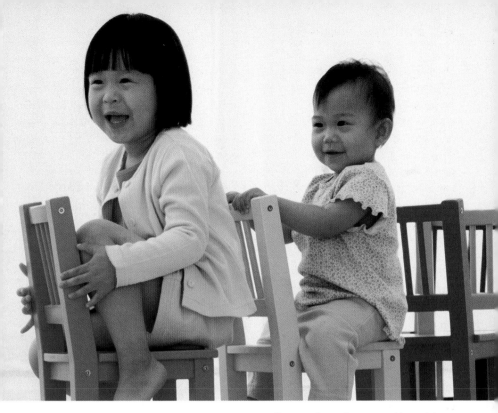

Make-believe games
Your child will love to create a little world of her own as part of her imitation of adults. Chairs can become a train or a car, and she can involve others in her game.

her world. There may be difficult choices to make, but your child has to learn to make decisions. Play helps your child to get to know herself. As she gets older, she has to learn to interact with others, but before she can do that successfully, she has to understand herself at least a little. Play allows her to discover her own physical and intellectual strengths as well as her weaknesses.

- Play is an important aid in helping your child mature. By the time your child is three, she will be showing signs of a sense of planning. She will keep her traffic jam of toy cars under the

surveillance of a police car, with a pickup truck standing alongside. This shows that she is thinking ahead. She'll start to exercise her capacity to delay when she plays with toys that need glue to harden or clay to dry. If she is prepared to share one of her toys with a friend who reciprocates by lending your child one of hers, then she is being taught the value of give-and-take.

Forming concepts
For your child to form concepts and put them to use in her world, she has to have mastered two things. First of all, she has to understand the basic concept of like and unlike. She learns to do this by recognizing similarities and differences in things and then fitting them together in her own mind. Once she can do this, she has made

an intellectual leap forward. From about 18 months to two years old, you'll find that your child does this sorting automatically when faced with objects that have some things in common and some differences. All things that roll and are round are sorted into one group. All things that have edges and are rectangular, like blocks, are sorted into another. Things that have four legs and meow are cats. Things that have two legs and fly are birds.

We give our concepts verbal labels (names), and in her third year your toddler develops her understanding of concepts by using language. It would be very difficult for your child to progress with concept formation if she couldn't talk. Your toddler might use the word "cat" for every cat she meets, including the family pet, the cat in a book, the cat she sees in a neighbor's backyard, and a toy cat. In her mind, she uses a single label for all these different things. But by the time she approaches three, she'll have made several sophisticated distinctions. She'll know that they are all cats so she'll have a concept of what makes "catness," but she'll also know that they are subtly different: "My cat," "Your cat," "Toy cat," "Cat in book," "Go see Grandma's cat."

Abstract ideas

When your child is two years old, it is impossible for her to describe things that are not real—things that she cannot see, and that she cannot pick up and touch. She doesn't know what pretty means, she hasn't quite got the hang of emptiness and fullness, and, while she knows that when she blows bubbles they will float, she can't yet distinguish lightness and heaviness. Your child may know the difference between one and several, but she has no idea of the magnitude of numbers, so anything more than one may be "lots." She has very little concept of time, she can't visualize what tomorrow or last week means, and she has difficulty coping with tonight. Her understanding, however, improves throughout this year.

To have abstract ideas and to think in the abstract, your child has to be able to picture things in her mind that are not actually there. If you ask her where a toy is, she has to remember when and where she last played with it. She has to see both

Picture card games
During his third year, your child will have learned to think in a more abstract way. Memory games such as pairing pictures, can help him develop this skill.

things in her mind and then go and retrieve the toy. Once she is able to do this, she can make plans about things that are not actually there. When you ask her where her boat is, she'll have a mental picture of the boat lying in the grass and will say: "Boat in backyard, me get it in a minute." She'll keep painting, finish it, wash her hands, then go out and get her boat without prompting. This means that she was able to carry the concept of getting the boat in her head, have it interrupted by her painting, then complete several unrelated tasks, and finally go back to the concept of bringing the boat in from the backyard.

How to help your child

The most important way you can help your child develop is to listen to what she's saying. Because her world is now expanding at a colossal rate, not only in terms of her physical capability but also her new intellectual development, it is very important that you communicate openly and freely with her. Listen carefully to everything she says, try to understand her thinking, and answer her questions in terms that she understands. She is constantly asking you questions, but ask her questions, too, so you are aware of what she's thinking and what interests her.

Every time your child asks you a question or you have a conversation with her, you have a golden opportunity to help her learn, even though the circumstances may be very casual and ordinary. If you are in the kitchen preparing lunch and your child asks you why you take the end off the carrots, you could start a discussion about how all plants have

roots because they need food in order to grow. Next time you are in the backyard, you could pull up a tuft of grass and show her its root system. If you are really ambitious, you could try putting a bean down the side of a jar lined with a wet paper towel and let her see the root actually appear and grow down. When you are out in the street, keep up a running commentary on what is going on around you: traffic lights changing, cars stopping at corners, crossing the road, a policeman stopping and waving on traffic, and so on.

Around the age of three your child naturally becomes rather sensitive to what other people are feeling. She may show the first signs of empathy by wanting to

EARLY READING

Some children have a natural inclination toward reading early and writing before their peers. If yours is one of them, encourage and help but never push. Your child can only master these advanced skills when the brain and intellect are sufficiently developed. You are not able to know whether your child's brain is capable of reading (and later writing), so take your lead from her. Until this happens, simply continue read to her, point out and name objects in books, and encourage her to repeat them.

I'm against using "flash cards" when your child finds it onerous and boring. In this instance you're only doing it for your own satisfaction and pride. This should never be the reason for making your child do anything. But if your child is eager to learn words and gets pleasure from remembering flash cards, do encourage her as much as you can. Don't try to make her read. When she's ready, she'll start pointing out words. Only then should you start to help her.

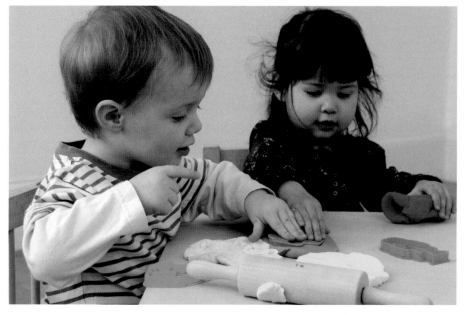

comfort you if you seem sad. Take advantage of this and start to teach her about the need to think of other people; that it is right to be kind and polite, helpful and thoughtful, cooperative and willing. Make sure she is introduced to people coming to your house like the housekeeper and the mail carrier. Tell her about their jobs and some of the problems they may have to cope with, and suggest ways she might help, for instance taking the letters from the mail carrier at the door and bringing them to you.

Nursery school

As your child reaches three years old, start thinking about whether she would benefit from going to nursery school. The advantages of a school are she will meet lots of new friends, as well as interested and sympathetic adults who are good at knowing how to widen a child's horizons.

Learning to play together
When a child starts nursery school it can be hard for her to learn to play with other children. Help her to learn with games that involve sharing toys with others.

She'll also have the opportunity to try new and interesting activities (things you might not have done at home), and she'll learn to socialize and be a member of a group. Lastly, and most importantly, she will have to be able to manage without you.

The decision about whether she's capable of doing without you for long periods of time will be one of the factors that you'll have to weigh when you are deciding the pros and cons of nursery school. If your child is very shy and clinging and doesn't talk easily to other adults and children, frets when you leave the room, and follows you wherever you go, then you are going to have problems with nursery school. You can, however, fall back on the knowledge that most children manage to get used to nursery school and, indeed, thrive on it so much that they miss school when they're on vacation. Bear in mind that with a little careful planning, you can help your child get over the frightening first stages and not feel deserted.

Assessing a nursery or playgroup

There are several different types of group for preschool children—playgroups, nursery schools and day nurseries. Do some research locally and ask other parents. Make a list of all approved preschool groups in your area. Choose two or three schools from this list that you can visit.

Go about your assessment in a thorough way. First of all, talk to the teacher in charge. Make an appointment to go and visit the group and sit in on some of the classes. If possible, spend a whole morning or a whole afternoon there so that you can get a feel for the routines—the amount of discipline, whether the teachers are strict, whether you approve of the way the children are treated, whether the environment is happy, informal and cosy, and whether the children seem happy. If you can, look at the facilities and talk to another mother whose child goes to that particular group.

Once you have chosen a nursery or playgroup, ask if you can take your child along to a session a few weeks before she is due to start, so that she can get used to everything. This will help her settle in more easily when she starts going regularly.

Speech birth to 1 year

The moment your child begins to speak is very exciting. Now you are getting precise information about what your child knows and thinks. It's as if language provides you with a window to look in on your child's mental ability. It's also the tool with which she can learn. She reaches a stage where she no longer has to rely on crying to communicate.

Despite a great deal of research, we still don't know exactly how a child acquires language. What we do know, however, is the general sequence that all children follow as their speech develops. We also know that your baby learns a lot about language before she starts to talk: long before she knows what the words mean, she'll listen to any changes in sound, and

to the rhythm and the intonation of your speech. She'll also learn about verbal rituals before she begins to speak, and will soon know that first one person speaks, and then another follows.

Early speech

For each month that your baby develops she will master new words and new grammatical rules. But learning to speak itself is infinitely more important than learning about vocabulary and grammar. Your child's main concern will be communicating and interacting with the people around her.

Children develop at their own speed, and this applies to speech well as other aspects of development. Don't worry if she doesn't seem to be as quick at picking up language as others—encourage her and let her take the time she needs.

How speech develops

Studies have shown that even a few days after birth, babies will respond more to speech than to any other noise.

Up to six weeks As soon as your baby is born she'll start to make sounds. Initially they will be cries—cries for food, for affection, or because she's uncomfortable. Along with these cries she'll start to make little burbling noises as a mark of pleasure and contentment.

Around six weeks She'll begin to respond to your smiling face as well as your voice with a more exaggerated gurgling. Although she's not literally talking to you she is communicating, and what's more she's learning to communicate in the way that adults do. For example, on seeing you vocalizing at her, your baby will respond

with mouth and tongue movements and wait for your reply before reacting again.

Three to four months Your baby will make soft, cooing noises. At this stage, the sound will be single syllables with an open vowel sound. The first consonants she'll use will be "p," "b," and "m," so it's hardly surprising that she'll say, "Maa" or "Paa," but she won't understand the significance of what she's saying at this time.

Seven months She'll be increasingly responsive to sounds, the human voice and music. She'll expand her cooing into two-syllable words by repeating the initial syllable: "Maama," "Beebe," "Daada." This stage will be followed by explosive sounds of exclamation: "Ai," "Imi."

Eight months Your baby will continue to babble, but she'll also learn how to shout to attract your attention. If she's near you when you're having a conversation with someone, she'll pay close attention to what you're saying and will then turn to watch any reply that's made to you. Her babbling may become quite musical, and she might try to imitate you when you sing a nursery rhyme to her or wind up her music box.

Nine months Your baby's speech will become noticeably more elaborate as she starts to join the syllables she knows and pronounce them with sentence-like phrasing. With the rising and falling intonation of adult speech she'll say, "Ca-mama-dah-ba." Once she starts to make up sounds like this, technically called jargoning, you'll know that she's just about to start talking.

Learning by imitation
Babies see their parents talking on the telephone and love to imitate. She'll enjoying "talking" to daddy or grandma on the telephone too.

Eleven to twelve months Your baby will probably say her first "real" words some time during this month. The emergence of these first words is as much controlled by your baby's physical ability to articulate and make speech sounds as it is by her intellectual ability to make connections between objects and labels. The words she chooses will almost certainly be the names of things that are important to her: people (like mama, dada), animals (dog, cat), and objects (cup, ball).

Simplifying words

The change from babbling to saying precise words means that your child has to change from making a stream of barely controlled sounds to planned, thoughtful, controlled speech. Furthermore, the sounds have to be in a certain sequence, so that the words are understandable to another person. This is a lot for a young child to cope with, so the pronunciation of early words will very often be simplified.

Nearly all children reduce the number of consonants that they say at the beginning (or the end) of words so that spoon becomes "poon" and smack becomes "mack." She might say "du" for duck, "be" for bed, "ca" for cat. This aspect of speech is one of the last to be mastered in English and children often have difficulty with consonants until they are four or five years.

Another way that children simplify the pronunciation of words is to put the consonants in the same place in the mouth that the basic sound of the word is made. This accounts for doggy being pronounced "doddy" or "goggy."

The other preference that children show at this stage is for substituting an explosive sound with a less explosive one. So, instead of saying "pie," your child may say "bie," and he may well use "doe" for "toe," and "bop" for "pop."

Helping your baby talk

- One of the first type of words your baby learns are label words that identify the names of things. In conversations with your baby, stress the names of objects and repeat them frequently. When you are feeding your baby, talk repeatedly about the spoon and the food. Make a special effort not to use pronouns. Say "I'll get your coat" instead of saying "I'll get it." Your child is learning the difference between herself and other people, so use her name constantly rather than "you." "Where are Harriet's shoes?" "Harriet and Mommy will go into the car."
- Don't expect too much of your baby's pronunciation—if she can't say a word properly but you understand what she means, don't make her try to say it

BILINGUALISM

Children thrive on having two languages to learn. When young babies are learning to talk, they can make all linguistic sounds. They find a new language much easier than adults do. It also seems to be easy for them not just to learn them, but also to think and speak in two languages. I remember watching my young godchild looking from her French mother who was speaking French, to her English father, who was speaking English. She was just two-and-a-half years old, but she replied to her mother in French and her father in English. I would encourage exposing children to more than one language.

perfectly. She'll only get frustrated.

- Make the effort to understand her own private, invented words or words that are mispronounced. If she is trying to explain something to you, go through all the alternatives until you find the word she actually wants. When you find it, her pleasure in having communicated with you will be enormous and will encourage her to try again.

- Help your baby learn about how to apply words by describing and talking about things that are in front of her. Your baby can make the connection between an object and what you're talking about if you repeat the word, especially if she can see, hold, touch, and play with it. While you are playing with a ball, repeat the word "ball" as often as you can, and discuss the innate properties of a ball— that it's round, and will roll and bounce.

- In teaching your baby to talk you really have to be something of an actor. You must bring drama and interest to what you are saying. This means exaggerating your pronunciation and your intonation. Make it clear that you're asking a

Reading can help speech
Point to pictures in her book when you read to her, and repeat the names of the objects. She will eventually start to copy you.

question. Show when you're pleased and when you're serious.

- Your baby learns language from you more easily than from any other person, but don't expect her to pick it up from the general babble of adult conversation. She won't be able to distinguish single sounds and sentences. Always stop what you are doing and look at your baby when she "talks" to you. Pay her the compliment of listening to her efforts when she tries to talk back.

- Ask your baby questions like, "Where's your teddy?" and "Was that nice?" She may not be able to answer you initially but she'll understand what you're saying and may point or nod.

SPOTTING IF SOMETHING IS WRONG

Don't worry if your baby doesn't speak in her first year. As in everything else, children develop speech at different rates. But if your child is still not combining words by age two, you need expert help. If hearing is deficient, it's crucial to have the faults attended to before she starts school. If you are concerned about your child's speech, discuss the issue with your pediatrician, who may refer you to a speech therapist or developmental specialist. Many problems can be corrected if identified early enough.

- Don't oversimplify what you say to your baby—she needs the stimulation of adult speech, not a kind of mushy baby talk.
- Take advantage of your baby's interests by talking about things on which she is already concentrating. She may not be interested in a story about a fictional character, but she will be riveted by a story in which she is the central character. She may not be particularly interested in animals, but she will be fascinated by all animals if they are discussed in terms of mothers and babies, because she can relate to that.
- Encourage her to use the few words that she has learned by using them in your conversations. She will be delighted to hear her own primitive conversation being spoken to her, and this will encourage her to be adventurous with speech and to try out new words.
- Never, ever scold or correct early errors of pronunciation or understanding. With my own children, I found some of these so charming that I left them uncorrected until a late age. In our house we all said "aterator" for radiator, "gamilla" for vanilla, and "binoclickers" for binoculars.

Speech 1 to 2 years

This year your child will make great strides forward in terms of both physical and intellectual development. She'll increase her vocabulary, and her grasp of grammatical construction will greatly improve. In order to be able to speak properly, she'll have to unlearn some of the habits she got into when her speech consisted of babbling. For example, in babbling consonants are frequently dropped and duplicated words are common. Once your child gains control of her speech, she'll correct the errors and substitutions that she used to make.

The beginning of classification

As your child learns to recognize and identify objects, she'll begin to classify and group them. However, at the beginning this process, she won't be completely accurate. She'll look at several objects and use the same word to identify all of them if they have one or more features in common. This is referred to as overextension. The reason she uses words like this is because she doesn't the ability to articulate all words, but her desire to communicate with you is so strong that she has to use the closest word that she can. Your child will link words together in the following way:

Shape Balls, apples, or stones may all be called "ball."

Size A purse, a plastic bag, and a shopping bag may all be called "bag."

Sound A whistle, a siren, and a car horn may all be called "beep."

Movement A bicycle, a car, a bus, and a train may all be "choo-choo." Although your child overextends in this way, she does know the difference between two things she calls by the same name. For example, she may use the word "guck" for "truck" and "duck," yet when faced with pictures of both of them and asked to point out a

THE FIRST SENTENCES

Some time before your child's second birthday she'll start to string words together. This is an important milestone because it shows that she's aware of the relationship between objects. Your baby's first sentences will be limited in meaning. They'll probably explain something that has just happened or describe what someone is doing. Her sentences will be concerned with:

What's happening	Me run
	Cow go moo
	Truck bump
Who possesses what	My dolly
	Mommy dress
	Grandma bag
Where things are	Doll in box
	Daddy in
	backyard
	Ball in bath
Repetition	Me more milk
	Play again
Where something's gone	Drink all gone
	No more toy

Her sentences won't follow adult grammatical rules—that develops later—but they have a logic of their own. She'll learn fairly early that certain words are used together. She'll repeatedly hear "Pick up," "Put on," "Go out," and will continue to use them as one word even when joining them to others. So she'll have "Car pick up," "Door go out." She'll make the past tense by adding "d" to anything—"I wented", "You goed," "I gaved." To make words plural, she'll add an "s" to the end—"Look, fishes," "Mouses," "Gameses."

truck and a duck, she'll make the distinction between the two.

In the same way, children can also underextend words. For most children, the word animal usually just applies to mammals and the animals that they meet in their everyday life; they often have difficulty understanding that fish, insects, and birds can be categorized as animals, too. Whatever early words your child learns, she'll soon begin to use them to mean a variety of things. A single word can be a label for a greeting, a demand, or a question. At the beginning, your child may often add gestures to single words to give them meaning. Later on, she will learn to change her speech intonation to signal different meanings.

Expanding vocabulary

Your baby's vocabulary will continue to expand and the words she'll learn most readily will be those whose use affects her daily life—people and animals, foods, and most things from her daily routine. Early words nearly always include the names of animals like duck, dog, cat, horse, cow, and the kind of noises that they make. Your child will also know the names of all her favorite toys and, very importantly, she'll know the words she can use to change or regulate the world around her by her interaction with you. There may be words like "no," "up," "more," "out," and "open."

Some children learn a great many words as soon as they begin to speak, but it's more usual for them to acquire between one and three a month. By the time she's two she should be able to say about 200 words.

Helping your child to understand

Understanding always precedes usage, and your 18-month-old child will understand a lot more of what she hears than her own language suggests. To help her, you should make available more information than your words alone provide.

- Talk to your child as often as you can and always look at her when you do so. In this way, your child will be given the maximum number of opportunities to learn and understand language.
- Help your baby's comprehension by acting out what you are saying with facial expressions and gestures, and make your words accompany actions that involve her. "Mommy will put on Jennifer's coat," or ''Mommy will take off Mommy's shoes.''
- For your child to learn that communication is always two-way, you shouldn't babble on with long sentences and stories without giving her the opportunity to participate and contribute. Punctuate your conversations with questions that demand a response of some kind.
- Your child finds it very difficult to understand language if there is a lot of background noise that obscures speech sound. If the television is on, keep the sound low, and don't play your radio or CD loudly.
- Give her the confidence to try talking to strangers by acting as her interpreter. In this way, she won't feel embarrassed and will have a try.
- Give her as many cues and clues about your meaning as you can, even though you know that she cannot understand exactly what you are saying. For example, at bath time take her into the bathroom, run the water, feel the temperature of the water, and undress her, giving her information about what you are doing all the time. Then say, "Now you are ready for your bath." Having had all the visual action and speech clues presented to her, she will certainly understand the meaning of your last comment.

Looking at books together

As with other aspects of her development, you are your child's first introduction to books. If she regularly sees you reading a book or magazine, she soon will start copying your behavior. You will find her sitting, studiously "reading" her book— which may well be upside down—and turning over the pages at intervals!

Gradually her attention will turn to the content of the pages as she starts to recognize objects. Books popular with two- to three-year-olds are those with clear, recognizable pictures of familiar, everyday objects that you can look at with them, pointing and referring to the object by name. As your child's vocabulary expands during this year, she will be able to point to objects herself when asked. She will soon start to appreciate simple, illustrated stories—especially those with a repeated "chorus," which she will start to anticipate and join in with—such as *The Gingerbread Man* or *The Three Billy-Goats Gruff*. In addition to a regular refrain, the most popular stories for this age group have simple, recurring themes—often involving the downfall of the big, fierce "baddie" (the wolf, the troll, the wicked witch) or the victory of the small or weak hero over her bigger and stronger opponent (like the little pig in *Three Little Pigs*). Toddlers often want the same story read over and over again; for some reason, they find something in the story that they need. If that is what your child wants, let her have it—even if you are bored with it.

The value of nursery rhymes

Children love nursery rhymes—from the first game of "This little piggy" to all the old favorites—and will join in enthusiastically with whatever actions are involved. As with storybooks, the attraction of nursery rhymes lies in their simplicity, drama, and recurring motifs and, above all, in the rhythm that babies and toddlers respond to from a very early age. Don't worry if you think you don't have a great singing voice: your child won't mind.

In fact, you'll never have had such an appreciative and adoring audience! Nursery rhymes play an important part in the development of your child's language skills, and also provide an enjoyable and entertaining form of communication. Many can be sung as the accompaniment to activities—like "See-saw Margery Daw" or "The Isty-Bitsy Spider"—thus teaching and reinforcing the concepts in an enjoyable and memorable form. All of them will expand your child's vocabulary, extend her powers of imagination, and encourage a love of music and rhythm.

Clapping games
Teach your child lots of nursery rhymes. Many have actions to help with understanding. Show her to clap her hands as you sing them together.

Speech 2 to 3 years

During the third year, the structure of sentences will become more complicated and your child will start to fit whole phrases together. She'll begin to understand and use negatives beyond a simple "no" and "not." She will also start to phrase words so that they make a question and not just put "why" in front. For the first time, she will begin to fully appreciate the relationship between one object and another. She'll start to use adjectives—big, small, fat, thin—and then comparative adjectives—bigger, smaller, fatter, thinner. She'll understand and start to use words that imply spatial relationships—this, here, that, there, and will learn the relationship between "I" and "my," "you," and "yours." She'll also learn how to use phrases with conjunctions including as "and," "then," and "but."

Having conversations

In her third year, your child becomes a natural chatterer, so take advantage of this tendency to show her how conversations are carried on: the to-and-fro pattern of verbal exchanges, making subjects interesting with questions, and moving on through the various points of interest on any subject.

One of the best ways of involving your child in a conversation is to ask her what she likes, what she is doing, or how things work. Having asked her the question, you have to show real and sincere interest in her response for her to learn that conversation is worthwhile. Similarly, when she approaches you with a question, an appeal for help, or just a request that you come and see something exciting, you have to show a genuine interest in what she is doing and saying. In this way, you can contribute to what she is thinking, understanding, and learning. If you respond to her running commentary of things she is doing with a series of absentminded "mms," she'll not only get little in return that she can learn from, but she'll quickly learn you're not interested and she'll stop trying to engage you.

Helping language to expand

You can help her by giving descriptions or instructions that are more detailed than you normally would. For instance, if she is having difficulty getting her sweater over her head, you can say something like, "Oh, dear, the opening in your sweater is too small for your head." With this elaborate way of saying "I'll help you," you're introducing her to at least three new ideas and three new words. If she can't lift something and you can, you can point out that you can lift it because you are stronger than she is and the object is heavy.

Talk about colors, shapes, and textures whenever possible. "You are going to have the red apple. I'll have the green one." "Look at the pretty blue flower with the long stem. Let's smell the flower." "Our car has four wheels. This truck has lots of wheels. Let's try to count them. One, two, three, four, five, six, seven, eight."

You can also help her out with conversation. If you ask her what she has been doing in the backyard and she can't get the words together, you could point her in the right direction by saying, "What did you make in the sandbox?" or "How did you get down from the top of the climber?" "Where did you go on your tricycle?" You can prompt her responses by asking, "What happened next?"

One of the things all my children enjoyed in a conversation, was for me to leave a blank that they could fill in with the word they knew. So, for example, in reference to getting down from the top of the climber, I could prompt them with "Oh, you mean you slid down the ___," and my children would gleefully contribute "slide." Or, if we were discussing what they had done in the sandbox that afternoon, I would say to them, "You made sand castles with your ___," and my children would shout "bucket."

HELPING WITH GRAMMAR

As your child begins to understand the more complicated aspects of grammar, you can help, as before, by simply repeating what she has said in the correct form. As she starts to apply the constructions more and more widely, help her to use them in the correct way with new words and expressions.

Negatives
With your help, your child can learn to put the negative where it belongs. By listening to you, she learns to use won't, can't, wouldn't, hadn't, wasn't.

Your child says, "I not eat biccit." You say, "You didn't eat your biscuit."

Your child says, "No candy left." You say, "Oh, dear—there isn't any more candy."

Questions
In the same way, you can teach her how to ask questions correctly and to use the appropriate words that precede questions.

Your child says, "Go out?" You say, "Where shall we go?"

Your child says, "More?" You say, "Would you like some more ice cream?"

Your child says, "Coat on?" You say, "Why do you put your coat on?"

In this way, your child learns to use the "wh" words, such as what, who, which, where, and why.

Adjectives
One of the best ways to teach your child about adjectives and the relationship of one object to another is to do it by opposites. If your child says, "big ball," you can look around for a smaller ball and then introduce her to the concept of opposites like big and small.

You will be able to show her that compared to each other, one is bigger than the other and one is smaller than the other. Similarly, you can introduce other concepts to your child, such as wide and narrow, thick and thin, deep and shallow, heavy and light, hard and soft. Always demonstrate with the appropriate objects and, if possible, make it into a kind of game.

Possessive pronouns
Your child says, "I bring book here," and you can say, "You were over there and you brought your book to me here."

Your child says, "I hate this biccit." You say, "Then I'll eat your biscuit and you can eat my biscuit."

Your child says, "This Jennifer coat, that Mommy coat." You say, "Yes, that is your coat, Jennifer, and this is my coat."

This way your child learns how to use the words "my" and "yours."

Asking and answering questions

When your child approaches her third birthday she'll constantly ask questions. You may get tired of answering the constant "whys," but you should be happy your child is so curious about what is going on around her and making so many attempts to try to understand the world and express her ideas in words.

Your child's questions should always be treated seriously, so give the most accurate, truthful answer you can. Don't fob your child off with an answer like, "Because that is the way it is," or "things are just made that way," because that can't advance her understanding at all. You have to give her information that adds to her knowledge in a form she can digest. When your child asks "Why is it raining?" don't respond with, "Because it is." Try, instead, a simple explanation, like clouds are full of water and the water is falling back to the earth in raindrops.

Your child's questions are usually very simple because she hasn't learned to use words to express her questions fully enough. Always examine the question to see what the point of it is. If your child asks, "What's that?" and you say, "A ruler," she may want more than a name. So you could say, "It's a ruler and you use it to measure things; look, this book is six inches long. It's also used to draw straight lines. Let's draw one together."

She may often ask questions that seem unanswerable at first, like, "Why birds fly?" But what she may really mean is "Why do birds fly? How do birds fly? Why do birds flap their wings?," so test out tidbits of information and then say to your child "Is that what you mean?"

Always answer truthfully

If you don't know the answer to a question, be truthful, and say that you don't know, but add, "Let's go and look at it in a book," or "Let's go and ask Daddy."

Sometimes parents shy away from giving truthful and accurate answers to children because they think a child won't be able to understand the truth. This is often the case with questions about death and sex. It's always best to answer these questions truthfully. Never avoid a difficult answer. However, don't make the mistake of thinking that when you tell the truth you have to tell the whole truth. You don't. It would be a mistake to do that because your child doesn't understand enough to cope with the complexities of the full reply. What you must always do is supply that part of the truth that she is able to digest and understand (*see p.259*).

LISPING

This is common speech defect in children who are just learning to talk. It occurs because the child simply has not mastered all the sounds needed to speak, so she substitutes a similar sound that she can make. The child may be copying another child with a lisp. This can become a habit, however. Neither of these is anything to worry about and usually stops without treatment.

Lisping may indicate a more serious underlying problem though. It may be caused by a degree of deafness, a cleft palate, or a faulty action of the tongue. Although these possibilities should have been excluded at your child's regular developmental checkups, if you are at all concerned about a child's persistent lisping, consult your pediatrician so that speech therapy can be started if necessary.

13 Social behavior

The foundations of your child's social behavior are laid in infancy. The way you treat your child and the way he responds to you and the outside world will be part of his makeup. Social development in early childhood goes through well defined stages. From being a very nongregarious newborn, your baby will join the surrounding social group by imitating others. One of the most important guides in this early period is the mother, or primary caregiver. Babies who establish warm, loving, outgoing relationships with their mothers are motivated to make friendly relationships with other people by the pleasure they feel in this early relationship.

Personal development birth to 1 year

Your baby is different from all others. He is unique, and no matter how many books you read, none of them can tell you about him. You are going to have to discover your baby for yourself. Little by little, by carefully observing, paying close attention to all the signals, you will come to know and prize his individuality. It is one of the most precious possessions a child has, and one of the most important jobs you do is to nourish that individuality. Help it grow and flower and maintain it intact.

Getting to know your baby as a person is like reading an exciting story very slowly. You'll find out if he likes very gentle treatment or slightly rougher handling; you'll discover if he has a sense of humor, enjoys a joke, and is eager to join in, or whether he prefers to be quiet. It may take you several weeks to know how he behaves when he's really well and happy, and until you do you may worry about whether he's ill. It may even take you a couple of months to know his crying patterns—an early signal of whether he's going to be a fretful baby or a placid one (*see p.158*). But don't worry. You'll gradually come to know all of your baby's idiosyncrasies: if he's a fast or slow feeder; if he needs a lot of sleep or is wakeful; he likes to be cuddled or not.

While you are learning about your baby, you will also have to make many reassessments and adjustments as you fit your daily routine to his needs.

Early socializing
You are your baby's favorite person and he will love to explore your face as way of saying "hello" and showing interest.

Social milestones

By the time your baby is six months old, he will have learned a lot about being a sociable human being. In ways that we do not quite understand, he will have become an expert at the flow of social exchange. He'll know how to start a conversation with you and how to get you to play. He will have learned how to hold your attention by smiling, by babbling, and by being interested and curious; and how to end a conversation by looking away or appearing bored.

The stages at which he acquires this ability are outlined below:

By three months Your baby won't like to be deprived of social contact and will quite often cry as soon as he is left alone. However, he'll stop crying when an adult reappears and when he is talked to or is diverted by a toy or a rattle. He'll turn his

Learning to laugh
Use laughter to show approval and punctuate games with laughs and jokes to develop your baby's sense of humor in social exchanges.

head when he hears human voices and will smile when an adult smiles at him or makes a kind of clucking sound. He'll express pleasure when others are present by smiling, kicking, and waving his arms. He'll recognize his mother and other familiar people by acting sociably, and will show fear of strangers by turning away and possibly even crying.

By the fourth month He may lift his arms in anticipation of being picked up. He will focus on faces and will almost always follows the direction of the person who leaves him. He'll smile at a person who speaks to him and when anyone pays special attention to him he'll show delight.

He'll laugh out loud when he is being played with.

Between the fifth and sixth month
He will show a different reaction to smiling than to a scolding tone of voice. Familiar people are greeted with a smile, and strange people with recognizable expressions of fear.

At six months Social behavior becomes much more active so he may pull the hair of the person who is holding him or rub their nose or start to pat the person's face.

At seven to nine months He will socialize by imitating speech sounds and gestures.

By 12 months He will refrain from doing things if told "No," and will show fear and dislike of strangers by rushing to his mother, and possibly even crying when the stranger approaches. He may become slightly clingy at this age.

Respond to his behavior

The generally accepted definition of a good baby is one who cries very little, settles down easily, and sleeps for long periods; the definition of a bad baby is the opposite. On the basis of these definitions, all of my friends had good babies and I had bad babies. However, I would not describe any of my babies as bad. My babies were demanding and occasionally difficult, but I am sure this arose only because they wanted my attention and, to me, this seems perfectly normal.

In the first few weeks, you and your baby have to get used to each other. Don't be put off by how your baby behaves initially. He has no control over how he responds to the outside world and may exhibit tendencies that will not remain beyond the first couple of months. He may be miserable, jumpy, excessively wakeful, or excessively sleepy. You must deal with your baby's needs as competently and calmly as possible, giving all the love that you have.

"Difficult" babies

A baby who is really difficult, who, for instance, cries and cannot be comforted by any of the usual methods (see p.162), is extremely hard to deal with calmly. The sound of a baby crying constantly is irritating and upsetting at the same time. If your baby also rejects your efforts to comfort him, you may feel spurned and inadequate. You may even become angry and believe that your baby is crying on purpose. This is absolutely impossible: your baby cries because he is biologically programmed to do so until his needs are understood and fulfilled. When you fail to do this, a vicious circle ensues. You become tense because the baby won't stop crying. When you're tense, you cannot cope calmly with your baby—as a result he'll cry even more. That way bad temper increases on both sides. Try very hard not to lose your temper or to get too worked up.

- Share the responsibility with your partner and take turns, wherever possible, to deal with your baby.
- Follow the advice on crying (see p.162–166), and don't forget, yours is not the only baby in the world who is going through this "difficult" period. Whatever you think, this spell will be brief.
- Don't treat your baby's behavior as a deliberate rejection of you—at the moment he can't help behaving like this as he's desperately trying to adapt to the

Keep him close
In the early weeks, carrying your baby with you in a sling as you go about your day gives him lots of close contact with you, and may help him sleep.

cry, won't be very alert, and won't take much notice of his surroundings. He may fall asleep while you feed him, he won't respond when talked to, and shows very little emotion.

A baby like this is marvelous initially, because he leaves you to regain your strength after delivery. But he's missing an awful lot in life and needs to be coaxed into realizing that being awake is much more fun.

- Don't try to keep your baby awake forcibly. He knows how much sleep he needs and you should respect this. However, you should make sure that he's not going for too long without food. If, for example, he can sleep through the night, you must wake him up before you go to bed, because it is too long for a new baby to go without liquid.
- Whenever he is awake, provide as much stimulation and affection as possible. Surround the crib with mobiles and photographs so that even if you're not there, he has something to focus on and be occupied by.
- Try carrying your baby in a sling so that at least he gets to know your warmth and smell, even though he's asleep.

Wakeful babies

Instead of sleeping the usual 16 out of 24 hours for the first few weeks of life, your baby may sleep as little as 12, and he'll take these in short bursts. He'll be full of life, interested in everything that's going

new world he's found himself in. You have to accept your baby as he is and deal with him accordingly; as he grows he'll change eventually.

- Accept any offer of help from friends and relatives so that you can take a break and recharge your batteries.
- Try talking to another parent or to your doctor about ways of coping, or contact a support group.

Sleepy babies

These babies are often called placid babies. Your baby may sleep 21 hours out of 24; he'll make few demands on you, will rarely on, and will be very eager to learn. Wakeful babies are usually very sociable and affectionate. Although he may exhaust you, he'll be very rewarding.

Until your baby's old enough to entertain himself, you and your partner will be his sole form of entertainment, and he may demand your attention at all hours of the day and night. If you don't work out some sort of shift system with your partner, you may become so fatigued that you cannot carry on. Don't be resentful of your baby's wakefulness; try to accept it and take practical steps to make sure that you get enough sleep.

- Carry the baby around in a sling.
- When you're at home, take the crib or carrier wherever you go, and place it safely on a table or work surface so that your baby can hear your voice.
- Have plenty of pictures and mobiles over the crib so that he'll be occupied.
- Prop him up in a bouncing chair or in the carriage or stroller (with straps on) from about six weeks.
- Keep the baby's room warm because this sometimes encourages sleepiness.

Discontented babies

You may have a discontented baby, one who is irritable when he's hungry yet doesn't enjoy feeding. He takes the feeding slowly and with difficulty. Afterward, he isn't very sociable and doesn't like to be held. When you talk to him, he doesn't seem to take much notice; he seems tired but fretful and not very relaxed. When laid down to sleep, he starts to cry.

Don't feel that you'll never succeed in making your baby comfortable and happy or you'll begin to feel inadequate and eventually resentful. Try to keep all negative emotions out of your head. Your baby's behavior is aimed at the outside world to which he's not yet acclimated, and not at you.

Never interpret your baby's unhappiness as a personal criticism. Try very hard, no matter how much your baby rejects you, to get him to smile at you. Try to engage him in play; sit with him on your lap and play, or even give him a massage. Get your baby to respond. Once he does this, then you know that you've turned the corner and you can get to know each other.

- When he cries, try all the crying remedies.
- Make sure his diaper is clean and dry and his room is warm and cozy before he's put down to sleep so he feels secure.
- Give as many feedings as he wants and never keep him waiting and crying.
- Put lots of mobiles above the crib to occupy his attention.
- Carry him around with you if that provides comfort.

Jumpy babies

All newborn babies are sensitive to loud noises and sudden, jerky movements, but jumpy babies overreact to normal stimuli. For example, when he gets hungry, he doesn't show hunger with the usual persistent cry but within a few seconds of waking is screaming hysterically. When he's picked up, his body stiffens and if he's put down again, his body may jerk. He'll seem to be alarmed by any kind of noise or rapid movement around him.

- Understand, once again, that your baby's behavior is not a rejection of you as a parent. It's just an inability to deal with the new world he's in.

- Hold your baby securely most of the time in such a way that there's no risk of his arms or legs flopping back, which can make him feel insecure.
- Pick him up gently and slowly. When you bend down speak softly and gently; you could even try singing a song.
- If he seems to feel more secure when he's near you, put him in a sling and carry him with you all of the time.
- Don't give your baby baths, just top and tail him every day (*see p. 72*). Never take all of his clothes off at once; always leave the T-shirt or the diaper on and try to keep his body covered, even by a towel, for as long as possible.
- Don't leave him in a noisy room. For example, avoid rooms that face noisy roads or schools, or rooms that have chiming clocks or telephones.

Your baby as part of the family
During the first few weeks of your baby's life, the household will revolve around him, but from then on he'll have to learn to fit in with the household and the rest of the family. It is important that your new baby learns to live with a group of people who have routines, accepted customs and modes of behavior, a number of guidelines, and a few rules.

However, your baby can't be expected to fit into family routines if he isn't introduced to them, so include your baby in family activities like mealtimes, games, outings, shopping, household chores,

caring for pets, and visiting friends as soon as possible. All of these encounters are important to your child because through the working of the family group he will learn about the ways of people in general. In this way he'll relate how he behaves with his own family to how he should behave with strangers.

Through the family, your baby will eventually learn the social customs and attitudes of your society. One of the most important ways your baby learns is by imitation—so by watching and copying how you behave, your child develops his own behavior patterns.

Involve your baby in family life
Include your baby in as many activities as possible. Give her a ringside seat at mealtimes for example, and let her get to know friends and family.

Boundaries birth to 1 year

Very few children under the age of a year need true discipline. Up to this age, a child is not open to reasonable argument and your main form of discipline will simply be to set boundaries and say "No" and, if your baby doesn't obey, to resort to the physical removal of either the baby or the object. Young babies should never be smacked or punished.

As they grow up, all young children need to be shown the boundaries of socially acceptable behavior by their parents. Many of these limits are implicitly set by the way members of the family behave to one another. Setting a good example by your own behavior is the best way to teach your child what good behavior is. It is part of your responsibility as the parent to give your child guidelines on behavior, so start to do this during your child's first year. If you don't, your child will soon find that other children and adults won't tolerate someone ill-mannered and selfish. You're going to have to keep some guidelines in your home, as in any other organized group of people, for the sake of efficiency, justice, and safety.

Understanding bad behavior

No baby behaves badly deliberately, although many a tired and exhausted parent feels convinced that they do. Your baby may cry constantly and be very irritable and grumpy, but this is usually because he is overtired, hungry, ill, anxious, or scared of your leaving or of meeting strangers. This is not your baby's fault, and he should never be blamed for what is beyond his control. Nor should you blame yourself if you've done everything within your power to prevent or correct what is causing your baby's unhappiness.

Toward the end of this year, one of the major causes of "bad behavior" will be frustration. Your baby may be a strong-willed character to begin with, and as he gets older and more independent, he's going to want to express this. A battle of wills will emerge and he will no longer accept that you have total control over his life. He'll challenge your preferences and begin to assert himself strongly. Objections to your choice of food are common, so let your baby choose what he wants to eat and the order that he eats it (see p.120). Equally, if he wants to wear certain items of clothing, let him go ahead and wear them. If you don't allow your baby some freedom at this time he will become frustrated and angry.

Help your child

Doing things alone may bring their own frustrations because your child's ambitions will often exceed his capabilities. He won't be able to make his body do what he wants it to, and he'll find that he cannot manage the world in the way that he wants to. This will inevitably result in tears and possibly temper tantrums (see p.166). Try not to get annoyed at this—every child goes through similar behavior—but give him your assistance. If you don't offer to help at this point, he may waste a lot of energy trying to do something that is completely beyond him, and repeated failure will be very demoralizing. When your baby is in this kind of mood, bullying and pressuring will cause more stubbornness. Be tactful, humorous even, and a little devious. If you let your baby feel that he is taking control, you'll find that he very often adapts to what you want. Instead of saying "Don't" to your baby, who is throwing plastic mugs everywhere, make the cleaning up into a game. Sit down and suggest that he try to pick them all up before you count to ten.

When to say "No"

During your baby's first year, there are very few reasons for saying "No." I had only one unbreakable rule in my children's first year. That was when they were doing something that was unsafe for them and others. In these instances, I would say "No" firmly and at the same time remove the object from my child, or stop my child from performing the dangerous activity. I did not wait for my child to stop. Since I was trying to teach my child what was unsafe, I always offered an explanation for why I was stopping him from behaving in a certain way. I simply stated what was dangerous about it and repeated it every time the same thing occurred, in the hope that my child would remember, learn, and not do it again. I did not chastise and I tried not to become angry. Only as they got older and learned the rule did I give them the opportunity to resist without my intervention first.

I believe the best way to teach a child how to behave is by praise and reward for good behavior, or by example with an explanation from other members of the family. However, this will only be successful when your child has the intellectual ability to recognize what's wrong and can decide what the correct way to behave actually is.

Possible concerns birth to 1 year

Many women believe that mother love will be turned on like a tap as soon as their baby is born. It can come as rather a shock when after even two or three days they don't feel anything for their baby that resembles love. They may feel tenderness and protectiveness toward this tiny new being who is dependent on them, but they don't feel a strong, binding love.

This is very common and not at all abnormal. Love usually does develop after one or two weeks. Until it does, concentrate on enjoying your baby physically: the feel of your baby against your skin; his smell as you put your nose into the crease of his neck; his grip as you put your finger into his tiny palm and feel it grasped tightly.

Postpartum depression

Most women have feelings known as the baby blues after childbirth. These are caused by the dramatic drop in hormone levels, and usually soon pass. About 10 percent of mothers, however, develop postpartum depression, which is more serious and can affect your relationship with your baby. Rapid medical attention is needed—the longer postpartum depression is left untreated, the longer it can take to resolve. Postpartum depression has many symptoms, and women experience these in varying combinations. As well as feelings such as hopelessness and despondency, sufferers can experience lethargy, anxiety, tension, sleep difficulties, loss of interest in sex, obsessive thoughts, feelings of guilt, and lack of self-esteem. If you have any of these symptoms don't bottle up your feelings—seek help. Go to your doctor or get counselling. The sooner treatment starts the better, and your depression should improve in a few weeks.

Antisocial babies

Just as there are adults who keep themselves to themselves, some babies are simply a bit antisocial. They don't smile much, they respond little to being talked to, they seem not to enjoy playing games, and they may not like being cuddled. On the other hand, they can become upset if left alone in a stroller or crib. They can be rather irritable and get upset easily. They tend to cry and are slow, fussy feeders.

When such a baby is tired he is fretful but doesn't go to sleep. Your best efforts fail to make this kind of baby sunny, and you may feel you are lavishing love to little effect. But don't blame yourself—some babies are just like this; you are not alone.

A baby who smiles a lot and exudes joy gets friendship, love, companionship, and help in return. The baby who acts miserable or who just stays in neutral gets less in return. Life is not as pleasant for him, so he may grow up to be a troubled individual. As a parent you may have to work hard to get your child to be more positive. Although you may find it difficult, you have to try your best to get your baby

to focus on you, to listen to you, to smile at you. If you can get to a stage where your baby is responding to your overtures, most of his unhappiness and yours will be a thing of the past.

Babies with disabilities

All babies develop at different speeds, from very fast to very slow. It can be difficult to judge what is normal and what is not. If you feel that your baby is not keeping up with the general social milestones (*see p.238*), consult your pediatrician. However, minor problems may not show up for several months, so always follow your instincts. If you suspect that your baby is not developing normally, seek early help. The earlier you get help, the greater the chance you have of dealing with an abnormality.

If your baby has a physical disability, it's often comforting and helpful to talk to people in similar situations, so contact any relevant agencies.

HEAD BANGING

Toward the end of the first year, some babies begin to bang their head against the end of the crib. This is rarely a sign of abnormality, and there's little risk of brain damage; most babies grow out of it quite quickly. However, minimize the risk by padding the ends of the crib with a quilted fabric, and by buffering the crib and the wall if it causes an irritating banging noise. Try giving your baby a relaxing bath at bedtime and an extra long cuddle—some psychologists think that such children may need more physical attention and stimulation. Music may also be soothing. If your baby continues to bang his head for several months, talk to your pediatrician.

Personal development 1 to 2 years

During the second year, much of your toddler's behavior is attention-getting. He will try to do this by speaking, by crying, by hitting, or by doing other things that he knows are forbidden. When he's successful at getting your attention, he'll show how satisfied he is by smiling or laughing.

Two-year-olds often seem to be very negative and their favorite word appears to be "No." This is a transitional stage between babyhood and childhood, and during it your toddler will be trying to assert his independence. He'll want to do everything immediately, and will frequently want a specific routine adhered to. Your toddler's mood may change frequently and his emotions may veer between extremes of lovingness and temper tantrums. One of the things that you must do is follow your child's mood when he shows this kind of negative assertiveness. Unless your child is given the opportunity to exert his independence at this stage, such early resistance can lead to strongly negative behavior now and later.

On a much more positive level, two-year-old toddlers become much more cooperative in play. Early play with an adult teaches toddlers how to be socially cooperative, as long as the adults are patient in showing children how to share. Your toddler will learn to share by being shared with. Gradually he will begin to cooperate with other children in play, although in the beginning other children may be unwilling to share. Encourage your child to persevere and don't give up teaching your child by your example.

Likes and dislikes

A child begins to show all kinds of assertiveness during this year and it is natural that he should demonstrate preferences dramatically. He is very eager to grow up and to show that he is growing up. He no longer sees himself as a mirror image of you; he now sees the two of you as separate people, and therefore finds no reason for doing exactly what you want. He will be determined to exercise his independence and will refuse offers of help and shrug off your assistance, even when he really needs it.

Your child is developing likes and dislikes, and has a very strong urge to fulfill his own desires, even though they may not be the same as yours—and yet the conflict this may bring can make him feel very unhappy. Your child is torn between the very strong drive to exert independence and the drive to be loved by you.

Even when he is trying to win a battle with you, he needs your help and emotional support because he is too immature to manage without them.

Balancing his needs

Your job is to take the middle road and try to balance your child's need for independence with the need for love and protection. It isn't always easy. Your toddler's thinking is immature, his memory is short, and his judgement is unreliable. He can't think ahead and may be impatient when things don't get done immediately.

At the same time, your child is eager to control and dominate the world around

Cooperation in play
Help your child learn about playing happily with other children by encouraging him to take turns when he plays with you.

him. His strength of will is ahead of his intellectual capacity, so you'll have to decide when it is time to baby your toddler, and when it's time to encourage him and push him on, allowing him independence and adventurousness while still guarding against any dangers. Be flexible in allowing your toddler to exercise his likes and dislikes, and don't enforce your will simply to win or to show your authority. You can always win a battle by pulling rank, but you shouldn't be unreasonable just for the sake of it.

Judge the situation carefully. You'll find that there are very few instances where it is important for you to get your own way (one would be if your toddler's safety or well-being was threatened, for example). Where it doesn't matter and no harm will come of it, it's best to let your child do what he wants to.

Personality

Your child is born with his own personality, which shows itself within the first few weeks of life. However, there are certain social situations that will develop a child's personality during early childhood. They can bring out both the good and bad aspects of his personality, so try to make sure that the good traits are accentuated and the bad ones played down.

THE TIMID CHILD

Some children are naturally shy; they keep to themselves, and speak very little. Don't immediately think that your child has problems and become overanxious and overprotective. A child who is talkative on home ground may be completely silent and withdrawn in a strange place or when confronted with strangers. This happens in many children around the age of one. In a new situation, don't increase your child's difficulties by insisting that he join in immediately. Allow him to sit quietly on your knee or to stand by your side while he takes in what everyone is doing and becomes familiar with it. After half an hour or so, when you can sense that he is feeling more comfortable, gradually encourage him to join in your conversation. Even a shy child, if encouraged in this gentle, slow way, will join in with new friends and new games after an hour or so. But remember to introduce new experiences slowly and allow your child to get used to them before moving on to other ones.

If your child is very timid and shy he may become very upset if you try to leave him with a babysitter. You must try to understand your child's feelings and still give him your love no matter how irritating the situation is. He'll grow out of this clinginess with your help, but he'll need to gain a sense of security first.

- If your child has a strong desire for approval, he will be motivated to fulfill the expectations of those around him. The desire for your approval and the approval of other adults usually comes before the desire for the approval of friends. Whenever you can, get your child to do the "right" things for your approval, then praise him for doing it.
- Young children express their sympathy by trying to help or comfort a person who is sad or in distress, but they are unable to sympathize until they have been in a situation similar to that of a person who is distressed.
- When children understand the facial expressions and speech of others, they develop the ability to empathize with them and to understand what the other person is feeling.
- Children who tend to be dependent, who like to be helped, and given attention and affection, are often motivated to behave in a socially approved way. The more independent children are motivated less by the desire for approval.
- Children who are friendly express their friendliness by wanting to do things for and with others. These children express their affection for others in all kinds of words and gestures.
- Children who are not allowed to be constantly in the limelight of family attention, and who are given opportunities and encouragement to share what they have, want to think of others and do things for them rather than simply concentrating on their own possessions, their own interests, and getting their own way.

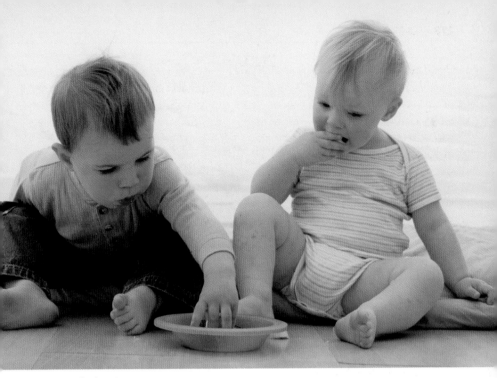

Playing and sharing

Your toddler should mix with others as soon as possible. In the first year your child becomes used to interacting, not only with members of the immediate family, but also with his extended family, such as aunts, uncles, cousins, grandparents, and friends who come to the house. Your toddler will be a great deal more comfortable with strangers and adults if he starts off by feeling that every friend of yours is a friend of his. He needs to know, too, that there are other members of the family who will help and care for him and whom he can rely on and trust.

If you help your child accept others readily then he won't have too much difficulty mixing with other children when expanding experience and the desire to strike out make him want the company of others of his age. At about the age of 18 months, children will usually tolerate other

Encouraging toddlers to share
Between the ages of one and two years, children play alongside rather than with each other. Giving them something to share can help them interact more.

children, although they won't necessarily play together. They may play side by side doing the same thing, but rarely interact with each other. A little later, when they start to play with toys, grabbing and hitting between children is not unusual. However, if your child does this repeatedly, you need to explain that it's not a good way to behave, and point out that he wouldn't like the same done to him.

While your child has to learn to share, it is not realistic to expect him to give a toy to another toddler if he wants it. This is not because your child is selfish or a bully; it is because he hasn't appreciated the concept of sharing. If your child makes a grab for a toy that another child is playing with, you can teach him about sharing by saying that if he has his friend's toy, he must give one of his to the friend. A child of two is usually able to understand the justice of this reciprocity.

You have to deal with sharing in very simple terms, because intellectually your child is not grown up enough to have more adult behavior forced upon him. It is not until he is about two-and-a-half to three that you can use reason and expect your child to be more altruistic.

ONLY CHILDREN

Although only children undoubtedly benefit from the constant love that they receive, and grow up feeling very close to both parents and friends, there are few who don't confess to having wanted brothers and sisters at some stage in their lives. This is rarely a serious problem, but one of the things you can do to mitigate any possible problems is to introduce your baby to other babies of the same age. As your baby reaches the sociable age, around 18 months to two years, make a real effort to find friends for him and invite them to visit you at home.

Try not to overindulge

It's easy for parents to overindulge an only child and to make him feel too important. You're going to have to curb your desire to give him all that he wants and, just as important, all your attention. It's important that he learns to accept that he can't have everything he wants and be the permanent center of your world, just as a child in a larger family has to (see p.242).

It may be tempting to be possessive and over-protective. This can be bad for you and your child. You'll feel bereft when he becomes independent and needs you less, but your child will lose out on a sense of curiosity, adventure, and independence and may become clingy. You mustn't shy away from disciplining your child either. Like any other child, he has to be shown the right way to behave if he's to grow up able to mix with others.

Encouraging generosity

You can encourage your child to be generous from a very early age. Since you are the most important person in his life it is easiest to be generous with you. You can take advantage of your child's desire to please you by teaching little generous acts (like giving Daddy a toy), and then go on to encourage more and more unselfishness in his behavior toward you and the other members of the family. It is only natural for your child to want to please you and be friendly with people who obviously care for him and love him and for whom he feels great affection.

Having accepted generous behavior toward people he loves as the norm, it is a fairly logical extension to show unselfish, generous behavior to people who are just friends. Ask your young child to give you a toy, to give Daddy a toy, or to give you one each. Or, if he finds a particular activity exciting and pleasurable you can ask him if you can join in and share the pleasure and excitement. Then you can encourage your toddler to do the same with the other members of the family or friends who come to your home.

By the time your child is about 18 months old, he should be able to share activities and treats with anyone who enters your home and is seen as a friend. If he can manage to do this, he is well on the way to being generous and unselfish with his peers.

Boundaries 1 to 2 years

Children like to know the boundaries of behavior and need them to be happy and well adjusted. Boundaries are essential to a child's development because they fulfill certain needs.

- By knowing the boundaries, children learn how to behave in ways that bring them praise. They interpret this praise as acceptance and love. Both are essential if your child is to adjust well to growing up and being happy.
- When discipline appropriate for the age of your child is applied, it serves as motivation. It encourages your child to strive to accomplish what is required and brings comfort and satisfaction.
- Boundaries help a child develop a sense of self-control and conscience. This inner voice will later guide him in making his own decisions and controlling his own behavior. Without them, he may be indecisive and act in an antisocial way.
- Undisciplined children are often scolded. This gives them a feeling of guilt and shame. These feelings will inevitably lead to unhappiness and poor adjustment.

When to use discipline

Discipline overdone or underdone can be equally bad for children; both extremes lead to insecurity. There is no place for ruling your child by fear, force, corporal punishment, or humiliation. While you can tell your child the reasons why you want some things to be a certain way, you cannot use reason until he's about two and a half or three. So disciplining has to be simple, easy to understand, and in direct relationship to the misbehavior being punished. There should be no delay between what your child does and the discipline he is given, and the action has to fit whatever it is your child has done.

If you're often extremely angry over minor misdemeanors, your child will be bewildered. Keep discipline for really serious matters like destructiveness, being physically violent, or telling lies. In this way your child gets very clear messages about what is tolerated and what is not. Your child's memory is short, and if you brood over what he's done he will simply not understand. He will think that you are purposely withdrawing love from him and be very perplexed, so make all discipline clear and swift, and then forget it.

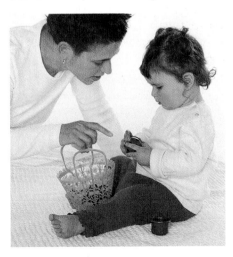

Understanding boundaries
Once you establish boundaries of behavior for your child, stick to them. Children thrive on consistency because they know where they stand.

Avoiding problems

Children are very receptive to fairness and justice, and if you adhere to these two principles you will probably avoid most difficulties in disciplining.

Avoid corporal punishment at all costs. Research has shown that children don't know why they are being smacked. They cannot remember, so they don't associate the punishment with the crime, so smacking doesn't act as a deterrent. Never punish a child as a calculated act. The child is much less damaged by a sharp word in the heat of the moment that is quickly forgotten when the air is cleared, than by a long argument with a threatened punishment as soon as you get home or, worse, when your partner gets home.

You will not go wrong if you are very clear about your motives for disciplining. Make sure that they are for the happiness and safety of the child, and not simply as a means of impressing on your child your authority and superiority.

BEHAVIOR GUIDELINES

Learning the rules of social behavior and learning self-control takes time; it doesn't take months, it takes years. Don't expect him to remember what you said last time. He isn't necessarily defying your previous instruction, he may simply have forgotten it. A child of two has a very short memory, so be forgiving and repeat your instructions. Words never mean as much as actions, and you really do have to show your child how to behave. Here are some of the things that you can do.

- Have as few "rules"—those instructions that cannot be broken under any circumstances—as possible. "Don't" is a very negative word and if you are not careful, by the time your child is two, you could be prefacing everything you say with "Don't." "Do" is a very positive word so reinforce with positive "dos" and cut down the "don'ts."
- Don't give vague instructions; try to be very clear. Instead of saying "Don't be naughty," tell him exactly what you don't want him to do.
- If you give your child instructions, always give a reason why. If you tell your child that his tricycle has to be put away when he's finished using it at night, explain that otherwise it may get rusty in the rain and not work. Try to avoid saying "Because I say so" when he asks you why.

- Always reward good behavior with praise and affection, possibly even with a treat if your child has accomplished something difficult. You can help him distinguish between good and bad behavior just by withholding praise and rewards from acts you don't approve of.
- There is no better way to get your child to do something than to show that you do it, too. If you want your child to take off his dirty shoes at the door, show him that you do it, too.
- Be consistent. Don't let your standards slide and give one instruction on one occasion and the opposite on another (although you can show that under certain circumstances you are prepared to be flexible). There is no reason why your child shouldn't have a lot of ice cream on his birthday, because he knows that that day is special, but he should learn not to expect the same on the following day.
- Always admit your mistakes to your child, no matter how young he is, and always be generous when you do something wrong. It makes your child feel that the world is fair and just. Don't be afraid to say, "naughty Mommy," or "Mommy shouldn't have done that," or "You are right. I won't do it again."

Possible concerns 1 to 2 years

The aggressive child

Aggression is a basic act of hostility and the ways in which we use it usually mean that it is unprovoked by anyone else. Most children have feelings of aggression to some extent and usually express them in verbal or physical attacks on another child—very often a child who is smaller than they are.

Aggressiveness, bullying, and destructiveness are modes of behavior that usually represent cries for help. They frequently result from parental neglect, absence, over-discipline, under-discipline, or too much smacking. A child who behaves this way is really not at fault, although he may be very hard to help. It is worth remembering that a nasty child is usually nasty because someone has been nasty to him. You shouldn't be too ready to blame the child but should look beyond the behavior to his home and his general environment. Weaning a child off his normal pattern of behavior, and his distrust of adults, may take many years, because he has to relearn the attitudes he has been absorbing from the day he was born.

If your child starts to show signs of being very aggressive, try to nip it in the bud. Don't punish and don't smack your child for being aggressive; this will only make the behavior worse. Instead, show him very firmly that you are not prepared to put up with it and that he will gain nothing but your disapproval if he continues with his current behavior. Show him that if he can change he will be highly rewarded, and will gain lots of praise for his good efforts. If your child seems to be highly disturbed, or if you're at all worried by an aspect of his behavior, seek expert help immediately.

Jealousy

Rivalry is a perfectly normal emotion for a child to feel. Sometimes it can have a positive effect and can act as a spur to make the child do his best. In this instance, it adds to his friendliness and his desire to socialize. However, if it leads to quarreling and boasting, your child will have a hard time with it.

A child feels one of the strongest forms of jealousy when a new baby arrives. This is because your child feels that he's been "dethroned" and that he has lost the special place he had in your life. He may try all types of attention-seeking actions and may even revert to such babyish behavior as losing bowel control, refusing to feed himself, or refusing to dress alone. He may direct his jealousy directly at the baby and try to hurt it. He might also feel unable to cope with these jealous emotions and may internalize them so that he becomes quiet and stays away from you; he may even reject you altogether.

It is very easy to understand all these emotions. You must try to help your child by preparing him for the arrival of a new baby and by showing that his place in your affections is secure. Make a special time when he has all your attention. Involve him in taking care of the baby by asking for assistance in certain easy tasks, and praise and reward him for helpful behavior, and whenever he shows love and affection for the new arrival.

Overindulgence

It is very easy for any parent to overindulge or spoil their child. After all, you have a natural desire to please your child and to make his life happy. It's all too easy to err on the side of giving a child too much, of making life too easy for him, and allowing him to become the center of your universe. You will have to control these desires in yourself for your child's sake.

One of the ways in which you can help your child not to be egocentric is to make sure from early on that he is not always the center of your attention. He must learn that the world does not revolve around him, that the household and the family do not see him as the pivot of their constant attention. If you let your child know quite clearly that there are times when he's expected to do without you and to do things alone, you will be doing him a favor. None of these should involve cruelty or force. You should show your child as much love as you can, but he should be made to see that everyone has certain boundaries

within which they live. As he gets older, teach him that you have a need for privacy just as he does, although you're always there if he needs you.

Don't make the mistake of thinking that overindulgence has anything to do with the number of possessions your child has or how much affection he gets. It has to do with allowing your child to grow up so that he impresses his will on you and on others by using power games like wheedling or bullying. It is a parent's duty to prevent this from occurring.

Temper tantrums

Between one and two years old, temper tantrums are normal, attention-seeking devices (see p.168). Children of this age have not yet acquired the judgment to match their strength of will, and clashes with parents are therefore frequent. If anger or frustration are excessive, they may culminate in a tantrum. Children usually throw themselves on the floor kicking and screaming because they do not have the control to do anything else. It is their way of showing their helplessness to overcome a problem in a controlled way.

Far and away the best thing to do is to stay calm. If you don't, your child will catch your mood and it will make his behavior worse. Ignore your child and, if possible, leave him alone. A tantrum loses much of its point if there is no audience.

As your child gets older, he will become better able to tolerate delays and accept compromises. At the same time, you will become more expert at anticipating problems and avoiding head-on clashes, and will become more skilled at finding distractions for him.

STUTTERING

Nearly all children of this age have jerky speech that, on occasion, may turn into a real stutter. This may be because your child has so many ideas in his head that he thinks more quickly than he can speak. It may also be that he is very excited and simply can't articulate properly. Stutters can also appear for a short time and then disappear again. Stay calm and don't draw your child's attention to the stuttering. Don't jump in with the word that you think your child is looking for. Simply accept his speech. Making your child feel nervous and self-conscious about the way he talks will only increase his tendency to stammer.

Conflicting desires
As your baby grows she can sometimes get confused and unhappy at the conflict between her urge to be independent and her desire to please you.

"Naughty" or disobedient?

There are some children who are habitually naughty and some who are habitually disobedient. These two things have to be handled differently.

To me, a naughty child is one who is immature and not able to exert sufficient self-control to do what he knows is right. A disobedient child is quite mature and knowingly flouts your wishes and rules.

A naughty child is often forgetful and simply forgets your remonstrances. You can correct him for doing something wrong and find him doing it again an hour later. He'll be genuinely surprised to find himself in the wrong again so quickly. Naughty children frequently get so wrapped up in an activity that rules go by the board. This kind of child needs more repeated tellings than the average, and careful, sympathetic correction. Usually, a naughty child will be apologetic and contrite, and this should be warmly received. However, there does come a point when a naughty child needs to be punished. I favor withdrawal of treats and pleasures that can be reinstated when a set goal has been achieved.

Your child may go on being naughty for a long time. Be prepared for this to happen and don't become too angry; sheer naughtiness is more of an irritation than a serious annoyance. You may feel you can sympathize to a certain extent with the naughtiness; even if you don't feel like this try not to be too hard.

Disobedience is another matter. Most of us feel little sympathy for a constantly disobedient child who rarely apologizes or expresses any kind of repentance. If you have a disobedient child you may have a constant stream of negatives, arguments, and recriminations. Guard against this if you can. A child has a limited repertoire with which to respond to your anger. Brutality in your behavior will lead to brutality in his. Physical punishment from you will encourage violence, truculence, and aggression in him. It's hard, but try a program of positive actions and words. Try to explain to him why he shouldn't be so disobedient; explain when his actions are dangerous or antisocial and suggest how he should behave. Outlaw punishments, reward all good acts. It often works. Whatever you do don't alienate your child. You are all he has. Show your love, and always let him know he can come to you.

Personal development 2 to 3 years

Your young baby's dependence on you stemmed from the fact that you were the center of his universe, and his primary caretaker and affection-giver. He couldn't get through life without your help and support, and he sought your approval and affection.

However, as he gets older and begins to see himself as an independent person, not just a reflection of you, he also begins to see you as a separate personality and as a whole person. He will be experiencing many different feelings and new emotions with which he has to become familiar. At this stage he begins to know real love for many of the things around him: his favorite toy, a pet, a favorite grandparent. All of these feelings bring your child closer to the adult idea of love.

Children respond to your moods

If he sees that you are tired he is genuinely concerned, and if you are unhappy he is sincerely sympathetic. When he is enjoying something, he will want to share the experience with you and will offer to share it. If you need help, he will offer it to you spontaneously because he really wants to give it. If you are upset or frightened, he feels profoundly sorry for you, and tells you so with words and expressions. He has a strong desire to make you feel better and happier, and does so in the only way that he knows, by telling you that he loves you and by hugging you.

This is quite a step forward in your child's personal development, because all these feelings and actions are truly unselfish. He is putting someone else before himself; he is genuinely caring and loving; he wants to understand someone else and do what is best for her; and he wants to bring her pleasure and comfort. These are very grown-up things to want to do. Always encourage these tendencies and make sure you praise him when he exhibits them.

Imitation and identification

Your child has always learned by imitation and as he gets older he begins to learn by "identification," too. He begins to put himself in your position and into the position of others and starts to behave as he would have others behave toward him. This means that he is starting to control himself and take command of himself. You may even overhear your child scolding himself when he has done something that he thinks you will disapprove of. The big difference is that he now disapproves of it in himself as well.

You will find your child observing and identifying with most of the adults who are close to him and any interesting ones who are not. He may give in to his imagination by dressing up and acting out roles and by being all kinds of different people. But most of all, what he is doing is practicing being you. He will play Mommy or Daddy with dolls and toys and you may even hear him imitate the exact phrases that you use with exactly the same intonation you have in your voice. These are all his ways of exploring and experimenting with the way he thinks the world works.

Making friends

Your child's galloping desire to learn brings with it the desire for the company of children of a similar age. He will probably be showing signs of gregariousness and of wanting to join in games with others during this year, and he'll need the stimulation of other children's ideas and their company.

You cannot make friends for your child, but you can help him find friends. Your child has to learn how to make friends slowly, just as he has learned all the other lessons in his life, so introduce your child to making friends with only one at a time.

Start off on home ground first and invite a child who lives nearby so that your child is in familiar surroundings and has a sense of confidence about what he is doing and where he's doing it. Make sure you are nearby to give him help and support if he needs it, and encourage him

Playing together
Children need to learn how to make friends. Invite first one, then several friends to your home for a tea party, or a picnic in the backyard.

to settle down to playing by playing along yourself. Once he has gotten over the first hurdle of making friends, try inviting two or three children to the house at the same time. Once your child becomes a member of a group of friends, make it clear to him that they are welcome at your home and that he can bring them into the house once he has asked your permission. As your child makes his first steps into the outside world, it is important that he has a comfortable feeling about it and has confidence about his own place within it. Helping him gather a small group of friends he knows and gets along with, is an important way of laying down the right patterns for later life.

Encouraging security

All children have fears. Anxiety and fear are normal emotions, but they make a child feel very unhappy and uneasy. It will be some time before your toddler has the ability to cope with fears or avoid the things that make him afraid (*see p.170*).

One of the most common early fears is of your absence or of being abandoned. The easiest way to cure this is to show your child that you will always come back as you promised and when you said you would. Fear will not be cured by staying with your child; that will only make him more fearful because he will never learn to cope without you.

Your young child also begins to feel anxiety if he finds that his own feelings like frustration, anger, and jealousy, are getting out of control. The way to help here is to listen and observe your toddler as closely as possible, so that you can pick up all the clues about what is causing his anxiety and then reassure him. Talking about some of the fears and explaining what's happening will give the reassurance that he needs.

Remember that whether you think your child's fear is reasonable or unreasonable, as far as your child is concerned, the fear is still the same. All fears have to be handled sympathetically and gently. Never suddenly present your child with whatever makes him most frightened. You wouldn't dream of asking your child to stay outside in a thunderstorm if he was afraid of thunder, so why should you expect him to pat the dog he's afraid of? Whenever your child shows fear, accept that fear as real, and don't brush it aside as nothing. Always tell your child when there is nothing to fear, but don't just tell him not to be afraid, because he won't understand that. Explain why there is no reason to be frightened, always tell him that you understand why he is, and sympathize with his fear. Never ridicule the fear; that will simply make your child secretive, and it is much harder for him to cope with a fear alone than to cope with your help.

Nudity and sexuality

A child's sex education begins with the first cuddle. All children take pleasure in physical contact and joy in their parents' reciprocity. They grow up realizing that people touch one another as an act of friendship as well as an act of love.

As your child gets older, he will become pleasantly aware of his body, without being at all self-conscious about it. You can encourage this by having an open attitude to nudity within the family. Like everything else, a child learns patterns of behavior and attitudes from you. The child who sees his parents unclothed and unembarrassed will take nudity as a matter of course and is unlikely to grow up concerned about nakedness. On the other hand, if you are worried about it, he will almost certainly worry about it, too.

It is natural for a child to be curious about the differences between male and female bodies. Your child will probably have been aware of the difference in genders since the age of 15 months or so, and once he sees his parents naked he'll be aware of sexual differences. Curiosity about his mother's breasts and his father's penis is best satisfied by a frank talk and a good look. Neither of these things is likely to stimulate sexual feelings in your child, and he'll only be embarrassed if you are.

Answering children's questions

Children who are encouraged to ask questions, and who are given explanations, take for granted that their parents will listen to them. These children grow up to be happier and less authoritarian than children whose questions are ignored and who are rarely supplied with explanations. Parents who take note of what their child says are showing that they consider him an individual with something useful to say. If your family believes and operates in this free and easy manner, it's going to be a much happier unit.

In the early years, your child regards you as omniscient and will naturally turn to you for advice on most subjects. If you remain approachable and welcome questions, your child will grow up feeling that he can talk to you about anything. Discouraging your child from asking questions when he's young and uninhibited will only make any inhibitions worse as he gets older. If you want to be the confidant of your children, it is important to try to keep the channels of communication open at any cost.

You should not avoid answering questions, even if they embarrass you. If you are concerned about when to tell your child about sex, the answer is you explain the first time he asks you. A child's curiosity should always be met by your willingness to answer truthfully. It is much better if he learns about sex in an accurate, matter-of-fact way from you than in a secretive, melodramatic way from friends who may well have some of the information wrong.

From about three years onward, a child can handle at least part of the truth about sexual questions, although it is not until he is about six or seven that he will be able to understand the mechanics of sex. I told my own children about conception, the growth of a child in the womb, and childbirth whenever they asked about it. I left talking about sexual intercourse until the age of six or so depending on the child. All discussions about sex must include aspects of caring, loving, and the responsibilities involved in intimate relationships.

HANDLING GENITALS

Babies usually become aware of their genital organs toward the end of the first year, but handle them without any obvious pleasure. Handling eventually does bring a pleasurable sensation, and then fondling becomes more like real masturbation. Most children of both sexes masturbate, and it's simply unreasonable to expect them not to. Despite the myths, it will not lead to blindness or insanity.

It is perfectly normal for a boy to handle his penis. After all, he handles every other part of his body that sticks out. In young children, this is rarely done for any length of time or for any purpose. The pleasure it brings is more general than sexual. It is not until children are much older that they feel sexual excitement.

Don't scold your child

There is no reason to discourage a child from handling genitals, nor should you stop him from masturbating. That will only cause furtiveness, and worse, it may stop your child from discussing anything about genital organs in later life. Unless masturbation is an obsessional means of escaping from reality, the best way to treat it is by paying no attention to it at all. If by accident it happens in public, distraction is the best course of action, but never, ever, scold your child for it.

Boundaries 2 to 3 years

As your child becomes old enough to reason with you, you can explain what discipline is. This way he will grow up knowing that discipline is based on mutual responsibility and participation in decisions. Don't expect blind obedience from a child. It is far better to reason and persuade. If, however, you take the trouble to discuss why it is wrong to behave in a certain way and right to behave in another, you'll find that your child is interested in motives and is much more likely to do what you want because he understands why you want it.

On the other hand, don't make the mistake of talking over every decision, and never just telling your child what to do. When you think the situation warrants it, give a simple order, unless you feel that your child is going to be recalcitrant and a softer approach may be better.

Good discipline should give your child the opportunity to make a choice. Part of growing up is about exercising choices and options, and he has to learn this skill like any other. Choose very carefully when you are going to give him a choice: let it be one he will find fairly simple, one you don't really think is important whichever way the decision goes. Don't try to fool your child by giving a choice when your decision is already made; you won't fool him.

When to insist

To my mind, there are just a few instances when you have to insist on discipline.

- When your child's safety or the safety of another person is threatened, there have to be rules; for instance, whenever fireworks are used or whenever you make a campfire or have a barbecue.
- Children have to grow up learning that the wishes and comforts of other people must be honored. I have been very strict on matters where thoughtfulness, helpfulness, unselfishness, and courtesy with anyone are concerned.
- I feel that there can be few concessions about honesty. With my own children I was always severe with lying and stealing. I didn't do this with punishment but by proving to the child that it was better and easier on them to tell the truth, no matter how bad it was, and no matter how dreadful the crime seemed, than to tell a lie. I wanted my children to know that I appreciated the courage it takes to own up to something.

Understanding right and wrong
Your child will only be able to learn the differences between right and wrong if they are clearly pointed out by you and explained every time.

Possible concerns 2 to 3 years

An aggressive antisocial child

We've all experienced feelings of aggressiveness toward other people, especially when we feel that our security is being threatened. It is only by great self-control that we conquer such feelings, and that's something that takes many years of learning and maturity to achieve. It is not surprising, therefore, that many children give full rein to aggressive instincts.

When aggressive behavior in a child becomes a regular feature, however, it is usually a response to two things: a lack of effective restraint and discipline from the time he was born, and a feeling of insecurity in the child, who may be experiencing a lack of parental attention, love, and affection. In both ways, the parents are almost entirely responsible for the child's difficult behavior.

If you have an aggressive child, look closely at the way you and your partner behave, and if you're honest with yourselves you'll almost certainly find you are falling short in your position as teachers and role models for your child. It is fairly easy to prevent a child from ever becoming aggressive, but it is very difficult to retrain an aggressive child. One of the first and most important ways to teach gentleness and flexibility in your child, is to be flexible, tolerant, and gentle yourself in all your dealings with him. Don't forget your child will imitate everything you do, including being aggressive.

If your child suddenly becomes aggressive or starts bullying, this is a sure sign of some tension or unhappiness in the child's life, and you should look carefully for the cause of it. In a young child it will nearly always be found in his relationship with you, your partner, or the rest of the family, or to tension in the home. Don't think that you can pull the wool over a young child's eyes by sweeping things under the carpet; children will always pick up on the atmosphere, and this can cause great insecurity.

Shyness

Some children are shy by nature, and studies show that up to ten percent of infants are born with a nervous system that predisposes them to shy behavior. Such children show their shyness by giving evidence of disliking new experiences; even when taken to a family gathering or party, they will spend most of the time clinging to their mothers' legs or hiding their faces.

STEALING

Most young children are used to taking things that belong to others—their mother's makeup, a sibling's toy, or their father's keys—just because they want to play with them, and at home this isn't usually a problem. However, young children are incapable of understanding the "property rights" of others, and you may discover that your child has taken something while you were out shopping or visiting a friend's home. If this is the case, explain to the child that this is stealing, and that stealing is not allowed. Eventually, your child will get the idea. It isn't necessary to have the child accompany you when you return the object, unless the habit has become persistent and you feel that extra enforcement is necessary. Most children feel penitent enough on being found out.

"HABITS"

Nail-biting, thumb-sucking, and carrying a comforter are not abnormal in a young child. Don't try to stop them, and certainly never by force, ridicule, or deprivation. They are nearly always caused by tension of some kind and they happen in about half of otherwise normal schoolchildren. For the most part, they are unconscious, nervous habits and are best cured by encouraging pride in appearance. For example, the majority of children stop nail-biting when they become more concerned about their appearance and become interested in the opposite sex. At this age, social considerations begin to outweigh personal habits.

I don't believe in discouraging these habits. As they get older, children sense what is acceptable, impose self-control, and only indulge in their habit in private. No one can persuade me that this mature behavior needs correcting.

Comfort habits
Thumb-sucking and carrying a comforter can continue right into the teens, but eventually a child will give up the habit of his own accord.

They also show reluctance in conversing with strange children or adults, and typically prefer to play alone rather than in a group. When such a child grows older and attends school, he may be diffident about making new friends.

If your child is shy, my advice is not to criticize him or to try to change his nature—not only is this unrealistic, but it also may add to the problem. Instead, when you know that a new experience is in coming up, try to prepare him ahead of time so that any strangeness is diminished. When he is meeting new people, allow him plenty of time to get used to them before you expect him to learn to feel comfortable in their presence.

A fresh child

It is not always easy to draw the line between freshness and impertinence. Occasional freshness is, to my mind, a perfectly acceptable trait. I like it in a child because it suggests spirit, mischievousness, and a healthy attitude toward authority.

There is also the mistaken belief that questioning decisions is being fresh. This is because some parents feel that freshness undermines their authority. However, if you encourage your child to talk things over with you, you will encourage his sense of responsibility for disciplining himself rather than blindly obeying your decisions. In this way, he will grow up aware of the value of persuasive argument. On the other hand, if you always encourage your child not to say what he thinks because you always interpret arguing as being naughty, he will rarely get the chance to understand the reasoning behind your decisions.

The other good aspect of being fresh is that it provides a verbal mechanism for getting rid of anger and frustration. Anger is a perfectly acceptable emotion in a child, but it isn't acceptable if he is venting his anger in a physical way. It is much better for your child to shout than to hit someone. So when your child is fresh, weigh why you think he is being so and if the reasons are healthy, and keep it in check. Insolence goes beyond freshness because it flouts good manners. It ignores thinking about how the other person feels and it may be hurtful. If your child goes over the boundary into insolence, you'll need to teach him that this isn't acceptable.

Selfishness in children

All children are naturally selfish, but as your child comes out of toddlerhood the most important lesson to learn is "Treat others as you would like to be treated." This means learning that he can't always have the treats he wants because they have to be shared with others; he may not have the biggest, rosiest red apple because there is only one and another child may want it; he has to learn to lose because only one child will win and it will not always be him.

The most important way of convincing your child that he should not be selfish is to try to get him to feel how other children will respond to selfishness. If he can understand that generally speaking all other children are feeling the same way as he is, then it is obvious that people have to take turns at getting what they want, whether it is being the top dog or having more turns on the swing than anyone else. It's up to you, by your actions, to show your child the benefits of unselfishness.

An overindulged child

A child who is overindulged is a self-centered child. Here are some of the things that you may have been doing that will make your child egotistical:

- If you are overprotective, you can make your child feel that he is extra-special. Children who are waited on hand and foot by others and protected from experiences, grow up to expect that others will continue to do things for them instead of making the effort to do them themselves. This stifles independence and cooperativeness.
- If you show favoritism toward a child you encourage a sense of self-importance. Children who are not favored have feelings of inferiority or martyrdom. Either way, it encourages the child to become self-centered rather than outgoing and thoughtful about others.
- Some parents set too high a goal for their children, and encourage them to become egocentric when they strive for these goals.

One of the best cures and possibly the only cure—if you won't change your ways—for an over-indulged child is to let him go to school early. He really needs the leveling process of a playgroup or a nursery school, and getting used to mixing with a group and being considered the same as anybody else. Later in life, he may respond well to boarding school. If neither of these things is possible, an overindulged child can still be pulled down a peg or two by choosing bright, outgoing, intelligent friends for him. Contact with another sensible adult can help your child through the painful process of losing this sense of self-importance.

14 Playing

Play has a vital role in your child's development and provides a platform for learning, especially about becoming sociable. To learn to become sociable, a child has to have contact with children of the same age, and these contacts will mainly be made through play. Parents now know that for their children to be healthy and happy and to grow up well adjusted, they need to be given liberty to play for as long as possible. To this end, parents provide their children with all sorts of play equipment and toys, with an emphasis on their educational value.

Play birth to 1 year

During the first year, your baby will go through what is called the exploratory stage. Until she is about three months old, play will mainly consist of observing people and objects and of making random attempts to grab hold of anything that is held in front of her. After three months, your baby will gain enough control over her hands and arms to enable her to grasp hold of, and examine, small objects. As soon as she can creep, crawl, or walk, her world will explode. She'll be able to forage for herself and will examine everything within her reach.

TOYS AND GAMES FOR BABIES

Never in a baby's development is play more synonymous with learning than in the first few years of life. She is learning to see properly and discovering how to use her hands and how to master hand-eye coordination (see p.195). She may learn quite a lot simply by watching and moving her own hands, but she'll practice and perfect her new skills with any toys you give her.

Suitable toys

• Mobiles • Rattles • Mirror • Music box • Large/small balls • Soft toys • Squeaky toys • Bendy toys • Activity center • Books • Cooking utensils

What toys to give

From about five weeks Her visual field will be increasing now and she'll enjoy watching anything that moves, so you can hang mobiles above her crib and changing mat. They're easy to make from household

Developing skills
You can help your baby improve her skills by giving her a variety of toys that encourage the development of hand–eye coordination.

items if you don't want to buy them (*see opposite*).

By three months She'll love objects that make a noise, so provide her with a rattle or any form of toy that she can shake or strike out at. Choose a brightly colored lightweight, unbreakable, washable rattle that has a small enough handle for your baby to grasp easily (at this stage she won't have the muscle strength or coordination to grip on to anything for more than a few seconds).

By four months Plastic cups filled with beans, or water-filled containers will also make interesting noises, and she'll be able to hold them between both hands.

By six to ten months Any object that is small and has crevices, holes, or handles that your baby can poke her fingers into or wrap them around will be ideal. They should be brightly colored and, if possible, make a noise, like rings with bells on them.

Put a fairly large, specially designed baby mirror in her crib—she'll love staring at her own face. Never be tempted to put one of your own mirrors in the crib—it could easily break.

Music boxes seem to provide endless fascination for small babies and can play a part in your bedtime routine (*see p.144*). The best ones have a string that the baby can pull herself.

Activity centers that have a series of knobs and buttons that your baby can push or turn to make noises can be attached to a piece of furniture or the tub. As your baby's manipulation abilities improve, she'll love playing with this.

Ten to 12 months Once your baby has learned to pick up something small, she'll be able to hold chalk, pencils, crayons, and, eventually, paintbrushes. She'll be more mobile now and she will enjoy being able to pull or push toys like trains, cars, or walking dogs. Provide her with some toys on strings so that as she sits on the floor she can draw them toward her.

Games to play together

Play Peek-a-boo with your baby, either when she's in her crib or if she's sitting on your lap. You can vary the game by hiding your face behind a scarf or a towel instead of your hands.

SAFETY TIPS

- Make sure the toys you buy are for the appropriate age group.
- Never give your child anything to play with that is so small that she might swallow it by accident or gag on it, or push it up her nose or into her ear.
- If you buy an second-hand painted toy make sure that the paint is leadfree. Young children put everything into their mouths and children have been known to get lead poisoning from toys covered with paint containing lead. (This applies to second-hand furniture, too.)
- Never leave your baby alone while she is playing, not even in a playpen.
- Always provide nontoxic crayons and pencils. For your own sake, make sure that the crayons, pencils and felt-tips markers you provide will wash off surfaces and fabrics.
- Don't buy toys made from thin rigid plastic. They break easily and leave sharp edges.
- When you buy soft toys, check for a safety label. If there's no label, make sure that there are no sharp pieces of wire used to hold any pieces on, and check that eyes and noses are firmly secured to the fabric.

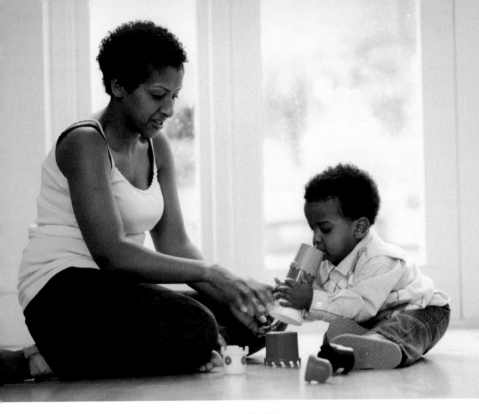

Buy a large inflatable beach ball and gently roll it toward your baby. Once she can sit unsupported, she'll be able to bat a ball back to you with her hand. You could even throw a small ball gently into your baby's lap for her to "throw" back to you. Show your baby how to fill up a container with a selection of toy animals or plastic spoons—anything that isn't breakable. Then encourage your baby to try and you'll soon find that she'll sit for hours filling up and emptying her container.

Babies seem to have endless patience with stacking cups or rings, both of which help your baby develop coordination. They come in a variety of styles, though the basic principle is the same. The ones with large pieces are better for younger babies because they're easier for uncoordinated hands to grab hold of.

All fall down
Play games with bricks: your child will try to make a tower and you can demonstrate cause and effect by knocking them down and saying, "All fall down."

Making use of household objects

A baby under one year old really doesn't need formal toys, although she'll inevitably be given some. Everything she comes across is fascinating. Any object that smells, looks, or sounds interesting will appeal to your baby. Many household items that we take for granted will hold a world of excitement for your baby. Here are a few everyday things that you might like to try as "toys" for your child:

• Wooden spoons and spatulas, small saucepans and their lids, plastic or metal colanders and sieves, funnels, plastic measuring spoons, plastic cups with lids, plastic bottles of different sizes with their caps taped on securely, small plastic food storage boxes, plastic ice-cube trays, a whisk, an old egg carton, or old loaf and muffin pans, or baking trays. Just hand them to your baby as they are, she'll soon work out what she wants to do with them.

- Anything that rolls, including the cardboard tube inside rolls of paper towels, kitchen film, or foil.
- Round objects like balls—balls of wool, balls of string, grapefruit, oranges, lemons or apples.
- Things that are very light: sponges, or foam rubber.
- Anything that rattles: transparent plastic jars with beans, colored beads, or paper clips inside. Make sure that the lid is firmly taped on.

- Things that are flat and hard: a wooden plate, a place mat, a ruler.
- Things that are stretchy: stretchy fabric, long strips of elastic, a piece of cloth that's been cut on the bias.
- Anything that has a hole large enough for a baby to poke her fingers through: for example, a roll of adhesive tape, a napkin ring, a set of shaped plastic cookie cutters.
- Things that are large and heavy but perfectly safe, like a cushion, a football, a soft-backed book, rice or dried fruit in a tough polythene bag, a loaf of bread (not bread with seeds, though).
- Objects that have different textures that will be interesting for your baby to feel. Good examples are pieces of felt, strips of fine sandpaper, thick strands of wool, a fabric-filled bean bag.

FUN WITH EVERYDAY THINGS

Noisy toys
Wooden spoons and metal pots and pans or a toy drum make a lnoise and help your baby understand how to exert control over things and himself.

Trying to reach
When your baby is starting to be able to lean forward, put something just out of his reach to encourage him to stretch forward and try to pick it up.

BABY MASSAGE

Massage is a wonderful way to express your love for your baby; in the early days it helps the bonding process between you and your child—it helps to calm an unsettled baby and can help an anxious mother come to terms with handling her precious new baby. Older babies and toddlers also benefit from massage; it is an effective way of soothing a fretful baby and can help an overexcited toddler relax. Work from the head down, with light strokes, ensuring that both sides of the body are massaged symmetrically. Use sweeping strokes and do each part two or three times. On small areas, use only your fingertips. On some parts of her body you will need two hands and on others one.

1 Lightly massage the head with a circular motion, then stroke down the sides of the face. Massage the forehead, working from the center out.

2 Gently stroke the neck from ears to shoulders and from chin to chest. Then stroke the shoulders working from the neck outward, toward her arms.

3 Stroke down the arms to the fingertips. With your fingers and thumb gently squeeze the arm from top to bottom. Massage the wrist and hand; stroke her fingers.

4 Continue down her chest, following the ribs. Massage the abdomen in a circular motion working outward from the navel, using fingertips or fingers and palm.

5 Massage down her legs, as with the arms. Massage ankles and feet and stroke each toe. Finish with long, light strokes the whole length of her body.

6 Once you have massaged your baby from head to toe on the front, turn her over and massage her back, again working from the head down.

Play 1 to 2 years

Like almost everything else your child is doing and experiencing, play develops. Your child is now entering what I call the real "toy" stage. This usually begins toward the end of the first year and goes on to reach its peak when a child is between five and six years old.

When children first play with toys, they just examine them and explore them. As they get older, they use their imagination to breathe life into the toys. They like toys that imitate the adult world. Dolls, toy houses, and cars, for example, allow children to act out the scenes they see in real life. At this age, they endow toys with human qualities. They set up houses, homes, and camps, and imagine that their toys are capable of talking and feeling just like themselves.

TOYS AND GAMES FOR TODDLERS

Your toddler's coordination will improve greatly this year, as will her manipulative skills. Toys that make use of both of these will provide the most enjoyment, but be prepared for your child to be a bit clumsy at first and give her large items. Household objects will continue to be popular, but other toys may stretch coordination and mental processes further.

Suitable toys

• Shape sorters • Stacking blocks • Building blocks • Hammering table • Push/pull toys • Dolls • Cars • Crayons and felt markers • Paints and brushes • Blackboard • Books • Modeling clay • Sandbox • Wading pool • Slide • Swing • Climber frame • Wagon

Toys to help manipulation

"Fitting" toys, where your toddler has to fit a shaped block into the correct hole, are ideal. A variation of this is sometimes called a shape sorter and consists of a plastic box or cylinder with shaped holes cut into the surface. Your toddler can put her appropriately shaped blocks through the correct holes with the extra pleasure of them disappearing with a clunk. Stacking blocks provide hours of fun because they can be used in the tub, in the backyard, and on the beach, as well as on the floor. If you don't already have them, building blocks are perennial favorites with children because they can be used as part of imaginary play to make so many shapes or objects—towers, forts, corrals, houses. Buy the ones sold with a wagon and you'll combine manipulation and walking.

Playing with paint

All children love to paint and draw, but during this year you may find it difficult to interpret exactly what's been drawn. Make sure that you prepare both the painting area and the child by covering the table and floor with a waterproof covering or newspaper and your child with an coverall or smock.

Two paint techniques your child might enjoy trying out are block painting and butterfly painting. In block painting, you have to provide the equivalent of a rubber stamp. This can be a small sponge, a ball of cotton, a cork, half an apple, or a potato—anything, really, that your child can hold easily and use in a stamping movement. Make the stamp pad by putting several colors of paint in a plastic egg carton, in plastic bowls, or a flat plastic dish. Show her how to dip the sponge or cotton and stamp it on the paper.

In the second technique blobs of colored paint are dropped on a piece of thick paper. Fold the paper so that the two sides mirror each other. If your child has learned how to blow through a straw, she can blow the paint into different shapes before you fold the paper.

Only keep paintings that you and your child both agree are worth keeping. Display them with magnets on the refrigerator door or, if you find a place where your child's fingerprints always seem to mark the walls, such as along the side of the staircase, cover these with your child's drawings. Your toddler's pictures can make ideal cards to send to relatives or to say "thank you" for presents; they're also easy to make into calendars, which make lovely little presents for grandparents.

FUN WITH PAINT

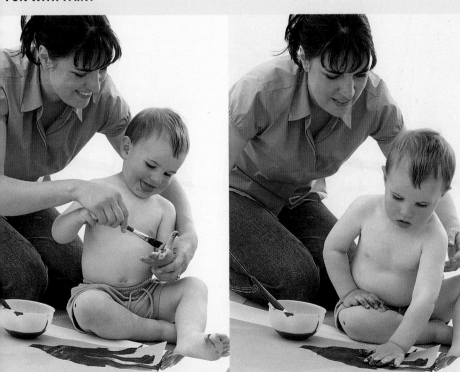

Finger painting
To make some finger paints, mix 2 fluid ounces (60 milliliters) of liquid starch with four drops of food coloring. Then let your child daub some on his hands.

Using his hands
Once the paint is on his hands, let him make handprints and other shapes on some huge pieces of paper; he will soon get the idea.

- Keep paint in small plastic jars, preferably the nonspill variety that have a hole in the top for the paintbrush.
- Plastic egg cartons make a difficult-to-spill artist's palette for your child.
- Children love making their own paint, so make up a little liquid starch in a small container and provide some bottles of food coloring. Children can add the food coloring until they have the color they require.
- Cleaning up is easier if you add a little bit of detergent to finger paints.
- You can make a paint that will stick to a shiny surface like glass or aluminum foil by mixing a few drops of food coloring, an egg yolk, and powdered detergent. However, if you are using egg, make sure your that the child is not allergic to eggs.
- If you buy your child felt-tip markers or crayons, make sure they're the fat, chunky ones because they're easier to hold. Make sure they are washable, too.
- Take a fairly large block of synthetic foam rubber and cut different-sized holes in it. Stand up all your child's bottles, brushes, and jars in it so they won't fall over.
- A utensil tray makes very good storage for bottles, jars, and paintbrushes.
- Put drawing paper on a paper towel dispenser and attach it to the wall in your creative corner.
- Keep your old newspapers for floor covering, or use a large plastic tablecloth.

What paper to use

Inexpensive makes of paper, wallpaper, shelf paper, old envelopes, brown paper bags, even old newspaper, can be painted on. Or you can buy a roll of brown paper and cut off what your child needs. Make a reusable coloring board by covering a piece of cardboard with clear, stick-on paper. In this way, paintings can be washed off with a damp cloth or paper towel (experiment with paints to see which one sticks on the surface best).

What brushes to use

When your child begins to paint, use thick brushes so that she sees immediate, bold results. Provide pastry brushes, cotton balls, corks, straws, and pipe cleaners for variety. Let her use her fingers or her feet from time to time. Make an alternative brush from an old roll-on deodorant bottle: take the ball from the neck of the bottle with a spoon, fill with paint, and replace the ball.

Preserving drawings

You can preserve a crayon drawing by ironing it on to a piece of cloth. Lay it face upward on the ironing board, cover it with a piece of light-colored cloth, and then iron it firmly at a low-to-medium temperature. The drawing will transfer to the cloth. Make sure you let it cool before you move it from the ironing board. Another tip is to spray drawings with fixative, or hair spray if you use it. This will keep the colors from being rubbed off. There is also a "magic" solution that is estimated to keep a drawing for 200 years! Dissolve a tablet of Milk of Magnesia in a quart of seltzer or sparkling water and let it sit overnight. The

Water fun
Give your child lots of empty plastic bottles, cups, and colanders to play with in a bowl of water in the garden and another set in the bathtub.

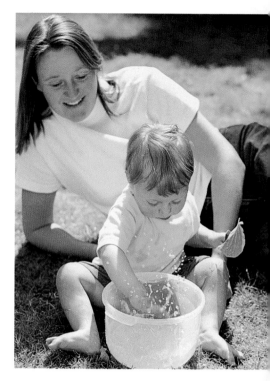

following day, soak a paper drawing in the solution for an hour, then remove it from the solution and let it sit until it is completely dry.

Playing with water

Most children love playing with water, and by the time they're in their second year will have forgotten about any fears they may have had. Try some of the following, but never leave your child alone near water:

- Wading pools are ideal summer playthings. The small, round variety that you blow up are just as much fun as a more elaborate, permanent one.
- In the summer, lay a tarp on the ground and spray a hose or sprinkler over it. When it's completely wet, it'll make a perfect slide for your child.
- Make a small hole in the bottom of a plastic container and fill it with colored water. Attach it to the back of your child's tricycle (and later, bicycle). She'll be able to see the colored trail the water has left as she cycles along.
- If you have a tap in the backyard, put a container of soil near it so that she can mix water with the soil and make up her own mud. It's messy, but lots of fun.
- Make an "iceberg" that can be played with in the bathtub or in a wading pool. Put some food coloring into a balloon then fill it with water. Put it in a pan and place it in the freezer. When it's solid, prick the balloon and peel it off—you'll be left with a perfect, round "iceberg."

CREATIVE MATERIALS

Glue
Mix 8 ounces (250 grams) flour with a teaspoon of salt in a pan. Add 20 fluid ounces (600 milliliters) water slowly until it's absorbed into a paste. Simmer for five minutes then cool and refrigerate in an airtight container until required.

Modeling dough
Mix three parts of flour to one part of salt, then stir in one part of water. Color with food coloring and store in an airtight container.

Mock play dough
Mix together equal parts of salt and flour. Add a little oil and then add enough water to mix to a stiff dough. Knead until soft and stretchy.

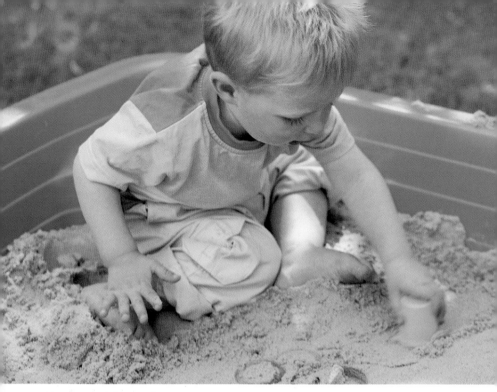

Playing with sand

Sandboxes are marvelous play areas for children. Whether you buy one or make your own by filling an old plastic wading pool, an old rubber tire, or a cement-lined hole, you should always use washed river sand. Although it is more expensive than builders' sand, it doesn't stain like the latter. Always cover the sandbox over when it's not in use or every cat in your area will use it as a litter tray.

Slides, frames, and swings

As your toddler becomes more coordinated throughout the year you may want to invest in a large piece of play equipment. If you decide to buy a swing, buy the kind that your toddler has to be lifted into and out of. If you buy a climber or a slide, make sure it has safety sides and no parts that will splinter.

Sandbox play

A sandbox can give young children hours of fun pouring sand, digging, or making castles. Make sure it is shallow, however, so your child can't get buried.

Rough and gentle games

Not all children like the same sort of game, nor does the same child like the same kind of game all the time. Some children have an obvious preference for more athletic, boisterous games, while others prefer quiet, contemplative activities.

Two of my sons were of the former type, and two of them the latter. I indulged the two who preferred rough and tumble games from an early age by providing large, soft cushions and foam-filled soft furniture for them to jump on and do their acrobatics. Outdoors there was a rope to climb, a tree with a favorite way up and down, a jungle gym with rope ladders and netting for them to cling to, and a tire swing. I think they each had their first tricycles around the age of about 13 or 14 months. Ball games like soccer or baseball were always favorites with my children and had the definite advantage that they tired them out.

For the other two children, we had to provide lots of books and countless sets of paints, easels, and drawing boards. At a very early age, the children made toy ships or toy steam engines from household junk like empty egg cartons, paper towel tubes, yogurt containers, and plastic margarine containers, and as they got older they went on to making paper airplanes. One of our sons became an expert on origami at the age of three. Both of these children loved musical instruments and they had recorders, toy xylophones, toy flutes, and toy guitars before graduating to proper instruments at a later age.

Are the toys creative enough?

There is hardly any toy or game that isn't creative for your child. Whatever she plays with or sees when she's awake will help her create imaginary worlds. She'll create patterns with colors and shapes and will create miniature models of her own home all the time she's playing.

By far the most enjoyable and beneficial are games that don't need much supervision from you. They allow your child to follow any interesting development if the fancy takes her, and concentrate on doing something of her own choosing. She can use her own judgment so that her interest is completely fulfilled. If you constantly interrupt her and tell her to be clean and tidy, or careful, or if you try to

help her too much, her interest in the game will wane. She will lose sight of the point of her game and she will become disheartened. This sort of adult interference can also result in a child being unable to concentrate when she gets to school.

Is my child stimulated enough?

If you provide the right environment and the right equipment, you don't have to worry about whether your child is being stimulated enough. At this stage, she is developing her thinking about playing, and what she needs is freedom to allow her thought processes to expand so that she can follow new ideas as they occur to her, and see play through to its conclusions.

Your child is attacking play very much like an explorer. She must be given privacy and time to herself with no interruptions (unless she asks for them). It is your job to be an assistant and make sure that she has all the facilities that she needs. Once you have provided all these facilities, it is up to your child to decide what to do, not you. It's best to let her alone to use her own imagination and not interfere.

SAFETY TIPS

- Keep her far away from any kind of pool containing water. No matter how small or shallow it is, even if she can swim, she should never be left unattended.
- Any game that involves metal implements is potentially dangerous, for example, metal buckets and spades or toy pistols. So is any game with sharp or pointed instruments, such as bows and arrows or toy knives.
- Never let your toddler go anywhere near or handle fireworks or matches.

How you can help

You can't teach your child to use her imagination, but you can encourage her natural gift for fantasy by doing the following:

- Play a variety of make-believe games with your toddler.
- When you tell a story, act out the characters' parts and make up all the different voices. If your child has a favorite, suggest that she takes that part for herself.
- Play games of "What's this?" Get your child to shut her eyes then gently stroke some object across her skin. She has to guess what the object is.
- Help your child in her imaginary world by giving her some glove puppets—either bought ones or brown paper bags with faces drawn on them.
- Start to fill a dressing-up box. Put in some of your old shoes, shirts, skirts, dresses, hats, and scarves. Have some special cheap jewelry as well. If you can find some authentic uniforms from second-hand stores, so much the better. Make a cape from a length of fabric and attach a clasp at one end.
- Provide good fantasy toys like dolls; children of both sexes love dolls because they're so easy to incorporate into their imaginary worlds. Stuffed animals, house cleaning sets, tea sets, and gardening or carpentry sets are also ideal.
- Play at being an animal. Get down on all fours and move about the floor making all the animal noises that you know. This will show your toddler how to do it.
- Play telephone conversations. If you've given your child a toy telephone, pick up the real phone and pretend to have a telephone conversation with her.

STORAGE TIPS

- Save plastic containers with lids for storing blocks or other small toys. Those made for ice cream or margarine are ideal.
- Use brightly colored labels for easy identification of what's inside your containers.
- Large glass jars are good for storage because you can immediately see what's inside them.
- Never throw out any shoe boxes—they make good beds for dolls as well as houses or barns.
- Loop a plastic mesh basket over the faucets in the tub to store all bathtub toys.
- Use a flat-topped chest for storing larger toys. This can double up as a table.
- Your child's toys are bound to get strewn around your home. Try to keep a basket in each room to make for quick and easy neatening.
- Keep a special bag or box of toys in the car.

CLEANING AND PREPARING TOYS

- Always buy machine-washable stuffed toys.
- You can use a vacuum cleaner clean stuffed toys in between washes.
- Try to buy plastic toys that can be put into the dishwasher when they are dirty.
- If plastic toys have got out of shape, you can soak them in hot water and then re-mold them with your fingers.
- Clean and deodorize smelly toys by sponging them with a cloth that has been soaked in a solution of baking soda.
- You can dry clean your child's soft toys by shaking them in a bag containing a generous amount of baking powder.

Play 2 to 3 years

Your child will probably still play with some of her existing toys although the ways in which she plays with them may be different. She may continue to play with building blocks, but instead of piling them on top of each other will use them as part of a larger project: she may use them to make the wall for an imaginary house.

During this third year your child will want to imitate the way you behave and the way you look. Manipulation skills will be improved, so larger jigsaw puzzles and more challenging puzzles will be popular.

Imitative games

As part of her imitation of the adults around her, your child will create a little world of her own. You don't need to buy a playhouse for her to do this. A couple of chairs or a small table draped with a large blanket will make an instant tent or playhouse, as will an old playpen covered with a sheet. Children love playing in the dark, so draw the curtains if that's what they want. All of my children loved playing with cardboard boxes of any size, as long as they were big enough to climb into. Small ones became boats and cars, piles of them were made into castles, forts, and houses. Boxes laid on their sides became tunnels and when laid end to end became trains. More elaborate "houses" can be made by putting several large cartons together and cutting out doors and windows. Your child can draw in curtains and put pictures on the wall inside. She can draw shutters, a door, and a knocker on the outside. If you put several stools or

TOYS FOR 2- TO 3-YEAR-OLDS

Children of this age are gaining steadily in independence, control of language, and new skills. They like to build things up and knock them down, and they love "let's pretend" games.

Suitable toys
• Large-piece jigsaw • Modeling clay • Plastic building bricks • Scissors (blunt-ended) • Glue • Carriages and strollers • Tea sets • Toy washing machines, cooking utensils • Playhouse • Tricycle • Cars and trucks • Jungle gyms

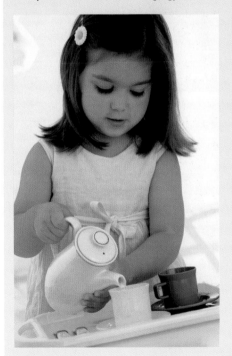

Imaginative play
Toys such as tea sets, play groceries, dolls' house furniture, and dressing-up clothes all encourage imaginative play.

small chairs in a line across the room, your child will make them into a train, a bus, a boat, or an airplane.

Games to help manipulation

Your child will use her hands to explore objects and discover what they do—it'll be an important part of the learning process for her. All of the games and ideas listed below require good coordination.

- During this year your child will have enough coordination to help with tasks in the house, and she'll see this as a form of play because she's so eager to copy what you do. She'll enjoy helping you wash fruits and vegetables, and she'll be able to snap the tops off beans and tear lettuce leaves.
- Many children love taking anything

Encourage manipulation skills
Construction toys such as building blocks or train sets with lots of pieces help stimulate your child's manipulation skills as well as his imagination.

mechanical apart, so don't throw away old clocks, old motors, cameras, or CD players when they break. Let your child have fun taking them to pieces. And if there is anything around the house that needs to be dismantled, such as cardboard boxes to be broken down, let your child join in.

- Your child might enjoy trying out spatter painting. To do this, she places leaves, grass, coins, or any shape she wants flat on a piece of white paper. She then takes a toothbrush, well soaked with paint, and gently draws her thumb or a plastic knife across it so that the paint is spattered randomly across the paper. To make it look even more exciting she can try different colors. When the paint is dry she can remove the objects and see their shapes on the paper.

• Give your child a small plot in the garden that is entirely hers. Provide her with her own trowel and a watering can and help her plant some quick-growing flowers such as marigolds, or vegetables such as radishes, runner beans, or peas.

Jigsaw puzzles

Your child will probably be able to deal with jigsaw puzzles of up to six pieces. Whenever possible you should try to buy ones with easily identified pieces when the jigsaw puzzle's apart. Your toddler will find it much easier if she can see what's a leg or an arm or a tree rather than just a shape. Buy wooden jigsaw puzzles when you can; they're much easier to handle and don't bend like the cardboard variety. If you find your child still can't hold them, make it easier by gluing on small plastic hooks from the hardware store. Start off with the inset puzzles where the pieces fit into precut areas on a tray. Your toddler will soon figure out how it works.

With some jigsaw puzzles you may have to show your child exactly how to assemble the pieces. When you do this explain to her why certain pieces go together and interlock. "Look, this piece has two bumps that look like eyebrows... this piece is for the head that always goes on top of the body." Once you've done this and helped your child through it a couple of times, she'll happily sit and do the jigsaw puzzle over and over again.

If you have a number of jigsaw puzzles, make them easier to sort by marking the back of each piece with a different color.

Make your own puzzles out of your child's favorite picture by pasting it onto heavy cardboard and covering it with contact paper. With a craft knife, cut the puzzle into about six pieces made up of triangles, diamonds, and squares.

Learning through play

There's no time in your young child's life when play does not contribute to her development. Quite often your child's needs and desires can be fulfilled in play when they cannot satisfactorily be met in any other way. For instance, a child who's unable to be a leader in real life may gain great satisfaction from being the leader of her collection of play people or bossing around her stuffed animals.

For most children, play involves experimentation. Through trial and error, your children can discover that creating something new, something that they haven't met or done before, can be very satisfying. Once they have fulfilled their creative interests in play, they can then transfer them to the real world as they grow and mature.

At home and in school, children learn the generally accepted roles of the different sexes. Knowing what they are, accepting them, and taking on the relevant role are different things. Soon after joining a playgroup, your child learns that she must play that role if she wants to become an accepted member of the group. It may be in this group that your child meets the most rigid enforcement of moral standards that she'll ever experience. There is nothing like a group of children at play for encouraging the development of desirable personality traits. By contact with friends, your child will be given lessons every day in how to be cooperative, generous, and truthful, how to be a good sport, and how to be pleasant to be with. These lessons are especially forceful because your child constantly seeks the approval of friends and the playgroup in general.

Learning about colors

Always mention the color of something that you are using or looking for. For instance, "I'm looking for the green package." "Where's that red tin gone?" "Oh, I've found the jar with the blue label," or "I'm going to use this yellow pencil." Always describe the color of your child's clothes: "That's a pretty pink dress." "What a nice red sweater." Always point

TELEVISION

Some babies are introduced to television while they are still in their cribs. Their parents see television as a built-in babysitter to keep children amused. For a lot of children television is more popular and consumes more of their playtime than all other play activities added together. Here are some of the reported facts about television:

- Television is at its least useful when a child is left to watch it alone. Even if she's watching a highly educational program she'll get less out of it if she watches it in an entirely passive way. But if she watches with other children who comment on it, or with an adult who asks questions and makes observations, the program can act as a springboard for ideas and discussion.
- Some parents let television interfere with the usual eating and sleeping routines, leading to upset digestion and tired children.
- Watching television can curtail other activities, especially outdoor play and playing with other children; it may leave little time for creative play.
- Television often presents information in a more exciting and dramatic way than schoolbooks and schoolteachers. Children therefore often find books and schoolwork boring.
- Television cuts down on conversation and other social interactions in the family.

- Characters on television are often presented as exaggerated stereotypes and children come to think that people in a given group have the same qualities as the people portrayed on the screen and this influences their attitude toward them.
- If a child watches too many programs portraying crime, torture, and cruelty, this may blunt a child's sensitivity to violence so that she accepts violent behavior as normal.
- Two groups of children were studied for the effects of violence on television. One group saw violent programs, the other did not. The studies showed that the young children in the group who watched the violent programs were noticeably more aggressive, both with other children and with their toys, than those children who had not been exposed to the same programs.
- Children are great imitators and as the lawbreakers often seem more glamorous than the heroes, children tend to identify with the villains.
- Television can present models for the behavior of the different sexes and for life roles and careers. This in turn gives rise to similar expectations in children that are not always the best.
- If children are really interested in programs they have seen they may want to find out more by reading or asking grown-ups about the subject.

out the color of flowers, in your garden, your windowbox, or in the park, and show your child the different colors that animals, and birds especially, can have. Show your child how colors are made. "Look, if we mix a little bit of red with white we get pink; yellow mixed with blue makes green." Teach her the colors of the rainbow; rainbows are magical to children.

Learning about numbers

Always take the chance to count while you are doing routine things. For instance, count one, two, three as you fasten the buttons on your child's jacket, or when you're washing her hands or feet. Help with number learning by counting things as you shop. Ask your child to bring you two oranges or three carrots.

Count bottles and jars and arrange them into groups such as two bottles, three cans, and four boxes. Draw numbers on small sheets of paper and help your child number little groups of her toys, for instance, three balls, five blocks, seven farmyard animals. When you go for walks count the number of houses or gates, trees in a garden, or ducks in a pond.

Learning about letters

Take every opportunity to help your toddler become familiar with letters. Teach your child the alphabet song so that remembering letters is easier. Serve alphabet soup or alphabet spaghetti and

help your child to spell out her name with the letters. Alternatively, buy your child some magnetic letters that she can play with on the refrigerator door. Children love moving the words around.

My children liked us to spell out words by drawing the letters in the palms of their hands while their eyes were closed, and they tried to recognize the letters and build up the word. Play word games when you read a story. As you read a sentence, leave out a word and get your child to say what it is. "The cat was sitting warming itself by the..." As you point to the fire in the picture your child can shout out "fire."

Have fun learning
Bring learning into your child's games in a relaxed way. Ask her to count her toy figures or dolls as she plays with them and give them simple names she can spell out with you.

15 Outings and travel

No baby is too young to take on an outing. In fact, with a young baby you can go just about anywhere and, provided he can look around, he'll enjoy the change of scene even if he doesn't understand quite what's going on. Planning ahead is the secret, and the younger your baby the more carefully you need to plan. If you are well organized, outings with your baby can be a great joy, and the sooner that you start after bringing your baby home from the hospital, the better. Looking after a baby doesn't preclude parents from resuming the active life that they had before. One word of warning, though: don't be too ambitious or undertake very long trips at first.

Local outings birth to 1 year

Planning your outings

It's always worth spending a little time planning how you're going to get to your destination, what you need for the trip, where you're going to feed your baby when you get there and how you're going to change him. Until you feel confident, take your partner or a friend along with you. An extra pair of hands to share the load, and an ally to share the novelty and possibly any problems, will make any trip with your baby more enjoyable.

When you're out and about, you'll need to make sure that there's somewhere that you can feed your baby in peace, especially in the first months when he won't have settled into a predictable feeding routine. You'll have to change your baby, too, so try to find out if there's a nearby department store with a mother-and-baby room you can use. There should be a countertop at waist height for easy changing, which will save you having to change your baby on the floor— or even worse, on your lap. In the summer, it's fun to sit in a nearby park to feed your baby.

WHAT TO TAKE FOR A YOUNG BABY

- A changing surface (that can be a fold-up plastic mat or a cloth diaper)
- Disposable diapers
- Baby wipes
- Breast pads if breast-feeding
- Bottle and milk powder if bottle-feeding
- Hat (sun hat for summer, warm one for winter)
- Sweater
- Toys for distraction
- Plastic bag for dirty diapers

Get out and about
Simply taking your baby out for a walk in the park in his stroller is good exercise for you while being fun and stimulating for him.

Using a baby sling

Slings are one of the most convenient methods of carrying a baby as well as one of the oldest. They hold your baby securely against your chest so that you and your baby have the security of being close to each other; they also leave your hands free. Buy a washable sling because your baby is bound to spit up on it, and try it on before you make your final choice. It has got to be easy to put on and to wear. The shoulder straps must be wide enough to support your growing baby's weight comfortably, and both you and your partner must feel relaxed wearing it. It has been said that a baby shouldn't be carried in a sling until he can support his own head. This is not true. You can carry your baby in a sling as soon

as you and he are happy about it—your baby will find close contact with you so soothing and reassuring that he'll probably curl up and doze.

Using a stroller

A stroller is absolutely essential if you don't want to carry your baby in a sling or when he's too heavy to carry. Strollers with seats

WHAT TO TAKE FOR AN OLDER BABY

- A changing surface
- Disposable diapers
- Baby wipes
- Baby food and spoon
- Non-messy snacks
- Feeding cup and some water
- Bib
- Hat
- Sweater
- Toys for distraction
- Plastic bag for dirty diapers

that lie completely flat are essential for very young babies. Although babies fit quite snugly into the curved shape of a stroller, it is important to make sure they are well supported. Even a tiny baby, if awake, can be propped up to take in the interesting sights around him. Always make sure that your baby is safely strapped in.

Using a backpack

A backpack is a useful means of carrying an older baby who can sit up well and who has become heavy to carry in a sling, too. Once again, it leaves your hands free, but it also allows your baby to see much more of what's going on around him. Before you buy a backpack, do the following:

- Try on the backpack in the store, with your baby in it.
- Check that the baby's seat comes halfway down your back. This is very important because it places the strain on your back and not on your shoulders; it also keeps the baby stable.
- Make sure that the pack has a safety strap to keep the baby in place and a waist belt for you to keep it secure. Check that the shoulder straps are well padded.

Know your stroller
You'll often have to collapse the stroller when you're out, so make sure that you can kick it shut and open it up while holding your baby.

TIPS FOR STROLLERS

- Never leave your baby unattended.
- Always make sure that the stroller is fully extended and that the frame is locked in position.
- Never let go of the stroller for a moment without putting the brakes on first.
- Always put the safety harness on your baby.
- Never, ever, put shopping on the handles of the stroller; it could tip over backward.
- From an early age, teach your child to keep his fingers away from the wheels.

- One disadvantage of strollers compared to carriages is that in cold weather your child is more exposed. If you don't have a padded chair cover, lay a blanket over the stroller seat before you put the baby in. Wrap the blanket around him.
- If your baby falls asleep before you get home either put the stroller down into the lie-back position or tuck him up comfortably with pillows.
- If you have an older child and a baby, fit a stroller board onto the stroller to save the toddler's legs.

- Check that your baby can sit comfortably and that the leg openings don't restrict him in any way.
- Try to buy a pack with a built-in loading stand so that you can put it on without any help; such backpacks often convert to free-standing seats.

Going shopping

Try to shop early in the morning when the stores are less busy. When you go to a supermarket, always strap your baby into your shopping cart. Wheel the cart down the center of the aisles. Your baby will want to grasp everything in sight, which can cause chaos with a supermarket's carefully stacked boxes or cans. If you're still breast-feeding your baby, plan to shop between feedings. If you're going to be out for a while, have most of your shopping done before you have to find somewhere quiet for his next feeding.

Having a car is one of the greatest freedoms a new parent can have. There's no concern about how to manage public transportation, and it provides an ideal feeding and changing area.

Eating out

In the first months your baby will doze off almost anywhere, so eating out will be quite easy. However, by the time he's nine months old he'll be capable of keeping himself awake; he'll be keen for any new experience and a restaurant, with strange people doing even stranger things, will fascinate him. Choose your restaurant carefully and try to find a child-friendly place that provides highchairs. Always take your own snacks with you, and as soon as you've settled your baby in his seat, give him these to occupy him. Have plenty of toys for distraction (rearranging paper napkins is also a good activity). You may find it works better if you feed your child before you and your partner start.

Using public transportation

If you're shopping on your own, with a stroller, a changing bag, and a grumpy baby, getting on public transport can seem like the last straw. However, there are some tips to get over the worst problems.

- Avoid traveling during rush hour.
- When possible, carry your baby in a sling or backpack. This leaves your hands free and makes getting on and off a bus or train easier.
- Carry distracting toys with you, and tie one or more to the stroller or backpack.
- If you're asked to leave your stroller in a special luggage section, make sure you get up in plenty of time to retrieve it before your stop.
- Never be embarrassed to ask for help.

TIPS FOR SHOPPING WITH BABIES

- When you're carrying your child in your backpack remember your child's grasping fingers can reach bottles and cans in a store.
- When you take your child into the supermarket, keep him supported and under control by using your own harness to strap him into the cart.
- For emergencies keep a few disposable diapers, wipes, and plastic bags in the glove compartment of the car for quick changes.
- Shopping seems to make children hungry and therefore fretful. Avoid this by taking a snack.
- You can use the opened trunk of the car, with a blanket laid over it, as a surface on which to change your child.

Local outings 1 to 3 years

By the time your child is walking you may find that your greatest problem is keeping him safely restrained and happily occupied when you go out. You'll also have to be prepared for very slow trips with endless stops to look at the many objects that strike your child's fancy. Most parents continue to use their stroller, although harnesses, backpacks, and bicycle seats are useful alternatives and can sometimes be more fun for your child.

Using the stroller

As your child gets older, he won't be happy just sitting in the stroller, but will want to walk along with you. This may be inconvenient, especially if you are shopping, and you will have to do your utmost to persuade your toddler to stay in it. In my experience, the best way of doing this is to take along one of your child's favorite toys and a snack.

If your child is so restless that he makes shopping impossible, you could put your child in a harness. Make a game of it if he resists. He will feel a sense of freedom and independence, but you know that he can't wander away from you and get lost. A wrist link that's securely attached to the harness will help prevent your child from becoming separated from you.

Using a bicycle seat

If you have a bicycle you may find it fun to take your toddler on the back. There are two kinds of bicycle seat—front-mounted and rear-mounted. These lightweight plastic structures fit neatly and securely onto a bicycle frame and can accommodate a child of up to 48 pounds (22 kilograms). Make sure that your child's feet are away from the wheels and that there's a strong safety harness for your child. If you decide you do want to use this method of transportation, both you and your child must wear protective cycle helmets.

SHOPPING WITH TODDLERS

- Encourage your child to become familiar with shopping. Give him the wrappers or boxes of things on your shopping list and suggest he find them for you by matching them up with products on the shelves.
- Toddlers can get lost in stores. Dress yours in an easily spotted coat or hat in a bright color.
- As soon as possible, teach your child his name, address, and telephone number. In the meantime, insert a label with this information inside his coat in case he does get lost.
- I used to use a referee's whistle on a string around my neck to summon my children. We had a code: one whistle—come quickly; two whistles—run; three whistles—emergency.
- Any outing can be a lesson in disguise. In the supermarket you can teach your child about healthy eating (that beans are better than spaghetti) or bargains (that buying large cans works out cheaper than getting small ones).
- It's a scary prospect but you can make sure your child could find his way alone when he's near home by giving the same running commentary as you approach your house. "And here's that big tree on the corner, now we turn right, past the mailbox, and here's our street, and our house, the fourth one on the left."

Shopping with an older child

As soon as your child can toddle, you'll be faced with a new problem: how to keep an eye on, and occupy, a lively young child and concentrate on what you have to do. The only efficient way of getting around, especially when shopping, is to take your partner or a friend along with you. In this way, one adult can get the shopping done, while the other occupies the child. (There is also the added bonus of another pair of hands to help carry the shopping home.)

The most important tip is to keep your toddler in a harness so that you can concentrate on what you're doing without having to worry about what he's doing. Or you can put your child in the supermarket cart so he can't run away; use the straps so he can't climb out either. As you go around the store, ask your child questions like, "Can you see the baked beans?" "Which is the largest can?" "Which apples do you want—the red or the green ones?" Most children love being involved in this way; you can even let them choose their favorite foods and put them in the cart.

My supermarket solution for keeping my children quiet was to let them put anything into the cart as we were going around and then take it all out when we got to the checkout (unbeknownst to them): it was time-consuming, but it was more peaceful.

If you aren't going food shopping but, say, clothes shopping instead, still keep your toddler in a harness, but take his

favorite books along. When you go into the changing rooms, sit your child on the floor beside you and encourage him to look at the pictures, maybe telling you what's in them, or what the story is about.

Special excursions

Going to the store or to the park will probably be part of your toddler's daily routine but there will be occasions when you want to plan a special excursion like the zoo or a boat trip. In your plans, take your child's personality into account. What's his attention span? Is he very active? If he is, don't plan to go anywhere where he's going to be confined to his stroller for long or you'll ruin everybody's day. If, when the day arrives, your toddler's in a bad mood, postpone the outing; similarly if you no longer feel like it. Take enough snacks for the whole day and include a variety of them.

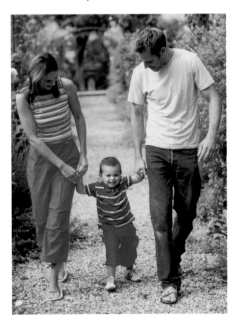

Family outings
Your toddler will love going out with his mom and dad. Be prepared to make endless stops to look at anything that catches your child's attention.

Car trips birth to 1 year

Traveling in cars is a normal part of everyday life, and the sooner your baby learns about it the better.

Car safety

The most important aspect of traveling by car is the safety of your baby. Never sit in the front or back of the car with your baby on your lap. Always use a car seat suitable for your baby's age, weight, and size and make sure that the seat complies with current state and safety regulations. Before choosing a restraint, seek independent consumer and safety advice.

Feeding your baby

Obviously feeding on the go is much easier if you're breast-feeding. If you're bottle-feeding, never try to keep a made-up bottle warm—any germs will quickly multiply. Instead, plan ahead by packing separately some powdered formula, and a thermos of boiled water. Then mix the formula (in a sterilized bottle) as you need it, using water from the thermos.

Once your baby's weaned you'll need to take baby food, a feeding dish, a plastic spoon, and a drinking cup with a spout. You can feed your baby from the jar, but remember to throw away anything he doesn't finish, because the food will be contaminated with saliva, and germs will grow in it very quickly.

Changing your baby

Disposables are by far the easiest to use when you're traveling. There's no need to do more than top and tail your baby when traveling, so all you need are some baby wipes and a plastic bag for dirty diapers.

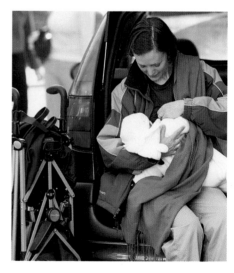

Travel with your baby
Car trips can be easier than public transportation with a young baby. You can keep changing kit in the car, and you'll have somewhere you can feed in peace.

CAR TIPS

- Never leave your child alone in the car.
- When the temperature is very hot, avoid heat exhaustion and heatstroke by only taking your baby on essential short trips early in the morning and at night when it is cooler.
- Secure a blind or piece of thick cloth on the car window to protect a baby from the sun.
- Remove all loose objects from the back ledge in case of accident.
- Always keep a bag with spare diapers and changing equipment in the car.
- Have a blanket or crib quilt to put over the baby when he falls asleep.

Car trips 1 to 3 years

It's between the ages of one- and two-and-a-half that car trips become most difficult. Your child will hate being made to sit still in one place and he'll want to assert himself. A new sense of independence emerges at this time and he'll be eager to express what he wants to do, especially when you don't want him to do it. Here are some tips that may help.

- Make an early start or travel at night. Pack soft clothing that will do double duty. For example, ski jackets in a pillow case make good car pillows.
- Buy or make seat backs with pockets for the front seats of the car and put games, snacks, drinks, and books in them.
- Curb restlessness by stopping for five minutes every hour or so, so that the children can stretch their legs.
- Always tape knives, forks, and spoons to the inside of the food containers.
- To minimize mess in the car, have a supply of garbage bags to put trash in and a supply of tissues and baby wipes to clean sticky hands and faces.
- Have nutritious snacks, for example, raisins, cornflakes, or pieces of cheese, in plastic bags so that you never have to say no if your child wants to nibble.
- Always take more drinks, such as small, sealed containers of milk or juice, than you think you'll need.
- Most children love grapes (the seedless kind), which quench thirst as well as satisfy hunger.
- Music and stories to listen to will keep most children happy in the car.
- Get your child to take some responsibility for his own entertainment by letting him select a few of his toys and put them in his own case or bag.
- Magnetized games prevent pieces from getting lost in the car. Sew or stick Velcro to toys or games so that they will stay steady or in one place.
- Keep a few treats hidden away for the moment when your child gets grumpy.
- Don't put up with any misbehavior like screaming or kicking. Pull off to the side of the road and say that you're not going any further until he behaves.

PREVENTING CARSICKNESS

Some children are more prone to carsickness than others. Most grow out of it as they get older, but there are ways to minimize the risks:

- If your child gets carsick, ask your pediatrician to suggest a suitable medicine.
- Keep your child occupied.
- Don't give your child rich or greasy food within a few hours of leaving.
- If your child wants a snack during the trip, give him dry cookies or a candy.
- Don't become overanxious. Children quickly pick up on their parents' moods and this can make them apprehensive and more prone to carsickness. Excitement and apprehension play a part, and children tend to suffer more on the outward trip than on the return one.
- If your child gets very pale or very quiet, stop the car. Provide a plastic bag or bowl to be sick in, if necessary.
- Keep a supply of plastic bags in the car, baby wipes to clean your child up, a change of clothes, and something to take away the taste.

Air travel birth to 3 years

When you make your reservations say that you're going to be traveling with an infant. Ask to be put on a flight that's not crowded and ask for a bulkhead seat, because there's more legroom there. Ask if the plane has a bassinet; if it does, order one so that your baby will be comfortable during the flight. Bulkhead seats are advisable if you have a toddler, too, because you can lay a towel on the floor in front of you for him to play on. If your baby is small enough, carry him in a sling so that you have both hands free. If you don't use a sling, bring a stroller. You'll probably have to walk a long way to reach the boarding area and if you're trying to manage hand-luggage and a baby you could find it exhausting. A stroller can usually be checked at the gate.

Arrive at the airport with plenty of time to spare. This means that you'll be able to check-in before the lines are long and take your time to get organized. Carry everything that you need in a lightweight shoulder bag or backpack—toys as well as diapers and changes of clothing—so that your hands are free. Families with young children are usually allowed to board first, or you can arrange for priority boarding. Ask your travel agent about this or check on the Internet.

WHAT TO TAKE WITH YOU

- Child's passport and immunization record, if necessary.
- Lightweight bag for baby's equipment.
- Folding travel crib, if crib unavailable.
- Stroller, carrier, backpack, or sling.
- Plastic mat for diaper changing.
- Bouncing chair if used.
- Pack of disposable diapers; buy supplies at destination.
- Diaper changing equipment.
- Potty if needed.
- Plastic bags for dirty diapers.
- Thermos flask for days on beach.
- Bottle-feeding equipment if required.
- Nonspill cup, plastic dish, and spoon if weaned.
- Toys and games.
- Comforters if used.
- Quick-drying, noncrease clothes.
- Sun hat, if necessary.
- Long-sleeved shirts and long-legged pants.

Making the best of plane trips

There are several ways you can make the trip easier for you and your child.

- Ask the airline if they carry baby food.
- Change your baby's diaper just before you board the plane.
- Keep some food or drink or a pacifier ready to give your baby at takeoff or landing to help equalize the pressure in his ears and avoid discomfort.
- Shortly after boarding, ask one of the flight attendants for help and find out if and when it will be possible for him or her to warm your baby's food and drink.
- Make sure your in-flight diaper bag, with bottles, equipment, and changes of diapers and clothing, is clearly labeled in case it gets mislaid during the flight.
- Amuse your child with the same kinds of games you play in the car (see p.289).
- Take along a few of your child's favorite

toys, but only bring them out one at a time and at intervals through the trip.
- Don't try to eat or drink hot food while you're holding the baby.
- Let your baby play with all the in-flight equipment—spoons and forks from the food tray, plastic safety instructions from the seat pouch, headphones for the movies or for music.

Toward carefree foreign vacations

Your baby's never too young to travel (although airlines will probably require a doctor's note if the baby is less than two weeks old). The type of vacation you choose is up to you and your individual tastes—it may be camping, staying in a luxury hotel, or swapping houses with another family. Wherever you go, make sure that they have adequate facilities for young children. Without them, you're not going to enjoy the vacation yourselves. If it is a hotel, ask if they provide highchairs, wading pools, laundry service, early meals for children, or babysitting. If you're going to a beach it's advisable to choose one that's sandy. Ask your doctor's advice well in advance of your trip about health precautions, vaccinations (*see p.343*), or any medication that you should take. Also enquire about food, facilities, and hygiene in the country or area that you're going to visit.

If you're adventurous with the family diet at home, let your children eat what they want. If you or they are more conservative and you're not planning to cook for your family, make arrangements with the hotel for them to have simple meals. Don't try to introduce a very young child to exotic food for the first time in a foreign country.

SAFE SUN TIPS

Keep babies in the shade at all times. Do not expose them to the sun. Babies have little skin pigment so they have much less protection from the sun than adults, and exposure to the sun's ultraviolet rays can lead to skin damage and skin cancer in later life.
- In very hot weather, avoid taking your baby out in the sun between 11 a.m. and 3 p.m. when the sun is at its highest.
- Dress your baby in a wide-brimmed hat and loose, light clothing that covers her shoulders and neck, such as a shirt or dress with sleeves and a collar.
- Be aware that your baby is still at risk on cloudy days.
- Make sure the carriage or stroller has an adjustable sunshade to shade your baby.
- Be particularly careful near snow and water where reflected light is strong.
- Apply sunblock of at least SPF 30 to your child before he goes out and reapply often. Use waterproof sunblock when swimming.

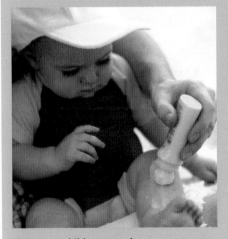

Keep your child protected
A young child's skin is easily damaged by the sun. Always protect your child by using sunscreen, cotton clothing, and a hat.

16 Home safety

Accidents in the home cause a large percentage of deaths of children between the ages of one and four. Most of these incidents are avoidable, so take the time and care to minimize the chances of anything happening in your home. Most accidents are caused by a chain of events rather than a single occurrence—for example when someone is ill or tired, or when something unusual is happening.

Room-by-room safety

All children are naturally adventurous and inquisitive, and it is all too easy to underestimate the dangers your child may face when she becomes mobile. Common household items can be dangerous to children. However, many of the accidents children have at home can been avoided with a little forethought.

General tips
- Buy all medicines in childproof bottles, and always keep them out of the reach of your child in a locked medicine cabinet. Ask your pharmacist if he or she can supply any prescription medicines in childproof bottles.
- Always keep medicines and chemicals in the labeled containers that they originally came in. Never put a poison into a bottle that previously held a harmless liquid such as fruit juice.
- Store all drugs and chemicals as far away from food as possible.
- Don't leave aerosol cans lying around— the nozzle could easily be depressed by your child and could cause eye damage.

RISK FACTORS

The chances of an accident happening are increased by the following factors:
- If your child is tired, ill, or hungry.
- If parents are tired or ill or if the mother is premenstrual or pregnant.
- When there's great excitement in the home, such as when you're going on vacation or expecting the arrival of a new baby.
- If your child is considered hyperactive.
- If you and your partner aren't getting along, or if you're actually fighting.
- If your child doesn't have anywhere safe to play.
- If correct safety precautions haven't been followed.
- If the equipment you use for your baby doesn't comply with safety standards.

- Fit safety covers in all electrical outlets that are not in use.
- Make sure that cords and electrical appliances are kept out of the reach of your child.
- All electrical cords should be in good condition and not frayed or otherwise damaged; replace them if necessary.
- Install window locks or safety catches to prevent windows from opening more than 4 inches (10 centimeters). Windows can be an essential escape route in case of fire, so make sure the window keys are easy to find in an emergency.
- Never leave anything near windows that your child can climb up on.
- Keep pins, needles, matches, lighters, sharp knives, and scissors out of your child's reach, in a childproof drawer.
- Cover hot radiators and pipes with towels

Stair gates
Put a gate across the kitchen doorway so your child can see you but won't be under your feet while you are cooking. Put one at the bottom of the stairs, too.

or seal them off with pieces of furniture that your child can't move. Teach your child from an early age that radiators are hot and shouldn't be touched.
- If you own a gun always store it, with its ammunition, in a locked safe.
- Buy flame-proof clothing for your child.
- Make sure furniture is too solid and heavy for your child to pull over. Brackets can also be used to anchor furniture.
- Install smoke alarms to ceilings on each level of your home. Check them regularly to make sure that they are still working.
- Replace old foam furniture; it gives off toxic fumes if it catches fire.

The bathroom

- Make sure that it is possible to open your bathroom door from the outside in case your child locks the door.
- Medicine, scissors, and razor blades should be kept out of your child's reach in a locked cabinet.
- Don't leave any perfume or cosmetics lying around.
- Keep the toilet bowl lid closed.
- When you run your child's bath always run the cold water first so there's no risk of her being scalded; test the water before putting your child in.
- Fit thermostatic taps to reduce risk of scalding.
- Install handles to the sides of the tub.

- Use a nonslip bath mat in the tub.
- Have a nonslip floor surface.
- Teach your child how to swim as soon as possible.
- Make sure bathroom windows have locks or safety catches.
- The medicine cabinet, which must have a childproof lock, should be out of the reach of your child.
- Don't put a bathroom medicine cabinet above the toilet—your child could climb up on the seat to open it.
- Never leave your child alone in the bath.
- Heated towel rails should be covered with towels, and your child should be taught from an early age that they're hot and shouldn't be touched.
- Don't mix bathroom cleaners with bleach as they can give off dangerous fumes.
- Keep all cleaning agents, bleaches, and disinfectants in a locked cabinet.

The kitchen

- The floors should be nonslip.
- All work surfaces should be well lit.
- The floor should be uncluttered.
- Windows and glazed doors should have toughened safety glass.
- Keep cupboard doors closed and fitted with child locks.
- Keep drawers shut and put child locks on them if possible.
- Always wipe up spilled liquid at once.
- Keep work surfaces as clear as possible so that sharp implements such as knives can be spotted immediately.

Safety in the bath
Put a nonslip mat in the bottom of the bathtub so your baby does not fall. This is just as important when your child is older, as he may try to climb in and out.

- Install a guard around the stove.
- Never leave a boiling pot or hot pan unattended on the stove.
- Use the back burners of the stove, and always turn the pan and pot handles towards the back of the stove.
- Never reach across a heated burner or ring; you could burn yourself, or knock a pan off the stove.
- Whenever using electrical equipment, always follow the manufacturer's instructions exactly.
- Don't use tablecloths. Even a crawling baby can reach up and pull whatever's on the table down on himself.
- Keep matches in a safe, cool place.
- Don't cook with your toddler around you. Arrange a safe play area in a special part of the kitchen so that you can still talk to each other.
- Keep the cord on any electrical equipment short and out of the way.
- Don't store things that you use frequently on a high shelf. When you have to reach into a high place, stand on a secure kitchen ladder, and make sure that your balance is good before you reach up.
- Always keep dishcloths away from the stove in case of fire.
- Make sure your dishwasher, washing machine, and dryer have safety locks.
- Keep a fire blanket next to the stove in case anything catches fire.
- Keep all plastic bags or kitchen film out of your child's reach.
- Your child's fingers could easily catch in a swinging door. Either get rid of it or secure it in an open position.
- Never leave a room with the iron on; it's all too easy for your child to topple both the board and iron.

- Any "glasses" that your child uses should be unbreakable.
- Always keep your baby and her toys away from the immediate cooking area so that there's no risk of you tripping and spilling hot liquid over her. Put her in a playpen, baby bouncer, or highchair while you are cooking.
- If you put your child in a playpen in the kitchen, make sure that it is out of reach of your work surfaces.
- Store all cleaning materials—such as bleach and detergents—out of reach.

In the highchair
A baby should be strapped into his highchair every time you put him in it— even if you think he can't climb!

Children's bedrooms

- Install safety locks on all windows and don't leave furniture near them.
- All furniture should have rounded corners; if it doesn't, put on special plastic safety corners.
- Store toys and games at a low level so that your child doesn't have to stretch or be tempted to climb up to get at them.
- Don't leave toys lying around on the floor.
- Don't put an electric heater anywhere near your child's bed at night because she could throw off her blanket or quilt and cause a fire.
- Buy flameproof pajamas.
- Wall-mounted lights are safer because they have no cords trailing on the floor.
- Never leave your baby in her crib with the side down.
- Never leave your baby alone on the changing table, even for a second.
- Keep a baby monitor by your child's bed so you can hear if she wakes up in the night.
- Put a gate across your child's bedroom doorway once she is crawling. Don't put one at the top of the stairs because you might trip over the bar.

The living room

- If you have an open fire, always keep a screen in front of it as well as a safety guard that is fastened to the wall.
- Run cords around the walls.
- Disconnect appliances when not in use.
- Keep cords on electrical appliances short.
- Don't place a hot or heavy object on a low table where your child could reach it.
- All shelving should be securely fixed to the wall and should be well out of reach of your child.
- Keep the television out of reach.

Sturdy furniture
When your child is nearly ready to walk, she will pull herself up on everything. Put unstable furniture out of her reach even if it is only until she is more stable.

- Anything breakable should be kept out of reach of your child.
- Windows that are near the floor, especially patio windows, should have toughened safety glass, so that it won't shatter even if your child falls on to it. In addition put stickers on the glass.
- Make sure your houseplants aren't poisonous.
- Never leave hot or alcoholic drinks lying around within reach of your child.
- Don't leave lighters or matches lying around. Lock them away.

Halls, stairs, and passageways

- Fit a safety gate across the bottom of the stairs; don't put one across the top because you can trip on it.
- Light switches should be positioned in convenient places.
- Never leave anything lying on or near the

stairs. Make sure that doors, hallways, and stairs are well lit.

- Balusters should be secure; check them regularly and replace loose posts.
- The gaps between the baluster posts should be no more than 2½ inches (6.5 centimeters) apart.
- Don't have open staircases in your home—your child could easily fall off the side or between the steps.
- Stair carpets should be fitted well so that they don't slip. Any tears or holes should be patched immediately.
- Put safety locks and a chain on your front door; make sure the lock is well out of your child's reach.

The backyard

- Put childproof locks on all gates.
- Fence off a swimming pool or pond and supervise a child when he is near them.
- Never leave a wading pool with water in it; empty it and either deflate it or store it upside down.
- Fit rainwater butts or similar water-collecting devices with a secure lid. Your child can drown in as little as 2 inches (5 centimeters) of water.
- Remove all poisonous plants from the backyard; ask your local plant nursery if in doubt.
- Pull up any mushrooms or toadstools as soon as they appear.
- Bury any animal excreta before your child has the chance to poke it, play with it, or even try to eat it.

Garden plants
Let your child do some gardening, but remove all
poisonous plants; ask your local nursery if in doubt.
Tell your child not to eat any plants or berries she finds.

- Your clothesline should be high up out of a child's reach. If you have a round clothesline, cover it up when not in use.
- Store all your gardening tools and machinery in a locked shed or garage.
- When mowing the lawn, or cutting a hedge, keep your toddler well away.
- Never work on your car when your child is playing outside.
- Lock away all pesticides, plant sprays, and car cleaners.
- Never leave rope lying around.
- Fence off your garbage cans so that your child can't get in and rummage around inside them.
- Make regular safety checks on any swings, slides, or climbing frames in your yard. Always watch your child on them.

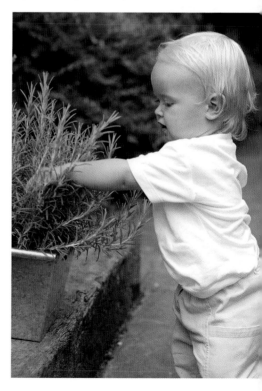

Out and about

Your child will enjoy playing out of doors—she will be able to run around freely, get dirty, and explore a different environment. The main danger associated with playing outside is that she may run out of the play area and into the road. You can prevent this by making sure that your child always plays in an enclosed environment and that backyard and playground gates are locked with childproof locks.

Your child must learn that streets are dangerous places and that she must never run out into the road.

Playground safety

Young children need challenging equipment to test their skills and use up energy, but make sure they're safe.

The play area should be surrounded by a fence so that animals can't get in.

- Young children should sit in box swings, not open ones.
- Swings should be enclosed by a fence.
- Climbing equipment should be situated on a rubber surface, grass, or sand, so children don't injure themselves.
- Tell your child she should not to put her feet under a merry-go-round or jump off one when it's still moving.
- Slides constructed on an earth mound will break a fall.
- The surface of a slide should have no joins in it.
- Playground equipment that is at ground level, like tubes and tires, is safest for toddlers and younger children.

ROAD SAFETY

It's never too early to teach your child the safety code for crossing the street. Whenever you want to cross the street, always go to a pedestrian crossing if possible or find the safest place to cross—one where you can see clearly in all directions and drivers can see you. Stop by the curb, hold your child's hand or her harness, look in both directions for traffic, and listen. If traffic is coming, let it pass. Look in both directions again and when nothing is coming, walk across; don't run. Continue to look and listen as you cross. Keep up commentary about what you're doing, looking for, and listening for.

Keep safe
Make sure your child understands that she must never run into the street. Hold hands or use a harness when out walking with her.

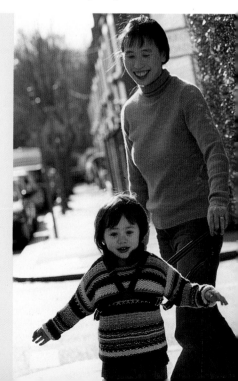

Emergency first aid

Choking

If your child chokes on a piece of food, her airway can become blocked, she will be unable to get oxygen into her lungs and may lose consciousness. If the blockage is mild, she will be able to cough, cry, and breathe; if severe, she can't cough, breathe, or make any sound. Normal breathing may return if she loses consciousness and the muscles relax. If she is not breathing, start resuscitation (*see pp.300–302*).

For a baby under one year

1 *Lay your baby face down along your forearm, keeping her head low and supporting her head and shoulders on your hand. Give her five sharp blows between the shoulder blades with the heel of your hand.*

2 *Turn your baby face up, support her neck and head, and look in her mouth. If you can see the obstruction, pick it out with your fingers.*

3 *Put your first two fingers on the lower half of her breastbone (see right), and give five downward thrusts. Check the mouth again. If the blockage hasn't cleared, repeat steps 1 and 2 three times, then call an ambulance. Continue back blows and chest thrusts until help arrives, or the baby is unconscious.*

For a child

1 *If choking is severe, and she can't cough or breathe, check her mouth and pick out anything you can see.*

2 *If that fails, use the heel of your hand to deliver five sharp blows between the shoulder blades. If she is still choking, stand behind her and place one fist, thumb inward against her abdomen, just below the rib cage. Cover it with your other hand, thumb inward, and pull sharply inward and upward. Repeat up to five times.*

3 *Check her mouth again. If necessary, repeat steps 1 and 2 three times, then call an ambulance. Continue alternating back blows and abdominal thrusts until the ambulance arrives, or the child loses consciousness.*

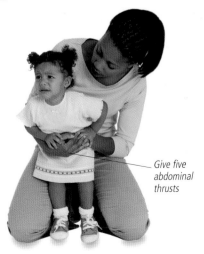

Give five abdominal thrusts

Unconsciousness

If your child is unconscious and isn't breathing, she's at risk of brain damage and her heart may stop. If your child collapses, assess her condition quickly so you know what first aid treatment to give. If she is unconscious but still breathing, call for help and place her in the recovery position (*see opposite*). If she's unconscious and not breathing, you will need to give rescue breaths (*see opposite*) to get oxygen into her body, then give chest compressions with rescue breaths to get the oxygenated blood circulating (*see p.302*). This is called cardiopulmonary resuscitation (CPR).

Assessing a baby under one year

1 *Find out if your baby is conscious by calling her name and tapping the sole of her foot. If she doesn't respond, shout for help.*

2 *Open the airway by lifting the chin with one finger and tilting the head back.*

3 *Look, listen, and feel for signs of breathing. Look along your baby's chest and abdomen to see if there is any movement. Listen for sounds of breathing and feel for breaths on your cheek for up to 10 seconds.*

• If there are no signs of breathing, you should give five rescue breaths (*see opposite*). If you have help, get someone else to call an ambulance. If on your own, do CPR for one minute, then call an ambulance.

• If she is breathing, hold her in your arms with her head lower than her chest and call an ambulance.

Assessing a child

1 *Find out whether your child is conscious by tapping his shoulder. Keep calling his name. If he doesn't respond, shout for help.*

2 *Open the airway. Tilt his head back by placing one hand on his forehead. Put two fingers under your child's chin and lift his jaw.*

3 *Look, listen, and feel for signs of breathing. Look along your child's chest and abdomen for movements. Listen for sounds of breathing, and feel for his breath on your cheek.*

• If he is not breathing, give five rescue breaths (*see opposite*). If you have help, get someone else to call an ambulance. If you are on your own, do CPR for one minute, then call an ambulance.

• If he is breathing, place him in the recovery position and call an ambulance.

Look and listen for signs of breathing

Rescue breathing for a baby under one year

1 If your baby has stopped breathing, keep her head tilted and lift the chin with one finger. Check the baby's mouth for obvious obstructions. Pick out anything you can see.

2 Put your mouth over baby's nostrils and mouth and breathe out so that her chest rises—one second. Remove your lips and let the chest fall. Do this twice. Begin chest compressions (see p.302), performing 30 chest compressions, then two rescue breaths, and repeating if necessary. If you can't get breaths in, victim is choking: give back blows and abdominal thrusts (see p.299).

Breathe into the baby's mouth and nose

Rescue breathing for a child

1 If child has stopped breathing, keep his head tilted, and lift his chin with two fingers on the point of the chin. Check the child's mouth for obvious obstructions.

2 Lift chin. Using the finger and thumb, pinch child's nostrils closed. Inhale, put your mouth over his mouth, making a complete seal, and breathe out until his chest rises—one second. Remove your lips and let the chest fall. Give two rescue breaths. Perform 30 chest compressions (see p.302), then two rescue breaths, repeating if necessary. If you can't get breaths in, the victim is choking: give back blows and abdominal thrusts (see p.299).

Lift the chin with two fingers

RECOVERY POSITION

For a baby under one year
Cradle your baby in your arms with her body facing slightly toward you. Keep her head lower than her body to help keep the airway open.

For a child
An unconscious child who is breathing should be placed in the recovery position to keep her airway open and to allow liquids to drain from her mouth. Roll your child over onto her side with the uppermost leg bent and the lower leg straight. Make sure her lower arm is clear of her body. Bend her upper arm at the elbow so that it supports her body, place her upper hand under her cheek to help keep the head back.

Chest compressions for a baby under one year

1 Lay your baby down on a firm surface and position two fingers only on the center of the chest.

2 Press down sharply on the chest with the tips of your two fingers to a depth one-third of the depth of the chest; release the pressure, but don't remove your fingers. Give 30 compressions at a rate of about 100 compressions a minute.

3 Give two rescue breaths (see p.301). Continue alternating 30 chest compressions with two rescue breaths. After two minutes, call an ambulance, if this has not already been done. Take your baby to the phone with you if necessary. Continue resuscitation until the ambulance arrives, the baby starts breathing, or you are too exhausted to keep going.

Chest compressions for a child

1 Lay your child on his back on a firm surface. Place the heel of one hand in the center of the child's chest.

2 Press down sharply to a depth one-third of the depth of the chest. Release the pressure, but don't remove your hand. Give 30 compressions at rate of 100 compressions per minute.

3 Give two rescue breaths (see p.301). Alternate 30 chest compressions with two rescue breaths for two minutes. After two minutes, call an ambulance if it has not already been called. Then continue resuscitation until the ambulance arrives, the child starts breathing, or you are too exhausted to keep going.

Serious bleeding

Severe bleeding can lead to a serious condition called shock and eventually unconsciousness. Act quickly and calmly. If bleeding is severe treat for shock (opposite).

1 Expose the wound—cut away clothing if necessary—and press on the wound with your hand or over a clean dressing or cloth. If there is glass sticking out of the wound, don't remove it. Instead, apply pressure on either side of the object to compress the ends of the damaged blood vessels.

2 Raise the injured part so that it is above her heart. This will slow down the blood flow to the injured area. If possible, lay her down, keeping the injury high. Call an ambulance or take your child to the hospital.

3 If blood appears through the bandage put another one on top. If it comes through the second bandage you may not be applying pressure in the right place. Take both dressings off and start again.

Shock

After a serious injury such as severe bleeding or burns, recurrent vomiting, severe diarrhea, or extreme pain or fear, a child may suffer from shock. Symptoms include: pale, cold, clammy skin; shallow and rapid breathing with yawning and sighing; sickness and vomiting; and, eventually, unconsciousness. If you notice any of these symptoms, especially if there is no obvious bleeding, act immediately. Send someone for help while you attend to her. If she becomes unconscious, see p.300.

1 *Lay your child down, preferably on a blanket, and keep her head low.*

2 *Raise her legs, unless you suspect a broken bone, to keep the circulating blood in the center of the body. Loosen any tight clothing and, if it is cold, cover your child with a blanket. Call an ambulance.*

Warning
- Do not give your child anything to eat or drink. If she's thirsty, simply moisten her lips with water.
- Do not warm her with a hot-water bottle or electric blanket; it takes blood away from the vital organs.

Electric shock

Your child may get an electric shock from frayed cords or wires, light switches, defective electrical appliances, or from touching an appliance with wet hands.

In severe cases, your child may lose consciousness. In mild cases, she may have burns—often at the point of entry and exit of the electricity.

1 *Break the contact between your child and the source of electricity. Turn the electricity off or pull the plug out of the wall.*

2 *If you have to break the contact manually, make sure you do it safely: push your child away using an object made of a nonconducting material, such as wood or plastic, and stand on an insulating material; or drag your child away by his clothes—your hands must be dry and you must not touch his skin.*

3 *Examine your child for burns. If burns are severe or your child is unconscious, call an ambulance. In the meantime, treat the burns (see p.304).*

Break the contact with a nonconducting material

Burns and scalds

These are described in terms of the amount of damage to the skin. Superficial burns are the least serious and can result from a minor spillage or from touching a very hot surface. Partial-thickness burns are more serious, and fluid-filled blisters form on the skin. Full-thickness burns are very serious as all layers of the skin, and possibly nerves, are damaged, and fluid loss is high because of weeping of the skin. Seek medical help for any burn on a child. If the burn is large, or deep, take her to the hospital.

1 *Cool the area by running cold water over the affected part of the body for about ten minutes. If there is no water available, you can use another cool liquid such as milk.*

2 *Remove or cut away any burned clothing, shoes, or jewelry before the damaged tissue begins to swell.*

3 *Cover the injury with a sterile dressing to protect it from infection. (Clean plastic wrap can be used as a temporary dressing; don't wrap it around the limb.)*

4 *Call for medical advice, or an ambulance. You may need to treat her for shock (see p.303). If she loses consciousness, assess her condition (see pp.300–302).*

Warning
- Do not touch the affected area or attempt to burst any blisters that form.
- Don't put lotion or fat on the area.
- Don't cover a burn with an adhesive dressing.
- Don't cover the burn with a "fluffy" dressing or any cloth that sheds lint.
- Don't remove anything that is sticking to the burn: you may cause further damage to the skin or tissue and introduce infection.
- Don't overcool your child; it could cause hypothermia.

Clothing on fire

1 *If your child's clothing catches fire, the first priority is to stop him from moving. Any rapid movement will make the flames worse.*

2 *Stop him from running around in a panic because this will fan the flames. Lie him on the floor with the burning side uppermost.*

3 *Wrap him in a heavy wool coat or blanket to stifle the flames. Never use nylon—it's flammable.*

4 *Roll him on the ground to put out the flames. Douse him with water if you have some, or with another nonflammable liquid.*

Wrap the child up to stifle the flames

Heat exhaustion and heatstroke

These can occur when the body becomes overheated. Heat exhaustion is caused by loss of body mineral salts. Heatstroke develops when the temperature-control mechanism in the brain fails. Your child's temperature may rise above 104°F (40°C). and in extreme cases she may lose consciousness. Her skin may look and feel hot, but is dry. Your child will seem drowsy and lethargic, and may have a rapid pulse. In severe cases your child may be confused, and may even lose consciousness.

1 *Take your child's outer clothes off and lay her down in a cool shady place.*

2 *Call a doctor if your child's temperature is as high as 104°F (40°C) and, while you are waiting, sponge her with tepid water or wrap her in a cool wet sheet. Place a covered ice pack on her forehead, give her water to sip and direct a fan onto her body.*

3 *Monitor her pulse rate and temperature closely. Check her temperature every minute until it lowers to 99°F (37.2°C), then stop cooling her, but continue to monitor her temperature.*

4 *If she loses consciousness, treat as directed on pp.300–302. Call an ambulance.*

Hypothermia

This is a condition that develops when the body temperature falls below a certain level—usually because of exposure to extreme cold outdoors or inadequate heating in your home. A baby who has become dangerously chilled will appear quiet, drowsy, and limp, and will refuse food. Her hands, feet, and face may be bright pink. If you suspect hypothermia in your baby, request urgent medical help. It is very important to warm your child gradually.

Cuddle your child to warm her

1 *Replace any wet or damp clothes, dress your child in dry clothes and put a hat on her head. Wrap your baby in a blanket. Call for medical advice, or call an ambulance for a baby.*

2 *Use your body heat to warm your baby or child. Take her to bed with you, or get into a sleeping bag with her and cuddle her against your body.*

Broken bones

Rough play not infrequently results in broken bones. Children are most prone to greenstick fractures, where the bone doesn't break completely and there is minimal damage to the skin. Suspect a fracture if your child cannot move the affected area normally or without pain; if there is bruising and/or swelling around the site of the injury; or if the area appears deformed.

1 *Support the joints above and below the affected area with your hands to prevent worsening of the injury.*

2 *For extra support, put an affected arm in a sling; immobilize a leg by tying knees and ankles together.*

Support the affected area

3 *Take your child to the nearest emergency room if someone else can support her while you drive, or call an ambulance.*

Warning
- Never straighten any bent or curved limb.
- Do not touch an open wound. (If there is an open wound or if bone is sticking through the skin, cover the area with a sterile dressing.)
- Do not give your child anything to eat or drink because she may need to be given a general anesthetic.

Poisoning

1 *If you suspect that your child has swallowed poison, call an ambulance immediately. Tell the dispatcher what you think she has taken and how much.*

2 *Your child may have severe stomach pains and will probably vomit. Hold her head lower than her body so there is no risk of her inhaling and choking on any vomit.*

Assess her condition

Warning
- Never attempt to induce vomiting—you could cause more harm if what she's swallowed is corrosive. Corrosive substances include caustic soda, weed killers, paraffin, disinfectant, bleach, and other ammonia-based household cleaners. Look for signs of burning around her mouth. If there are any, she's probably swallowed one of these substances. Give water or milk to drink to cool the burning.
- If your child is unconscious, assess her condition. If she is breathing, place her in the recovery position (see p.301); if she's stopped breathing, begin resuscitation (see pp.300–302). If available, use a plastic face shield to give rescue breaths, or seal her mouth and breathe into her nose.

Find out what your child has swallowed

Head injury

This is a potentially serious injury. A blow to the head can cause injury to the skull or the brain, and there may be a delayed reaction to the injury hours or even days later. It's important, therefore, that you watch your child after any head injury.

1 *Help your child to sit or lie down, and place a cold pack against the injury.*

Apply pressure to control bleeding

2 *If there is an wound, cover it with a dressing and apply direct pressure to stop the bleeding.*

3 *Watch your child and monitor for any changes in his level of consciousness. If he was slightly dazed but recovers quickly, he may be concussed (his brain was "shaken" in his skull). If he appears fine initially but deteriorates later, he may have a serious condition called a hematoma, caused by bleeding within the skull, or a fractured bone fragment pressing on the brain.*

4 *Seek medical treatment for all head injuries.*

Warning
- Never shake your child to check his level of consciousness.
- If your child is unconscious, assess his condition. If he is breathing, place him in the recovery position (*see p.301*); if he's stopped breathing, begin resuscitation.

FIRST AID KIT

Always have a first aid kit in your home (and a separate one in the car). Keep it out of reach of your children in a cool dry place. Check the contents regularly and restock as necessary.

- Sterile gauze squares in various sizes for cleaning wounds.
- A box of adhesive dressings in various sizes.
- Sterile dressings with bandages attached in various sizes.
- Small and large roller bandages such as gauze or crêpe bandages.
- A roll of 1 inch (2.5 centimeter) hypoallergenic adhesive tape.
- A sterile eye pad with bandage attached.
- 2 triangular bandages
- Safety pins

- Blunt-ended tweezers and scissors
- Disposable gloves
- Protective face mask for rescue breathing
- Antiseptic cream
- Calamine lotion

Other useful items
- Children's acetaminophen and/or ibuprofen liquid
- Insect repellent
- Antihistamine syrup
- Sunscreen with the highest protection factor
- Digital thermometer

17 Home medicine

All parents are worried when their child is sick. The difficulty can lie in not being able to identify what's wrong with the child (especially when he's too young to tell you how he feels) and in not knowing how serious the ailment really is. All children get sick at some stage, but modern medicine is so efficient that few illnesses now pose the threat that they once did. Health care professionals can identify and prescribe for the ailment; it's the parents' job to provide the essential nursing and comfort. Sometimes it's difficult to know when to ask for help, but if you're worried, it's always best to seek medical advice.

When to ask for medical help

Doctors, nurses, and other health care professionals won't mind if you consult them for reassurance if you're worried about your child's health. There is always 911 or your local hospital's emergency room. Like many doctors, I quickly learned that one person whose opinion can't be dismissed is the mother's. When in doubt, always seek medical advice, but especially if you notice any of the following:

Temperature
- If your child's temperature rises above 100.4°F (38°C) and he is obviously sick.
- If the temperature rises above 103°F (39.4°C) even if there are no apparent signs of illness.
- When a child's high temperature drops and then rises again.
- When a baby has had a temperature of 100.4°F (38°C) for 24 hours.

- When your child has had a temperature of over 100.4°F (38°C) for three days.
- When child has a high temperature that is also accompanied by febrile seizures (see p.332).
- When your child has a stiff neck, a headache, and sensitivity to light, as well as a fever.
- When your baby's skin feels cold and he is drowsy, unusually quiet, and limp, although his face, hands, and feet are pink (possibly hypothermia).
- If the child has a high temperature that is accompanied by a rash, especially of red or purple blood spots that don't disappear when pressed. Check this by pressing a glass to the skin and looking through it to see if the rash is still visible. If it is, get medical help immediately.

Ask for advice

If you suspect your baby isn't well, don't hesitate to get medical advice. You know your baby and you're the best judge of when she is unwell.

Pain and discomfort
- When your child feels sick and dizzy and complains of headaches.
- When your child complains of blurred vision, especially after having had a blow to the head.
- When your child has severe gripping pains at regular intervals.
- When your child has a pain in the right side of his stomach and feels sick.

Breathing
- If your child's breathing is labored and you notice that his ribs are being drawn sharply inward with each breath.

Loss of appetite
- If your child is normally a good eater.
- If your baby is under six months.

Wounds
- When your child has had any kind of serious accident or burn.
- When your child has lost consciousness, no matter how briefly.
- When acid gets into your child's eye.

- When the wound is deep or has caused serious loss of blood.
- When your child has been bitten by an animal, a human, or a snake.
- When the eye has actually been pierced by an object.

Vomiting
- If the vomiting is violent, prolonged, or excessive.
- If your baby is very young, as it may cause rapid dehydration.

Diarrhea
- If your baby is very young as it could cause dehydration.
- If it is accompanied by abdominal pain, temperature, or any obvious illness.

Questions you may be asked
When you seek medical advice, you are likely to be asked a number of questions and it's important to answer these as accurately as you can.

Some specific questions may include the following: has your child vomited or had diarrhea? Does he have any pain? Where is it? How long has it lasted? Have you given him anything for it? Does he have a raised temperature? How quickly did the fever come on, and what was his highest temperature? Has he lost consciousness? Have you noticed swollen glands or a rash? Has he had any dizziness or blurred vision? You may be asked about your child's appetite and sleeping patterns.

Examining your child
If you take your child to your pediatrician's office, expect him to be examined once you have answered all of the pediatrician's questions.

Using a thermometer birth to 3 years

Your child's temperature will probably fluctuate between 97.5°F and 99.5°F (36°C and 37.5°C). It will be at its lowest at night when your child is asleep and highest in the afternoon; it will also be high if your child has been running around.

Although you'll probably be able to tell your child is feverish just by looking at him and laying your hand on his brow, there may be occasions when you need to take his temperature. Don't, however, rely on the temperature reading as an accurate reflection of your baby's health. Children can be very sick with no fever, or well with a high temperature—so always take account of any other symptoms.

TYPES OF THERMOMETERS AVAILABLE

Never use a mercury thermometer in your child's mouth; he may bite it and swallow mercury, which is poisonous. Digital thermometers are harder to break and easy to use with children of all ages and can be used in the mouth, under the arm, or rectally.

A baby's temperature should be taken rectally for the most accurate reading. To take the mouth temperature, ask your child to open his mouth and raise his tongue. Place the thermometer under his tongue and ask him to place the tip of his tongue behind his lower front teeth to hold the thermometer in place. Ask him to close his lips, but not his teeth, over it. Wait until the thermometer beeps and read the number in the window. Ear thermometers are accurate and give a reading in seconds. Strip thermometers are less accurate than the others, but simple and safe to use. Always wash a thermometer after use in soap and cold water.

Using a digital thermometer
With a young child, you may find it easier to take his temperature under his arm than in his mouth. Put the thermometer into his armpit and lower his arm over it. Hold his arm down until the thermometer beeps, then remove and read it.

Using an ear thermometer
Digital ear thermometers are a quick, safe method of taking a child's temperature. Gently insert the tip into your child's ear and read the temperature from the display. The ear thermometer has a hygienic disposable tip.

Using a strip thermometer
Carefully position the heat-sensitive side on your child's forehead and hold it there for a minute or so, keeping your fingers off of the panels. One of the panels on the outside of the strip lights up to indicate the child's temperature.

Giving medicine birth to 1 year

When your baby is sick, your doctor may prescribe a medicine, such as liquid acetaminophen or an antibiotic. Always give the dosage recommended by the doctor or as instructed on the bottle. Follow any instructions exactly. If using a teaspoon, make sure it is the correct size.

Most medicines for children come in syrup form with a spoon, dropper, or syringe to administer them. The syringe is the easiest method for giving medicine to babies and for measuring the amount accurately. Ask your pharmacist to give you an adapter to put in the top of the bottle. Put the adapter in the bottle and the fit the syringe into it. If your baby refuses to take medicine, get your partner to help you, or wrap your baby up in a blanket so that you can hold him steady. Your baby may start to cry when he takes the medicine. Don't worry about this; it's far more important that your baby swallows it and keeps it down so that he can recover from his illness. Try to stay calm when giving the medicine, as your baby will sense your own anxiety. When a child is sick, the importance of getting him to take his medicine outweighs every other consideration; this is one situation in which blackmail is justifiable. Use the most powerful reward you can think of to get your baby to take the medicine.

GIVING MEDICINE TO A BABY OR CHILD

If you are using a syringe or a plastic measuring spoon to administer medicine to your child, measure out the dose before you start. Make sure that you have understood your doctor's instructions if you're giving a prescription medicine and follow them precisely. When giving over-the-counter medication, read the directions on the package very carefully. If you are at all unsure, check with your doctor or pharmacist.

You'll need to hold your child securely. It's best to hold his hands gently out of the way to prevent him from knocking the medicine out of your hand.

Using a syringe
Sterilize the spoon with boiling water or sterilizing solution. Draw up the correct amount of medicine from the bottle into the syringe. Hold your baby in the crook of your arm. Place the end of the syringe into the side of his mouth and push the plunger down gently. This will gradually release the medicine into his mouth.

Using a spoon
Sterilize the spoon with boiling water or sterilizing solution. Pour the medicine into the spoon. Hold your child in a semi-reclined position and pull his chin down with your finger, then place the spoon on his lower lip. Raise the angle of the spoon so that the medicine trickles into his mouth.

Giving medicine 1 to 3 years

Medicines for older children usually come in a liquid form, that can be taken on a spoon. Ear or nose drops should be given in the same way as for a younger baby (*see below*). If your child is making a lot of noise about taking drops it's important to stay as calm as possible so your child doesn't panic. Get your partner to help you by holding the child firmly while you administer the drops.

As your child gets older, try not to make a fuss, or be very insistent that he takes the medicine because this will make your child respond negatively. It usually helps if you show your child that you are willing to take some yourself. If your child

really doesn't like the taste of medicine, then try diluting it with his favorite drink.

Tips for giving medicine

- Suggest your child hold his nose while taking the medicine, which lessens the effect of the taste. Don't hold his nose yourself, however, because he may inhale some of the medicine.
- Show your child that you have his favorite drink ready to wash away the taste of the medicine.
- Help your child clean his teeth thoroughly after taking any liquid medicine to prevent the syrup from sticking to his teeth.

ADMINISTERING DROPS TO A BABY OR CHILD

Eye drops
Lay your baby on his back and tilt his head in the direction of the affected eye. Put the dropper into the medicine and draw up the right amount. Gently pull his lower eyelid down with one finger and raise his upper lid with another. Let the drops fall into the corner of his eye. Get someone to help if necessary.

Nose drops
Lay your baby on his back with his head tilted backward. Put the dropper into the medicine and draw up the right amount. Hold the dropper above your baby's nostrils and let the required number of drops fall into each nostril. Keep your child lying down so the drops run into the nose.

Ear drops
Lay your baby on his side. Put the dropper into the medicine, and draw up the right amount. Hold the dropper over your baby's ear opening and let the required number of eardrops fall into the center of his ear. Keep him still for a few moments while the drops spread into the ear canal.

Being a nurse to your child

Few mothers will escape being called upon to act as a nurse—all children get sick at some time. Mothers, however, make excellent nurses because they put the health and comfort of their children before almost anything else. Many children become "babyish" when they are sick and want to be with their mothers all the time.

Very often it's not just the mother's company they require but also the mother's physical contact. Sick babies need a lot more nursing, cuddling, and affection than usual. If you're still breast-feeding you'll probably find that your baby wants more "comfort sucks." However, at the same time as being as loving as possible, guard against starting habits you don't want to continue.

Should he go to bed?

Unless your doctor advises otherwise, it's best to trust your own common sense and your child's natural inclinations. If he wants to stay up he should be allowed to do so. Even if he has a temperature, he should be allowed to stay up if he wants to. But do make sure that he gets plenty to drink so that he doesn't become dehydrated, that he rests when he feels tired, and that the room temperature is kept even and warm.

There is nothing sacred about bedrooms either. One of the most potent medicines is the sight and sound of you and the reassurance you bring, so your sick child will be very much better off being near you. If possible rig up a couch, sofa, or comfortable chair so that he can be in the same room with you. This way your child will have the opportunity of seeing, talking to, and being entertained by anyone who comes into the house rather than being cut off from the rest of the family in his bedroom. When your child is tired, however, it is time to put him to bed. But don't just leave him alone. Make sure that you visit him at regular intervals (every half hour), and find the time to stay and play a game, read a book, or do a puzzle. If you have other children, encourage them to do the same thing. If he is asleep check him to make sure he is not too hot.

When he's on the road to recovery, make sure that enough happens in his day to make the distinction between night and day clear. Allow your child to watch television for diversion during the daytime. Then read him a story to calm and quiet him at bedtime, as you would usually do.

Feeding your sick child

There are no longer any hard and fast rules about the sort of food that you should give your child when he's sick. Unless directed by your doctor, you can feed your child whatever he wants to eat. It's time for you to relax most of the rules, dietary and otherwise. Let him eat and drink what he wants, and as much as he wants. You'll probably find that he prefers to eat little but often—never force him to eat.

Even though your child will seem to eat very sparsely while he's sick, he will quickly make up the deficit as his appetite increases. The return of his appetite is invariably the sign that your child is getting better. When he is on the road to recovery,

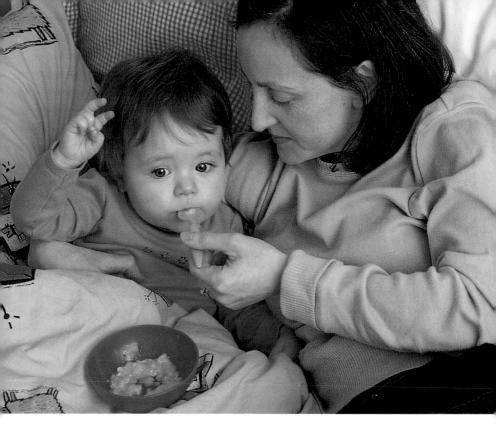

Stay close
Give your child as much comfort and love as you can when he's sick. Stay with him as much as you can and give him his favorite foods and drinks.

spoil him with his favorite foods and perhaps those that have been previously restricted to treats. He'll be eager to make up for all the lost meals, and any weight loss will be made up.

Giving drinks

It is essential that your child drinks a lot when he's sick—when he has a fever, diarrhea, or is vomiting—because he will need to replace lost fluids to avoid becoming dehydrated. The recommended fluid intake for a child with a fever is 1½–2½ fluid ounces per pound (100–150 milliliters per kilogram) of body weight per day, which is the equivalent of 2 pints (1 liter) per day for a child who weighs 20 pounds (9 kilograms). Encourage your child to take fluids by leaving a drink at his bedside (preferably water or fruit juice), by putting drinks in glasses that are especially appealing and by giving him flexible straws.

Treating your child's temperature

The first sign of a raised temperature is often a hot forehead, but to check that your child is feverish take his temperature (*see p.311*). Call your doctor if a fever lasts more than 24 hours for a baby (or three days for a child), or if there are other symptoms.

Temperatures over 100.4°F (38°C) should be taken very seriously in children acetaminophen to help control the fever, but do not give more than four doses in 24 hours. Check his temperature regularly. It is important for the child to drink a lot as he will lose fluid through sweating. Ibuprofen can be given to a child instead of acetaminophen, or they can be alternated to help control the fever. Never give aspirin to a child under the age of 16.

Keeping your sick child amused

Illness is an occasion when you can indulge your child. When he is not resting, spend time playing games and talking to him. Relax all rules and let him play whatever games he wants to.

If your child wants to do something messy like painting, let him—just spread an old sheet over the bed first. If you can, move a television with a DVD player into his room temporarily. This will keep him entertained and make him feel special, too.

under six months, so you must take action to reduce a high temperature as soon as possible. Children are at risk of febrile seizures when there is a rapid change in temperature. To reduce fever, lower the temperature in your child's room and give him iced drinks. Try to cool your child by removing his clothes. If he is in bed, use only light bedclothes. Give the recommended dose of children's liquid

COMFORT AND RECUPERATION TIPS

- Give your child treats. If he has a sore throat give him ice cream.
- Cool cotton sheets are soothing to a feverish child. Change the bed regularly.
- When your child is vomiting, always be there, and support his forehead with the palm of your hand. Give him some water to rinse his mouth with, and perhaps a mint to suck afterward to take away the bad taste.
- Put a table next to the bed for his toys, books, fruit juices, or water.

- Make a worktable by cutting a semi-circle out of an inverted cardboard box. This can be placed over your child's lap. You could also support a sanded wooden plank on two chairs placed either side of the bed.
- Buy some new toys for your child. Don't give them to him all at once, but one at a time.
- If your child isn't feeling too sick you could try wrapping the toys up so that you can play a game together. Ask him to guess what's in the packages by feeling them, then let him tear off the paper.

Also read aloud to him. Alternatively, you can get out some of his old toys and play with them together; buy him small presents and let him unwrap them; sing songs or make up a story together; ask him to draw a picture of what he is going to do when he feels better; and, unless he has an infectious illness, let some friends visit him for a brief period during the day. As your child begins to feel better, you can let him play outside, but if he still has a fever, discourage him from running around.

If your child goes to the hospital

At some point in your child's life he may have to be admitted to the hospital. Given a little forethought, a stay in hospital does not have to be upsetting or frightening. If you don't like hospitals and you convey this feeling to your child, you may inadvertently make his stay much more difficult than it has to be. Try to teach him that a hospital is a friendly place where people go to get better. Whenever the chance arises—if you have a friend or a relative in the hospital, for instance—take your child along when you go to visit and be matter of fact, not gloomy, about the illness. If a child's first experience of being in hospital is when he becomes sick, it will seem even more alien than it would otherwise.

Preparing a child for the hospital

If you know that your child is going to the hospital, read him a story about a child who goes into the hospital, and role play

doctors and nurses with toy stethoscopes. Be as honest as you can about why he's going into the hospital, and emphasize that it's to make him better. Reassure him that you will be with him as much as you can while he's there, and if he is old enough to understand, tell him when he'll be well enough to come home. If your child needs to have an operation, he's bound to be curious about what's going to happen to him and what the doctors are going to do. Answer his questions as honestly as you can—if he asks you if the operation will hurt, don't pretend that it won't, but tell him that doctors have medicines to make the pain go away and that he'll soon be better.

Packing for the hospital
Involve your child in the preparations for going into the hospital if possible and make sure she takes some of her favorite toys and books.

Medical index

■ Asthma

In a person suffering from asthma, the allergic reaction shows itself in the lining of the air passages. This lining is very sensitive. It not only responds to an allergen with wheezing, but it also responds more than usual to exercise, infection, and emotional disturbances. The lining of the airways goes into spasm and secretes mucus. Your child will have difficulty breathing out, and you will hear a wheezing noise when he does this. His face may become pale and he could look anxious and perspire. If his lips turn blue, this indicates a late stage and a serious need for urgent medical help.

The allergen that causes your child's asthma may be dust, pollen, feathers, animal hair, or fungal spores. Many young babies wheeze if they have an attack of bronchitis or bronchiolitis (inflammation of the smaller tubes). This baby can legitimately be labeled a wheezy baby, but it is wrong to assume that all babies who wheeze are asthmatic. They are not. Once they grow a little bigger and the bronchial tubes become wider, the wheezing will stop. This condition is not allergic in origin, and the wheeze associated with respiratory viral infections is not necessarily asthma.

What to do If your child has an attack of wheeziness, seek medical help. This usually means making an appointment to see your doctor. If the doctor diagnoses asthma, your child will be given medication, and if necessary you will be taught how to administer it. Your child will be followed by your pediatrician or he may be referred to a specialist depending on the severity of his asthma.

As your child gets older he may be tested with various allergens to see if he is sensitive to a specific substance. If this substance is isolated, you can then do something about avoiding it. For instance, if your child is sensitive to feathers and dust (both of these being very common causes of allergy), try to get rid of any bedding that contains feathers, down, or hair, and make sure that the furnishings, carpets, and curtains in your child's room do not hold a lot of dust. Dust allergy is commonly caused by a microscopic mite (the dust mite) that lives in house dust. There are nearly always more mites in damp houses than in dry ones, so there is a scientific rationale for asthma being worse in a damp house than in a dry one.

Besides an allergic component of asthma, there may be an emotional one. If your doctor suggests that emotional factors are playing a part in your child's asthma, it is up to you and your family to see what you can do to improve the atmosphere and minimize stress for your child.

It is very important that you and the rest of the family don't get asthma out of perspective. Many parents of asthmatic children are overanxious and overstress the condition so that eventually whole household revolves around the child. This is unwise because the child may soon learn how to manipulate the household around his asthma attacks. The treatment of asthma is complicated, so you will be given very clear instructions about what you should do under certain circumstances, and certainly what you should do if an asthma attack comes on out of the blue.

Balanitis

This is an inflammation of the tip of the penis in uncircumcised boys. It may be caused by diaper rash, which is often a reaction to detergent, or it can be caused by an infection. It is not serious, but for the child's comfort, you should treat it promptly. The penis will be red and swollen, there may be a pussy discharge from the tip, and the foreskin cannot be drawn back.

What to do If you notice any redness around the tip of the penis, try to draw back the foreskin very gently, wash, and apply some antiseptic cream until you can get medical advice. If the foreskin won't draw back, leave it and see your doctor as soon as possible. Your child may be prescribed both topical and oral antibiotics.

Bites

The chances of your child being bitten by an animal such as a dog or another child are relatively high; the chances of your child being bitten by a snake depend on where you live.

What to do The treatment given for a cat, dog, or other mammal bite depends on the depth of the wound and whether your child's tetanus immunization is up to date. If the bite is superficial, clean the wound and leave it open or put a loose-fitting gauze dressing on it if necessary. If, however, the wound is serious, or on your child's face, then you must seek medical

advice as soon as possible. Animal bites are usually deep and dirty, so your child may be prescribed an antibiotic.

Bites from other children can be even more septic than animal bites. These should be cleaned and left open, and if you're at all worried by them you should seek medical advice.

If your child is bitten by a snake, dial 911 for an ambulance. Do not let him walk, but lay him down. While you are waiting for medical help, wash the surface of the skin and apply a pressure bandage from above the bite as far up the limb as possible. If possible, identify the snake. If you are in an area where poisonous snakes are prevalent, seek advice as to whether you should keep emergency serum on hand.

Blisters

These may be formed as a protection to the body where it has been chafed, burned, or rubbed.

What to do A blister should be left intact. Never prick it; leave it intact as long as you can. If a blister is on an exposed area, simply cover it with a small pad of gauze kept in place with surgical tape. The blister will subside of its own accord and the skin becomes dry and hard. It will change its color to a rather dark pink and will gradually fall off. Don't do anything to disturb this natural process.

Bruise

This is a purplish-red stain in the skin, usually resulting from a blow or a knock that ruptures the small blood vessels near the skin's surface. It usually takes ten to fourteen days for a bruise to disappear completely; as it fades, it changes color to maroon, then green or yellow as the blood pigments break down and are reabsorbed by the body. Resting, cooling, and raising the affected part will soothe any pain. A bruise is rarely serious. If a bruise appears without any reason, this could relate to uncommon but serious conditions such as leukemia and hemophilia.

What to do A minor bruise needs no treatment at all, just a cuddle and reassurance if your child is upset. If the bruise is large, apply a cold compress for half an hour or so. This will contain the bruising. Seek medical advice immediately if the pain and bruising aren't getting better within 4–6 hours; this might suggest an underlying fracture. Also seek medical advice if a bruise appears spontaneously with no apparent cause.

▄ Burns

It is almost inevitable that your child will burn himself on a radiator or hot faucet at some point, despite your efforts.

What to do Cool the burn by placing it under cold running water for ten minutes, or until pain subsides (see p.304). The best treatment is to protect the burn with a non-stick dressing. Otherwise use a sterile gauze dressing or non-fluffy material (a clean cotton handkerchief will do). Don't remove any clothing that is sticking to a burn.

Seek medical advice. If your child has been severely burned he must be taken to the nearest hospital emergency room for proper medical treatment.

▄ Congested or runny nose

Neither persistent yellow mucus (mucus which continues for longer than five or six days), nor a runny nose is normal. Both of these signs indicate that your child may be suffering from a viral upper respiratory infection. If yellow secretions go on for more than six or seven days, your child may need antibiotics. A clear watery nasal discharge over a long period is more likely to be caused by allergic rhinitis.

What to do As the ear, nose, and throat, and the lungs are connected by a small set of tubes, anatomically speaking, an infection in any one place can very quickly creep along the tubes to infect another place. For example, a chronic infection of the middle ear can lead to a condition called serous otitis media, or otitis media with effusion, which may affect hearing and the development of speech. See your doctor if you suspect your child may have an ear infection.

▄ Chicken pox

This is a very common infection that children invariably catch, as it's one of the most contagious of all childhood diseases (see p.340). Your child will be contagious from one to two days before the rash starts to the time when the blisters scab over. The chicken pox virus is the same one that causes shingles (herpes zoster), which may affect adults, particularly older ones.

Chicken pox often starts with a temperature of 100.4–102°F (38–39°C). In very young children, however, there is hardly any rise in temperature; the rash may be the first sign. This will appear in crops over five to seven days and will be extremely itchy. At first, the spots are like dark red pimples, but within a couple of hours they will have developed a small blister on top that resembles a drop of water. The spots will eventually scab over and drop off. The rash usually starts on the child's trunk and then spreads to his face, scalp, arms, and legs. In the worst cases, the spots can also appear inside the child's mouth, nose, ears, vagina, and anus. Your child will be contagious for one or two days before the rash starts until the time when the blisters scab over.

What to do The most important thing to do is to stop your child from scratching the spots. If you don't do this the scab may come off and the resulting wound may become infected and can leave a scar. The best treatment for this is a moisturizer containing antiseptic, such as calamine lotion, applied at regular intervals. Keep your child's nails short to minimize the risk of infection should he pull the scabs off. Your child may find the itchiness so intense that he can't get to sleep, so your doctor may prescribe an antihistamine for relief. Give your child the recommended dose of acetaminophen to control his temperature and make sure he drinks plenty of fluids. If your child is still wearing diapers, leave them off as much as possible to prevent possible infection.

▦ Colds

A cold is caused by a virus that we cannot treat specifically. There is no antibiotic to which the virus is sensitive, so it cannot be killed. This means that it has to be overcome by the body's own defense mechanisms, which usually takes ten to fourteen days. The virus infects and inflames the membranes of the nasal passages and throat, producing the well-known symptoms of sore throat and runny nose.

Sometimes the viral infection weakens the body and allows a secondary bacterial infection to develop. The tonsils and adenoids may become swollen, and so may the glands in the neck. If the tonsils become infected (tonsillitis), antibiotic treatment may be required, so seek medical advice (see p.336).

Colds are common in young children, and to have five or six colds a year is quite usual. Babies under six months are less likely to catch colds because of the antibodies they receive from their mothers, especially if they're breast-fed.

What to do In a young baby a cold can cause quite a lot of distress because it may block the nose and prevent breathing during feeding. Don't let your child suffer this way; seek medical advice. You will probably be given nose drops to use before each feeding, and these will keep the nasal passages clear long enough for the baby to eat. Never use nose drops unless they are prescribed by your doctor.

Because all the upper air passages, the nose, and the sinuses in an infant are connected by short tubes, an infection of one part can quickly spread to another. For this reason a cold may rapidly become bronchitis (an infection of the respiratory tract), tonsillitis (see p.336), and sometimes otitis media (infection of the middle ear). If your child complains of a sore throat or earache (see p.325), seek medical advice because he may need antibiotics. Older children seem to feel the symptoms of a cold less than adults, so there is no reason to use over-the-counter cold medicines for a child in the way one might for an adult.

◼ Cold sore/Herpes simplex

Despite their name cold sores have nothing to do with a cold, other than the fact that a cold affects the immune system and reduces resistance to infection, which may allow the herpes simplex virus to activate. Primary herpes simplex infection may occur in young children. This is an acute illness with a very high fever, lots of painful mouth ulcers, and great difficulty swallowing.

What to do If you notice a herpes blister coming up, contact your doctor. She may prescribe oral acyclovir or recommend acyclovir cream, which is available over the counter. If used early enough, this can contain or minimize the attack of herpes.

The herpes virus is passed on by direct contact. Most children who get cold sores, usually around the lips, nose, and possibly on the cheeks and chin, get them from adults who kiss them. It is quite common if one parent in the family has a cold sore for others to catch the virus from that one parent; it is equally possible for your child to infect others as well.

◼ Colic

In a baby under four months of age colic describes a crying spell, during which the baby's face becomes very red and both legs are drawn up to his stomach as if he is in great pain. This crying spell usually comes in the early evening; during the rest of the day the baby is generally contented. The crying can reach screaming pitch and last from one to three hours. The baby doesn't usually respond to soothing techniques that work at other times. Colic is so common that it is regarded by pediatricians as normal, but for parents it can be difficult to endure. The cause is not known. It is often at its worst at six weeks but disappears by three to four months.

What to do Try all the ways of soothing your baby that work at other times of the day. This may mean you are constantly offering the breast or bottle; changing diapers; burping; nursing and rocking; walking with the baby on your shoulder; putting the baby in a sling against your body; playing music for constant background noise; or walking him in a carriage or stroller. Try offering your baby a pacifier if he seems to want to suck all the time. Having a warm bath relaxes most babies and helps when the crying is at its worst.

If you find it hard to cope, seek medical advice to reassure you that your baby is healthy and will grow out of the colic eventually. Your doctor or nurse practitioner can provide valuable advice and counseling while your baby is still having attacks.

◼ Conjunctivitis

This is an inflammation of the conjunctiva, which is the outer covering of the eye. It makes the child's eye look red, and it can feel itchy or sore.

What to do If your child develops "pinkeye," examine the eye to see if there is a foreign object trapped underneath the lid. If there is, try to rinse the eye with tepid boiled water to see if you can wash the foreign body out. If not, go to your pediatrician. If there is not a foreign object or trauma, the cause of the "pinkeye" could be viral or bacterial infection or an allergic reaction. In case your child's conjunctivitis needs antibiotic treatment, seek medical advice.

▓ Coughing

A cough is the body's natural reflex to irritation of the throat, the very back of the nose, and the membranous lining of the air passages. It often accompanies an infection of the upper airways, the throat, or the lower airways, and the purpose of the cough is to remove excess mucus or phlegm. By coughing the phlegm is loosened, brought up into the mouth, and then swallowed. Any germs existing in it are then killed by the acid in the stomach. (A common cause of coughing at night is mucus dripping from the nose and sinuses into the back of the throat.) However, coughing can also be due to allergy or asthma and not infection.

What to do A cough that is merely a response to irritation and not to the presence of excess mucus is called an unproductive cough because it doesn't cough out any phlegm. A cough that does get rid of mucus is called a productive cough. An unproductive cough serves no useful purpose and can be extremely irritating to a young child; it can even prevent sleep. It is important to differentiate between a dry, unproductive cough and a wet, productive one that produces phlegm.

Cough medicines in general are not effective, but cough suppressants may be prescribed for a child with a very severe,

dry, unproductive cough that's disturbing his sleep. Over-the-counter cough medicines are no longer recommended for children under the age of two, and infant preparations are no longer available over the counter.

You can ease the irritation of a night-time cough by turning your child on his side or his front, or by propping him on pillows (if he's over one year old). Never let the coughing become so severe that a long bout causes your child to vomit.

A productive cough, however, should not be suppressed because it's serving a useful purpose. It is helping to overcome infection by clearing mucus from the air passages. Seek medical advice for a productive cough that lasts for more than 24 hours as it may need treatment.

▓ Cradle cap

A thick yellow encrustation on the scalp, cradle cap occurs mainly in babies, although children up to the age of three can have it. The yellow scales appear in small patches or can cover the entire scalp. Cradle cap is not caused by poor hygiene. Babies who suffer from it probably just have greasier scalps. Cradle cap may look unsightly, but it is quite harmless unless it is accompanied by red, scaly areas elsewhere on your baby's body, in which case your baby may have seborrheic eczema.

What to do Don't try to remove the scales with your fingers. If they won't brush out, they must be loosened first. Smear a little baby oil or aqueous cream on your baby's scalp and leave overnight. This makes the scales soft and loose, and they will wash away when you shampoo the next day. If the cradle cap becomes hard and thick, you may need to continue the treatment over a ten-day period. Seek medical advice if you're worried, or if your baby has red scaly areas elsewhere.

■ Croup

In children between the ages of one and five, croup quite often accompanies a cold. The name describes the sound of air being inhaled through a constricted windpipe, past inflamed vocal cords. Your child may go to bed feeling quite well, but wake with a tight chest and have great difficulty breathing in; exhaling is easier.

What to do If you notice this kind of breathing you should seek medical advice. Occasionally, the breathing can be so labored that there's a risk of suffocation. If this is the case try to keep your child calm and in an upright position in a moist, humid atmosphere and call an ambulance. Stay with your child until help arrives. If necessary, take him to the hospital yourself.

To make breathing easier, prop up your child in an upright position with pillows, and make sure that he is comfortable. If he's very alarmed, take him on your lap, hold him firmly, and try to get him to copy your breathing. Listening to you breathing in and out will take his mind off his fear; if he's relaxed, breathing will be easier.

Make sure that the air in your child's bedroom isn't too warm, as this can dry and irritate the already-inflamed air passages. Open the window and let some cool air blow in. Moistened air is soothing to the passages, so try taking him to the bathroom and running the hot water of the shower with the door and the windows shut. Sit in this steamy atmosphere with your child on your lap (maybe telling him a story at the same time). If you can't do anything else, place a pan of boiling water in your child's room. Never leave your child with boiling water in the room. After the first episode of croup, seek advice about treating croup so that you can deal with it should it happen again.

■ Cuts and abrasions

Examine any wound to see how deep it is and whether it is bleeding profusely. If it is both deep and bloody, get medical help.

What to do If it is a small graze, wash the area with clean water and apply a clean, dry, non-stick dressing that's larger than the injury. If the cut is bleeding, apply pressure directly over the wound and raise it above the level of the heart (see p.302). Cover the wound with a sterile dressing.

■ Diarrhea

The main symptom of diarrhea is the frequent passage of loose, watery stools. Diarrhea is a sign of irritation of the intestines. Bear in mind, however, that it is normal for breast-fed babies to pass frequent watery stools.

Diarrhea in a baby is always serious because of the danger of dehydration. If accompanied by vomiting in a young child, it is serious for the same reason, especially if it is also accompanied by fever and sweating.

What to do Seek medical advice immediately if your baby is under one year old and has had diarrhea for six hours, or if a child has diarrhea with fever and vomiting, if he still has diarrhea after twelve hours, or if the stools are greasy or contain mucus or blood. Give your child frequent small sips of an oral rehydration solution. This contains sugar and electrolytes that help reduce the amount of fluid lost and replace fluid in the body.

Pay close attention to hygiene when a child has diarrhea. The infection could spread throughout the family if your child doesn't wash his hands after going to the toilet or if you don't wash yours after changing his diapers.

▉ Drowsiness

In a normally alert child drowsiness can be a symptom of a fever, hypothermia (when the body temperature falls below normal), or dehydration. It can also occur before or after a febrile seizure, following a blow to the head (*see p.307*), or as a result of medication such as antihistamines.

If your child is drowsy but contented, is eating well, and has a normal body temperature, there is no cause for alarm; your child is probably just feeling a little sleepy. If, however, your child becomes drowsy while recovering from an infectious disease such as measles or chicken pox and complains of a headache and neck pain, this could indicate encephalitis or meningitis—both of which are serious conditions and require immediate medical attention.

What to do Check your child's body temperature. If it's over 100.4°F (38°C), he has a fever; if it is under 95°F (35°C), he is suffering from hypothermia. In either case, seek medical advice.

If the drowsiness is accompanied by diarrhea and vomiting, keep up your

child's fluid intake to prevent the risk of dehydration. If his condition does not improve, seek medical advice.

Check to see if your child has received a blow to the head; ask if your child has a headache or neckache; smell your child's breath and check the liquor cabinet—he may have drunk alcohol. Check the medicine cabinet for sleep-inducing drugs. In any of these cases, seek medical advice.

If your child has had a seizure, let him rest after the seizure has passed and seek medical advice.

▉ Earache

The main reason that earache is a common ailment in babies and young children is the anatomy of the ear. Think of the ear as two sections separated by a membrane, the eardrum. The first section is a passage leading from the opening of the ear to the eardrum. This is the auditory canal. The second section, behind the eardrum, is the middle ear. Inflammation of the outer ear is called otitis externa; inflammation of the middle ear is called otitis media. The Eustachian tubes, which are short and wide in young children, link the middle ear to the back of the throat. The purpose of the tubes is to equalize pressure in the ears, but they are often the source of ear problems in young children.

Otitis media is the most common ear ailment both because of the construction of the Eustachian tubes and because babies spend most of their time lying down. The combination of these two factors makes it much easier for bacteria to travel from the nose and throat straight to the middle ear. Inflammation of the mucus membrane of the Eustachian tubes causes them to become blocked. This traps the bacteria in the middle ear, where they multiply. Obviously, a very young child cannot tell you that his ear hurts, but if he has inexplicable fever, vomiting, diarrhea, and loss of appetite, and certainly if he pulls at his ear, you may be right to suspect that his ears are troubling him.

What to do Seek medical advice if you suspect your child has earache. He will need to be examined to confirm the diagnosis and, if the cause is otitis media, your doctor may recommend acetaminophen for the pain, and possibly nasal drops to clear the upper airways. If the pain has gone on for more than 24 hours, your child may need antibiotics.

Never, ever put anything into your baby's ears, and don't apply hot compresses to the outside of the ear. Similarly, if the cause of the earache is a boil or something else in the outer ear, don't treat it yourself. Seek medical advice.

▣ Eczema

Infantile eczema often goes hand in hand with asthma, and the two are commonly seen together. Eczema produces a generalized rash on the face, behind the knees, and on the inner side of the arms and wrists. The rash is usually itchy, dry, red, and scaly; in its worst state, it can weep quite profusely. You will notice that the eczema waxes and wanes. It may be brought on by a cold or if the baby has had a sleepless night or a tummy upset.

Often asthma or other allergic conditions may run throughout the family, so you may find that a relative has penicillin sensitivity, another has

asthma, another has eczema, another has hay fever.

What to do You'll need to seek medical advice for your child and you may be referred to a skin specialist if the eczema is difficult to treat.

The story on infantile eczema is rather good: many children improve by the age of two, and many more do so by the age of seven. Usually it will have disappeared by the teens, although the person retains the possibility of eczema flaring up in later life if he should suffer severe mental or physical trauma.

For the everyday care of a baby with eczema of the skin, I would suggest the following: avoid overbathing, since soap and water are dehydrating. Instead, use baby lotion on cotton balls, which will do the same job just as well.

Pay attention to cleanliness, particularly around the diaper area and face. Dress your child with cotton next to the skin at all times and avoid wool as it can be irritating and make the eczema worse. Rub in soft, bland creams and ointments exactly as prescribed.

▣ Epilepsy

After febrile seizures, the next most common cause of seizures in children is epilepsy. Epilepsy can take two forms: absence seizures and general seizures.

With an absence seizure your child suddenly "blanks out" for a couple of seconds and looks very pale and vacant. He won't fall down or become incontinent but he'll be completely unaware of his surroundings. When he snaps out of it he'll continue as if nothing had happened.

A child suffering from a general or grand mal seizure, will have similar symptoms to febrile seizures (*see p.332*).

What to do You should deal with epileptic seizures in the same way as febrile seizures (*see p.332*), then seek medical advice. Your child may have tests to assess the likelihood of the seizures recurring, and will then receive medical treatment.

It is psychologically inadvisable to treat children suffering from epilepsy as "epileptic." Treat your child as you normally do, but take certain precautions—leave the bathroom door open in case an attack occurs in the bathtub and keep a close eye on him when he's swimming.

▥ Eye discharge

A sticky eye is fairly common in the first week or so after your baby is born and it is nearly always caused by a little blood or amniotic fluid getting into the baby's eye during birth.

What to do There is always the possibility that the sticky eye is caused by a bacterial infection, so seek medical advice just in case. However, usually all that is needed is careful cleansing with a clean cotton balls soaked in sterile water. When you wash your baby's eye, you should always draw the swab from the inside corner, near the nose, to the outer corner, and then throw it away. It's important to use a separate swab for each eye.

▥ Fever

The range of normal body temperature is 96.8–98.6°F (36–37°C). Anything over 100.4°F (38°C) is a fever, although the height a temperature reaches is not necessarily an accurate reflection of the seriousness of the sickness. A fever is not in itself an illness but a symptom of one. Apart from any illness, your child's temperature will reflect the time of day and activity level: After a strenuous game of soccer, for example, the temperature could temporarily be over 100.4°F (38°C). A temperature of over 100.4°F (38°C) could be serious in a baby under six months old. If the temperature remains high, there is also a slight risk of a febrile seizure (*see p.332*).

What to do If you suspect that your child has a fever, take his temperature, then check it again in 20 minutes to see if it has varied. Write down each reading.

Put your child to bed and remove most of his clothing, even if the room is cool. A child with a fever needs to be covered only by a light cotton sheet. Give children's liquid acetaminophen in the recommended dose to help bring down the temperature. If the temperature is high, give alternate doses of acetaminophen and ibuprofen to reduce in fever and then to control the temperature. Never give aspirin to a child under 16 years of age as it has been linked to the development of Reye's syndrome.

Encourage your child to drink as much liquid as possible by offering him small amounts of fluid at regular intervals. Ask for medical advice promptly if: your child is under six months old; your child has a seizure; he has had a seizure before or seizures run in the family; your baby has a fever that lasts more than 24 hours (or three days in a child); you are worried about any of the other symptoms.

■ Fingers caught in door

Until your baby learns how doors work, there's always the risk that his fingers may become trapped.

What to do If the skin is badly broken and there is any serious bleeding, take your child to the nearest emergency room immediately. If the finger is bleeding profusely, press on the place where it is bleeding and hold your child's hand up in the air. When the bleeding stops, put on a dry, clean, nonfluffy dressing if possible and put your child's arm in a sling for the trip to the hospital.

■ Gluten sensitivity/celiac disease

This is a problem that occurs when gluten (a protein contained in most cereals except for rice and corn) damages the lining of the intestines, which causes a gluten sensitivity. Unwittingly, therefore, you may feed your baby with an allergen, sincce some baby cereals contain gluten.

A child with gluten sensitivity initially shows a "failure to thrive." This means that the child will perhaps not have as much energy as you'd expect, may be a little sleepy, and won't gain weight quite as quickly as he should. You will also notice that the stools alternate between a fatty consistency, so that when you to try to flush them away they won't go—they stay and float—and loose stools. This is because the allergic reaction in the lining of the bowel prevents the correct digestion and absorption of fatty substances. Your child may have frequent bouts of diarrhea and be pale and irritable a lot of the time. He will also have abdominal distension and vomiting. If this condition goes undiagnosed in young girls it can lead to a delay in the onset of menstruation.

In its very advanced stage, gluten sensitivity, or celiac disease, produces abnormal body configuration. The abdomen becomes distended with hardly any fat on the limbs or body, the muscles of the legs and arms become wasted, the tongue becomes smooth, and there may be swelling of the ankles. The hair will be thin. However, gluten sensitivity is not very common and the fact that it is caused by a very common foodstuff should not make you unnecessarily wary or overanxious about your child's diet.

What to do Once a diagnosis has been made, your child has to be given a gluten-free diet, which means that wheat, rye, barley, and oats will have to be excluded. Your child will have to remain on a gluten-free diet for life.

The first thing that you will notice is an improvement in the mood of your child. This usually appears within a few days, and is followed by a greatly improved appetite and consequent weight gain. You will then notice a change in the appearance of the stools and the frequency of bowel movements, although this may take weeks. After being on a gluten-free diet for six months to a year, your child should be within the normal range for weight, although his height will take about two years to recover.

■ Hay fever

Hay fever, or allergic rhinitis, is similar to asthma except that the allergic reaction occurs in the mucus membranes of the nose and eyelids, not the chest.

The condition is also known as allergic rhinitis and causes sneezing, a runny nose with clear discharge, and itchy, watery, red-rimmed eyes. It mostly occurs in spring and summer and is usually caused by a reaction to plant pollen. Hay fever is troublesome, but is not usually serious.

What to do If your child is sneezing a lot, check his temperature to make sure that he isn't ill with an infection such as influenza or a common cold. Discourage your child from rubbing his eyes; this will make them worse. Bathe his eyes with cool water to ease the irritation. Seek medical advice as soon as possible if you think your child may be suffering from a more serious infection, or if the hay fever is making your child miserable. If your child's condition is severe, he may need to see an allergist and have a series of tests to track down the allergen that is causing his symptoms.

There are various measures you can take to try to minimize the severity of attacks. Watch the pollen count each day and, if it is high, discourage your child from playing near freshly mown grass, for example. Use synthetic stuffing for your child's pillows and duvet, rather than feathers. Keep your house as dust-free as possible. Even if your child isn't allergic to dust, a dusty atmosphere always makes hay fever worse.

Prepare an emergency pack for outings. It should contain paper napkins, eye drops to reduce the eye irritation, a moist towel to soothe your child's eyes, and whatever medication has been prescribed. Your doctor may be prescribe a steroid nasal spray or an oral antihistamine to help relieve the condition.

▦ Hives (see Urticaria)

▦ Infectious fevers (*see p.340*)

▦ Measles

This is a highly infectious disease; it can also have quite serious complications, namely pneumonia (*see p.331*) and meningitis (*see p.330*). Your child is most likely to catch the disease between the ages of one and six; it takes its most serious form under the age of three.

It generally takes ten to fourteen days for the symptoms of measles to appear after your child has been infected. The first symptoms are similar to that of a normal cold—runny nose, a hoarse cough, and a fever. For the first two days the temperature will be about 100.4–102°F (38–39°C). It may fall briefly before becoming as high as 104°F (40°C). It's at this stage that the rash generally starts as brownish-red spots behind the ears, and then spreads to the face and the rest of the body. There may be small red spots, each with a white center in the mouth (Koplik's spots) before the rash starts. Your baby's eyes may become red and sore.

At around the age of 13 months your child will be immunized against measles when he has his MMR (measles, mumps, and rubella) immunization (*see p.339*).

What to do Look in the child's mouth for signs of Koplik's spots. Ask for medical advice to confirm measles. While your child has a fever, follow the general instructions for coping with high temperatures (*see p.315*). Bathe his sore eyes with lukewarm water and dim the lights if that makes him more comfortable. He probably won't be very hungry when he's feverish, but make sure that he drinks adequate amounts of liquid by providing small but frequent drinks. Seek medical advice immediately if your child has any of the following: a high temperature four days after the rash has appeared; earache or labored breathing; a phlegmy cough; or if he becomes semi-conscious.

▥ Meningitis

An inflammation of the meninges, the membrane that surrounds the brain and spinal cord, meningitis is caused by viral or, much more seriously, bacterial infection. The illness starts with flu-like symptoms, high temperature, mottled skin, limb pain, and cold hands and feet. As the infection develops, the child will have a headache, stiff neck, sensitivity to bright light, increasing drowsiness, and vomiting. Bacterial meningitis may also lead to a rash that does not fade when pressed. Check this by pressing a glass onto the rash. If it is caused by meningococcus the small purplish-red spots will not disappear.

What to do Meningitis is life-threatening and the disease can develop very quickly, so it needs urgent action. If you suspect meningitis, be prepared to insist on urgent medical attention. Take your child to the nearest emergency room of the nearest hospital or call 911 for an ambulance.

Meningitis is confirmed by taking a sample of cerebro-spinal fluid through a lumbar puncture. Your child will be treated in the hospital, and, in the case of bacterial meningitis, all close contacts will also be treated to prevent further spread of the disease.

▥ Mumps

This disease is uncommon due to good vaccination rates (*see p.340*). It usually takes 16 to 21 days for the symptoms to appear after infection. When the infection does occur, you may first notice that your child seems under the weather. The positive symptom will be if the glands swell up in front of and under the ear on one or both sides of your child's face. This swelling will be accompanied by fever and the glands will be tender.

What to do Ask for medical advice to confirm the diagnosis. Although there's no specific treatment, you can do a lot to make your child more comfortable. Reduce his fever using the recommended dose of children's acetaminophen (*see p.327*). Offer liquid foods if he finds it difficult to chew, and plenty to drink. At around the age of 13 months your child will be immunized against mumps when he has his MMR (measles, mumps, and rubella) immunization (*see p.339*).

▥ Nettle rash (see Urticaria)

▥ Nosebleeds

Hemorrhaging from the nose, or nosebleeds, are most often caused by damage to a patch of small blood vessels lying very near the surface of the skin just inside the nose. Nosebleeds are usually caused by a blow or injury to the nose during rough games, or simply because your child persistently picks his nose.

What to do This small patch of blood vessels can bleed a lot, but try not to panic. Never tip your child's head back, because blood that is swallowed can irritate the stomach and cause vomiting. This increases the blood pressure in the head and creates a tendency for the nose to bleed again.

Apply gentle pressure with your thumb and first finger on either side of the nose until the bleeding has stopped. This will usually happen in two or three minutes. If nosebleeds occur frequently seek medical advice. Your child may be referred to a specialist for cauterization of the delicate areas inside the nose.

▦ Pertussis (whooping cough)
Like most childhood illnesses, whooping cough starts off with a cough, a runny nose, and a slight temperature. This period can last for up to two weeks. This will be followed by severe, paroxysmal coughing when your child will have difficulty drawing breath. This is when the characteristic "whoop" occurs. Breathing difficulties are even greater for babies, who may not develop the technique of whooping to get air into the lungs.

What to do Ask for medical advice. Antibiotics are effective in the runny nose stage. People who've been in close contact with the infected child may be protected from whooping cough if given antibiotics during the incubation period. When your child starts on a coughing bout, hold him firmly and try to calm him down. If he's tense he'll find it even more difficult to catch his breath. Support him in a sitting position to make breathing easier. Eating may provoke vomiting. Try giving small amounts of easily eaten food (mashed if necessary) immediately after a coughing fit.

Your child will be vaccinated against whooping cough as part of his routine immunizations.

▦ Pin worms
This is the most common type of infecting worm. These thin, ¼-inch (6-millimeter) white worms live in the rectum and the females crawl through the anus to lay their eggs on the surrounding skin. This produces the classic symptoms of itching, especially at night. When a child scratches his bottom he may pick up the eggs under his fingernails. If he puts his hand in his mouth, the eggs will be ingested again.

What to do If you notice your child scratching his bottom, especially at night, save your child's stools and examine them for the threadlike worms. If you find them, get medical advice. Medicine to eradicate the worms is available with a prescription from your pediatrician. Because infection spreads easily, everyone in the family should be given the treatment. Keep your child's nails short, and insist he wash his hands after going to the bathroom.

▦ Pneumococcal infection
This is caused by a strain of the *streptococcus bacterium*. In most people the bacterium is carried in the nose and throat without causing any harm, but infection can lead to meningitis, ear infections, and pneumonia, so it is potentially serious in young children.

What to do Pneumococcal infections can be treated with antibiotics. Babies are now routinely offered a vaccination against pneumoccal infection (*see p.339*).

▦ Pneumonia

Common childhood viral infections and rarer infectious diseases such as measles and whooping cough may be accompanied by pneumonia. In this situation the infecting organism enters the lungs and weakens their defenses. The bronchial tubes become inflamed and produce excessive mucus, and lung function begins to deteriorate so that the lungs can't expel the mucus. It then forms into little pools in the lungs, which become infected.

The initial signs of pneumonia are an increased breathing rate and difficulty breathing. Bluish color around the mouth indicates an advanced stage. When pooling of mucus occurs in a small air passage, the deeper part of the lung beyond the blockage becomes sealed off. The fluid may collect to the extent that it renders a little section of the lung completely solid; this is a small area of pneumonia. If a larger air passage becomes blocked off, the area of pneumonia can be extensive.

What to do If you notice any of the above signs, seek medical advice immediately. Meanwhile, stay calm and try the following measures to help your child: keep the air moist by running a bath or the shower and sitting in the bathroom with him. Make him feel comfortable and secure. Try to support your child in an upright position to make breathing easier.

▦ Rashes

Most rashes have an internal cause and in young children they are a classic symptom of some of the more common infectious fevers (see p.340). They may also be the result of an allergy.

What to do Rashes usually involve damage to the small blood vessels in the skin and there is very little you can do to correct this by applying anything to the skin's surface. However, try to relieve the symptoms of itching and burning by applying a cooling lotion, like calamine, since prolonged scratching may break the skin and introduce infection. It is better not to use anti-sting or anti-burn sprays on a rash because they may contain local anesthetics that can trigger allergic reactions in the skin. If you are concerned about your child's rash, or if the rash becomes infected, seek medical advice.

▦ Roseola infantum

This disease is often confused with rubella (see p.340). Your child will suddenly get a high fever of about 102°F (39°C) without any other symptoms. As the child's temperature returns to normal, he'll develop a rash of pale red spots. Roseola infantum is most common in children under the age of two.

What to do Seek medical advice to get an accurate diagnosis. There is no specific treatment is needed, other than keeping the fever down (see p.315), and making sure that your child is comfortable.

▦ Rubella (German measles)

This is a viral disease, like measles, and is now rare due to good vaccination rates (see p.340). The initial symptoms resemble a mild cold with a runny nose, a sore throat, and a temperature of 100.4°F (38°C). The rash usually appears a couple of days after your child starts to feel unwell. The spots, which start behind the ears and on the forehead before moving down to the body, are pale and flat and are not as close together as those in measles. They only last for two to three days. The glands on the back of your child's neck will almost definitely be swollen and they may stay like this after the rash has gone. The symptoms usually last about ten days.

What to do Get an accurate diagnosis so you can notify any pregnant woman with whom your child has been in contact; it's also important in relation to possible immunization at puberty. The infection is so mild that there is nothing you can do other than keep your child comfortable and give him plenty to drink. Keep him indoors until the rash has been gone for a few days.

At around the age of 13 months your child will be immunized against rubella when he has his MMR (measles, mumps, and rubella) immunization (see p.339).

▥ Scarlet fever

Also known as scarlatina, this is a throat infection that is caused by a strain of streptococcus bacillus that is no longer common. It starts with a sore throat and a fever, the tonsils become swollen and inflamed, and your child may have headaches and vomit. After about three days, a rash of tiny spots may appear around the neck and in the armpits, spreading over the whole body. The tongue's surface may become red and swollen, and looks like a strawberry.

What to do Get medical advice so you have an accurate diagnosis. Penicillin is the antibiotic of choice for this condition

provided your child is not allergic to it. Other than this, there is nothing specific that you can do to help, except to treat the fever and make sure your child has plenty of fluids.

▥ Seizures

In some children we never discover the cause for seizures, but in the majority of children between the ages of six months and five years seizures are caused by a rise in body temperature. Young children's brains are more easily affected by this than adults; the irritation stimulates the nerves that control the muscles, which in turn react by contracting violently.

When having a seizure your child will become unconscious and will twitch uncontrollably. His eyes will roll up and he may froth at the mouth slightly. His breathing will be heavy and his teeth will be firmly clamped; he may become incontinent during the seizure. When the seizure is over, your child will fall asleep— he may drift straight into sleep, alternately, he may briefly wake up and then fall into a deep sleep.

What to do Never leave your child alone. Although you may desperately want to call for help you must stay by your child until the seizure is over to make sure he doesn't hurt himself. Loosen his clothing and remove any nearby furniture in case he kicks or rolls against it, but don't try to restrain him. Don't try to place anything in his mouth. Contrary to popular belief, people rarely bite or swallow their tongues during a seizure and you could do more damage by trying to pry open his jaws. Once the seizure is over, place him in the recovery position and call for medical help.

If your child has a seizure of this sort, try to prevent high fevers from occurring in the future. Remove extra clothing and blankets when he gets hot and give him regular doses of children's acetaminophen and ibuprofen. Alternate the two in order to bring a reduction in fever and then a steady control of the temperature.

▥ Sleepwalking

A sort of "mobile dreaming," sleepwalking occurs when a child wanders around the house while asleep. A sleepwalking child does not walk with his eyes closed and his arms held straight out in front of him. His eyes will be open but he will be asleep; he won't see you and won't understand anything you say to him. Many children go through a short phase of sleepwalking.

What to do If you find your child sleepwalking, don't try to awaken him. Lead him slowly and gently back to bed. There is no need to get medical advice unless the sleepwalking is very frequent and you need reassurance that nothing is seriously wrong. Protect your child, for instance, by putting a barrier at the top of the stairway at night so he can't fall down the stairs, and by making sure that no windows are left open. Try to reassure your child if you think you know the underlying cause of the sleepwalking.

▥ Splinters

All splinters carry a risk of infection because they are rarely clean, so they should always be dealt with promptly.

What to do Usually a splinter can be removed with tweezers. Gently clean around the splinter with soap and warm water. Grasp the splinter and draw it out at the same angle as it went in. Clean the area and check that the child has been immunized against tetanus. If the splinter is deeply embedded, lies over a joint, or is difficult to remove, take your child to the emergency room.

▥ Sprains

Because children are so active and may not have very good coordination when young, they can sprain their wrists and ankles quite easily. In a sprain a ligament is often stretched or torn, and this causes swelling. Your child won't want to put pressure on the joint, and will find it painful to move.

What to do The best treatment for a sprain is rest; any kind of strain on the sprained part should be avoided. You can also help by putting an ice pack on the sprained joint and elevating the limb to reduce swelling and bruising. Then surround the joint with padding and secure it with a bandage. Check the circulation beyond the bandage every ten minutes to make sure that the bandage isn't too tight. Loosen if necessary.

▥ Stings

It's almost inevitable that your child will be stung by a bee or wasp at some stage, and that he'll be very upset when it happens. A wasp or bee sting is rarely serious, but if it causes an allergic reaction, if your child is stung in the mouth, or if he is stung by a number of insects, dial 911 for an ambulance immediately.

What to do If your child has been stung, do not try to squeeze the sting as this may spread the irritating chemical in the sting into deeper parts of the skin. Instead, scrape it off with your thumbnail or the side of a credit card. Don't use over-the-counter sting preparations that contain antihistamines; they may cause an allergy of the skin and are better avoided. If your child is stung in his mouth, call 911 for an ambulance. Cool his mouth with sips of water while you wait.

▓ Strabismus

Your baby's eyes may seem misaligned until the age of eight or ten weeks, by which time he'll have learned to use his two eyes together (stereoscopically).

What to do There's nothing wrong with this early squinting, but if it persists after three months seek medical advice. Early treatment is important or the imbalance of the muscles of the eye, which usually causes a squint, may remain uncorrected.

▓ Stys

A sty is an infection in the hair follicles of the lower eyelashes. It looks like a small boil on the eyelid—a red swelling with a central area of pus.

What to do Eyes are very precious. Never take chances, and get medical advice if you are at all worried. Don't use any over-the-counter treatments, as they may make specific antibiotics less effective should they be prescribed. You may notice that the eyelash is loose and if your child is cooperative you can release the pent-up pus just by pulling the hair out. It won't

hurt because the infection will already have dislodged the hair from its follicle. You can also bathe the sty with a cotton swab dipped in cool water.

▓ Sunburn

Sunburn is inflammation of the skin caused by excessive exposure to sunlight. The best cure is prevention. You'll need to be strict with children, who may not appreciate the dangers and the potential for long-term damage. Most children's skin is very sensitive to sunlight—more sensitive than adults'—so be careful about exposing their skin to the sun at any time.

What to do Preventing sunburn is a lot better than treating it. Protect exposed parts of the skin with a generous application of sunblock of at least 30 SPF about 20 minutes before going outside. Repeat at least every two or three hours and every time your child has been in the water.

Always cover your baby's head with a wide-brimmed hat and dress him in loose, light clothing that covers the shoulders and neck, such as a shirt with sleeves and a collar. Make sure the carriage or stroller has an adjustable hood or sunshade with which to shade your baby. If the sun is extremely strong, it is better to keep your child indoors, especially between 11 a.m. and 3 p.m. when the sun is at its highest. Remember that your baby is still at risk of ultraviolet rays even on cloudy days.

If by chance your baby does get sunburned, calamine lotion is a good cooling application, and children's acetaminophen will do a lot to relieve the soreness in the skin and bring his temperature down. If your baby is restless and ill, take his temperature; if it is raised this may mean heatstroke. You should seek medical advice immediately.

◼ Teething

This is the term used to describe the eruption of a baby's first teeth. Teething usually begins at about the age of six or seven months, with most of the teeth breaking through before your baby is 18 months old. Your baby will produce more saliva than usual and will dribble; he will try to cram his fingers into his mouth and chew on his fingers or any object he can get hold of. He may be clingy and irritable, have difficulty sleeping, and may cry and fret more than usual. Most of these symptoms occur just before the teeth erupt. It is important to realize that the symptoms of teething do not include bronchitis, diaper rash, vomiting, diarrhea, or loss of appetite. These are symptoms of an illness and should be treated as such.

What to do If you can't figure out why your child is so irritable, and he has no other symptoms of illness, feel his gums. If a tooth is coming through you will feel a hard or sharp lump, and the gum area will be swollen and red. You should not need to get medical advice unless your baby has other symptoms that cannot be attributed to teething. Nurse your baby often. Teething babies need comfort and closeness. Don't think that the arrival of teeth means you have to speed up the weaning process. Babies with teeth breast-feed with no discomfort to the mother.

Distract your child with a chilled teething ring (never freeze the ring or your baby may get frostbite) or a piece of carrot or apple—something firm. Stay with your baby in case he chokes on the food. If your child seems to be in a lot of pain, give children's acetaminophen or ibuprofen, but never exceed the recommended dose. If your child refuses food, encourage him to eat by giving him cold, smooth foods such as yogurt, ice cream, or flavored gelatin.

◼ Tonsilitis

Although tonsilitis can be caused by the *streptococcus bacterium* or by a variety of viruses, it is often called "strep throat." The job of the tonsils is to trap infections as they enter the body through the mouth, and localize them in the throat. For this reason tonsilitis is usually part of a throat infection. The tonsils also send warning signals to the rest of the body when an infection is beginning so the body can alert all its defenses. The adenoids serve exactly the same function, but are at the back of the nose instead of in the throat. It is fairly logical, therefore, for the tonsils and adenoids to be thought of together. Tonsils are most important to a child up to the age of ten years. This coincides with the time they are most likely to meet infection and their defenses have to be very strong. If your child has tonsilitis he will complain of a very sore throat and his tonsils will look red and swollen; they'll probably have white patches on them.

What to do You'll need to seek medical advice—usually, your child will be prescribed an antibiotic to combat the infection if he has a positive throat culture. To make your child's throat feel better, give him as much ice cream and cold liquid as he wants.

Despite their useful function it used to be fashionable to remove tonsils and adenoids. Today, ear, nose, and throat surgeons feel that certain criteria must be met before tonsillectomy can be considered, as it is quite a major operation with some risk involved. The criteria for performing a tonsillectomy may be met by any one of the following three conditions: the child had six throat infections in a single year, or four throat infections in six months, or if the child experiences sleep apnea, a condition in which snoring causes the child to periodically stop breathing or to gasp for breath during sleep.

▥ Toxocara

This roundworm lives in cats and dogs. Its eggs are passed on in their feces, so your child is at risk when he plays on ground where animals have defecated. He can ingest the eggs if he puts his dirty hands into his mouth. The eggs burrow through the intestinal wall and are carried in the bloodstream to the lungs. They are then coughed up, swallowed, and continue to develop in the intestines. There are generally no symptoms, although if your child has more than one worm he may have abdominal pain and suffer from a loss of appetite.

What to do Prevention is better than cure. Don't allow pets into your child's play area at home and be careful when you go to public parks. If your child is diagnosed with toxocara he will need a prescription to get rid of it. Follow the instructions carefully. The most serious effects of this illness involve the eyes, so your child may need to see a specialist.

▥ Urticaria

A general term used for an allergic skin reaction, urticaria is also known as hives. Most children have a tendency to develop hives, but this is gradually lost as they grow older. It is very easy to diagnose because it is the only skin rash that will disappear completely within a few minutes.

The rash, which is very itchy, often looks like a fairly bad nettle sting; it can also form large red patches with uneven edges. It may result in swelling of the eyes, the lips, and possibly the tongue. If the latter occurs, you must call 911 for an ambulance immediately.

What to do You can do a lot to relieve the itchiness by cooling it with applications of calamine lotion. There is no need for any specific treatment unless the attacks are persistent. In that case, you should ask for medical advice.

There is a particular form of urticaria called *papular urticaria,* which is caused by flea bites, usually from the fleas on the family cat. I remember a case of a child who used to appear in our clinic once a month and it turned out that it was always the day after she had been to visit her grandma and it was her grandma's cat who had the fleas. The cure for this is to treat the cat for fleas, not to get rid of it.

▥ Vomiting

This is the expulsion of the contents of the stomach through the mouth. A baby may spit up small quantities of curdled milk after a feeding, but this should not be confused with vomiting. Vomiting has many causes, but in the majority of cases there is little warning and after a single bout your child should be comfortable and back to normal.

Vomiting can be a symptom of a specific disorder of the stomach such as pyloric stenosis, or a symptom of an infection such as an ear infection. It frequently accompanies a fever, and even the common cold can cause vomiting if your child swallows enough nasal discharge to irritate his stomach. If your child has a bad cough this can cause him to vomit up food that he has recently eaten. Other causes of vomiting include appendicitis, meningitis, migraine headaches, food poisoning, and travel sickness. Some children vomit because of excitement and anticipation, but this is usually limited to toddlers. Vomiting should always be taken seriously because it can rapidly cause dehydration, particularly in a baby or young child.

What to do Put your child to bed and place a bowl within easy reach for him to vomit into. Offer frequent, small amounts of liquid, preferably cool water. Check his temperature. If he has a fever, treat it and make sure he does not become too hot (*see p.327*). Get him to brush his teeth to take away the taste. Seek medical advice if your child continues to vomit over a six-hour period; if vomiting is accompanied by diarrhea or a fever over 100.4°F (38°C); or if the vomiting is accompanied by other symptoms such as earache or abdominal pain. Feed your child bland foods when the nausea and vomiting have passed. Reintroduce solid foods slowly.

▮ Warts

These are small benign lumps caused by the wart virus. They are made up of an excess of dead cells that protrude above the surface of the skin. They can appear singly or in alarming numbers over all parts of the body, including the face and genitals. If they occur on the soles of the feet, they are known as verrucae. It takes about two years for the body to build up resistance to the wart virus, and after that time the warts usually disappear spontaneously. Warts are spread by direct contact with an infected person.

What to do If your child wants the warts removed, or they appear on a part of the body where they can easily infect other people, try the over-the-counter wart treatments from your pharmacy. These work by the application of a weak acid solution to the wart and the daily removal of the resulting burned skin. Follow the manufacturer's instructions carefully and avoid applying the solution to healthy skin. Don't use these wart cures on warts that appear on the face or genitals: you may cause scarring.

Ask for medical advice as soon as possible if you are unsure whether the lumps are really warts. Any growth or lump on your child's skin that you are uncertain about should be checked. Get medical advice as soon as possible if the warts continue to multiply or if they appear on the face or genitals and you want to have them removed.

Immunization

Immunization is one of the most successful forms of preventive medicine and has helped to eradicate many formerly lethal diseases throughout the world. However, its continued success depends on strict maintenance of an immunization program in the community, and it is the responsibility of all parents to ensure that

AGE	VACCINATION	HOW GIVEN	REACTION
Birth– 1 month	• Hepatitis B	One injection	Generally well tolerated, reaction at injection site possible, but rare
2 months	• Pneumococcus	One injection	Possible redness and swelling at injection site, mild fever
	• Diphtheria, tetanus, pertussis (whooping cough), polio and Hib	One injection	Slightly raised temperature; sickness and/or diarrhea, small lump at injection site that will disappear in a few weeks
4 months	• Hepatitis B	One injection	Generally well tolerated, reaction at injection site possible, but rare
	• Diphtheria, tetanus, pertussis (whooping cough), polio, and Hib	One injection	As above
6 months	• Hepatitis B	One injection	As above
	• Pneumococcus	One injection	As above
	• Diphtheria, tetanus, pertussis (whooping cough), polio, and Hib	One injection	As above
Around 12 months	• Hib	One injection	As above, fever; rash; generally unwell/malaise
	• MMRV (measles, mumps, rubella, and chicken pox)	One injection	As above
15 months	• Pneumococcus	One injection	As above
	• Hib (if not given at 12 months)	One injection	As above
18 months	• Hepatitis A	One injection	As above
2 years	• Hepatitis A booster	One injection	As above
4–5 years	• Diphtheria, tetanus, pertussis (whooping cough), polio	One injection	As above
	• Measles, mumps, and rubella (MMR) or MMRV	One injection	As above

their children are fully protected. Some parents are anxious about the possible side effects that may occur as a result of a vaccination. If you have concerns, it's important to discuss them with your doctor. The risk of complications is very small compared to the harmful effects of the diseases themselves, which are far more serious. However, if your baby develops side effects at any stage of the vaccination program, your doctor may delay or stop immunizations.

COMMON CHILDHOOD INFECTIOUS DISEASES

Disease	Incubation period	Symptoms
Measles (see p.329)	10–14 days	Runny nose, cough, inflamed eyes, fever, vomiting, diarrhea, Koplik's spots on the inside of the cheeks at first then after four days a rash behind the ears, then on the face, then on the body.
Rubella (German measles) (see p.332)	14–21 days	Slight temperature, enlarged glands at the back of the neck, rash behind the ears then on the forehead, then the rest of the body. Rash lasts three days.
Roseola (see p.331)	4–7 days	A high temperature with slight cold symptoms; a pink rash after three days when temperature goes down.
Chicken pox (see p.320)	10–21 days	Dark red, irritating groups of spots that emerge every three or four days. Initially look like blisters then scab over.
Pertussis (Whooping cough) (see p.338)	Around 7 days	Slight temperature, runny nose, slight cough then a convulsive cough followed by whooping breath, vomiting, cyanosis (blue coloring to skin) during coughing spasms, then exhaustion.
Mumps (see p.330)	17–21 days	Swelling and soreness of the glands at the sides of the face, and in front of the ears, painful swallowing, and dry mouth. Fever and generally unwell.
Scarlet fever or Scarlatina (see p.332)	2–5 days	Sore throat, lack of appetite, fever, vomiting, swollen glands, tiny red spots, scarlet facial flushing, and strawberry-colored tongue.

New vaccines go through an intensive testing procedure that ends with approval, then recommendation. Rotavirus vaccine, an oral vaccine for babies, preventing diarrhea, and HPV vaccine, to be given in adolescence, preventing genital warts and cervical cancer, have just been approved. Two more vaccines are recommended for adolescents: Tdap (tetanus, diptheria, and acellular pertussis) at age 11–12, and meningococcal conjugate vaccine at age 11 or entrance to high school or college.

Treatment	Complications	Immunity	Prevention
No specific treatment other than children's acetaminophen to reduce the fever. If secondary infection of the ears or lungs occurs antibiotics will be necessary.	Ear infection, pneumonia encephalitis, gastroenteritis.	Lifelong	Immunization combined with mumps and rubella vaccine around 13 months and 4 years.
No specific treatment.	None to your child but fetal damage could occur in a pregnant woman.	Lifelong	Immunization combined with measles and mumps vaccine around 13 months and between 4 years.
No specific treatment.	Rarely infantile convulsions.	Usually lifelong	None
Relive itching with calamine lotion.	Encephalitis, pneumonia.	Lifelong	Varicella vaccination at 12 months, booster at 4–6—may be combined with MMR.
Antibiotics must be given early to be effective; fresh air. Possibly raise your child's head in bed to make breathing easier.	Possibility of seizures, bronchitis, or pneumonia.	Lifelong	Immunization at 2, 4, and 6 months, with booster at 15–18 months and then at 4 years.
Plenty to drink, soft food if chewing is painful.	Meningitis, inflammation of the testes.	Lifelong	Immunization combined with measles and rubella vaccine around 12 months and between 3½ and 5 years.
Penicillin with bedrest as long as fever lasts.	Rheumatic fever.	Lifelong for each strain	None

Immunization and traveling abroad

If you are planning to take your baby or toddler abroad, it is vital that you find out beforehand about the health risks in the country you will be visiting and the precautions, including vaccinations, that you may need to take. You can get the information from your travel agent, the embassy of the country you are going to visit, the Department of Health, or the Centers for Disease Control. The CDC publishes a new edition of the *Yellow Book: Health Information for International Travel* every two years, giving up-to-date information on health risks throughout the world, and you should consult it well before your departure date. The *Yellow Book* can be ordered through the CDC web site, at www.cdc.gov/travel; but much of the information, including updates, is available on the CDC site.

Your child should be current for his age on all vaccinations listed in the immunization schedule (*see p.339*). If vaccination is required, you should see your doctor, or pediatrician, at least two months before departure because some vaccines take time to be effective, and some cannot be given at the same time as others. Other vaccines and medications, while safe by adults, should not be administered to pregnant or breast-feeding mothers, or to children, because their safety for the fetus, breast-feeding infant, or child has not yet been determined. You can obtain specific information from the CDC web site regarding the vaccinations for travel to any particular area, as well as outbreaks of diseases that are rare in the US.

Vacation health precautions

First aid kit Be sure to take a first aid kit, which should contain a package of adhesive dressings, sterile needles, insect repellent, antiseptic cream, water sterilization tablets, alcohol-based hand sanitizer, child-safe hand wipes, diaper rash ointment if appropriate, oral rehydration solution (ORS) sachets, and any medicines that have been prescribed by your doctor.

Water safety If you or your child wants to swim while on vacation, be aware that the local water may be contaminated and parasitic infections can be picked up if any water is swallowed. In areas where shistosomiasis or other parasites are common, do not allow your child to swim in unchlorinated water.

Water Babies' food should, of course, be mixed with boiled water as usual. Otherwise, unless you know that the local water is safe, use bottled water or sterilize it by boiling or using sterilization tablets. This applies not just to drinking water but also to the water you use for cleaning teeth or rinsing the mouth out.

Food Beware of raw vegetables, salads, unpeeled fruit, cream, ice cream, ice cubes, underdone meat or fish, and uncooked or reheated food.

Taking medicines abroad

If you need to take any prescribed medicines for your baby or toddler with you, you should check if there are any restrictions on taking drugs, prescribed or over-the-counter, into the country you are visiting. It is advisable to have a letter from your doctor with details of any medicines prescribed, to avoid problems with Customs.

Traveling restrictions

Check with the Transportation Security Administration (www.tsa.gov) or your airline before you leave home to ensure that you have followed any security rules currently in force. In addition, make sure that your baby has his own passport— many countries now require that every person, regardless of age, has a passport.

Travel insurance

Whatever countries you intend to visit, it is very important that you take out adequate private medical insurance, especially if you have a preexisting medical condition.

DISEASE AND PRECAUTIONS

Disease	Risk Area	Vaccination
Cholera	Africa, Asia, Middle East, especially in conditions of poor hygiene and sanitation.	None available in the United States. Cholera is contracted from eating or drinking contaminated food or water.
Malaria	Africa, Asia, Central and South America; possibly southern Europe and United States (check before traveling).	None, but antimalarial pills must be taken before, during, and for a month after your trip.
Polio	Everywhere except Europe, North America, Australia, and New Zealand.	Given as a routine to babies in the US.
Rabies	Many parts of the world, including Europe.	Not routine, but ask for advice because it may be more common in remote areas.
Tetanus	Occurs worldwide, but greatest risk in areas where children are not immunized.	Given as a routine to babies in the US.
TB	Africa, Asia, Central and South America, some poorer inner-city areas elsewhere.	Skin test and injection, preferably three months before travel. Not necessary for short visits and when staying in modern hotels, but advisable for longer visits if you will be living or working closely with the local population.
Typhoid	Everywhere except Europe, North America, Australia, and New Zealand, in conditions of poor hygiene and sanitation.	Two injections, 4–6 weeks apart. Typhoid is contracted from drinking contaminated water.
Yellow fever	Africa and South America.	One injection at least ten days before traveling. Infants under nine months should not be vaccinated, and should not be exposed to the disease.

Index

A

abscesses, breast 101
acetaminophen 202, 316
adventurousness 198
aggression 253, 261
air travel 290–1
allergies
  asthma 318
  food allergy 114, 128–9
  gluten sensitivity 327–8
  hayfever 328–9
  urticaria 337
alphabet, learning 280–1
animals
  bites 319
  hygiene 83
antibodies, in breast-milk 88
antisocial babies and children
  245, 261
anxiety see fears and
  anxieties
appetite, loss of 122, 310
asthma 318
attention-seeking 246

B

babbling 226, 227
babies see newborn baby
backpacks 36, 55, 284–5
back strain, avoiding 55
backyards, safety 297
balanitis 319
baskets, baby 36, 143
bathing 70–85
  bathtubs 74–5, 79–80
  birth to 1 year 70–81
  equipment 34
  1 to 3 years 82–5
  safety 74, 76, 82–3
  see also washing
bathrooms, safety 294
bed-wetting 140–1
bedding 144

bedrooms 38–9
  safety 296
beds 36
  moving from crib into 151
  sick children 314
  taking child into parents'
    bed 152
bedtime routines
  birth to 1 year 142–3, 147
  causes of crying 168–9
  1 to 2 years 151
  reading books 155, 169,
    209–10
  2 to 3 years 154–6
bee stings 334
behavior
  newborn baby 25–7
  see also social behavior
bilingualism 227
bibs 35, 118
bicycle seats 286
bilirubin 23
birthmarks 24
bite wounds 319
biting, and breast-feeding 99
bladder control 46, 69, 132,
  138–9
  at night 139–40
  bed-wetting 140–1
  late developers 140
  regression 140–1
bleeding
  cuts and abrasions 324
  nosebleeds 330
  serious bleeding 302
blisters 319
blood, in stools 134, 136
body temperature
  babies 144
  causes of crying 163
  fevers 315–16, 327
  heat exhaustion and
    heatstroke 305

hypothermia 305
  thermometers 311
  when to call the doctor 308
bonding 16, 19, 28–31, 92
bones, broken 306
boredom, crying 165
bottle-feeding 102–9
  on car journeys 288
  equipment for 35
  frequency of feedings 107
  making up bottles 104
  night feedings 110, 148
  nipples 102, 104
  problems 108–9
  sterilizing bottles 102–3
  supplementing breast-
    feeding 94–6
  weaning 111
bouncing chairs 37, 185–6
boundaries
  birth to 1 year 243–5
  1 to 2 years 251–5
  2 to 3 years 260
bowel control 46, 69, 132
  1 to 2 years 136–7, 138–9
  2 to 3 years 139, 140
bowel movements see stools
bowel problems 135–6
  diarrhea 324–5
brain
  handedness 196
  vision 201
bras, breast-feeding 93, 100
breakfast menu 123
breast-feeding 88–101
  advantages 88–9
  bras 93, 100
  on car journeys 288
  and contraception 89
  equipment for 35
  expressing milk 96–7
  frequency of feedings 94
  milk supply 89

night feedings 110, 148
positions 93–4
problems 98–9
supplementary bottles 94–6
twins 94
weaning 111
breast pads 100
breast pumps 35
breasts
care of 100–1
exercises 100
newborn baby's 23–4
problems 101
breathing
asthma 318
breathholding 168, 176
croup 324
newborn baby 25
rescue breathing 301
when to call the doctor 310
broken bones 306
bruises 319–20
brushes, painting 272
bullying 253, 261
burns 304, 320
burping 108–9

C

Cesarean section 94
calories 121, 126
carbohydrates 87, 120
carriages 32, 36, 37, 144
carrier 36, 143
carrying babies 52–5
cars
car journeys 288–9
car seats 32, 37, 288
car sickness 289
road safety 298
catarrh 320
celiac disease 328
cereals 119, 122, 126
changing equipment 34
chest compressions 302
chicken pox 320–1, 340–1
choking 118, 299

cholera 343
circumcision 78
citrus fruits 122
classification, intellectual
development 215, 229–30
clinginess 146, 165–6, 248
clothes 40–9
birth to 1 year 40–5
for breast-feeding 93
dressing-up games 215,
220, 276
on fire 304
1 to 3 years 46–9
for sleeping 144
washing 44–5
see also undressing
coordination 194–8, 214–15
cold sores 321–2
colds 321
colic 164, 322
color
baby's room 38
color vision 199
of eyes 22
learning about 280
of skin 23
colostrum 88, 104–5
comforters 146, 166, 262
concentration span 216
conjunctivitis 322–3
consciousness, loss of 300–2
constipation 135
contraception, breast-feeding
and 89
conversations
with babies 209, 210
speech development 212–
14, 233
cooking 116
corporal punishment 252
cotton diapers 64
cots 36, 143, 151
coughing 323
counting games 281
cracked nipples 92, 101
cradle cap 75, 323–4

crawling 186–7
"crawling" reflex 26, 27
creative play 216, 273, 275–6
crib bumpers 36, 145
crib death 36, 52, 145
croup 324
"cruising" 188, 190
crying 158–77
birth to 1 year 158–66
coping with 163
crying spells 161
cures 162
"difficult" babies 239–40
leaving baby to cry 160
night waking 148
1 to 2 years 167–9
responding to 158–9, 161
2 to 3 years 170–7
cuddling 55–6
cups, weaning on to 117
cuts and grazes 324

D

dairy products 122, 126
dark, fear of 156–7, 171
day nurseries 225
death, crib 36, 52, 145
dehydration 136, 315
delaying tactics, bedtime
problems 156
dental hygiene 204–5
dentists 205
dermatitis 68
diapers
birth to 1 year 58–67
bladder control 138
on car journeys 288
changing equipment 34
diaper pins 64
disposable diapers 61–2
fabric diapers 64–5, 67
liners 64, 65
1 to 3 years 69
washing 66–7
diaper rash 65, 68–9
diarrhea 324–5

birth to 1 year 135–6
toddler diarrhea 141
when to call the doctor 310
diet *see* food and feeding
"difficult" babies 239–40
dinner menu 123
diphtheria immunization 339
disabled babies 245
discipline 15, 243–5, 251, 260
discontented babies 241
diseases
infectious 340–1
traveling abroad 343
disliking your baby 244–5
disobedience 255
disposable diapers 58
doctor, when to call 308–10
dolls 216, 220
doors, locked 157
drawings 216, 272–3
dreams 157
dressing *see* clothes
drinks
introducing solids 117
sick children 315
weaning on to a cup 117
drowsiness 325
drugs *see* medicines
dummies 166
duvets 36

E

early wakers 147–8, 152
ears
care of 77
ear drops 313
earache 164, 325–6
hearing problems 228
eating out 285
eczema 326
electric shock 303
emergency first aid 299–307
emotions 8
jealousy 253
personal development 256
engorged breasts 101

epilepsy 326–7
episiotomy 94
equipment 32–9
exercises, breast care 100
expressing breast-milk 96–7
eye contact, with newborn
baby 28, 209
eyes
care of 77
color 22
conjunctivitis 322–3
discharge 22, 334
eye drops 313
hand-eye coordination 194,
195
newborn baby 15, 22
sticky eye 22, 327
strasbismus 22, 335
stys 335
vision 199–201

F

fabric nappies 58, 64–7
family
baby as part of 242
conflict in 177
in history 10–11
fathers 12
bonding with baby 19
bottle-feeding 102
night feedings 148
fats
in diet 87
feeding toddlers 122, 128
fears and anxieties
of bathing 78–80
bedtime problems 156
about breast-feeding 99
causes of crying 165–6
of the dark 156–7, 171
dealing with 171–3
encouraging security 258
irrational fears 172–3
nightmares 157
of parenthood 8
phobias 176–7

preschool nerves 173
of separation 167, 170
of thunder 171
of undressing 78
of water 85
febrile seizures 316
feces *see* stools
feeding *see* bottle-feeding;
breast-feeding; food and
feeding
fever 327
treating 315–16
when to call the doctor 308
finger foods 119
fingers, caught in door 327
fire, clothing on 304
first aid
emergencies 299–307
first aid kit 307
fleas 83
fluoride toothpaste 87, 203,
204–5
fontanelles 20–2, 75
food and feeding 86–131
buying food 115–16
cooking and reheating 116
establishing solids 113–20
food fads 125
food intolerance and allergy
114, 128–9
introducing solids 111–12
nutritional needs 86–7
1 to 2 years 121–6
preparation 115
ready-prepared foods 116
safety 112, 114
self-feeding 118–19
sick children 314–15
snacks 130–1
storage 115–16
2 to 3 years 126–9
see also bottle-feeding;
breast-feeding
foreskin, care of 78
fractures 306
freezing food 115–16

freshness 262–3
friends 257
fruit
    finger foods 119
    1 to 2 years 121, 122
    2 to 3 years 126
frustration
    and bad behavior 243–4
    causes of crying 166, 168
    play 216
    temper tantrums 175–6

G

games
    birth to 1 year 266–7
    imitative games 277–8
    for manipulation 278–9
    1 to 2 years 215, 216
generosity, encouraging 250
genitals
    care of 78
    handling 259
    newborn baby 24
German measles see rubella
glue, creative play 273
gluten sensitivity 327–8
grains, finger foods 119
grasp reflex 27, 184, 194
grazes 324
growth spurts 184
guidelines, behavior 252
gums, tooth care 205

H

"habits" 262
hair
    dislike of washing 80–1,
        84–5
    newborn baby 24
    tangles 84
    washing 75–6
halls, safety 296–7
handling babies 50–5
handling children 55–7
hands
    coordination 194–8

handedness 196
    washing 82, 83, 114
harnesses,
    highchairs 35, 118
    for walking 287
hay fever 328–9
head
    fontanelles 20–2, 75
    head banging 245
    injuries 307
    newborn baby 20–2
hearing tests, newborn 25
hearing problems 228
heart, chest compressions
    302
heat exhaustion 305
heatstroke 305
hernia, umbilical 23, 78
herpes simplex 321–2
Hib immunization 339
hiccups 25–6
highchairs
    buying 35,
    using 118, 123–4
hives see urticaria
holding babies 50–5
home safety 292–7
hormones, and bonding 30
hospitals, children in 317
household objects, games
    with 267–8
hunger, and crying 162
hygiene
    bottle-feeding 103
    food safety 112, 114
    kitchens 114–15
    pets 83
    toddlers 83
hypothermia 305

I

identification, personal
    development 256
illness 308–17
    and breast-feeding 99
    immunization 339–43

infectious diseases 340–1
imaginary friends 216
imitation
    games 277–8
    personal development 256
immunization 339–43
infectious diseases 340–1
injuries
    bleeding 302
    broken bones 306
    burns 304
    cuts and abrasions 324
    dealing with 172
    head injury 307
    shock 303
insecurity 146, 167, 248
insurance, travel 343
intellectual development
    206–35
    abstract ideas 222–3
    birth to 1 year 206–11
    classification 215, 229–30
    forming concepts 221–2
    by imitation and
        identification 256
    learning from experiences
        218–19
    learning spurts 210–11
    milestones 212, 218
    nursery school 224–5
    1 to 2 years 212–17
    and playing 214–17, 220–1,
        279–81
    2 to 3 years 218–24

J

jaundice, newborn baby 23
jealousy 253
jigsaw puzzles 279
joints, sprains 333
jumpy babies 241–2

K

kitchens
    hygiene 114–15
    safety 294–5

L

language *see* speech development
lanugo 24
laundry services, nappies 67
learning *see* intellectual development
left-handedness 196
letters, learning 280–1
ligaments, sprains 333
lightning, fear of 171
likes and dislikes 246
lip blisters, newborn baby 22
lisping 235
living rooms, safety 296
love
  for baby 8, 16, 19, 30–1
  older children 56
lunch menu 123

M

malaria 343
manipulation
  coordination 196
  games 278–9
  milestones 189, 193
  toys for 270
massage, baby 269
mastitis 101
masturbation 259
mattresses, cot 36
mealtimes 123–4, 126–7
measles 329, 340–1
  immunization 339
meconium 24, 132, 134
medicines
  and breast-feeding 101
  giving 213
  safety 292
  traveling abroad 342–3
meningitis 329–30
  immunization 339
menus, for toddlers 123
messy eaters 124
messy play 217

milestones
  intellectual development 212, 218
  physical development 179–84, 189, 193
  social behavior 238–9
  speech development 226–7
milia 24
milk
  bottle-feeding 102, 104, 105
  breast-feeding 88–9, 95
  expressing breast milk 96–7
  feeding toddlers 122, 128
  introducing solids 111, 113, 117
milk ducts, blocked 101
milk teeth 202–3, 204
minerals needed 86–7
MMRV immunization 339
modeling dough 215, 273
Mongolian blue spots 23
Moro reflex 27, 50
mothering instincts 31, 161, 245
mouth, newborn baby 22–3
mumps 330, 340–1
  immunization 339
music
  bedtime routines 155, 169
  musical instruments 216
  singing 29, 155, 169, 216
muslin squares 64

N

nails
  biting 262
  care of 77
naps 147, 149–50, 154
naughty children 255
navel 23
  care of 77–8
needs
  of child 13–14
  of parents 14
newborn baby

appearance 20–4
behavior 25–7
bonding with 28–31
bottle-feeding 102–9
breast-feeding 88–99
clothing 40–5
crying 158–65
diapers 58–67
equipment for 32–9
handling 50–5
intellectual development 206–9
night feedings 110
nursery 38–9
nutrition 86–7
sleeping 142–6
toddlers and 170, 253
vision 15, 199
washing 70–8
night
  bladder control 139–40
  crying problems 161, 168–9
  establishing a routine 142–3
  fear of the dark 156–7, 171
  night feedings 110, 148
  nightlights 156, 157, 171
  nightmares 157
  night waking 148–9, 151–3
nightmares 157
nipples
  bottle-feeding 35, 96, 102, 104
  breast-feeding 92
  nipple shields 101
  sore nipples 92, 101
"No," saying 244
nose
  care of 77
  catarrh and runny nose 320
  nosebleeds 330
  nose drops 313
nudity 258
numbers, learning about 281
nursery
  preparing 38–9
  rhymes 216, 232

temperature 23, 38
nursery school 224–5
    introducing children 173–5
nursing sick children 314–17
nutrition *see* food and feeding

O

obesity 125–6, 128
Onesies 40
only children 250
outdoor safety 298
outings 282–7
overindulgence 250, 254, 263
overfeeding
    bottle-feeding 108, 109
    breast-feeding 99
overtiredness, crying 173
overweight
    bottle-feeding and 108
    toddlers 125–6, 128
oxytocin 89

P

pain
    cause of crying 164
    when to call the doctor 310
painting 270–2
pants
    plastic 64, 67, 68–9
    trainer 69
paper, painting 272
penis
    balanitis 319
    care of 78
    circumcision 78
    handling 259
personal development
    birth to 1 year 236–42
    1 to 2 years 246–50
    2 to 3 years 256–9
personality 248
pertussis 331
    immunization 339
pets, hygiene 83
phobias 176–7
physical development 178–205

birth to 1 year 178–88
coordination 194–8
milestones 179–84, 189, 193
1 to 2 years 189–92
teeth 201–5
2 to 3 years 193
vision 199–201
walking 190–2
pimples, newborn baby 24
pin worms 331
placid babies 240
plastic pants 64, 67, 68–9
playgrounds, safety 298
playgroups 225
playing 264–81
    birth to 1 year 264–9
    and learning 214–17, 220–
        21, 279–81
    1 to 2 years 270–6
    safety 275
    and sharing 249–50
    sick children 316–17
    2 to 3 years 277–81
    with household objects 267
playpens 37
pneumococcal infection
    330–1
    immunization 339
pneumonia 331
poisoning 306
polio 88, 343
    immunization 339
postpartum depression 244–5
potties
    introducing 137
    travel 141
potty training *see* bladder
    control; bowel control
praise 14, 248, 252
premature babies 50, 98
propping babies up 185–6
protein
    birth to 1 year 86, 120
    1 to 2 years 121, 122
    2 to 3 years 126
public transportation 285

pumps, expressing breast-milk
    96
punishment 252
puzzles, jigsaw 279

R

rabies 343
rapid-return technique,
    sleeping problems 153
rashes 331
    chicken pox 320–1
    diaper rash 68–9
    eczema 326
    measles 329
    newborn baby 24
    roseola infantum 331–2,
        340–1
    scarlet fever 332
    urticaria 24, 337
    when to call the doctor 308
reading
    bedtime rituals 155, 169,
        209–10
    learning letters 280–1
    learning to read 223
    to toddlers 231–2
recovery position 301
reflexes 26–7, 184, 194
regression, bowel and bladder
    control 141
reheating food 116
rescue breathing 301
restaurants 285
resuscitation 300–2
right-handedness 196
ringworm 83
rituals
    at mealtimes 126–7
    at bedtime 155–6
road safety 298
role models 15–16
rooting reflex 26
roseola infantum 331–2,
    340–1
rubella 332, 340–1
    immunization 339

S

safety 186
bathing 74, 76, 82–3
car journeys 288
food 112, 114
home safety 292–7
outdoor safety 298
playing 275
pushchairs 284
saying "No" 244
self-feeding 120
sun protection 291
toddlers 191
toys 266
salmonella 114
sand, playing with 215, 274
scalds 304
scalp, cradle cap 75, 323–4
scarlet fever (scarlatina) 332,
340–1
school
introducing children 173–5
nursery school 224–5
preschool nerves 173
seborrhoeic dermatitis 68
second-hand equipment 32
security
personal development 258
security objects 146
and sleep problems 146
toddlers 55–6
seizures 316, 332–3
self-feeding 118–19
selfishness 263
separation
prolonged 169
separation anxiety 167, 170
sexuality 258–9
shampoo 75–6, 81
sharing, playing and 249–50
shields, hair washing 81, 84
shock 303
electric 303
shoes, toddlers 49
shopping 285, 286, 287

shuffling 187
shyness 248, 261–2
singing 216
bedtime rituals 155, 169
to newborn baby 29
sitting down 187–8
sitting up 184–6
skin
blemishes 24
blisters 319
bruises 319–20
burns and scalds 304, 320
cuts and grazes 324
diaper rash 68–9
eczema 326
newborn baby 23, 76–7
splinters 333
sun protection 291
sunburn 334–5
warts 338
see also rashes
sleep-walking 157, 333
sleeping 142–57
birth to 1 year 142–9
during breast-feeding 98
equipment for 36
naps 147
and night feedings 110
1 to 2 years 149–53
safest position 145
sleepy babies 240
2 to 3 years 154–7
wakeful babies 240–1
sleeping bags 36, 144, 188
slides 274
slings, using 36, 53, 162, 283
smacking 252
smell, sense of 29
smiling 209
snacks 123, 130–1
sneezing 25
snuffling 25
soap 76, 82
social behavior 236–63
boundaries 243–5, 251–2,
260

guidelines 252
milestones 238–9
personal development
236–242, 246–50, 256–9
possible concerns 244–5,
253–5, 261–3
socks 47, 49
solid foods
establishing 113–20
introducing 111–12
sounds, newborn baby 25–6
speech defects 228, 235
speech development
bilingualism 227
birth to 1 year 225–9
conversations 233
expanding vocabulary 230,
233–4
grammar 234
helping your baby 227–9
lisping 235
milestones 226–7
1 to 2 years 212–14, 229–32
problems 228
questions 223, 235
sentences 230
simplifying words 227
stuttering 254
2 to 3 years 219–20, 223,
233–5
understanding and 231
spitting up 109, 337
splinters 333
spoiling babies and children
16, 158–9, 160–1
sponge baths 74
sprains 333
stain removal 45
stairs, safety 157, 296–7
standing 187, 188
startle reflex 27, 50
stealing 261
sterilizing
bottles 102–3
diapers 66
feeding equipment 112, 114

stings 334
stools
  of bottle-fed baby 134
  bowel problems 135–6
  of breast-fed baby 88, 134
  changes in 134
  frequency of 132
  newborn baby 24, 134
storage
  in baby's room 38
  food 115
  toys 39, 276
strabismus 22, 335
stretchies 40, 44–5
strollers 36–7, 283–4, 286
stuttering 254
stys 335
sucking reflex 26, 106
"sucky" babies 98
Sudden Infant Death
  Syndrome 36, 52, 145
sugar
  overweight toddlers 128
  tooth decay 131, 204
sun protection 291
sunburn 334–5
supermarkets 285
swallowing reflex 26
sweets 122
swimming 85
swings 274

T

talking *see* speech
development
tangles, in hair 84
tantrums 168, 175–6, 254
TB (tuberculosis) 343
teeth 201–5
  brushing 202–3, 205
  cleaning 83
  decay 131, 204
  teething 201–2, 204, 335
television 281
temper tantrums 168, 175–6,
  254

temperature
  baby's room 23, 38, 143
  of bottle-feedings 105
tetanus 343
  immunization 339
thermometers 311
thirst 95
three-dimensional vision 199
thrush 68
thumb sucking 166, 262
timid children 248, 261–2
tiredness, and crying 165, 173
toddlers
  bedrooms 38–9
  bowel and bladder control
    139–41
  car journeys 289
  clothing 46–8
  coordination 197–8
  crying 167–9
  diapers 69
  diarrhea 141
  feeding problems 125–6,
    128–9
  food 121–6
  handling 55–6
  learning 212–17, 218
  and new babies 170, 253
  playing 270–6
  safety 191
  shoes 49
  shopping with 287
  sleeping 149–53
  snacks 130–1
  speech development
    229–32
  teeth 204–5
  vision 201
  walking 190–2
  washing 82–3
toilet training *see* bladder
  control; bowel control
toilets 140
tongue-tie 22–3
tonsilitis 336
toothpaste 87, 131, 203, 205

topping and tailing 72
touch, importance of 16–18,
  56
toxocara 336–7
toys
  in bath 75
  birth to 1 year 264–6
  and creativity 275
  for early wakers 147
  learning process 215
  1 to 2 years 270–6
  playing without 217
  safety 266
  sharing 249–50
  storage 39, 276
  2 to 3 years 277
trainer pants 69
travel
  air travel 290–1
  car journeys 288–9
  foreign travel 342–3
  with newborn baby 36–7
  potties 141
  public transportation 285
twins 57
  breast-feeding 94
typhoid 343

U

umbilical cord 77
umbilical hernia 23, 78
umbilicus 23
unconsciousness 300–2
underfeeding 99, 108
undershirts 43
underweight toddlers 126
undressing
  cause of crying 163
  fear of 78
  newborn babies 45
urine
  babies 132
  diaper rash 68–9
  see also bladder control
urticaria 337
urticaria neonatorum 24

V

vacations 291, 342–3
vaccinations see immunization
vegetables
  fingerfoods 119
  1 to 2 years 121, 122
  2 to 3 years 126
vernix 23
violence, on television 281
vision 199–201
vitamins 86–7
vitamin D 86, 204
vomiting 337–8
  car sickness 289
  forcible vomiting 109
  when to call the doctor 310
  spitting up 109, 337

W

wakeful babies 240–1
  see also night waking
walking 190–2
  "cruising" 188, 190
  "walking" reflex 26–7
warts 338

washing
  birth to 1 year 70–81
  clothing 44–5
  diapers 66–7
  hair 75–6, 80–1, 84–5
  plastic pants 67
  sponge baths 74
  toddlers 82–3
  topping and tailing 72
  see also bathing
wasp stings 334
water
  drinking 117, 121
  fear of 85
  water play 215, 273
wax, in ears 77
weals, newborn baby 24
weaning 111–12
weight gain 178–9, 189
weight problems, toddlers
  125–6, 128
whooping cough see pertussis
wind, burping 108–9
working mothers 11–12
worms 83, 336–7
wounds

  cuts and abrasions 324
  serious bleeding 302
  when to call the doctor 310

Y

yellow fever 343

Acknowledgments

Medical consultants for new edition:
Dr. W. John Fysh MBBS FRCP FRCPCH;
Dr. Aviva Schein MD.

Cooling Brown would like to thank:
Constance Novis for proofreading; Hilary Bird
for the index.

Picture library: Romaine Werblow

The publisher would like to thank the
following for their kind permission to
reproduce their photographs:
Corbis: Cameron 29; **Getty Images:**
Photodisc Green; 9; **Mother & Baby Picture
Library:** EMAP: 287

Photograph of breast pump on page 35
provided courtesy of Avent Ltd.

Jacket images: Front and spine: Photolibrary:
Marina Raith. Back: Author portrait: Carolyn
Djanogly for DK; Punchstock: Brand X
Pictures.

All other images © Dorling Kindersley
For further information see:
www.dkimages.com